THE AFTERLIFE OF OVID

BULLETIN OF THE INSTITUTE OF CLASSICAL STUDIES SUPPLEMENT 130
DIRECTOR & GENERAL EDITOR: GREG WOOLF

DIRECTOR OF PUBLICATIONS: RICHARD SIMPSON

THE AFTERLIFE OF OVID

EDITED BY
PETER MACK
AND
JOHN NORTH

INSTITUTE OF CLASSICAL STUDIES
SCHOOL OF ADVANCED STUDY
UNIVERSITY OF LONDON

2015

The cover image shows the *Ara Grimani*, Museo Archeologico Nazionale, Venice (1st century BCE/1st century CE). See discussion of the *Ara Grimani* in Hérica Valladares, 'The *Io* in Correggio: Ovid and the metamorphosis of a Renaissance painter' at pp. 142-43 in this volume. Photo: Art Resource, NY. All rights reserved.

ISBN: 978-1-905670-60-4

© 2015 Institute of Classical Studies, University of London

Reprinted 2017

All rights reserved. No part of this publication may be reproduced, stored in a retrieval system, or transmitted, in any form or by any means, electronic, mechanical, photocopying, recording, or otherwise, without the prior permission of the publisher.

The right of the contributors to be identified as the authors of the work published here has been asserted by them in accordance with the Copyright, Designs and Patents Act 1988.

Designed and typeset at the Institute of Classical Studies

Also available to download free at
http://www.humanities-digital-library.org

TABLE OF CONTENTS

Peter Mack & John North	Introduction	vii
Ingo Gildenhard	Dante's scriptures: *Metamorphoses*, Bible, *Divina commedia*	1
Caroline Stark	Reflections of Narcissus	23
Frank T. Coulson	Bernardo Moretti: a newly discovered commentator on Ovid's *Ibis*	43
Hélène Casanova-Robin	From Ovid to Pontano: myth, a *forma mentis*? Elaborating *humanitas* through mythological *invention*	61
John F. Miller	Ovid's Janus and the start of the year in Renaissance *Fasti sacri*	81
Gesine Manuwald	Letter-writing after Ovid: his impact on Neo-Latin verse epistles	95
Fátima Díez-Platas	*Et per omnia saecula imagine vivam*: the completion of a figurative corpus for Ovid's *Metamorphoses* in fifteenth- and sixteenth-century book illustrations	115
Hérica Valladares	The *Io* in Correggio: Ovid and the metamorphosis of a Renaissance painter	137
Elizabeth McGrath	Rubens and Ovid	159
Maggie Kilgour	Importing the Ovidian Muse to England	181
Philip Hardie	Milton as reader of Ovid's *Metamorphoses*	203
Victoria Moul	The transformation of Ovid in Cowley's herb garden: Books 1 and 2 of the *Plantarum Libri Sex* (1668)	221
Index		235

INTRODUCTION

From the Middle Ages onwards Ovid (Sulmona 43BCE – Tomis 17 CE) was the most influential and widely imitated of all the Roman poets. He mastered an astonishing range of tones, subjects and poetic genres from love elegy, female complaint, mock-textbook, and calendrical encyclopaedia to mythological epic and exilic lament. Reading Ovid inspired countless poets and artists, including Dante, Petrarch, Chaucer, Spenser, Marlowe, Shakespeare, Milton, Goethe, Pushkin, Botticelli, Titian, Rubens, and Picasso.[1] He was an obvious choice for the conference on the afterlife of classical literature, organized by the Institute of Classical Studies and the Warburg Institute, with the assistance and invaluable advice of Philip Hardie (Trinity College, Cambridge) on 6 and 7 March 2013, of which this volume is the permanent record.

Ovid himself was famously preoccupied with the passage of time and with the future survival and reputation of his own work:

quaque patet domitis Romana potentia terris,
ore legar populi, perque omnia saecula fama,
siquid habent veri vatum praesagia, vivam.
Metamorphoses 15.877-79

Wherever Roman power stretches over defeated lands. I shall be read out (or perhaps 'gathered up') on the people's lips and, if the foresight of bards has any reality in it, I shall live on in fame through all the ages.

Ore legar populi has been interpreted, not as meaning 'read out', but rather 'gathered up on the lips', as though not just his poetry, but his spirit will live on forever. Either way, we can hope that the new age of Classical Reception and Ovid's own prominence in it will have soothed his Manes. We hope that the publication of this conference will make a small contribution to making Ovid's wish come true.

The works that play the greatest part in this book are the *Heroides*, the *Fasti* and the *Metamorphoses*. It is not an accident that the emphasis should be placed on the central period of Ovid's output rather than on his earlier sunnier and wittier phase or on his last

---

[1] Ann Moss, *Ovid in Renaissance France* (London: The Warburg Institute, 1982), Leonard Barkan, *The gods made flesh: Metamorphosis and the pursuit of paganism* (Yale: Yale University Press, 1986), Charles Martindale ed., *Ovid renewed: Ovidian influences in literature and art from the Middle Ages to the Twentieth Century* (Cambridge: Cambridge University Press, 1988), Jonathan Bate, *Shakespeare and Ovid* (Oxford: Oxford University Press, 1993), P. R. Hardie ed., *The Cambridge companion to Ovid* (Cambridge: Cambridge University Press, 2002), Liz Oakley-Brown, *Ovid and the cultural politics of translation in Early Modern England* (Aldershot: Ashgate, 2006), J. Clark, F. T. Coulson and K. McKinley eds, *Ovid in the Middle Ages* (Cambridge: Cambridge University Press, 2011), J. F. Miller and C. E. Newlands eds, *A handbook to the reception of Ovid* (Oxford: Wiley-Blackwell, 2014).

years: only a humanist commentary on the *Ibis* evokes the later poetry of suffering and exile. But it is the *Metamorphoses* that dominates the range of these studies. There are many reasons why the *Metamorphoses* should play such a major role in the reception of classical poetry in the years from Dante to Milton. First, the process by which classical models are adapted and re-thought in the Renaissance is itself a form of metamorphosis, and Ovid himself frequently foreshadows this re-use of his work by the combining of radical change of shape with continuity of certain characteristics: as for instance when Lycaon in Book 1 (199-243) is changed from man to beast, but retains the very savage characteristics that had brought Jupiter's vengeance on him: 'He was a wolf, but kept some traces of his former shape: the grey hairs were the same; same was the violence in his face, his eyes had the same glitter, his image the same savagery'. Then again, the appropriation of pagan stories, often involving gods failing to resist their lustful impulses, could offer obvious targets for Christian religious amelioration. In the end, as Book 15 makes clear, the poem is an extended meditation with copious illustration on the mutability of every aspect of human life. Undoubtedly, the theme of metamorphosis is a linking element but it would be a mistake to think that all the stories end the same way; rather there is endless variety and ingenuity, with metamorphosis itself providing the climax in only some of the stories. As our contributors so successfully demonstrate, different authors and artists could take the Ovidian material into widely different areas and for widely different purposes, without being untrue to the inheritance.

Thus in any account of the afterlife of Ovid, his *Metamorphoses* must take pride of place. As 'the most witty and ingenious book which has come down to us from classical antiquity' (E. J. Kenney), it incorporates vast reading in earlier poetry and mythology into a varied and entertaining conspectus of the history of the world from its creation onwards. The *Metamorphoses* has provided later poets with an inexhaustible treasury of astounding stories of transformation and with many rich ways of thinking about time, change, and love. French commentators provided Christian moralizations of the stories culminating in the fourteenth century in the 72,000 line French verse *Ovide moralisé* and the Latin prose *Ovidius moralizatus* which sanctioned their use by Christian poets. In *Inferno 25* Dante commands Ovid to be silent, insisting that the transformations of hell are much greater than the transformations of the *Metamorphoses*, which frequently suggested them. Chaucer and Shakespeare were inspired by the *Metamorphoses* more often than by any other book. In this volume, Caroline Stark reflects on the implications of the myth of Narcissus starting from the reasons for Alberti's choice of Narcissus as the inventor of art, to show how the appropriation of Ovid's story by Dante, Ariosto, and Tasso reveals at once the power and danger of art. Maggie Kilgour discusses the use of the *Metamorphoses* in Thomas Lodge's *Scillaes metamorphosis* (1580) and John Weever's *Faunus and Melliflora* (1600) to translate the muses of Roman poetry to England. Philip Hardie adds a study of the use of Milton's reading of the *Metamorphoses* to develop and complement previous studies of Milton and Ovid by Charles Martindale, Maggie Kilgour and others.[2]

---

[2]   Charles Martindale, 'Paradise Metamorphosed: Ovid in Milton', *Comparative Literature* 37 (1985) 301-33, Mandy Green, *Milton's Ovidian Eve* (Aldershot: Ashgate, 2009), Maggie Kilgour, *Milton and the Metamorphosis of Ovid* (Oxford; Oxford University Press, 2012).

INTRODUCTION

Long known as 'the Bible of the painters', the *Metamorphoses* has provided visual artists with subject-matter since the Pompeian frescoes, which must have been painted within a generation of the publication of the poem. In the 1470s Pollaiuolo painted an *Apollo grasping a Daphne* whose arms have already changed into the leaf filled branches of trees, a painting now in the National Gallery, London. In the mid-sixteenth century Titian painted a series of *poesie* based on episodes from the *Metamorphoses*, including *Venus and Adonis*, *Diana and Actaeon*, *Diana and Callisto*, *Danae*, *The rape of Europa* and *Perseus and Andromeda* for Philip II. In the seventeenth century Poussin painted *Narcissus*, *Cephalus and Procris*, and *Acis and Galatea*, while Bernini sculpted *Pluto and Proserpina*, and *Apollo and Daphne*. As Svetlana Alpers has observed, the *Metamorphoses* 'was first of all the most popular and convenient source for mythological narratives'.[3] The very substantial impact of the *Metamorphoses* on the visual arts is represented in this volume by Fátima Diez-Plazas's study of illustrations in printed editions of the *Metamorphoses*, starting from the Venetian edition of 1497, and making a particular study of the two editions from Parma in 1505 which set the format for many later sixteenth-century illustrated editions, by Hérica Valladares's investigation of Correggio's *Io* (*c.* 1530), and by the studies of Rubens's *Banquet of Tereus* and *Pythagoras advocating vegetarianism* in Elizabeth McGrath's essay on Rubens and Ovid.

In the Middle Ages and the Renaissance, Ovid was particularly revered as the poet with the greatest interest in love, on the basis of his early elegies, the *Amores*, which were partially translated into English by Christopher Marlowe and were imitated by John Donne, and of the *Art of Love*. The *Amores* and the *Ars Amatoria* were not a focus of this conference though Elizabeth McGrath shows the influence of the *Ars Amatoria* on Rubens' painting of the *Rape of the Leucippides* and his designs for a tapestry cycle on the *Life of Achilles*. The *Heroides*, the letters in which spurned heroines write to reproach their former lovers, were discussed by Gesine Manuwald who assesses their influence on the development of Neo-Latin verse epistles by offering two examples, Bodius – the Scot, Mark Alexander Boyd (1562-1601) – and the German Hessus, Helius Eobanus Hessus (1488-1540), who wrote letters from *Heroides Christianae* published in 1514.

In recent years the *Fasti* have been seriously revalued by classical scholars. The process tracing their afterlife, which was especially strong in the Renaissance and involved commentaries by Poliziano (1481), Paolo Marsi (1482) and Antonio Costanzi (1487), as well as the inspiration for Botticelli's *Primavera* and paintings by Piero di Cosimo and Giovanni Bellini. John F. Miller's essay in this volume examines a crosssection of the Renaissance Latin poetic calendars, including those by Lodovico Lazzarelli (1484), Baptista Mantuan (1516), Ambrogio Novidio Fracco (1547) and Girolamo Chiaravacci (1554), by comparing their discussions of the first day of the year and their treatment of the myth of Janus. In her essay on Rubens and Ovid Elizabeth McGrath argues that Rubens's *Boreas and Orithyia* and *Feast of Venus* (Prado) were based on a close reading of passages from the *Fasti*.

Ovid's later work, and the Renaissance tradition of scholarship on Ovid, is represented in this collection by one essay. Frank T. Coulson provides a study of the commentary on the *Ibis*, by Bernardo Moretti, a Bolognese rhetorician working around 1460, which has survived

---

[3] Svetlana Alpers, *The decoration of the Torre della Parada* (London, 1971), 151.

in four manuscripts. The difficulty of the *Ibis* encouraged many fifteenth-century scholars to write commentaries on it. Moretti also composed one verse and two prose lives of Ovid. The verse life receives its first printed edition in this volume (59). Coulson traces Moretti's references to Latin poets and historians, his explication of points of grammar, his occasional comments on textual issues and his explication of the myths to which Ovid refers.

Looking at the question of reception from the side of the receiving culture, the essays by Frank Coulson, John Miller and Gesine Manuwald have already broached the topic of neo-Latin poetry, which evidently owes so much to the study of Ovid. Neo-Latin poetry is the major topic of two further studies in this collection. Hélène Casanova-Robin's essay discusses the impact of Ovidian myths and metamorphoses on the Latin poetry of Giovanni Pontano (1429-1503). She shows how myth nourished Pontano's poetry, acting as a method of thinking and a foundational language. Thus Pontano uses the myth of Phaeton as a basis for his last collection of elegies *Eridanus*. In his *Eclogues* he uses Ovidian myth to celebrate the landscape of Campania. Pontano uses Ovidian myth for consolation in *De Tumulis* and to teach temperance in *Eridanus*. Victoria Moul presents a study of the first two books of Abraham Cowley's *Plantarum libri sex* (1668) which shows how Cowley draws on various Ovidian works, on the *Amores* for style, on the *Fasti* and the *Ars amatoria* for the combination of wit and instruction and on the *Heroides* for the women (now plants) lamenting their mistreatment. She shows that Cowley cites Ovid in his commentary, while his plants refer to Ovid explicitly in their own speeches. She sees Cowley's work as a challenge to Ovidian poetics, in that Cowley's female plants survive their transformations and claim the power to prevent or ameliorate the sufferings of women both physical and in the myths depicted by Ovid.

The focus of Ingo Gildenhard's essay is comparative, trying to understand the ways in which Dante uses Ovid through a comparison between the Bible, the *Metamorphoses* and the *Divina Commedia*, seen as 'grand narratives about humanity and the sacred'. He treats the *Metamorphoses* as an anthropological epic, making a detailed comparison between the opening chapters of Genesis and the first four hundred lines of the poem. He shows how his three chosen works use metamorphosis to explore what it is to be human in a cosmic setting. Like the Bible and Ovid, Dante claims to give a true account of what happened, but his text goes further in anticipating the reader's incredulity about his claim. Allusions to Glaucus and Semele frame the beginning and end of Dante's quest. It would have been logical for Gildenhard to have moved directly on to Milton, but, for the purposes of this collection, that claim had already gone to Philip Hardie. He explores Milton's technique of 'Combinatorial imitation', that is to say, imitation based on the combining of a range of different episodes from the *Metamorphoses*. When this analysis is applied to Milton's layered characterization of Eve, Hardie reveals a Renaissance way of reading Ovid which corresponds to one of the ways in which Ovid himself in the *Metamorphoses* sought to meet the challenge laid down by Virgil's *Aeneid*.

This volume, and the conference from which it originated, is the first of a series of collaborations between the Institute of Classical Studies and the Warburg Institute, funded by the Dean's Development Fund of the School of Advanced Study, University of London. This collaboration aims to build a bridge between the flourishing field of Reception Studies, which now forms a large part of the research activity of Classics Departments throughout the world, and the long tradition of study of the afterlife of the ancient world. A tradition which was established by Aby Warburg in his private library in Hamburg, and which is now the main topic of the Library and Photographic Collection of the Warburg Institute. Before these conferences there had been surprisingly little contact between these two related fields of research; some classicists were unaware of the bibliographic and photographic riches available in the Warburg Institute, while scholars associated with the Warburg Institute had not paid much attention to the new field of Reception Studies growing within Classics. It turns out that both sides have a great deal to learn from each other. The conferences aimed to serve as a platform for classicists to explore the Warburg Institute and for Renaissance scholars to appreciate what was being carried out in the field of Classics and what was available in the extraordinary library of the Institute of Classical Studies. Since these great libraries sit between the incomparable collections of the British Museum to the south and the British Library to the north east, this collaboration helps to show the extraordinarily rich resources of London for the study of the classical tradition. The joint conferences were first suggested by Professor Mike Edwards, and since they have come into existence they have been steered by Professors John North and Peter Mack. We are grateful to the School of Advanced Studies and its Dean, Roger Kain, for financial support, to Philip Hardie for his invaluable advice, and to Jane Ferguson and Richard Simpson for the practical assistance which made possible the conference, held at the Warburg Institute, and the book, published by the Institute of Classical Studies. We must also thank François Quiviger for arranging a photographic exhibition of illustrations of Ovid and classical mythology to accompany the conference. Future volumes, reflecting conferences which have already taken place, will consider the afterlives of Plutarch, Virgil, Herodotus, and Thucydides, as well as Greek Tragedy and Cicero. Greg Woolf, Raphaële Mouren, and David Freedberg will now take on the responsibility for the future of this collaboration.

DANTE'S SCRIPTURES:
METAMORPHOSES, BIBLE, *DIVINA COMMEDIA*

INGO GILDENHARD

Introduction

Ovid, unlike his fellow classical *auctores* Virgil or Statius who guide Dante through *Inferno* and *Purgatorio* before handing over to Beatrice and St. Bernard of Clairvaux for *Paradiso*, has hardly any *narrative* presence in Dante's *Divine Comedy*. In fact, he is only named twice. Dante encounters him in person while traversing the unorthodox limbo of *Inferno* 4, populated as it is by classical poets rather than un-baptized infants: together with his guide Virgil, 'sovereign' Homer, 'satirist' Horace, and Lucan, Ovid belongs to '*la bella scola*' of ancient authors who welcome Dante in their midst.[1] And in *Inferno* 25, he figures as the creator of his *magnum opus Metamorphoses*, who receives, jointly with Lucan, the order to be silent. The reason: their stories of transformation pale in comparison to the perverse and polymorphous permutations sinful humans are forced to undergo in Dante's Hell.[2] The modes of transformative change Dante observed on his infernal journey and has put on record in his poem surpass even the most *outré* figments of Ovid's outlandish imagination: the pagan fantasies fall short of the peerless novelty and horror of Christian realities, defined as they are by the omnipotence and justice of God. And unlike Virgil and the *Aeneid*, which are at least recognized as an inferior sort of scripture that gives way to the Bible in the course of Dante's spiritual ascent, he nowhere acknowledges the *Metamorphoses* as a key contributor to his poetics. *Prima facie*, then, Ovid remains a marginal figure: neither he nor his *oeuvre* seems to make a significant contribution to Dante's mission.

Appearances deceive. In the *Divine Comedy* (as in Dante's earlier works) Ovid and his poetry resonate powerfully, throughout. Indeed, Ovid, much more so than Virgil, qualifies as Dante's classical *alter ego*, insofar as their (literary and political) careers feature striking

---

[1] *Inf.* 4.88-90: *quelli è Omero poeta sovrano;/ l'altro è Orazio satiro che vene;/ Ovidio è 'l terzo, e l'ultimo Lucano.* For Dante's violation of theological protocol in his handling of Hell see T. Barolini, 'Arachne, Argus, and St. John: Transgressive Art in Dante and Ovid', in *Dante and the origins of Italian literary culture* (Fordham 2006) 158-71 (159-60). The strategy of situating predecessors in the Underworld (the literary equivalent to the notion of supersession in Christian theology) has a distinguished classical pedigree, from Homer to Virgil: P. R. Hardie, *Virgil's Aeneid: Cosmos and Imperium* (Oxford 1986) 69-83; *The epic successors of Virgil: a study in the dynamics of a tradition* (Cambridge 1993) 103-05; G. W. Most, 'Il poeta nell'Ade: catabasi epica e teoria dell'epos tra Omero e Virgilio', *Studi italiani di filologia classica* n.s. 10 (1992) 1014-26. For '*la bella scola*' more generally see *e.g.* the papers in *Dante e la 'bella scola' della poesia: Autorità e sfida poetica*, ed. A. A. Iannucci (Ravenna 1993).

[2] *Inf.* 25.94-99.

similarities, which Dante deliberately exploits in his authorial self-fashioning:[3] both ascend from youthful trifles in the poetry of love to more mature forms of literary expression; both find themselves exiled from their native city;[4] and both stake their hope for a return home and crowning recognition in part on their respective literary masterpieces, the *Metamorphoses* and the *Divine Comedy*.[5] Moreover, if one takes pseudo-epigraphical evidence into consideration, both authors, in their final literary moments, experience an ultimate revelation of Christian truth, to which they pay homage in a prayer to the Virgin Mary: Dante invokes her at the outset of the final canto of *Paradiso* and Ovid at the conclusion of his long-lost autobiography, which, as luck would have it, was rediscovered shortly before Dante was born.[6] Most strikingly, perhaps, like few others both poets cultivate poetry in a range of genres as imaginary autobiography.[7] And just as the 'autobiographical' poetological fictions of Ovid's amatory verse inform the 'inspirational scenarios' Dante sketches out in his *Vita Nuova*, so the personalized re-readings of ancient myth (not least as set out in his very own *Metamorphoses*), Ovid performs in his exile poetry have their equivalent in Dante's encounters with figures from ancient myth and legend (often in their Ovidian incarnation) during his journey through the beyond. In purely quantitative terms, Ovid makes a significant contribution to the allusive texture of the *Divine Comedy*. With *circa* 100 references he comes in fourth after only the Vulgate (c. 500), Aristotle (300+), and Virgil (c. 200), and well before Cicero and Lucan (c. 50 each), Statius or Boethius (between 30 and 40).[8] Figures from the *Metamorphoses* such as Arachne, Argus, Glaucus, Io, Narcissus, Phaethon, or Semele are part of the personnel that populates Dante's literary world or are invoked in figures of speech (such as similes) that he employs to articulate

---

[3] On the literary careers of ancient authors and their influence see now *Classical literary careers and their reception*, ed. P. Hardie and H. Moore (Cambridge 2010), especially the paper by A. Barchiesi and P. Hardie: 'The Ovidian career model: Ovid, Gallus, Apuleius, Boccaccio'.

[4] For Dante's use of Ovid's exile poetry see M. Picone, 'Ovid and the *exul immeritus*', in *Dante for the new millennium*, ed. T. Barolini and W. Storey (New York 2003) 389-407.

[5] For these biographical parallels (and their exploitation by Dante) see in general W. Ginsberg, 'Dante's Ovid', in *Ovid in the Middle Ages*, ed. J. G. Clark, F. T. Coulson, and K. L. McKinley (Cambridge 2011) 143-59.

[6] The poem, entitled *de vetula*, records the transformation of Ovid's youthful erotomaniac self into a convert to Christianity. For the argument that Dante knew and used it, see M. Picone, 'Auctoritas classica e salvezza cristiana: una lettura tipologica di *purgatorio* xxii', *Italianistica* 21 (1992) 379-95 and 'Canto XIX', in *Lectura Dantis Turicensis: purgatorio*, ed. G. Güntert and M. Picone (Florence 2001) 287-306, cited by Ginsberg, 'Dante's Ovid', *Ovid in the Middle Ages* (n. 4, above) 152 n. 18.

[7] For Ovid, see I. Gildenhard and A. Zissos, 'Inspirational fictions: autobiography and generic reflexivity in Ovid's proems', *Greece & Rome* 47 (2000) 67-79.

[8] See E. Moore, *Studies in Dante, first series: scriptures and classical authors in Dante* (Oxford 1896) cited, with discussion, by D. Pietropaolo, 'Whipping Jesus devoutly: the dramaturgy of catharsis and the Christian idea of tragic form', in *Beyond the Fifth Century: interactions with Greek Tragedy from the Fourth Century BCE to the Middle Ages*, ed. I. Gildenhard and M. Revermann (Berlin and New York 2010) 397-424 (402–03).

his – ultimately ineffable – experience in discourse.[9] Distribution, too, is important. Thus Virgil may account for about twice as many references in the *Divine Comedy* as Ovid; but they tend to peter out towards the end of *Purgatorio*. Whereas the import of the *Aeneid* diminishes, we find '*escalating* use of Ovid as the poet of transgression and metamorphosis in all senses' once Dante reaches *Paradiso*.[10] As we shall see, Ovid is even an intertextual bystander in Dante's concluding encounter with God.

At one level, Dante's engagement with Ovid's *oeuvre* features the same 'spiral-like configuration of confiscation and correction' that characterizes his attitude towards *auctores* more generally, whom he reread from a Christian point of view – as heir to a long tradition of theological exegesis that saw in both the Jewish scriptures and the pagan classics preliminary and necessarily inferior figurations of Christian Truth.[11] The unbridgeable nature of the watershed in world-history effected by the incarnation, death, and resurrection of Jesus Christ which Dante has built into his initial encounter with Virgil, with Virgil identifying himself as someone who lived during 'an age of false and lying gods' (*Inf.* 1.72: *nel tempo de li dèi falsi e bugiardi*) programmatically establishes his undeniable and unconditional superiority over classical authors in eschatological terms. Material taken from Ovid and other classical authors tends to undergo the same aggressive revision. The placement of '*la bella scola*' in Dante's underworld topography is emblematic here: 'the hopelessness of limbo is the consequent fate of Classicism: without access to the proper name of Christ, without a mastery of the Word, it is forever condemned to a tragic state of hermeneutic suspense, forever alienated from its own words and meanings'.[12] Confiscation and correction, however, only captures one side of Dante's Ovidianism. Ovid, and in particular his *Metamorphoses*, proved profoundly enabling for Dante – as enabling, even, as Virgil (if in different ways). As Sowell puts it: 'the Dante-Ovid connection reaches beyond the placement of classical myths in Christian contexts. It reaches to the core of Dante's

---

[9] For Arachne and Argus, see *e.g.* Barolini, 'Arachne, Argus, and St. John' (n. 1, above); for Glaucus, S. Botterill, *Dante and the mystical tradition: Bernard of Clairvaux in the Commedia* (Cambridge 2005) 234-35; for Io, J. Levenstein, 'The Pilgrim, the Poet, and the Cowgirl: Dante's Alter-"Io" in Purgatorio xxx-xxxi', *Dante Studies* 114 (1996) 189-208; for Narcissus, K. Brownlee, 'Dante and Narcissus (*Purg.* xxx, 76-99)', *Dante Studies* 96 (1978) 201-06; for Phaethon, K. Brownlee, 'Phaeton's fall and Dante's ascent' in *Dante Studies* 102 (1984) 135-44; for Semele, K. Brownlee, 'Ovid's Semele and Dante's Metamorphosis: *Paradiso* 21-22', in *The poetry of allusion: Virgil and Ovid in Dante's Commedia*, ed. R. Jacoff and J. Schnapp (Stanford 1991) 224-32.

[10] Barolini, 'Arachne, Argus, and St. John' (n. 1, above) 171.

[11] Barolini, 'Arachne, Argus, and St. John' (n. 1, above) 158. See also T. Barolini, *Dante's poets: textuality and truth in the Comedy* (Princeton 1984), P. S. Hawkins, 'Transfiguring the text: Ovid, Scripture and the Dynamics of Allusion', *Stanford Italian Review* 5 (1985) 115-39, the papers in *The Poetry of Allusion: Virgil and Ovid in Dante's Commedia*, ed. R. Jacoff and J. Schnapp (Stanford 1991) and *Dante and Ovid: essays in intertextuality*, ed. M. U. Sowell (Binghamton and New York 1993), and K. Brownlee, 'Dante and the Classical Poets,' in *The Cambridge Companion to Dante*, ed. R. Jacoff (Cambridge 1993) 100-19.

[12] J. T. Schnapp, *The Transfiguration of History at the Center of Dante's Paradise* (Princeton 1986) 4 (on *Inf.* 4.52-54).

poetics – to how and why he creates poetry'.[13] Dante, though, refuses – cannot *but* refuse – to recognize Ovid's inspirational value with a tribute similar to the one that Virgil receives at *Inferno* 1.85 ('Tu se' lo mio maestro e 'l mio autore') because of his status as literary anti-Christ and the function of the *Metamorphoses* as a veritable counter-Bible.

This paper looks into the reasons for this strange relationship by appraising the Christian Bible, Ovid's *Metamorphoses*, and Dante's *Divine Comedy* as works that have several key hallmarks in common, on account of which they qualify as 'scripture' – grand narratives about humanity and the sacred. A systematic and detailed *syncrisis* of the three texts as typologically federated works that stand in various forms of creative dialogue with one another could easily fill a volume of its own. This paper offers some exploratory (and experimental) soundings that, for reasons of space, go light on close readings and engagement with the scholarly literature.[14] The following *syncrisis* focuses on five features that all three texts (and very few others) have in common. All three belong to a genre of writing one could dub 'anthropological epic' (section 1). All three endorse (variants of) metamorphosis as a dynamic principle that defines the potential of the human species for degeneration *and* elevation, damnation *and* salvation (section 2). All three are, at their core, invested in a rhetoric designed to render believable supernatural interventions in our world that are *prima facie* incredible since they blatantly defy empirical plausibility (section 3). All three practice an imperial 'poetics of supersession' that includes a linguistic dimension (section 4). And all three celebrate the figure (but also the failure) of the artist (section 5). We will have occasion to consider whether Ovid read the Bible (Genesis, in the Septuagint version), but the main emphasis will be on how the family-resemblance between the Christian Bible and the *Metamorphoses* inform the proto-Hegelian scenario in Dante's *Divine Comedy*, whereby the pagan work functions as the antithesis to Christian writ and both are transformed and sublimated in 'the *Commedia*'s imitation of God's way of writing, in defiance of all theological protocol' – or, put differently, Dante's conceit to have authored a vernacular Scripture.[15]

1. Anthropological epic

Classicists agree: on account of its idiosyncratic eccentricities the *Metamorphoses*, despite its formal filiations with epic (it is a narrative of substantial length written in hexameters), is virtually impossible to classify in generic terms. As the following table illustrates, Ovid's poem both belongs to, and radically breaks with, the Greco-Roman epic tradition:

---

[13] M. U. Sowell, 'Introduction', in *Dante and Ovid* (n. 11, above) 1-15 (13).

[14] This paper is in many ways a spin-off from work on *Transformative change in Western thought: a history of Metamorphoses from Homer to Hollywood*, ed. I. Gildenhard and A. Zissos (Legenda: Oxford 2013). Many of the issues only touched upon here are treated at further length there.

[15] The quotation comes from T. Barolini, 'Detheologizing Dante: for a "new formalism" in Dante studies', *Quaderni d'italianistica* 10 (1989) 35-53 (42).

Author	Title	Length	Main Theme	Protagonist
Homer	*Iliad*	24 Books	Wrath and War	Achilles
Homer	*Odyssey*	24 Books	Return and Civil War	Odysseus
Apollonius Rhodius	*Argonautica*	4 Books	Travel and Adventure	Jason
Ennius	*Annals*	15/18 Books	Men and their deeds	Roman nobles
Virgil	*Aeneid*	12 Books	Arms and the Man	Aeneas
Ovid	*Metamorphoses*	15 Books	Transformation	?

The tally of fifteen books, while marking a conscious deviation from the 'multiple-of-four-or-six' principle canonized by Homer, Apollonius Rhodius, and Virgil, has at least a precedent in Ennius' *Annals*.[16] But Ovid's main theme (and hence the title) is unequivocally – and shockingly – unorthodox: before his *Metamorphoses*, transformative change was a *sujet* principally cultivated in Hellenistic catalogue poetry, which is about as un-epic in scope and conception as literature can get.[17] To use this theme as basis for a universal history not merely bent, but actually shattered prevailing generic norms. From Homer to Virgil, the stuff of epic was war and adventure, men and their deeds. In Ovid, it is – a fictitious phenomenon.[18] A related curiosity pertains to the protagonist. In all the other epics in the table, the main character is easy to identify (even if there are several, as in Ennius' *Annals*). That is decidedly not the case in the *Metamorphoses*: Ovid's frequently un-heroic personnel changes from one episode to the next, to the point that some scholars have suggested that the hero of the poem is the poet himself – the master-narrator who holds everything together and, in and through his poetry, performs a deed worthy of immortality. There is some truth to this 'composition myth' (as we shall see in Section 5 below), but it does not rule out the possibility of pinpointing a protagonist on the level of plot as well. As Ernst Schmidt has argued, the question mark in the last box could be replaced with 'the human being'.[19]

There are some difficulties with this suggestion (one may well ask: what about the gods?); but overall the thesis that humanity *as such* takes centre-stage in the *Metamorphoses* is attractive and compelling. At its core, the poem offers a sustained meditation on what it is to be human within a wider cosmic setting defined by supernatural agents, and explores the potential of our species for good and for evil. These anthropological concerns are set

---

[16] *Annals*, year-by-year chronicles, are anyway difficult to contain within even multiples since they defy closure: the next year is always just around the corner, and annals therefore tend to fray at the end, a fact that compelled Ennius to add three further books to the *editio princeps* of his poem when Roman history had moved on. See generally P. R. Hardie, 'Closure in epic', in *Classical closure: reading the end in Greek and Latin literature*, ed. D. H. Roberts, F. M. Dunn and D. Fowler (Princeton 1997) 139-62.

[17] The various sections on Ovid's *Metamorphoses* in this paper are based on I. Gildenhard and A. Zissos, 'Introduction to Part I: Antiquity and Archetypes', in *Transformative Change* (n. 14, above) 36-87 (65-77).

[18] That Ovid chose to write, for the most part, fiction did not prevent him from presenting his fictions as historical facts: see Section 3 below.

[19] E. A. Schmidt, *Ovids poetische Menschenwelt. Die Metamorphosen als Metapher und Symphonie* (Heidelberg 1991).

6   THE AFTERLIFE OF OVID

up by the various forms of anthropogenesis at the beginning of the poem, which trace the origins of humanity to such diverse material as earth and a divine spark, stones, or the blood of giants, which yields a gamut of possibilities that covers the full range from quasi-divine and ethically impeccable (divine spark and golden-age bliss) to bestial and blasphemous (blood of giants and iron-age criminality).[20] As we proceed through the poem, encounters with such atrocious human beings as Tereus or such admirable individuals as Baucis and Philemon serve as vivid reminders that the accursed blood of the giants and a salvific element are equally part of our DNA.

Ovid shares this interest in anthropogenesis and the paradigmatic significance of the early history of humanity with the Bible. It is possible to adduce circumstantial evidence that Ovid (could have) read Genesis in the Septuagint version. Translated during the reign of Ptolemy II (309-246 BC), it entered the holdings of the library of Alexandria. There is some evidence of Alexandrian poets engaging with the Septuagint (even beyond the Pentateuch) – and Ovid, too, may well have considered it another piece of Alexandrian literature if he was able to lay his hands on a copy in Rome.[21] It seems reasonable to assume that the Septuagint translation circulated among the significant Jewish community in Augustan Rome given that a large number of them (as we know from grave inscriptions) spoke Greek.[22] It may even have been part of the holdings of one of the public libraries which were set up by Asinius Pollio and Augustus in Rome during Ovid's youth.[23] But for our purposes it is ultimately immaterial whether Ovid actually read the Bible (however interesting the question is in its own right). What matters is that both the Bible and the *Metamorphoses*, at or from the outset, establish humanity at their centre. Indeed, the opening of the *Metamorphoses* is in many ways closer to the beginning of Genesis than any other ancient source. Consider:

---

[20] In the Deucalion and Pyrrha story, Ovid makes the aetiological connection between the kind of material from which humanity is moulded and our respective qualities explicit: originating from stones, 'we are hence a hardy race and experienced in toil and give testimony from what source we are born' (*Met.* 1.414-15: *inde genus durum sumus experiensque laborum/ et documenta damus, qua simus origine nati*).

[21] The possibility is mooted by J. Lightfoot, *Lucian: On the Syrian Goddess* (Oxford 2003) 341 n. 26, with further bibliography.

[22] See A. S. Hollis, *Ovid, Ars Amatoria I: edited with an introduction and commentary* (Oxford 1977) 47: 'After the capture of Jerusalem by Pompey in 63 BC many Jews came to Rome as prisoners of war, later gaining their liberty and staying in the capital (*cf.* Philo, Legatio ad Gaium 155)' and, more generally, J. M. G. Barclay, *Jews in the Mediterranean Diaspora from Alexander to Trajan (323 BCE-117 CE)* (Edinburgh 1996).

[23] See most recently M. Nicholls, '*Bibliotheca Latina Graecaque*: On the Possible Division of Roman Libraries by Language', in *Neronia VIII: Bibliothèques, livres et culture écrite dans l'empire romain de César à Hadrien*, ed. Y. Perrin (Brussels 2010) 11-21. There is circumstantial evidence that suggests that Asinius Pollio, who was a prominent presence in Rome's literary scene in the generation of Virgil and Horace, entertained diplomatic relations with high-ranking Jews. See L. H. Feldman, 'Asinius Pollio and his Jewish Interests', *Transactions of the American Philological Association* 84 (1953) 73-80.

INGO GILDENHARD: DANTE'S SCRIPTURES

	Metamorphoses	Genesis
Initial condition	Chaos	God
Theogony	n/a	n/a
The (uncreated) demiurge sets to work, fixing the cosmic sphere of heaven, earth, and waters	1.22–31	1.1–9
Some special attention to the earth, not least its waterways and flora	1.32–44	1.10–13
Further fiddling with the cosmos, in particular lighting up of the stars	1.45–71	1.14–19
Population of the different habitats with fish, fowl, land animals	1.72–75	1.20–25
Anthropogenesis in God's image as the climax of creation; the human being to rule over all other life-forms	1.76–88	1.26–31
Human existence in Paradise, a Golden Age of innocence and bliss	1.89–112	2
Loss of Paradise, rise of crime	1.113–50	3.1–6.3
Giants, a hybrid humanoid race pose a threat to the established order	1.151–62	6.4
Moral degeneracy of humanity reaches insufferable levels; the supreme deity reconsiders the wisdom of anthropogenesis	1.163–252	6.5–6
The supreme deity decides upon destruction of humankind (and most other life-forms) by means of a universal Flood	1.253–312	6.7–7.24
Repopulation of the earth by means of a couple, selected for survival on account of its piety	1.313–415	6.8–8.22

As one would expect, Ovid's creation sequence is a *melange* of elements scooped from an encyclopaedic range of predecessors, notably Hesiod, from whom he adopts the notion of primeval chaos and the succession of the ages (from gold to iron, but leaving out the age of (semi-divine) heroes which, in Hesiod, momentarily interrupts and reverses the story of decline),[24] but also other Greek and Latin sources, from Homer to Plato, from Empedocles to Lucretius and Virgil. But the reminiscences of classical authors that Ovid has woven into his text are arguably less remarkable than the striking parallels between the opening of the *Metamorphoses* and the biblical account of creation. There is, to be sure, no *creatio ex nihilo*. But both Genesis and the *Metamorphoses* feature an omnipotent demiurge in charge of setting up the universe.[25] Just as crucial, neither text features a theogony.[26] Its absence is as unremarkable in Genesis as it is unexpected in Ovid – and not just because the rise and

---

[24] See Hesiod, *Works and Days* 109-201. Omitting this (important) chapter of Greek cosmic history (important since it concerns the generations of humans who fought the 'epic' wars at Thebes and Troy and hence Homer) is a natural corollary to the even more striking omission of a theogony (on which see below).

[25] Ovid pairs him with *melior natura* (*Met.* 1.21).

[26] The other peculiar absence from Ovid's account of creation is Love/ Amor, either as a divinity or as a creative principle – again in oblique defiance of Greek cosmogonic thought, not least that of Hesiod and Empedocles. This absence chimes with the omission of theogonic thought, in which Eros and various acts of a sexual nature play major roles, can also be read as part of Ovid's 'composition myth': see I. Gildenhard and A. Zissos, 'Inspirational Fictions: Autobiography and Generic Reflexivity in Ovid's Proems', *Greece & Rome* 47 (2000) 67-79.

fall of successive generations of divinities constitute important chapters in cosmic history within the Greek mythographic tradition.[27] The gods, after all, are major players in Ovid's narrative, but just pop up as if they always already existed. This silence in the text is all the more pronounced since Ovid occasionally gestures to theogonic material in later books.[28] In both texts, the world's flora and fauna is put into place before the narrative moves on to the moulding of the human being in the image of God as the climax of creation. Christian readers from late antiquity onwards (Lactantius, Conrad of Hirsau, Arthur Golding, among others) have considered the following verses one of the nuggets of insight hidden within the pagan filth that pullulates elsewhere in the poem (*Met.* 1.76-88):

> Sanctius his animal mentisque capacius altae
> deerat adhuc et quod dominari in cetera posset:
> natus homo est, siue hunc diuino semine fecit
> ille opifex rerum, mundi melioris origo,
> siue recens tellus seductaque nuper ab alto   80
> aethere cognati retinebat semina caeli,
> quam satus Iapeto mixtam pluuialibus undis,
> finxit in effigiem moderantum cuncta deorum.
> pronaque cum spectent animalia cetera terram,
> os homini sublime dedit caelumque uidere   85
> iussit et erectos ad sidera tollere uultus.

A living creature more holy than these, more capable of lofty thought, and able to have dominion over all the others was still lacking. Born was man: be it that the craftsman of things, the creator of a better world, fashioned him from some divine seed; be it that the earth, recently created and only lately drawn apart from the heavenly ether, retained seeds of its kindred sky – the earth, which the son of Iapetus, once mixed with rain-water, moulded in the image of the all-governing gods. While all the other animals are prone and gaze upon the earth, he gave to man a face held high and ordered him to stand erect and raise his face upwards to the stars.

Humanity begins its stay on earth with a period in Paradise or a Golden Age, which, however, does not last. In both texts the rising crime-rate that follows upon the loss of Paradise or Golden-Age bliss coincides with the appearance of giants. The account of the giants at *Metamorphoses* 1.151-62 has its counterpart in the giants that appear in the Septuagint version of Genesis 6.4.[29] Ovid's inclusion of this chapter in cosmic history here

---

[27] See J. Strauss Clay, *The politics of Olympus: form and meaning in the major Homeric hymns* (Princeton 1989) and *Hesiod's cosmos* (Cambridge 2003).

[28] See *e.g. Met.* 4.536-38 where Venus, pleading with sea-god Neptune for a favour, refers to her Greek name 'Aphrodite', which signals her origin from the foam (in Greek *aphros*) of the sea. At the same time, she passes in silence over what caused the sea to foam in the first place: Uranos' cut-off, yet still procreative genitals hitting the waters.

[29] οἱ δὲ γίγαντες ἦσαν ἐπὶ τῆς γῆς ἐν ταῖς ἡμέραις ἐκείναις καὶ μετ' ἐκεῖνο, ὡς ἂν εἰσεπορεύοντο οἱ υἱοὶ τοῦ θεοῦ πρὸς τὰς θυγατέρας τῶν ἀνθρώπων καὶ ἐγεννῶσαν ἑαυτοῖς· ἐκεῖνοι ἦσαν οἱ γίγαντες οἱ ἀπ' αἰῶνος, οἱ ἄνθρωποι οἱ ὀνομαστοί. [There were giants in the earth in those days; and also after that, when the sons of God came in unto the daughters of men, and they bare children to them; those were the giants of old, men of renown.]

is decidedly unorthodox – in Greek sources, the giants are primeval divinities who belong much earlier in the creation sequence. Hesiod's *Theogony*, for instance, features them as offspring of the blood that gushed forth and scattered in drops from Uranos' severed and far-flung genitals and the (thereby inseminated) Earth when the world was young.[30] In contrast, in both Ovid and the Bible they emblematically represent, quite literally, sky-rocketing levels of hubris, which in turn entails the decision of the supreme divinity to wipe out (human) life on earth in a cleansing flood. The universal flood is a widespread motif in the literary traditions of Greece, Anatolia, and the Near East (though Hesiod passes over it in silence).[31] And yet it is not impossible to detect textual traces in the *Metamorphoses* that point to a direct engagement of Ovid with the biblical deluge. *Met.* 1. 293-94, for instance, has been read as a sly Ovidian allusion to Genesis 8:4:[32]

Occupat hic collem, cumba sedet alter adunca | et ducit remos illic, ubi nuper ararat.

This one occupies a hill-top, another sits in a curved skiff and rows where only recently he had ploughed.

Genesis 8.4: καὶ ἐκάθισεν ἡ κιβωτὸς ... ἐπὶ τὰ ὄρη τὰ Αραρατ.

And the ark rested on the mountains (in the region) of Ararat.

The logic of such a reference, if it is one, perfectly enacts the technique of allusive one-upmanship via a sly 'Alexandrian footnote' of which Ovid was the undisputed master: by way of intertextual contrast, the biblical flood, unlike Ovid's, barely reached the height of a modest hill. Righteous Noah and his (rather faceless) wife find their match in the pious couple of Deucalion and Pyrrha – though Ovid suppresses (or knows nothing of) the ark and the other members of Noah's family (his three sons Shem, Ham, and Japeth and their wives) who floated to safety and then helped to repopulate the earth by means of sexual procreation (rather than petro-genesis as in Ovid), resulting in the 'table of nations'.[33]

While in Hebrew Scripture, the anthropological opening soon takes an ethnic turn and focuses on the interaction of God with one privileged community, the Christian Bible with its promise of universal salvation re-establishes humanity as such as the protagonist of the story. There is a similar dynamic at work in the *Metamorphoses*. Just as the

---

[30] Hesiod, *Th.* 178-87. Other members of this brood include the Erinys and a branch of tree-nymphs.

[31] Lightfoot, *Lucian* (n. 21, above) 338, with further bibliography in n. 17. See also M. L. West, (2004), 'The Flood Myth in Ovid, Lucian and Nonnus', in *Mitos en la literatura griega helenística e imperial*, ed. J. A. López Férez (Madrid 2004) 245-59.

[32] K. F. B. Fletcher, 'Ovidian "Correction" of the Biblical flood?', *Classical Philology* (2010) 105, 209-13. Further bibliography includes A. Griffin, 'Ovid's Universal Flood', *Hermathena* (1992) 152, 39-58 and W. Speyer, 'Spuren der Genesis in Ovids Metamorphosen?', in *Kontinuität und Wandel: Lateinische Poesie von Naevius bis Baudelaire; Franco Munari zum 65. Geburtstag*, ed. by F. Wagner *et al.* (Hildesheim 1986) 90-99.

[33] Lightfoot, *Lucian* (n. 21, above) 345: 'Other classical sources know the tradition that the rest of the world was wicked, but do not generally explain Deucalion's survival by his special virtue. Reference to his justice or piety (Ov. Met. I. 322-3 and Bömer *ad loc.*, 327) seem late, sporadic developments, perhaps under the influence of Near Eastern tradition...'

New Testament shifts the emphasis from 'God's chosen people' to a new covenant that covers all of humanity, so Ovid's *Metamorphoses* rewrites Greek mythic material that often has a decidedly local, aetiological slant, in a universalizing key. The *telos* of the narrative is Rome, but imperial Rome corresponds to the world: in the *Metamorphoses* the equation of *urbs* and *orbis*, *imperium* and cosmos, finds its most sustained and programmatic articulation. As Ovid puts it at the end of his narrative '*terra sub Augusto est*' (*Met.* 15.860), shortly before signing off with a *sphragis* that proclaims his fame *urbi et orbi* (*Met.* 15.871-79).[34]

Apart from Ovid's *Metamorphoses* and the Bible, there are very few other literary texts of the first rank that treat the human being as the protagonist of a grand narrative. Milton's *Paradise Lost* and *Regained* belong here – as does Dante's *Divine Comedy*. In fact, it is Dante who offers the best definition of what I have dubbed 'anthropological epic' when he explains to Can Grande what the *Commedia* is all about (*Epistle to Can Grande* 34: '*man* according as by his merits or demerits in the exercise of his free will he is deserving of reward or punishment by justice' (*subiectum est homo prout merendo et demerendo per arbitrii libertatem est iustitie premiandi et puniendi obnoxius*).[35] The biblical and classical personnel that populate his literary world bear the same anthropological, universalizing imprint also on display in Ovid and the Bible. A case in point is Dante's re-profiling of the figure of Ulysses in *Inferno* 26, whom 'he extends ... from the conniving Greek hero to an image of unredeemed Man'.[36] In Ovid, Dante, and the Christian Bible historical and legendary characters partly lose their cultural specificity and become focal points for a meditation on humanity as such.

2. Metamorphosis as a principle of cosmic dynamism

Metamorphosis plays a crucial role in a tradition of anthropological thought that emphasizes the eccentricity and pliability of human nature and links those qualities to free will. For the Renaissance philosopher Pico della Mirandola, for instance, God anticipated Sartre in positing that our existence precedes our essence, giving humanity, in contrast to all other beings, the freedom to define his or her own position in the world:[37] 'We have given you, Adam, no fixed seat nor features proper to yourself nor endowment peculiar to you alone', so Pico imagines the Lord as saying, 'in order that whatever seat, whatever features, whatever endowment you may responsibly desire, these same you may have and possess according to your desire and judgement.' Adam is thus released into the world with the exhortation: 'as the free and extraordinary shaper of yourself, fashion yourself

---

[34] See further Section 4 below.

[35] For the letter and its (disputed) authorship see (*e.g.*) R. Hollander, *Dante's Epistle to Cangrande* (Ann Arbor 1993); A. R. Ascoli, 'Access to authority: Dante in the *Epistle to Cangrande*', in *Seminario Dantesco Internazionale/ International Dante Seminar 1*, ed. Z. Baranksi (Florence 1997) 308-52; or Z. G. Baranski, 'The Epistle to *Can Grande*', in *The Cambridge History of Literary Criticism, vol.2: the Middle Ages*, ed. A. Minnis and I. Johnson, Cambridge, 583-89.

[36] B. Reynolds, *Dante: the poet, the political thinker, the man* (Emeryville/ CA 2006) 196.

[37] *De hominis dignitate* 4. I quote the translation of Pier Cesare Bori from the Pico Project at Brown University (www.brown.edu/Departments/Italian_Studies/pico/).

in the form you will prefer' – though God notes, presciently, that this self-fashioning may not necessarily result in a rebirth into the higher orders of being (which are divine): it could also entail a degeneration into lower, brutish forms of life. In a breath-taking syncretistic sweep, Pico then goes on to cite various authors and systems of thought (Near Eastern, Jewish, Christian, pagan, mystic, hermetic) as evidence for the entwining of anthropology and metamorphosis in support of his argument that the defining hallmark of our species is the divinely sanctioned capacity for transformative change, which enables us to turn ourselves into any other creature we like.[38]

The (Christian) Bible, Ovid's *Metamorphoses*, and the *Divine Comedy* are main tributaries to this wider tradition: all endorse modes of metamorphosis to explore and define what it is to be – and cease to be – human within a wider cosmic setting. Ovid in particular sounds out the limits and possibilities of being human within a transforming and transformative universe, especially at the extreme ends of the spectrum at which humanity touches upon, perhaps even morphs into, the divine or begins to resemble, maybe even turns into, the bestial. Transformation and the related phenomenon of conversion occupy an equally central place in the New Testament, which revolves around the 'metamorphic moments' of incarnation, transfiguration – or, to use the Greek term Matthew and Mark use to describe the event, 'metamorphosis' – and resurrection after crucifixion.[39] The sequence finds ritual remembrance in the celebration of the Eucharist, which Jesus instituted during the Last Supper when he took the bread and wine he served at table and proclaimed them (turned them into?) his body and his blood – a transformative event that has given rise to numerous theories of transubstantiation ever since the early middle ages and still preoccupies the theological imagination.[40] Paul picks up on the idiom of metamorphosis in Mark and Matthew and applies it to the consequences of imitating Christ. His use of μεταμορφοῦσθαι captures the 'before' and 'after' of experiencing divine revelation, coinciding with an assimilation of the believer to Christ. Like Mark and Matthew with reference to the transfiguration, Paul uses the notion of metamorphosis as a dynamic principle at work in the universal and personal history of salvation, which is grounded in the precarious – indeed, polymorphous – ontology of Christ, in which God's plan for humanity 'materialized': 'The Son's hominization as the Second Adam in Jesus of Nazareth, a particular human being in

---

[38] See § 9: *Ecquis hominem non admiretur? Qui non immerito in sacris litteris Mosaicis et Christianis, nunc omnis carnis, nunc omnis creaturae appellatione designatur, quando se ipsum ipse in omnis carnis faciem, in omnis creaturae ingenium effingit, fabricat et transformat.* ('Who, then, will not admire man? Not undeservedly, in the Mosaic and Christian Scriptures he is called at times with the name of every flesh, at times of every creature, for he fashions, shapes and transforms his own look into that of every flesh, his own mind into that of every creature'.)

[39] Metamorphoses are marginal in, if not entirely absent from, the Old Testament. See *e.g.* Genesis 5:22-24 (the possible deification of Enoch), 19:15-26 (the transformation of the wife of Lot into a pillar of salt), or Exodus 7:1-12 (the stick-into-snakes competition between Moses and the Egyptian Magi). Metamorphosis becomes more rampant in apocryphal texts. See *e.g.* H.-J. Klauck, 'Christus in vielen Gestalten: Die Polymorphie des Erlösers in apokryphen Texten', in *Die apokryphe Bibel: Ein anderer Zugang zum frühen Christentum* (Tübingen 2008), who begins his discussion with the programmatic quotation of the proem to Ovid's *Metamorphoses*.

[40] See *e.g. 'Dies ist mein Leib': Philosophische Texte zur Eucharistie-Debatte im 17. Jahrhundert*, ed. A. Scheib (Darmstadt 2008).

history, was conceived as the ultimate ratification of God's commitment to the *material* creation and as the definitive outworking of God's original plan for the world.'[41]

Christian theologians are generally rather keen on putting up a *cordon sanitaire* between Christian and pagan thought on transformative change. Not so Dante: throughout the *Divine Comedy*, Christian and Ovidian notions of metamorphosis are in constant dialogue, and in various ways. Most obviously, Dante operates a corrective contrast between the sterile perversity of 'Ovidian' metamorphosis and the salvific sequence of incarnation, transfiguration, and resurrection. But a simple contrast does not do justice to his complex engagement with the *Metamorphoses*, which evolves on the way from *Inferno* to *Paradiso*: 'Every reference to Ovid's poem ... is part of an extended meditation on the reach and the shortcomings of its idea of metamorphosis. In Hell, Dante refitted the conceit of "forms changed into new bodies" ("in nova ... mutatas ... formas/ corpora", *Met.* 1.1-2) so that it could underwrite the exhaustion of form in the damned and their dissolution into the inert matter of non-being. In Purgatory he baptised it, so that it subtends the soul's reformation. In Paradise, he sanctified it, so that it dimly foreshadows the perfection of bliss the resurrected will enjoy after the Second Coming'.[42]

In fact, it is possible to take the elevation of Ovidian change in Paradise even a step further (*Paradiso* 1.64–72):[43]

> Beatrice tutta ne l'etterne rote
> fissa con li occhi stava; e io in lei
> le luci fissi, di là sù rimote.
>   Nel suo aspetto tal dentro mi fei,
> qual si fé Glauco nel gustar de l'erba
> che 'l fé consorto in mar de li altri dèi.
>   Trasumanar significar *per verba*
> non si poria; però l'essemplo basti
> a cui esperïenza grazia serba.

Beatrice had fixed her eyes/ upon the eternal wheels and I now fixed/ my sight on her, withdrawing it from above./ As I gazed on her, I was changed within,/ as Glaucus was on tasting of the grass/ that made him consort of the gods in the sea./ To soar beyond the human cannot be described/ in words. Let the example be enough to one/ for whom grace holds this experience in store.

---

[41] P. M. Blowers, *Drama of the divine economy: Creator and creation in early Christian theology and piety* (Oxford 2012) 2, with reference to Eph. 1:3-14; 3:9; Col. 1:15-20, 26; 2:2-3.

[42] W. Ginsberg, 'Dante's Ovid', in *Ovid in the Middle Ages*, ed. J. G. Clark, F. T. Coulson, and K. L. McKinley (Cambridge 2011) 143-59 (156).

[43] I here and elsewhere cite the translation of *Paradiso* by Robert and Jean Hollander (New York 2007).

The neologism *trasumanar* evokes a potentially problematic mode of transformative change: apotheosis.[44] Bernard of Clairvaux, who, within the *Divine Comedy*, acts as Dante's last guide for the empyrean part of *Paradiso*, took great care to stress in his own writings that any change human beings undergo in either direction (upwards or downwards) does not – must not – unsettle God's natural order or basic principles of scholastic ontology. Thus in his Sermon on the *Song of Songs*, Bernard, with reference to Second Corinthians, endorses the notion of assimilation to the divine, rather than transformation into a god (*Sermo* 62.5):

> Etenim revelata facie speculantes, in eamdem imaginem transformamur de claritate in claritatem, tanquam a Domini Spiritu [~ 2 Cor. 3.18] *Transformamur cum conformamur*. Absit autem ut in majestatis gloria, et non magis in voluntatis modestia, Dei ab homine conformitas praesumatur!

> For when we see him face to face, we are transformed into that same image, from brightness into brightness, as if by the Spirit of the Lord. *We are transformed in that we are made to resemble.* May the thought be absent, however, that the resemblance of humankind to God be claimed to consist in the glory of majesty, rather than in the modesty of the will.

And likewise, in *Sermo* 82, while discussing the downward movement of the human soul towards the level of the beasts, he rejects the potential implications of several passages from the Psalms that seem to hint at the possibility of human-into-animal metamorphosis: the likeness of the soul to God may be covered up, he argues, but it can never be fully destroyed. In essence, then, the human soul may, to varying degrees, come to resemble, without turning into, God; and it may only ever become *like* a beast, but not a beast itself, by donning some of its characteristics, through a process of corruption and deformation. In all, Bernard draws clear boundaries within the domain of transformative change, and scholars have plausibly argued that Dante's 'trasumanar' evokes Bernard's theory of deification, in the sense of an assimilation to the divine that emphatically does *not* involve a transformative change in substance.[45]

As *Inferno* 25 makes clear, however, Dante was by no means beyond deconstructive play with the categories of scholastic philosophy, putting on record modes of punitive metamorphosis that defy Bernard's principles of ontological stability even more so than the Ovidian flux that is simultaneously dismissed as feeble in comparison.[46] And in *Paradiso* 1, he invokes Bernard's philosophy of deification but uses Ovid to hint at the possibility of a genuine 'transgression' of scholastic protocols of thought. Since the experience he here tries to capture in language defies *verbal* signification (*per verba*: Dante tellingly switches into Latin to make this point: see Section 4, below), he resorts to an illustrative 'example',

---

[44] For discussion of this technique (and its classical precedents), see *e.g.* B. D. Schildgen, 'Dante's neologisms in the *Paradiso* and the Latin rhetorical tradition', *Dante Studies* 107 (1989) 101-19.

[45] See Botterill, *Dante and the Mystical Tradition* (n. 9, above).

[46] See *e.g.* K. Gross, 'Infernal metamorphoses: an interpretation of Dante's "counterpass"', *Modern Language Notes* 100 (1985) 42-69; C. A. Cioffi, 'The anxieties of Ovidian influence: theft in *Inferno* XXIV and XXV', *Dante Studies* 112 (1994) 77-100; Gildenhard and Zissos, 'Introduction to part II', *Transformative Change* (n. 14, above) 200-03.

likening his soaring beyond the human to the transformation of the human Glaucus into a god of the sea caused by the consumption of magical herbs – a story that found its classic articulation in Ovid's *Metamorphoses*.[47] The pagan myth of apotheosis, however tightly integrated into Dante's Christian universe, at least evokes the possibility of far more radical transformations of the human being than Bernard, for one, is willing to entertain and thereby generates – is designed to generate – a surplus of meaning that enriches the nature of Dante's experience in Paradise – a journey into the beyond of language that requires recourse to an Ovidian idiom to articulate.

3. The historicity of fiction

Superficially, a document of faith (the Bible), a self-conscious exercise in what is largely fiction (the *Metamorphoses*), and what purports to be the autobiographical record of a journey into the beyond (the *Divine Comedy*) would seem to have little in common from the point of view of historicity. Yet, however differently readers are tempted to assess their documentary value, the three texts themselves all lay claim to re-present what *really* happened (even though in the case of Ovid at least this claim is of course made tongue-in-cheek).

Consider, first, the Bible and the *Metamorphoses*. Both works claim to trace a universal history of the cosmos and of humanity, from the moment of first creation to the present (or the end of time); and in both texts, this historical record revolves around a series of decisive interventions by supernatural forces (epiphanies, miracles, metamorphoses) that *prima facie* defy belief. Both texts feature a distinctive rhetoric of truth to authenticate their referential value, which involves, not least, the anticipation of incredulity, designed to pre-empt the audience's unwillingness to suspend disbelief in the face of the miraculous, marvellous, and metamorphic. In the New Testament, Jesus knows that he is at times preaching to 'those of little faith', and he faces the same challenge even after his passion: the emblematic figure here is 'doubting Thomas', who initially refuses to believe in the physical resurrection of Christ unless he can verify the fact on the basis of personal experience.[48] The equivalent figure in the *Metamorphoses* is Pirithous, who, at the very centre of the poem, challenges its key premise: the metamorphic powers of the gods. In response to a story by the river-god Achelous about the transformation of nymphs into islands, a *factum mirabile* that all other members in the audience accept as true, he flat-out denies that the gods have the power to cause miraculous transformations (*Met.* 8. 612-15).[49] To reaffirm divine omnipotence, Lelex then narrates the story of Philemon and Baucis and their transformation into trees as reward

---

[47] *Met.* 13.916-65.

[48] John 20:24-29.

[49] This portion of the epic has received much discussion. See *e.g.* F. Graf, 'Ovide, les *Métamorphoses* et la véracité du mythe', in *Métamorphoses du mythe en Grèce*, ed. C. Calame (Geneva 1988) 67-68; D. C. Feeney, *The Gods in epic: poets and critics of the Classical Tradition* (Oxford 1991) 230, and J. Fabre-Serris, 'Constructing a Narrative of *mira deum*: The story of Philemon and Baucis (Ovid, *Metamorphoses* 8)', in *Paradox and the marvellous in Augustan literature and culture*, ed. P. Hardie (Oxford 2009). A more detailed analysis is also available in Gildenhard and Zissos, 'Introduction to Part I', *Transformative Change* (n. 14 above) 72-76.

for their piety – a story that points forward to the poem's Roman end.[50] The tussle over credibility at the centre of the poem highlights particularly well that Ovid represents fiction as fact throughout the *Metamorphoses*, claiming historical value for events that defy belief.

Dante too puts on record experiences that are, to use an Ovidian tag, *maiora fide*. And just like Ovid, the rhetoric of the text adopts an unwavering commitment to the claim that his poetry is as faithful a record of reality as he (or anyone else, for that matter) is able to produce. He never budges from the conceit to report actual events, vouched for by empirical inspection: As Charles Singleton put it, 'Dante will never undermine the basic fiction of his poem, which is that it is not a fiction'.[51] The techniques he applies to endow his eye-witness account of the beyond with plausibility are strikingly similar (though not entirely identical) to those on display in the Bible and the *Metamorphoses*. Just like Ovid and the evangelists, Dante anticipates incredulity. In his account of Geryon, 'a monster derived from classical mythology whose patently fictional characteristics Dante first heightens and then uses as the stake on which to gamble the veracity of his poem', he concedes that what he reports may well strike readers as a 'truth that has the face of a lie' (*Inf.* 16.124: '...ver c'ha faccia di menzogna'), but goes on to insist, paradoxically and paradoxographically, on the reality of the impossible.[52] A related strategy is the incorporation of earlier authors' self-critique, again as a way of showing awareness of the *distinction* between fact and fiction. A programmatic instance occurs in *Inferno* 13, where Dante the poet has his character Virgil reflect critically on one of the few metamorphoses he decided to include in the *Aeneid*: the transformation of Polydorus into reeds, which start to bleed into speech when they are broken. The intricate design yields an assertive epistemology: 'The opening of canto 13 ... makes Virgil a reader of his own poem and reveals his inadequacy in foreseeing and speaking about the fulfilment of his marvel as revisited in Dante's *Inferno*', as part of Virgil's *and Dante's* "poétique de la démonstration"'.[53] The engagement with Ovid in *Inferno* 25 likewise features a *contrastive* commitment to standards of veracity, a separation of the marvellous chaff that is fictitious (associated with pagan authors and their imagination) and the marvellous wheat that is a true and authentic part of the Christian universe.[54]

More so than the authors of the Bible and Ovid, Dante also made the anticipation of incredulity part of his authorial self-fashioning. Throughout the *Divine Comedy*, he underscores the limits of language – as we shall see in the next section: *any* language – to represent adequately his autopsy of the beyond. Dante practices a poetics of the ineffable, in which constant appeals to the failure of language countersign the authenticity of his

---

[50] *Met.* 8. 618-19: ... *'immensa est finemque potentia caeli | non habet et, quidquid superi voluere, peractum est.'* For Philemon and Baucis (a 'Phrygian' couple) as anticipation of Rome, see I. Gildenhard and A. Zissos, 'Ovid's "Hecale": deconstructing Athens in Ovid's *Metamorphoses*', *Journal of Roman Studies* 94 (2004) 47–72.

[51] C. S. Singleton, *Dante Alighieri, the divine comedy translated, with a commentary: Purgatorio, 2. Commentary* (Princeton 1973) 702. See also T. Barolini, *The Undivine Comedy: Detheologizing Dante* (Princeton 1992) 3-20.

[52] Barolini, 'Arachne, Argus, and St. John' (n. 1, above) 161.

[53] D. Biow, *Mirabile Dictu: representations of the Marvelous in medieval and renaissance epic* (Ann Arbor 1996) 43.

[54] Gildenhard and Zissos, 'Introduction to part II', *Transformative Change* (n. 14 above) 201.

experience, thus shielding the encounter with divine truth from the pitfalls of representation, yet also suggesting that his endeavour at representation constitutes the closest possible approximation of divine truth.[55] For his apparent modesty has a counterpart in a striking megalomania: to complete his mission impossible, Dante musters every possible source of inspiration, essentially turning himself into an *auctor* and a prophet, suitably inspired to pen a vernacular scripture that comprises secrets of heaven even the apostle Paul considered beyond the remit of human speech.[56] Thus at the outset of *Paradiso*, Dante first proclaims, in an obvious allusion to Paul's *raptus* into Paradise mentioned at 2 *Corinthians* 12:2-4 (*quoniam raptus est in paradisum et audivit arcana verba quae non licet homini loqui...*), that anyone who comes down from where he has been can neither know nor tell what he has seen (1.4-6):

> Nel ciel che più de la sua luce prende
> fu' io, e vidi cose che ridire
> né sa né può chi di là sù discende;

> I was in that heaven which receives
> more of His light. He who comes down from there
> can neither know nor tell what he has seen

But whereas the Paul of the Christian Bible abides by his own injunction not to pass on the lessons he learned in Paradise, Dante follows the apocryphal tradition of Pauline writings and tries to express what he has seen in words.[57] For this impossible mission, he appeals to every biblical and classical source of help (including the Muses, Paul, and Ovid), to fashion himself as a vessel and vehicle of discourse inspired by Apollo-Christ, to endow his authorial voice and poetic language with divine legitimacy and claim to truth.[58]
From the point of view of reception, then, the Bible, the *Metamorphoses*, and the *Divine Comedy* all issue a more or less serious challenge to the reader. Each work rebukes more or less implicitly as impious those who dismiss its contents as beyond belief. Those who do are nullfidians, *contemptores superum*, or heretics, who doubt the divinity of Christ, the omnipotence of the gods, or Dante's revelation, consisting in nothing less than a personal encounter with (the world of) God.

4. Politics of language and poetics of succession

A key dynamic that defines the argument and the poetics of Ovid's *Metamorphoses*, the Christian Bible, and Dante's *Divine Comedy* is the way in which they reshape the cultural heritage of an older civilization: in Ovid's case, Greek myth; in the case of the Christian

---

[55] Examples include again his faltering in the face of the new in *Inferno* 25 and *Paradiso* 1 (as discussed above). See also Section 4 and 5 below.

[56] For Dante as author see further A. R. Ascoli, *Dante and the making of a modern author* (Cambridge 2008).

[57] T. Silverstein, 'Did Dante know the vision of St. Paul?', *Harvard Studies and Notes in Philology and Literature* 19 (1937) 231-47.

[58] See in detail K. Brownlee, 'Pauline vision and Ovidian speech in *Paradiso* i', in *The poetry of allusion* (n. 11, above) 202-13.

editors of the Bible, the Hebrew Scriptures, which get re-organized and re-labelled as the 'Old Testament'; in the case of Dante, the pagan classics. In all three cases we are dealing with polemical acts of appropriation and more or less explicit assertions of 'supersession' (still a highly controversial issue in interfaith relations), by which Ovid, the authors of the New Testament and editors of the biblical canon, and Dante re-contextualize the chronological priority of another faith or civilization within a countervailing rhetoric of pre-figuration and completion. This includes a linguistic dimension. We get shifts from Hebrew into universalizing *koine* Greek; from Greek into imperial Latin to coincide with the universal sway of Roman power; from the artificial Latin of the classical past into the natural vernacular of Dante's present. In each case, the linguistic register that seems inferior becomes the medium for a reconfiguration of ultimate truth.

The passage from *Paradiso* 1 we already had occasion to cite earlier offers a good instance of the politics of language in the *Divine Comedy*:

> Trasumanar significar *per verba*
> non si poria

Dante here recalls an experience that, he says, is impossible to capture in human language altogether; and he stresses, obliquely yet programmatically, that this applies irrespective of which tongue one uses in the endeavour to meet the challenge: Italian, that is, or, indeed, Latin. The switch in linguistic registers here, from the vernacular to the universal language (*per verba*) is far from incidental. It recalls his preoccupation with the relationship between Latin and vernacular Italian throughout his career as author – from the paradoxical opening of the *de vulgari eloquentia*, where he announces that, inspired by God, the Word (*Verbum*), he will address the theme of vernacular eloquence in Latin (*Verbo aspirante de celis, locutioni vulgarium gentium prodesse tentabimus*) to *Convivio* 4.21 where he deems the generation of the human soul a process that cannot be expressed in words – words, he adds, in the vernacular ('Non è cosa da manifestare a lingua, lingua, dico veramente, volgare'). Yet here at the gateway to heaven, Dante, pushed, as he is, to the limits of his native Italian, intimates with supreme economy that the language of the *Biblia Sacra*, too, even though it contains the revelation of the *Verbum*, would not have been up to the task of articulating *per verba* his transporting and transforming vision of Beatrice. His own elevation of the vernacular as a medium in which to express divinely revealed truth contrasts with his implicit criticism of Latin as a medium of ancient pagan lies – not least those of Virgil and Ovid.[59]

---

[59] For further discussion of Latin and the vernacular in the age of Dante, see *e.g.* A. Mazzocco, *Linguistic theories in Dante and the Humanists: studies of language and intellectual history in late medieval and early renaissance Italy* (Leiden 1993), or A. J. Minnis, *Translations of authority in medieval English literature: valuing the vernacular* (Cambridge 2009) (with a discussion of Dante at 2-3).

5. The figure of the artist

From Moses, the alleged author of the Pentateuch, to David, who, as legend has it, wrote much if not all of the Psalter, Solomon (composer of the Song of Songs), the prophets, evangelists, Paul, and John, the author of Revelations, the Bible comprises a symphony of voices, orchestrated by the one voice that permeates the whole: the voice of God.[60]

The *Metamorphoses* features a similar line-up of verbal and visual artists *in* the text who variously inflect – and are orchestrated – by the artist *of* the text: Ovid himself. The artist in Ovid and Ovid as artist are by now well-explored phenomena.[61] For our purposes, four aspects are particularly pertinent. (i) Ovid highlights the world-making power of poetry which imposes form on matter – up to and including an argument for the superiority of form over substance. His comment on the divine craftsmanship of Vulcan, which is on display in the palace of the Sun, fashioned as it is out of the most precious metals, that 'the artistry outshines the material' (*Met.* 2.5: *materiam superabat opus*) could stand as a metapoetic motto for his own poetry. (ii) Ovid associates art with transgression – as betoken by the long series of hubristic artists who receive their comeuppance in the course of the poem and come to a sticky end. The daughters of Minyas? Turned to bats. Arachne? Transformed into a spider. Marsyas? Skinned alive. Orpheus? Torn to pieces. Their art, too, suffers: the stories of the Minyeides who try to defy Bacchus are ultimately infiltrated and inflected by their divine antagonist.[62] Arachne's perfect tapestry is shredded. Orpheus' voice is reduced to unintelligible muttering – a particularly poignant reduction of divine music to meaningless noise given that the same head could still call out 'Eurydice' in a plangent, plaintive, and profoundly tragic voice in Virgil's *Georgics*.[63] (iii) In striking contrast to the fate of art and artists in his text, Ovid elevates his poetry into a medium of immortality *for himself*: in his *sphragis* he outrageously breaks through the generic anonymity of epic and claims in a supreme gesture of defiant hubris that his poetry, which he advertises as his better part, will survive even the wrath of Jove and his annihilating thunderbolt (*Met.* 15.871-72: *Iamque opus exegi, quod nec Iovis ira nec ignis | nec poterit ferrum nec edax abolere vetustas...*), soar to the starts, ensure the immortality of his name, and thus ensure eternal

---

[60] See A. J. Minnis, *Medieval theory of authorship: scholastic literary attitudes in the later middle ages* (London 1984) 40-58 for a classic discussion of how the medieval commentary tradition rehearsed the issue of scriptural *auctores*. For a somewhat different, though no less illuminating take, see P. Barolsky, *A Brief History of the Artist from God to Picasso* (University Park, Penn. 2011).

[61] See in particular the magisterial treatment by P. Hardie, *Ovid's poetics of illusion* (Cambridge 2002).

[62] See A. Keith, 'Dionysiac theme and dramatic allusion in Ovid's *Metamorphoses* 4', in *Beyond the fifth century: interactions with Greek tragedy from the fourth century BCE to the middle ages*, ed. I. Gildenhard and M. Revermann (Berlin and New York 2010) 187-217.

[63] Contrast Virgil, *G.* 4.523-27: *tum quoque marmorea caput a cervice revulsum | gurgite cum medio portans Oeagrius Hebrus | volveret, Eurydicen vox ipsa et frigida lingua, | a miseram Eurydicen! anima fugiente vocabat: | Eurydicen toto referebant flumine ripae* with Ovid, *Met.* 11.50–53: *caput, Hebre, lyramque | excipis, et (mirum!) medio dum labitur amne, | flebile nescioquid queritur lyra, flebile lingua murmurat exanimis, respondent flebile ripae*, where the name of Eurydice turns into *flebile nescioquid*.

INGO GILDENHARD: DANTE'S SCRIPTURES

life for himself. The last word of the poem is the triumphant *vivam*: 'I shall live!'[64] The *sphragis* thus amounts to an act of self-deification that asserts the power of the creative imagination to withstand even the application of extreme physical force invested in the supreme deity that earlier on in the poem reduced Semele to cinder.[65]

Dante again intertwines the two traditions in defining his own authorial voice, using Ovidian hubris to throw his Christian modesty in relief – a modesty designed not least to take the sting out of his (Ovidian) hubris to have authored a vernacular scripture worthy of secular-Ovidian glory, more specifically the laurel crown. The dialectics of megalomania and modesty in Dante's authorial self-fashioning, which he develops in dialogue with Ovidian material, pervade *Paradiso* – and resonate until the very end.[66] To begin with, Dante explicitly rejects any hint that his poetry can rival his material. He explicitly puts both the divine *materia* and the divine *forma* he encounters on his journey beyond his powers of expression, however inspired his voice. Dante reinforces the point by a kind of ring-composition between the first and the last canto of *Paradiso*, marked by a *quasi*-platonic gesture of modesty that he will have succeeded if he has managed to convey in and through his poetry a mere shadow of the divine matter (*materia*) and form (*forma*) he encountered on his journey.[67]

At the same time, as the passage from *Paradiso* 1 makes clear, Dante wants a share of literary fame. Christianity strongly disapproved of this secular mode of immortality, but just at the time of Dante the ennobling power of poetry and the special status of the poet experienced a revival in the form of the *poeta laureatus* – an honour which Dante's rival Albertino Mussato received in 1315, and which Petrarch would come to elevate into an obsession to rival his Christian faith. The poet who provided the mythic aetiology for the custom was, naturally, Ovid with the first love story of the *Metamorphoses*, which ends in the transformation of Daphne into a laurel tree and the acclamation of the laurel as the tree of poets and – in the form of the triumphal crown – Roman emperors and princes. Dante

---

[64] *Met.* 15. 871-79. Ovid comes back to this boast in more sober terms in his exile poetry – after, that is, Jupiter (in the form of the *princeps* Augustus) has, if not incinerated his poem, at the very least zapped the poet. In this context, he even draws an explicit parallel between the fate of Semele and his own: see *Tristia* 4.3.67–70: *nec Semele Cadmo facta est aliena parenti, | quod precibus periit ambitiosa sui. | nec tibi, quod saevis ego sum Iovis ignibus ictus, | purpureus molli fiat in ore pudor*, further 4.8.45-50 (on Jupiter's omnipotence).

[65] It is possible to read the *sphragis* as at least in part a self-conscious inversion of the Semele-episode, in which an encounter with the fire of Jove proved fatal: Dante, arguably, did so: see below.

[66] For Dante's Janus-like authorial voice see for instance also Ascoli, 'Access to Authority' (n. 35, above) 338, who focuses on the fact that Dante endows (what are from a certain point of view) figments of his imagination with documentary value: 'Paradoxically, as "fabricating" poet he is most autonomous and god-like, most proleptic of the Renaissance author-God to come, while as *scriba Dei* he is most required to stress that he is a mere vehicle of divine vocalization.'

[67] See *Paradiso* 1.22-27 (*O divina virtù, se mi ti presti | tanto che* l'ombra *del beato regno | segnata nel mio capo io manifesti, | vedra'mi al piè del tuo diletto legno | venire, e coronarmi de le foglie | che la materia et tu mi farai degno*) and 33.91–96 (*La forma universal di questo nodo | credo ch'i' vidi, perché più di largo, | dicendo questo, mi sento ch'i' godo. | Un punto solo m'è maggior letargo | che venticinque secoli a la 'mpresa | che fé Nettuno ammirar* l'ombra *d'Argo*).

20 THE AFTERLIFE OF OVID

was keenly aware of the practice. At the opening of *Paradiso* 1 and 25 he imagines the power of his poetry to enable him to return from exile to his native Florence, the city of his baptism into the Christian faith, to receive the laurel crown.

The poem, of course, concludes not with a terrestrial, but a spiritual homecoming that promises true immortality rather than its secular substitute of literary glory. Noting (again) that his powers failed him to comprehend the final, ultimate *vista nova* of his journey, Dante recalls an act of succour from above (*Paradiso* 33.139-41): *ma non eran da ciò le proprie penne:/ se non che la mia mente fu percossa/ da un fulgore in che sua voglia venne.* ('But my wings had not sufficed for that/ had not my mind been struck by a bolt/ of lightning that granted what I asked'). The state he achieves resembles deification as conceived by Bernard of Clairvaux, his last guide.[68] But, as with the Glaucus reference in *Paradiso* 1, Ovid remains an intertextual presence as well in Dante's transfiguration. The phrasing here not coincidentally recalls the experience of Semele:[69] the Theban princess was motivated by the same desire as Dante, that is, to set eyes on the supreme divinity in his true shape. In Semele's case, as in Dante's, this desire resulted in their being struck by a bolt of lightning. Yet whereas the thunderbolt of sexual passion Jupiter is forced to unleash on the princess proves fatal (she ends up incinerated even though the Olympian 'came' only with his *tela secunda*), the *fulgore* of divine love that strikes Dante is salvific. Far from suffering combustion, he enters into perfect alignment with *l'amor che move il sole e l'altre stelle* (33.145).[70] Instead of physical pagan *eros* we get spiritual Christian *amor*, where Ovid offers a sordid tale of (it has to be said: truly divine) sex and death, Dante shares a sublime moment of union with God himself.

Here the *Divine Comedy* ends. Having reached the *telos* of his quest, there is nothing more for Dante to say. And just as his final experience of transformative salvation negatively invokes the doom of a character from the *Metamorphoses*, so his sense of closure inverts

---

[68] Botterill, *Dante and the mystical tradition* (n. 9, above) 241: 'Dante *personaggio* can be seen to aspire, throughout the poem, to reach a condition of Bernardine *deificatio*; and that might help to explain just why, when he does so, it should be through the intervention and under the auspices of Bernard of Clairvaux himself...'

[69] Dante sets up the intertext in *Paradiso* 21-23, where he explicitly rewrites Ovid's Semele-episode from *Metamorphosis* 3 in a positive, Christian key: see K. Brownlee, 'Ovid's Semele and Dante's Metamorphosis' (n. 8, above). Brownlee well works out how 'Dante's strategic fragmentation of his Ovidian subtext (*Met.* 3.287-315) involves the following basic pattern: Semele's request to Jupiter is correctively rewritten in *Paradiso* 21 and 22 in the three encounters between Dante and Beatrice, Dante and Peter Damian, and Dante and St. Benedict; the fulfillment of Semele's request to Jupiter is correctively rewritten in *Paradiso* 23 through Dante's successive (and profoundly complementary) perceptions of Christ, Beatrice, and Mary' (224). But he overlooks that the pattern arguably finds its (mind-blowing) climax only at the very end of the *Commedia*.

[70] In scholastic thought, the alignment of human and divine will that constitutes deification is an act of grace on the part of God. See *e.g.* Thomas Aquinas *Quaestio De raptu, ST*, IIaIIae.175 (*ad secundum dicendum quod ad modum et dignitatem hominis pertinet quod ad divina elevetur, ex hoc ipso quod homo factus est ad imaginem Dei. Et quia bonum divinum in infinitum excedit humanam facultatem, indiget homo ut supernaturaliter ad illud bonum capessendum adiuvetur: quod fit per quodcumque beneficium gratiae. Unde quod sic elevetur mens a Deo per raptum, non est contra naturam, sed supra facultatem naturae*), cited by Botterill, *Dante and the mystical tradition* (n. 9, above) 219, who argues that this is the condition that Dante achieves at the end of the *Commedia*. The concept is Christian; the imagery, arguably, Ovidian.

Ovid, the *auctor*, at the level of poetics. What babbles away at the end of Ovid's epic is *Ovidius loquax*, who 'seals' his poem in a hubristic act of self-immortalization through his poetry in explicit defiance of the thunderbolt of Jove; what resonates at the end of the *Divine Comedy* is the equally eloquent, yet also triumphantly modest sound of silence.

King's College, University of Cambridge

REFLECTIONS OF NARCISSUS[1]

CAROLINE STARK

> Quae cum ita sint, consuevi inter familiares dicere picturae inventorem fuisse, poetarum sententia, Narcissum illum qui sit in florem versus, nam cum sit omnium artium flos pictura, tum de Narcisso omnis fabula pulchre ad rem ipsam perapta erit. Quid est enim aliud pingere quam arte superficiem illam fontis amplecti?   Leon Battista Alberti, *De pictura* 2.26[2]

> Consequently I used to tell my friends that the inventor of painting, according to the poets, was Narcissus, who was turned into a flower; for, as painting is the flower of all the arts, so the tale of Narcissus fits our purpose perfectly. What is painting but the act of embracing by means of art the surface of the pool? (trans. C. Grayson)

In the beginning of the second book of *De pictura* (1435), Leon Battista Alberti credits Narcissus with the invention of painting. He is drawn to the story in Ovid because the reflection of Narcissus in the water brilliantly captures the use of Alberti's veil: for 'What is painting but the act of embracing by means of art the surface of the pool?', *Quid est enim aliud pingere quam arte superficiem illam fontis amplecti?* (2.26). Just as Narcissus attempts to embrace his reflection in the water, so also does the artist attempt to grasp the image in Nature and accurately recreate it on the canvas. But Alberti has other reasons for choosing Narcissus. Beyond representing a likeness of things, a painter should seek to improve upon Nature by selecting the most excellent parts of the most beautiful bodies (3.55). He cites as evidence the story from Cicero (*De inventione* 2.1.1-3) and Pliny (*Naturalis historia* 35.64) of the way in which the famous painter Zeuxis did not settle on one body alone for his portrait of Helen. Instead, he 'chose from all the youth of the city five outstandingly beautiful girls, so that he might represent in his painting whatever feature of feminine beauty was most praiseworthy in each of them', *ex omni eius urbis iuventute delegit virgines quinque forma praestantiores, ut quod in quaque esset formae muliebris laudatissimum, id in pictura referret*

---

[1] I would like to thank the conference organizers, Philip Hardie, Peter Mack, and John North; the other conference participants; and especially Emily Greenwood and Christina Kraus for their thoughtful comments and suggestions. I also would like to thank Karsten Harries, Giuseppe Mazzotta, and David Quint, whose seminars and scholarship inspired this study. An earlier version of this paper was presented at Yale University, Wake Forest University, SUNY Binghamton, University of Dallas, and Ohio Wesleyan University.

[2] The text and translation of Alberti is taken from C. Grayson (London 1972). For more on Alberti's use of Narcissus, see C. Baskins, 'Echoing Narcissus in Alberti's *Della Pittura*', *The Oxford Art Journal* 16.1 (1993) 25-33; U. Pfisterer, 'Künstlerliebe. Der Narcissus-Mythos bei Leon Battista Alberti und die Aristoteles-Lektüre der Frührenaissance', *Zeitschrift für Kunstgeschichte* 64.3 (2001) 305-30.

(*De pictura* 3.56).[3] In addition, the painter should so accurately depict the form and movement of bodies that the figures come alive and the viewer believes he sees the runner gleaming with sweat or gasping for breath (2.37). The emotions of the figures in the painting should also evoke a sense of empathy with the viewer. We should 'mourn with the mourners, laugh with those who laugh, and grieve with the grief-stricken', *lugentibus conlugeamus, ridentibus adrideamus, dolentibus condoleamus* (2.41).[4] Above all, a painting should be 'so charming and attractive as to hold the eye of the learned and unlearned spectator for a long while with a certain sense of pleasure and emotion', *ita amenam et ornatam exhibeat, ut oculos docti atque indocti spectatoris diutius quadam cum voluptate et animi motu detineat* (2.40, cf. *oculos et animos spectantium*, 3.52). For Alberti, then, a painting must not only accurately reflect Nature and, if possible, improve upon it, but it also must, as Narcissus' reflection succeeds too well in doing, entrance its viewer. Alberti sets as a corrective and as the ultimate test for a perfect painting if the painter can view its reflected image in a mirror without seeing any blemish:[5]

> Ac nescio quo pacto res pictae in speculo gratiam habeant, si vitio careant. Tum mirum est ut omnis menda picturae in speculo deformior appareat. A natura ergo suscepta speculi iudicio emendentur. (Alberti *De pictura* 2.46)

> I do not know how it is that paintings that are without fault look beautiful in a mirror; and it is remarkable how every defect in a picture appears more unsightly in a mirror. So the things that are taken from Nature should be emended with the advice of a mirror. (trans. C. Grayson)

A painting is only admirable and worthy of praise, then, when it successfully blurs the distinction between reality and illusion. For Alberti, Narcissus' reflection in the pool of water captures all of the desirable qualities in a painting: his perfect body, the semblance of movement, the conveyance of emotion, its bewitching effect on the viewer, and even Narcissus' *error*, mistaking his reflected form for a real person, is not lamentable but necessary.

---

[3] *De statua* 12; See also Xenophon *Memorabilia* 3.10.2, Aristotle *Politics* 3.6.5 (1281b), and Cicero *Orator* 2.7-10. For an excellent discussion of the changing conceptions of art from antiquity to the Renaissance, see E. Panofsky, *Idea: a concept in art theory* (Columbia SC 1968) translation from the revised 1924 German edition.

[4] *Cf.* Pliny describes the famous painters, Apelles portraying the *mores* of Penelope (*Nat.* 35.63) and Aristides, depicting the mind and feelings (*animus et sensus*, ἤθη) and emotions (*perturbationes*) of human beings (*Nat.* 35.98).

[5] Although Alberti's use of the mirror has practical applications for the artist, he could equally be interested in its metaphorical implications, especially given his interest in projecting the artist as a good and learned man (*De pictura* 3.52-56). For the thesis that Renaissance artists employed mirrors as an aid in painting, see especially D. Hockney, *Secret knowledge: rediscovering the lost techniques of the old masters* (New York 2001, revised 2006). For essays re-evaluating the Hockney-Falco thesis, see the special volume: *Optics, instruments, and painting, 1420-1720: reflections on the Hockney-Falco thesis*, especially Y. Yiu, 'The mirror and painting in early renaissance texts', *Early Science and Medicine* 10.2 (2005) 187-210.

Alberti's choice of Narcissus as the inventor of painting brings out three themes in Ovid on which I would like to focus my discussion: first, the ability of art (as represented in Narcissus' reflection) to blur the distinction between reality and illusion, and even, at times, to 'perfect' Nature; second, the power of art to entrance its viewer (and arouse potentially dangerous emotions); and finally, the self-corrective use of a mirror to see the truth.

After first analyzing Narcissus as a metapoetic figure in Ovid's *Metamorphoses*, I will then investigate how the Renaissance heroic epics of Dante, Ariosto, and Tasso appropriate the story of Narcissus to explore both the power and danger of art. In Dante's *La Divina Commedia*, Lodovico Ariosto's *Orlando Furioso*, and Torquato Tasso's *Gerusalemme Liberata*, the myth of Narcissus becomes a reminder that we should reject sensory pleasure in favour of the rational reflection that leads to a transcendent aesthetic experience.

Ovid's Narcissus

In the third book of the *Metamorphoses*, Ovid tells the story of Narcissus, an exceptionally beautiful youth, who unwittingly sees himself reflected in a pool of water. He is so filled with desire at his reflection that he forgets to eat and drink and eventually dies staring at the insubstantial image (*Met.* 3.339-510).[6] Narcissus' desire for himself is a consequence not only of his extraordinary beauty but also of art's ability, as represented in his reflection, to simulate reality. Narcissus believes the image in the water is another youth, who both reacts to his advances and gestures of love and reciprocates his feelings of desire and frustration. This mistaken belief in a false reality roots Narcissus to the spot and entirely transfixes him. Only when desire has utterly and irrevocably consumed him, does he realize the truth: that he is in love with an image of himself. For Ovid, Narcissus' *error* represents the power of art to immortalize the transient beauty of nature (when it is at its most powerful to 'bewitch'), to suspend time in the illusion of reality, and to arouse such insatiable desire in the viewer that it consumes all other desires.

Whether in painting or sculpture, art has the ability to express beauty in its most perfected form, even at times, as in the case of Pygmalion, to 'improve' upon nature (10.243-46). Narcissus' reflection captures just such a moment, when Narcissus' natural beauty precisely reflects the beauty of art. At the age of sixteen, on the cusp of manhood, Narcissus' beauty is at its apogee, when he is desirable both to youths and to young women (3.351-53, 455-56). When Narcissus first catches a glimpse of his own image reflected in the water, he both becomes and reflects the crystallized beauty of a statue:

adstupet ipse sibi vultuque immotus eodem
haeret, **ut e Pario formatum marmore signum**.

---

[6] For the history of the Narcissus story before Ovid, see L. Castiglioni, *Studi intorno alle fonti e alla composizione delle Metamorfosi di Ovidio* (Rome 1906, repr. 1964) 215-19; S. Eitrem, 'Narkissos', *RE* 16 (1935) 1721-33; L. Vinge, *The Narcissus theme in western European literature up to the early 19th century* (Lund 1967) 1-40; and G. Rosati, *Narciso e Pigmalione: illusione e spettacolo nelle Metamorfosi di Ovidio* (Florence 1983) 10-20. For the importance of the Narcissus/Echo episode in the larger Ovidian narrative, see P. Hardie, 'Ovid's Theban history: the first "anti*Aeneid*"?', *Classical Quarterly* 40.1 (1990) 224-35; I. Gildenhard and A. Zissos, 'Ovid's Narcissus (*Met.* 3.339-510): echoes of Oedipus', *American Journal of Philology* 121.1 (2000) 12947; and P. Hardie, *Ovid's poetics of illusion* (New York 2002) 165-72.

spectat humi positus geminum, sua lumina, sidus
et dignos Baccho, dignos et Apolline crines
impubesque genas et **eburnea colla** decusque
oris et in **niveo** mixtum **candore** ruborem,
cunctaque miratur, quibus est mirabilis ipse. (*Met.* 3.418-24)

> He looks in speechless wonder at himself and hangs there motionless in the same
> expression, like a statue carved from Parian marble. Prone on the ground, he gazes
> at his eyes, twin stars, and his locks, worthy of Bacchus, worthy of Apollo; on his
> smooth cheeks, his ivory neck, the glorious beauty of his face, the blush mingled
> with snowy white: all things, in short, he admires for which he is himself admired.
> (trans. F. J. Miller)[7]

Ovid describes Narcissus as if he were a statue of a beautiful youth, even a god. In book 10, Ovid similarly compares Adonis's beauty to a work of art: *laudaret faciem Livor quoque; qualia namque/ corpora nudorum tabula pinguntur Amorum,/ talis erat*, 'Even Envy would praise his beauty, for he looked like one of the naked loves portrayed on canvas' (10.515-17). Such beauty in nature, however, lasts for only a short period of time. As the narrator Lycinus in Pseudo-Lucian's *Erotes* jokingly says of one of his companions, Callicratidas, that he surrounds himself at all times with beautiful youths, but as soon as hair begins to show on their faces, he sends them away to manage his properties in Athens. Callicratidas manages to sustain the beauty of youth in his lovers only by constantly exchanging them as they grow older (*Erotes* 10). Art, however, has the power to suspend time – to freeze that perfect, youthful beauty forever. By capturing Narcissus at the height of his beauty, his reflection represents art's attempt to immortalize the transient beauty of nature and to capture beauty when it is at the climax of its bewitching power.

As several scholars have argued,[8] Ovid stresses the transfixing power of the gaze throughout the story of Narcissus. As soon as Narcissus catches sight of his reflection in the water, he is struck with wonder (*adstupet*), becomes completely immobilized (*immotus*), and is rooted to the spot (*haeret, Met.* 3.418-19). Hardie rightly connects Narcissus' reaction to that of Aeneas's, when gazing at the pictures in Juno's temple (*dum stupet obtutuque haeret defixus in uno*, Verg. *Aen.* 1.495). Just as Aeneas is caught in rapt gaze at the *inanis pictura* of Troy, so is Narcissus enraptured at the fleeting image (*fugacia simulacra*), the shadow of an image (*umbra imaginis*), and the lying form (*mendax forma*, Ov. *Met.* 3.432, 34, 39).[9] Unlike Aeneas, however, Narcissus loses all connection with reality – 'no thought of food or rest can draw him from the spot', *non illum Cereris, non illum cura quietis/ abstrahere inde potest* (3.437-38).

---

[7] The text of Ovid is taken from R. J. Tarrant (New York 2004) and the translation is taken from F. J. Miller (Cambridge MA 1999).

[8] M. Bettini, *The portrait of the lover*, trans. by L. Gibbs (Berkeley 1999) 94-108; J. Elsner, *Roman eyes: visuality & subjectivity in art & text* (Princeton 2007) 132-76.

[9] Hardie, *Ovid's poetics of illusion* (n. 6, above) 146-47.

Ovid here attributes a bewitching power to the visual arts similar to the power of the Sirens in Homer's *Odyssey* to 'fascinate' (θέλγουσιν) any man who hears them singing.[10] Lost in the beauty of the Sirens' song, the sailors forget all else, and their bodies rot on the island (12.39-46). In Plato's *Phaedrus*, Socrates describes a similar effect on the first men to hear song. When the Muses were born and song was created, these men were so overwhelmed with the pleasure of singing that they forgot to eat or drink and so died (259b-c). Narcissus' delusion is dangerous because the false image arouses such insatiable desire that it destroys him: 'he gazes on that false image (*mendax forma*) with eyes that cannot look their fill and through his own eyes perishes' *spectat inexpleto mendacem lumine formam/ perque oculos perit ipse suos* (Ov. *Met.* 3.439-40).[11]

In discussing Ovid's Narcissus, Bettini mentions a passage from Columella which describes a rare disease among female horses who waste away after having seen their reflection in water. These mares are so consumed with an empty passion for themselves (*inanis amor*) that they forget to eat and die from a disease of desire (*tabes cupidinis*, *De re rustica* 6.35.1). In order to cure the mare of her *error*, Columella prescribes disfiguring the mare's appearance and leading her back to the water. Her now ugly appearance in the water serves as a corrective for her former madness.[12] For Narcissus, however, even after he realizes his *error* and defiles his appearance in grief, rather than destroying his mad passion (*miser furor*, Ov. *Met.* 3.479), his actions only increase his desire (3.480-87). Ovid attributes the cause of his death to the bewitching and fatal power of the gaze: *lumina mors clausit domini mirantia formam*, 'death sealed the eyes that marveled (*mirantia*) at their master's beauty' (3.503). For Narcissus, even death is not an end, for he continues gazing at his image in the Styx (*in Stygia spectabat aqua*, 3.505).

What is ultimately tragic for Narcissus is desirable in art. Art has the ability to mystify and mesmerize its beholder not only by capturing perfect beauty but also by simulating reality. Narcissus is entranced at the sight of his reflection because he is smitten by what he sees and because he believes the image to be the beauty of another. Art aims to blur the distinction between reality and illusion. In book 35 of his *Natural History*, Pliny commends painters who successfully trick the viewer into thinking that what is represented actually exists. He tells numerous stories of famous painters who dupe animals. Zeuxis painted grapes so real that birds flew towards the painting (35.65-66), and in a painting contest,

---

[10] For the effect of the Sirens' song as 'self-obliteration', see C. Segal, *Singers, heroes, and gods in the Odyssey* (Ithaca 1994) 100-06, 134-35.

[11] For Ovid's interplay with Lucretius in this passage, see P. Hardie, 'Lucretius and the delusions of Narcissus', *Materiali e Discussioni per l' analisi dei testi classici* 20-21 (1988) 71-89.

[12] Betini, *The portrait of the lover* (n. 8, above) 96: *Rara quidem, sed et haec est equarum nota rabies, ut cum in aqua imaginem suam viderint, amore inani capiantur, et per hunc oblitae pabuli, tabe cupidinis intereant...Mentis error discutitur, si decidas inaequaliter comas equae et eam deducas ad aquam. Tum demum speculata deformitatem suam, pristinae imaginis abolet memoriam*, 'There is a form of madness which comes over mares and is rare but remarkable, namely, that, if they have seen their reflection in the water, they are seized with a vain passion and consequently forget to eat and die from a wasting disease of desire... this delusion (*error mentis*) is dispelled if you cut off her mane unevenly and lead her down to the water; then beholding at length her own ugliness, she loses the recollection of the picture which was formerly before her eyes' (Col. 6.35.1-2; trans. adapted from E. S. Forster and E. Heffner (London 1968)).

Apelles decimates his rivals when a group of horses neigh only at the sight of his painting (35.95).[13] Far greater than misleading animals is to fool a man capable of 'reason': although having won a contest after birds fly at his painting, Zeuxis himself owns defeat, when he asks his rival Parrhasius to draw aside his painted curtain (35.65). Exceptional art has the ability to deceive even the learned eye. The ancient reception of the Narcissus story shows it was read as exemplifying precisely this. In describing a painting of the story, Philostratus – a connoisseur of the visual – becomes himself a victim of Narcissus' *error*.[14] As he praises the painting's likeness to reality (ἀλήθεια), he cannot entirely distinguish what is real and what is not:

> τιμῶσα δὲ ἡ γραφὴ τὴν ἀλήθειαν καὶ δρόσου τι λείβει ἀπὸ τῶν ἀνθέων, οἷς καὶ μέλιττα ἐφιζάνει τις, οὐκ οἶδα εἴτ᾽ ἐξαπατηθεῖσα ὑπὸ τῆς γραφῆς, εἴτε ἡμᾶς ἐξηπατῆσθαι χρὴ εἶναι αὐτήν. ἀλλ᾽ ἔστω. Σὲ μέντοι, μειράκιον, οὐ γραφή τις ἐξηπάτησεν, οὐδὲ χρώμασιν ἢ κηρῷ προστέτηκας, ἀλλ᾽ ἐκτυπῶσαν σὲ τὸ ὕδωρ, οἷον εἶδες αὐτό, οὐκ οἶσθα οὔτε τὸ τῆς πηγῆς ἐλέγχεις σόφισμα, νεῦσαι δεῖν καὶ παρατρέψαι τοῦ εἴδους καὶ τὴν χεῖρα ὑποκινῆσαι καὶ μὴ ἐπὶ ταὐτοῦ ἑστάναι, σὺ δ᾽ ὥσπερ ἑταίρῳ ἐντυχὼν τἀκεῖθεν περιμένεις. εἶτά σοι ἡ πηγὴ μύθῳ χρήσεται; οὗτος μὲν οὖν οὐδ᾽ ἐπαΐει τι ἡμῶν, ἀλλ᾽ ἐμπέπτωκεν ἐπὶ τὸ ὕδωρ αὐτοῖς ὠσὶ καὶ αὐτοῖς ὄμμασιν, αὐτοὶ δὲ ἡμεῖς, ὥσπερ γέγραπται, λέγωμεν. (*Imagines* 1.23.2-3)

> The painting has such regard for realism that it even shows drops of dew dripping from the flowers and a bee settling on the flowers – whether a real bee has been deceived by the painted flowers or whether we are to be deceived into thinking that a painted bee is real, I do not know. But let that pass. As for you, however, Narcissus, it is no painting that has deceived you, nor are you engrossed in a thing of pigments or wax; but you do not realize that the water represents you exactly as you are when you gaze upon it, nor do you see through the artifice of the pool, though to do so you have only to nod your head or change your expression or slightly move your hand, instead of standing in the same attitude; but acting as though you had met a companion, you wait for some move on his part. Do you then expect the pool to enter into conversation with you? Nay, this youth does not hear anything we say, but he is immersed, eyes and ears alike in the water, and we must interpret the painting for ourselves. (trans. A. Fairbanks)

Despite his own inability to discern illusion from reality, Philostratus chides Narcissus for being duped by his own reflection – after all, he claims, a slight movement of Narcissus' hand or head could destroy the illusion (σόφισμα) in front of him. He implies that art should be more difficult to distinguish from reality than a reflection because art lacks movement – it suspends the time of the viewer and the subject alike. But as he goes on in his description, he sees the painted Narcissus as conveying movement and showing emotion:

> τὸ δὲ ἐν τῷ στέρνῳ ἆσθμα οὐκ οἶδα εἴτε κυνηγετικὸν ἔτι εἴτε ἤδη ἐρωτικόν. τό γε μὴν ὄμμα ἱκανῶς ἐρῶντος, τὸ γὰρ χαροπὸν αὐτοῦ καὶ γοργὸν ἐκ φύσεως πραΰνει τις

---

[13] *Cf.* Clement of Alexandria of the 'deceptive power of images' *Protrepticus* 4.

[14] Vinge, *The Narcissus theme* (n. 6, above) 29-32; Bettini, *The portrait of the lover* (n. 8, above) 95; Elsner, *Roman eyes* (n. 8, above) 143-46.

ἐφιζάνων ἵμερος, δοκεῖ δ᾽ ἴσως καὶ ἀντερᾶσθαι βλεπούσης αὐτὸν τῆς σκιᾶς, ὡς ὑπ᾽ αὐτοῦ ὁρᾶται. (*Imagines* 1.23.4)

Whether the panting of his breast remains from his hunting or is already the panting of love I do not know. The eye, surely, is that of a man deeply in love, for its natural brightness and intensity are softened by a longing that settles upon it, and he perhaps thinks that he is loved in return, since the reflection gazes at him in just the way that he looks at it. (trans. A. Fairbanks)

In Ovid's version, Narcissus does move and even attempts to embrace his reflection, but none of his actions dispel the illusion of the water. In fact, the reciprocity of emotion and movement only serves to encourage and further enflame Narcissus:

spem mihi nescioquam vultu promittis amico,
cumque ego porrexi tibi bracchia, porrigis ultro;
cum risi, adrides; lacrimas quoque saepe notavi
me lacrimante tuas (Ov. *Met*. 3.457-60)

Some ground for hope you offer with your friendly looks, and when I have stretched out my arms to you, you stretch yours too. When I have smiled, you smile back; and I have often seen tears, when I weep, on your cheeks. (trans. F. J. Miller)

Just as Ovid interjects into the story of Narcissus in a futile attempt to reason with his character (3.432-36), so Philostratus is lured into the drama unfolding before him and addresses the painting. His question to Narcissus could equally be posed to himself: 'Do you then expect the pool (or in his case, the painting) to enter into conversation with you?' In his rhetorical rebuke, Philostratus draws attention to the similarities between a masterful painting and the deception of the pool. Painting masters the art of deception, when it accurately and convincingly conveys emotion and movement – in other words, when it succeeds in being as lifelike and responsive as Narcissus' reflection.

Before we leave Ovid to explore the reception of Narcissus in Renaissance epic, I would like to draw your attention to another aspect of the story of Narcissus that becomes combined with its aesthetic implications in the later tradition, that is, the theme of pride (his *superbia*). While Narcissus' delusion lasts long enough to ensure its disastrous consequences, the story is made more poignant by the fact that Narcissus realizes his mistake but is powerless to do anything about it: *iste ego sum! sensi, nec me mea fallit imago*, 'Oh, I am he! I have felt it, nor does my image deceive me' (3.463).[15] The illusion of the water is shattered, but he is still caught in its trance. He foolishly thinks death will be an end to his grief, but instead, death guarantees its perpetuity.

Narcissus' eternal torment is punishment for his arrogance, which Ovid credits at the beginning of the story with causing him to remain chaste. Unable to find a lover worthy of his own beauty, Narcissus finds that perfection only in himself. This excessive pride in

---

[15] For excellent discussions of self-knowledge and the metaphor of the mirror in antiquity, see W. McCarty, 'The shape of the mirror: metaphorical catoptrics in classical literature', *Arethusa* 22.2 (1989) 161-95; S. Bartsch, 'The philosopher as Narcissus: vision, sexuality, and self-knowledge in classical antiquity', in *Visuality before and beyond the Renaissance: seeing as others saw*, ed. R. S. Nelson (Cambridge 2000) 70-97.

turn provokes a scorned lover to pray to Nemesis for retribution (3.405-06). Like Niobe (6.301-12), Anaxarete (14.753-58), and the daughters of Propoetus (10.238-42), who turn into statues as punishment for their arrogance, Ovid deliberately conflates the real Narcissus and a statue (3.418-24) – a statue which is lifelike and beautiful, and yet, is as cold, unyielding, and impassive as the real Narcissus. It is only when Narcissus at last feels the burning passion of love that he ceases to be an implacable and perfect work of art. As his beauty and life waste away, consumed by passion, Ovid turns his marble-like appearance into an ephemeral statue made of wax or frost that melts in the sun (3.487-93). Even Echo pities his fate as he loses all of his former beauty, his strength and vigor, and his youthful glow (3.491-93). His enduring pride (*dura superbia*), therefore, destroys the source of his pride, that is, his fragile beauty (*tenera forma*, 3.354). Unwilling to be 'touched' by the love of others (*tetigere*, 3.355), Narcissus suffers the same unfulfilled and consuming desire. Though his corporeal body vanishes, he remains transfixed at his reflection for all eternity.

Renaissance Epic

In the later tradition, the pride of Narcissus is closely connected with his *error*.[16] In the allegorical tradition of commentaries on Ovid's *Metamorphoses*, particularly those of the late twelfth and early thirteenth-century writers, Arnulf d'Orléans and Johannes de Garlandia, Narcissus represents the vanity of pride and ambition.[17] What I would like to emphasize in what follows is that in the Italian Renaissance Dante, Ariosto, and Tasso prove to be insightful readers of the *Metamorphoses*. In addition to the *vanitas* theme in Ovid's Narcissus story, they also recognize the importance of self-knowledge, which as Vinge has pointed out,[18] is absent in the early commentary tradition. Unlike Narcissus, who becomes aware of his self-love only too late and gives into despair, each hero recognizes and repents of his error. The moment of self-knowledge is revisited and 'corrected' in Renaissance epic. Not only does the mirror have the power of enchantment, but it also can become a vehicle for self-knowledge and correction.

---

[16] For the Christian and Neo-Platonic tradition that Narcissus' love for his reflection (a shadow, fleeting image, lying form) symbolizes the vain pursuit of false images and sensual pleasures, see especially Clement *Protrepticus* 4, *Paedagogus* 3.2; Plotinus *Enneads* 1.6.8; and Augustine *Confessions* 9.4. For more on the tradition of Narcissus before Dante, see Vinge, *The Narcissus theme* (n. 6, above) 55-106; K. Knoespel, *Narcissus and the invention of personal history* (New York 1985) 23-110; R. McMahon, 'Autobiography as text-work: Augustine's refiguring of Genesis 3 and Ovid's "Narcissus" in his conversion account', *Exemplaria* 1.2 (1989) 337-66; J. Rosenfeld, *Ethics and enjoyment in late medieval poetry: love after Aristotle* (Cambridge 2011) 45-73; and n. 17, below.

[17] Arnulf d'Orléans *Allegoriae super Ovidii Metamorphosin* 3.5-6 (ca. 1180) and Johannes de Garlandia *Integumenta Ovidii* 163-64 (1234); See also Giovanni del Virgilio (a younger contemporary and poetic correspondent of Dante) *Allegorie librorum Ovidii Metamorphoseos* 3.6. For recent scholarship on the medieval commentary tradition of Ovid and Ovid in the Middle Ages, see Knoespel, *Narcissus and the invention* (n. 16, above) 23-58; L. Barkan, *The gods made flesh: metamorphosis and the pursuit of paganism* (New Haven 1986) 94-136; M. Desmond, ed. *Ovid in medieval culture*. vol. 13, Special Issue, *Mediaevalia* (1989); J. Dimmick, 'Ovid in the Middle Ages: authority and poetry', in *The Cambridge Companion to Ovid*, ed. P. Hardie (New York 2002) 264-87; A. Keith and S. J. Rupp, ed. *Metamorphosis: the changing face of Ovid in medieval and early modern Europe* (Toronto 2007); and J. G. Clark, F. T. Coulson, and K. L. McKinley, ed. *Ovid in the Middle Ages* (Cambridge 2011).

[18] Vinge, *The Narcissus theme* (n. 6, above) 76.

In the Renaissance heroic epics of Dante, Ariosto, and Tasso the story of Narcissus represents both the power and danger of art. At various points along the way, the heroes Dante, Ruggiero, and Rinaldo fall victim to Narcissus' *error*. They become so enamoured with the beauty or spectacle before them that they lose all connection with reality and forget the purpose of their journey. Only when each hero restores his sense of reason and repents of his error through self-reflection, as a 'corrected' Narcissus, is he able to fulfill his divine destiny. For these poets, Narcissus' *error* symbolizes the vain pursuit of false images and sensual pleasures.

In *La Divina Commedia*, Narcissus appears in Canto 30 of *Inferno* (30.128) when Dante, the protagonist, becomes mesmerized by the heated argument between the disfigured souls of two falsifiers: Sinon and Master Adam.[19] Vergil, who is present as Dante's guide, interrupts at the very moment when Master Adam mentions Narcissus, thus highlighting the reference.[20] Vergil scolds Dante for his fascination with their base argument (*Inf.* 30.124-48):

[19]   The discussion on Dante that follows draws upon my previous work, see C. Stark, 'Dante's Narcissus', *The Classical Outlook* 86.4 (2009) 132-38. Ovid is an important classical author for Dante; not only does he appear in the *Commedia* among the poets of *la bella scola* in Limbo (*Inf.* 4.90) and by name again in *Inf.* 25.97, but Ovid is also mentioned frequently in Dante's earlier works: *Vita Nuova* 25.9, *De vulgari eloquentia* 1.2.7, 2.6.7, and *Convivio* 2.1.3, 2.5.14, 2.14.5, 3.3.7, 4.15.8, 4.23.14, 4.27.17-19. Ovid's *Metamorphoses*, as a universal history, is another model for the *Commedia*, the book that embraces the totality of experience (*Par.* 33.85-90), and numerous allusions to the *Metamorphoses* appear throughout the *Commedia*. See also I. Gildenhard's contribution in this volume. For discussions of the importance of Ovid in Dante's work, see A. Buck, 'Dante und die Mythologie', *Dante-Jahrbuch* 55/56 (1980/1) 7-27; R. Jacoff and J. T. Schnapp, ed. *The poetry of allusion: Virgil and Ovid in Dante's 'Commedia'* (Stanford 1991); M. Picone, 'La *lectio Ovidii* nella "Commedia". La ricezione dantesca delle "Metamorfosi"', *Le Forme e la Storia* 3 (1991) 35-52; M. U. Sowell, ed. *Dante and Ovid: essays in intertextuality* (Binghamton 1991); M. Picone, 'L' Ovidio di Dante', in *Dante e la 'bella scola' della poesia: autorità e sfida poetica*, ed. A. Iannucci (Ravenna 1993) 107-44; M. Picone, 'Dante and the classics', in *Dante: contemporary perspectives*, ed. A. Iannucci (Toronto 1997) 51-73; Dimmick in Hardie (n. 17, above); K. Brownlee, 'Dante and the classical poets', in *The Cambridge Companion to Dante*, ed. R. Jacoff (New York 2007) 141-60; W. Ginsberg, 'Dante's Ovids', in Clark and others (n. 17, above) 143-59. Ghisalberti hypothesizes that Dante used the 'Vulgate' commentary for interpreting the *Metamorphoses*; see F. Ghisalberti, 'Il commentario medioevale all' *Ovidius maior* consultato da Dante', *Rendiconti dell' Istituto Lombardo, Classe di Lettere e Scienze Morali e Storiche* 100 (1966) 267-75; F. T. Coulson, 'Ovid's transformations in medieval France (ca. 1100ca. 1350)', in Keith and Rupp (n. 17, above) 38; F. T. Coulson, 'Ovid's *Metamorphoses* in the school tradition of France, 1180-1400: texts, manuscript traditions, manuscript settings', in Clark and others (n. 17, above) 70. My thanks to Frank Coulson for reminding me of Ghisalberti's hypothesis.

[20]   While *Inf.* 30.128 is the only explicit reference to Narcissus by name, scholars have drawn attention to the number of allusions to the story of Narcissus throughout the *Commedia* that mark the progress of Dante's own spiritual and poetic transformation; see R. Dragonetti, 'Dante et Narcisse ou les faux-monnayeurs de l'image', *Revue des etudes italiennes* 11 (1965) 85-146; K. Brownlee, 'Dante and Narcissus (*Purg.* XXX, 76-99)', *Dante Studies* 96 (1978) 201-06; R. A. Shoaf, *Dante, Chaucer, and the currency of the word: money, images, and reference in late medieval poetry* (Norman 1983); R. McMahon, 'The Christian scripture of Ovid's Narcissus in the "Commedia"', *Pacific Coast Philology* 20.1/2 (1985) 65-69; R. McMahon, 'Satan as infernal Narcissus: interpretative translation in the *Commedia*', in Sowell (n. 19, above) 65-86; E. P. Nolan, 'Dante's comedic displacements of Ovid's Narcissus', in *The Influence of the classical world on medieval literature, architecture, music, and culture: a collection of interdisciplinary studies*, ed. Fajardo-Acosta (Lewiston 1992) 105-21.

32   THE AFTERLIFE OF OVID

Allora il monetier: 'Così si squarcia
la bocca tua per tuo mal come sòle;
chè s' i' ho sete ed umor mi rinfarcia,
tu hai l'arsura e 'l capo che ti dole,
e per leccar lo specchio di Narcisso,
non vorresti a 'nvitar molte parole.'
Ad ascoltarli er' io del tutto fisso,
quando 'l maestro mi disse: 'Or pur mira!
che per poco che teco non mi risso'. (*Inf.* 30.124-32)

Then the coiner: 'Thus thy mouth gapes, as usual, to put thee in the wrong, for if I have thirst and humour stuffs me, thou hast burning fever and aching head and wouldst need little persuasion to lap Narcissus' mirror'. I was fixed on listening to them, when the Master said to me: 'Now keep marveling. A little more and I quarrel with thee'. (trans. based on Sinclair)[21]

Vergil is angry because, instead of reflecting upon the eternal punishment decreed for Sinon and Adam, Dante delights in observing their petty squabble: *chè voler ciò udire è bassa voglia*, 'for the desire to hear it is a base desire' (*Inf.* 30.148).[22] Like a Narcissus, Dante has forgotten his journey and is enraptured (*mira*) with the image before him. Dante becomes *tutto fisso* in listening (*Inf.* 30.130), as Narcissus becomes *immotus* gazing at his image (Ov. *Met.* 3.418).

The valence of Narcissus as a symbol of what can happen when reason is lost to the pleasure of the aesthetic experience is strengthened by the fact that he is set amongst references to other Ovidian figures who have lost their minds and fallen prey to their desires: Athamas, Hecuba, and Myrrha. Dante 'corrects' Ovid by portraying each of his characters as animals in *Inferno* 30 to reflect their loss or rejection of human reason. The transformation of their bodies from humans to animals mirrors the transformations of mind. Dante turns Athamas into a lion: *i dispietati artigli*, 'his pitiless claws' (*Inf.* 30.9) and links Hecuba's 'madness' out of grief with her later transformation into a dog (*Inf.* 30.16-21).[23] Dante also emphasizes the effect of passions on Hecuba's mind: *forsennata latrò sì come cane;/ tanto il dolor le fè la mente torta*, 'being out of her wits barked like a dog, so distraught was her mind with grief' (*Inf.* 30.20-21). While Athamas and Hecuba were victims of either Juno or Fortune, Myrrha and Gianni Schicchi willfully deceived others for their own base desires. In the *Metamorphoses* when Myrrha goes to consummate her lust by deception, divine signs and her own conscience

---

[21]   The text and translation of Dante (unless otherwise stated) is from J. D. Sinclair (New York 1961).

[22]   *Cf.* Dragonetti (n. 20, above) 94-106 and Shoaf, *Dante, Chaucer, and the currency of the word* (n. 20, above) 44-45, who argue that Dante tries to understand the 'reason perverted' in their exchange.

[23]   When Hecuba first discovers the death of Polydorus, Ovid compares her to a lioness whose cub has been stolen (*Met.* 13.547-48), and when Hecuba finally gives into her wrath against Polymestor and exacts her revenge, she transforms into a dog (*Met.* 13.567-71).

make her fully aware of her transgression, but she persists (Ov. *Met.* 10.448-71). Therefore, instead of turning Myrrha into a tree, as Ovid does, Dante portrays her shade as a wild hog (*Inf.* 30.22-27).[24]

In this canto and at other points in his journey, Dante becomes Narcissus when he sees his own sins reflected in the sins of others. As a poet, he too is a 'falsifier'. Shoaf has argued that Dante places the Narcissus reference in the tenth *bolgia* among sinners guilty of fraud in order to address the charge that poetry is also deception.[25] For Dante, poetic imagery and rhetorical flourish without meaning are as shameful as his pleasure in the performance of the dispute between Sinon and Master Adam in *Inferno* 30. As he explains in *Vita Nuova*, 'deception' in poetry is permissible as long as, when the artifice is stripped away, some reason or truth remains (25.1-10).[26]

At the sculptured wall of figures of humility and the chiseled images on the terrace of pride in *Purgatorio* (10, 12), Dante, the protagonist, is transfixed by the art in the white marble that puts 'not only Polycleitus but nature itself to shame' (10.31-33). He praises the 'visible speech' (*visibile parlare*, *Purg.* 10.95) of the scenes of humility and lifelike quality of the sculpture on the terrace: *Qual di pennel fu maestro o di stile/ che ritraesse l'ombre e' tratti ch' ivi/ mirar farìeno uno ingegno sottile?/ Morti li morti e i vivi parean vivi*, 'What master of brush and chisel could have portrayed the shapes and outlines there, which would have filled with wonder a discerning mind? The dead seemed dead and the living living' (*Purg.* 12.64-67). Vergil initially encourages Dante to look at the didactic images in order to meditate on the sin of pride and its corresponding virtue. Dante is mesmerized at the figures of pride because he sees his own failings reflected in these penitents. In a conversation with a fellow artist, Oderisi, earlier in the poem,

---

[24] Ov. *Met.* 10.489-502. By turning Myrrha into a wild hog instead of a tree whose precious myrrh gives her eternal honor, Dante directly responds to Ovid's plea to his reader that if you believe his story, believe in the punishment of the deed (*Met.* 10.301-03).

[25] Shoaf focuses on falsifying the image and the corruption of reference in this canto. Building on Dragonetti's argument (n. 20, above) 94-106, Shoaf believes that Dante, by trying to reason out their argument, lends meaning and substance to Sinon and Master Adam's dispute (an otherwise empty image); see Shoaf, *Dante, Chaucer, and the currency of the word* (n. 20, above) 24, 39-48. Vergil's rebuke and Dante's shame (*Inf.* 30.133-34, 31.1-2), however, suggest that Dante does not contemplate the divine truth behind their punishment (and thus give meaning) but delights in hearing their taunts to each other.

[26] E.g.: *E acciò che non ne pigli alcuna baldanza persona grossa, dico che né li poete parlavano così sanza ragione, né quelli che rimano deono parlare così non avendo alcuno ragionamento in loro di quello che dicono; però che grande vergogna sarebbe a colui che rimasse cose sotto vesta di figura o di colore rettorico, e poscia, domandato, non sapesse denudare le sue parole da cotale vesta, in guisa che avessero verace intendimento. E questo mio primo amico e io ne sapemo bene di quelli che così rimano stoltamente*, 'So that some ungifted person may not be encouraged by my words to go too far, let me add that just as the Latin poets did not write in the way they did without a reason, so vernacular poets should not write in the same way without having some reason for writing as they do. For, if any one should dress his poem in images and rhetorical coloring and then, being asked to strip his poem of such dress in order to reveal its true meaning, would not be able to do so--this would be a veritable cause for shame. And my best friend and I are well acquainted with some who compose so clumsily' (*Vita Nuova* 25.10; trans. M. Musa (Bloomington 1973)).

Dante confronts the artist's overweening ambition in his own work and the vain pursuit of eternal renown (*Purg.* 11.79-119).[27] The effect of Oderisi's words on Dante reveals that Dante too suffers from the sin of pride, his poetic pride. But when he spends so long engrossed in the art on the terrace that he loses control of his mind (*non sciolto, Purg.* 12.75), Vergil scolds him: *Drizza la testa; non è più tempo di gir sì sospeso,* 'Lift up thy head! There is no more time to go thus absorbed' (*Purg.* 12.77-78).[28] Once again Vergil's call to 'reason' breaks his narcissistic trance.

One of the most dangerous obstacles for Dante in his ascent to Beatrice is his dream of the Siren. She represents the sins of the flesh and the pursuit of earthly good in the forms of avarice, gluttony, and lust.[29] The Siren initially appears in her true form, far from a vision of beauty (*Purg.* 19.7-9), but as Dante gazes, she transforms her appearance and begins to sing. The Siren's song bewitches Dante and he forgets his journey, just as he froze in *Inferno* 30 and *Purgatorio* 12: *cominciava a cantar sì, che con pena/ da lei avrei mio intento rivolto,* 'she began to sing so that it would have been hard for me to turn my mind from her' (*Purg.* 19.17-18). Vergil's usual call to Dante fails to break the trance of her enchanting song, but with the help of the angel of zeal, Vergil awakens Dante by revealing the Siren's true self (*Purg.* 19.25-36).

Narcissus is then 'recalled and corrected', as Brownlee has argued,[30] in *Purgatorio* 30, when Dante views his own reflection in the water and instead of awakening self-love, confesses his own poetic pride and his pursuit of false images of good. Again Dante proves himself to be an insightful reader of the *Metamorphoses* by incorporating Narcissus' moment of self-realization.

Dante's initial reaction at the sight of Beatrice in *Purgatorio* 30 is to turn to Vergil, only to find the poet is no longer there. At Beatrice's censure of his tears, Dante looks into the clear fountain. Instead of being captivated by his reflection, however, he draws his eyes away in shame. Thus, Dante has overcome the pride that had previously weighed on his brow in *Purgatorio* 12 (*Purg.* 12.121-26):

---

[27] A number of clues in this and the following canto reveal that Dante himself suffers from excessive pride: Dante bends down to speak to Oderisi, as if he also attempts to purge this sin (*Purg.* 11.73); Oderisi alludes to Dante surpassing the poets of his age (*Purg.* 11.98-99); to Oderisi's reflection on his vain pride and pursuit of glory and those of his fellow penitents, Dante replies: *tuo vero dir m' incora/ bona umiltà, e gran tumor m'appiani:,* 'Thy true speech fills my heart with good humbleness and abates a great swelling in me' (*Purg.*11.118-19; trans. Sinclair); and finally, the angel of humility removes this sin from his brow (*Purg.* 12.98).

[28] Vergil's scolding of Dante parallels the Sibyl's scolding of Aeneas, who spends too long gazing at Daedalus' images on the doors of Apollo's temple in *Aeneid* 6.37-39, my thanks to Christina Kraus for reminding me of this passage. See also n. 9, above.

[29] See R. Hollander, '*Purgatorio* XIX: Dante's siren/harpy' in *Dante, Petrarch, Boccaccio: studies in the Italian trecento in honor of Charles S. Singleton,* ed. A. S. Bernardo and A. L. Pellegrini, Medieval & Renaissance texts & studies 22 (Binghamton 1983) 77-88.

[30] Brownlee, 'Dante and Narcissus' (n. 20, above) 202.

Li occhi mi cadder giù nel chiaro fonte;
ma, veggendomi in esso, i trassi all'erba,
tanta vergogna mi gravò la fronte. (Purg. 30.76-78)

My eyes fell down to the clear fount, but, seeing myself in it, I drew them back to the grass, so great shame weighed on my brow. (trans. Sinclair)

Beatrice explains to the angels who protest her harsh scolding of Dante that she is doing it for his benefit. While Beatrice was alive, she had led Dante on the right path. After her death, when she became even more beautiful and virtuous, however, Dante abandoned her to follow false images of the good which lead no farther (*Purg.* 30.127-32, 31.34-36). Whereas the Siren's beauty is entirely artifice, Beatrice's beauty inspires Dante's soul upward to God and Truth. As Beatrice explains, the sin that the Siren represents, the pursuit of false images, is what Dante must confess (*Purg.* 31.34-36) and repent (*Purg.* 31.85-90) before he can pass through the River Lethe and obtain absolution: *Tuttavia, perchè mo vergogna porte/ del tuo errore, e perchè altra volta,/ udendo le serene, sie più forte,* 'Nevertheless, in order that thou mayst now bear the shame of thy wandering and another time, hearing the Sirens, be stronger' (*Purg.* 31.43-45). Unlike Narcissus, who realizes his self-love only too late and gives into despair, Dante's shameful recognition of his reflection in the water represents both a self-awareness of his own failings and a repentance of his poetic pride. His confession and absolution leads not to his death but to salvation. Narcissus' mirror becomes in *Purgatorio* a vehicle for rational reflection, self-knowledge, and absolution that leads the way to transcendence.

In *La Divina Commedia*, the story of Narcissus explores both the power and danger of art. When Dante becomes transfixed by the performance of the dispute in *Inferno* 30, by the chiseled figures of pride in *Purgatorio* 12, and by the Siren's song in *Purgatorio* 19, he falls victim to Narcissus' *error*. He is mesmerized by the reflection of his own sins in the sins of others. Unlike Narcissus, however, Dante is rescued each time and 'restored' to reason by Vergil or the angel of zeal. By recognizing himself, Dante achieves the selfknowledge of Ovid's Narcissus, but by also feeling ashamed, he 'corrects' the source of Narcissus' error. When he finally reaches Beatrice and repents of his pursuit of false images and pleasures, as a 'corrected' Narcissus, Dante is able to ascend to divine revelation and the transcendent aesthetic experience of *Paradiso*.

In Ariosto's *Orlando Furioso*, the hero Ruggiero similarly falls victim to the supernatural beauty and sensual delights of the 'Siren' Alcina (*OF* 6.40). After Ruggiero is taken away from his beloved Bradamant by a hippogryph, he lands in the magical realm of Alcina (*OF* 6.16-27). He soon learns from a myrtle tree, the transformed Astolfo, of Alcina's bewitching power. Like the sinners in *Inferno* 30, Alcina's former lovers have been transformed into wild animals and plants to signify their loss of reason and moral depravity.[31] As the myrtle tree describes his own folly in succumbing to her charms and sensual pleasures, he eerily foreshadows Ruggiero's own fate (*OF* 6.28-56). He explains: *né di Francia né d'altro mi*

---

[31] My thanks to David Quint for reminding me of this passage. The overt references to Alcina as Circe, (as later Armida as Circe and Calypso), who forestalls the hero's journey with pleasure, is reminiscent of the warning in Plotinus of the parable of Odysseus, which teaches readers to run from bodily beauty and to seek the Good (*Enneads* 1.6.8). See also n. 16 and n. 29, above.

rimembra: / stavomi sempre a contemplar quel volto: / ogni pensiero, ogni mio bel disegno/ in lei finia, né passava oltre il segno, 'Lost in contemplation of her looks, I quite forgot about France and all else – my every thought, my every good design ended in her, and never went beyond' (*OF* 6.47).[32]

Despite this warning, Ruggiero becomes entranced by the exceptional beauty of Alcina, whom Ariosto describes as a beautiful work of art:

> **Di persona era tanto ben formata,**
> **quanto me' finger san pittori industri;**
> **con bionda chioma lunga et annodata:**
> **oro non è che più risplenda e lustri**.
> Spargeasi per la guancia delicata
> misto color di rose e di ligustri;
> di terso avorio era la fronte lieta,
> che lo spazio finia con giusta meta...
> **Bianca nieve è il bel collo, e 'l petto latte;**
> il collo è tondo, il petto colmo e largo:
> **due pome acerbe, e pur d'avorio fatte**,
> vengono e van come onda al primo margo,
> quando piacevole aura il mar combatte.
> Non potria l'altre parti veder Argo:
> ben si può giudicar che corrisponde
> a quel ch'appar di fuor quel che s'asconde.
> **Mostran le braccia sua misura giusta;**
> **e la candida man spesso si vede**
> **lunghetta alquanto e di larghezza angusta,**
> **dove né nodo appar, né vena escede.**
> **Si vede al fin de la persona augusta**
> **il breve, asciutto e ritondetto piede**. (*Orlando Furioso* 7.11, 14-15)

She was so beautifully modelled, no painter, however much he applied himself, could have achieved anything more perfect. Her long blonde tresses were gathered in a knot: pure gold itself could have no finer lustre. Roses and white privet blooms lent their colours to suffuse her delicate cheeks. **Her serene brow was like polished ivory, and in perfect proportion.../ Snow-white was her neck, milky her breast;** the neck was round, the breast broad and full. **A pair of apples, not yet ripe, fashioned in ivory,** rose and fell like the sea-swell at times when a gentle breeze stirs the ocean. Argus himself could not see them entire, but you could easily judge that what lay hidden did not fall short of what was exposed to view. / **Her arms were justly proportioned, and her lily-white hands were often to be glimpsed: they were slender and tapering, and quite without a knot or swelling vein. A pair of small, neat, rounded feet completes the picture of this august person.** (trans. G. Waldman)

---

[32] The text of Ariosto is taken from A. Seroni (Milan 1981) and the translation from G. Waldman (New York 1983) unless otherwise stated.

Alcina's beauty is so perfect in every detail that it surpasses nature and even art. It is so dangerous and so seductive because it is entirely artifice. As Ruggiero spends the ensuing days basking in every sort of pleasure and luxury, Alcina's magic erases all traces of Ruggiero's true love for Bradamant and causes forgetfulness:

> né più memoria avea del suo signore,
> né de la donna sua, né del suo onore.
>   E così il fior de li begli anni suoi
> in lunga inerzia aver potria consunto
> sì gentil cavallier, per dover poi
> perdere il corpo e l'anima in un punto (*Orlando Furioso* 7.40-41)

> forgetful of his Liege, of his beloved, of his own renown./ And it might therefore have been the lot of so goodly a knight to pass the best years of his life in sustained idleness, only to lose his soul and body all at once. (trans. G. Waldman)

Like a Narcissus, Ruggiero is captivated by the pleasure of the illusion before him and loses all connection with reality.[33] Ruggiero is brought to his senses only when the enchantress Melissa destroys Alcina's deception using the ring of Reason and reveals to him the truth.[34] Just as Vergil rebukes Dante for his fascination with Sinon and Master Adam's dispute (*Inf.* 30.131-48),[35] so Melissa scolds Ruggiero:

> Ma perché tu conosca chi sia Alcina,
> levatone le fraudi e gli artifici,
> tien questo annello in dito, e torna ad ella,
> ch'aveder ti potrai come sia bella.
>   Ruggier si stava vergognoso e muto
> mirando in terra, e mal sapea che dire;
> a cui la maga nel dito minuto
> pose l'annello, e lo fe' risentire.
> Come Ruggiero in sé fu rivenuto,
> di tanto scorno si vide assalire,
> ch'esser vorria sotterra mille braccia,
> ch'alcun veder non lo potesse in faccia. (Ariosto *Orlando Furioso* 7.64-65)

---

[33]   See also F. Masciandaro, 'Ariosto and the myth of Narcissus: notes on Orlando's folly', in *Studi filologici e letterari in memoria di Danilo Aguzzi-Barbagli*, ed. Daniela Boccassini, Filibrary Series 13 (Stonybrook 1997) 147-58, who argues that Orlando is Narcissus when he is transfixed by Angelica's words inscribed on the trees in Canto 23.

[34]   See also B. Corrigan, 'The opposing mirrors', *Italica* 33.3 (1956) 165-79, who rightly connects Melissa's rescue of Ruggiero and Carlo and Ubaldo's of Rinaldo to Ulysses' discovery and 'calling' to war of Achilles in Statius' *Achilleid*. While noting the importance of the restoration of the hero in Ariosto and Tasso, Corrigan fails to note its parallel with Dante.

[35]   This passage also recalls Beatrice's rebuke of Dante in *Purg.* 30 for following false pleasures, especially the verbal parallels of the protagonist looking shamefacedly at the ground, *i trassi all'erba,/ tanta vergogna mi gravò la fronte* (*Purg.* 30.77-78).

'Now, that you may know who Alcina is, stripped of her artifices and deceits, put this ring on your finger and return to her, and you shall realize just how fair are her looks.' / Ruggiero stood shamefaced and silent, staring at the ground, not knowing what to say. The enchantress put the ring on his little finger, and brought him back to reality. Coming to himself, Ruggiero was so overwhelmed with shame that he wished himself a thousand feet below ground, so that no one could look him in the face. (trans. G. Waldman)

Recalled to reason, Ruggiero returns to Alcina and sees the truth behind the artifice: she is as ugly as the true image of the Siren. All of her former beauty is gone. Far from being a work of art, Alcina is a wrinkled and decrepit old hag (*OF* 7.70-74). As in Dante's encounter with the deadly Siren (*Purg.* 19.17-36), Ruggiero barely escapes from Alcina's clutches. He finds refuge in the land of Logistilla, whose beauty, like Beatrice's, leads to virtue and knowledge. Although his confession and absolution are deferred to his religious conversion and baptism by the hermit in Canto 41, Ruggiero experiences a similar moment of self-knowledge when he gazes into the jewels on Logistilla's palace:

> Quel che più fa che lor si inchina e cede
> ogn'altra gemma, è che mirando in esse,
> l'uom sin in mezzo all'anima si vede;
> vede suoi vizii e sue virtudi espresse,
> sì che a lusinghe poi di sé non crede,
> né a chi dar biasmo a torto gli volesse:
> fassi, mirando allo specchio lucente
> se stesso conoscendosi, prudente. (Ariosto *Orlando Furioso* 10.59)

What in particular gives these jewels their supremacy over every other is this: on admiring them, a man sees right into his own soul; he sees there reflected his vices and virtues, so that he no longer believes in the compliments he is paid, nor does he heed blame when he is charged unfairly. Gazing with wonder into these bright mirrors, he discovers himself, and learns wisdom (trans. based on G. Waldman).

These mirrors, unlike the opulence of Alcina's palace, lead to truth and selfknowledge. As a 'corrected' Narcissus, Ruggiero leaves the realm of Logistilla to rejoin his companions and to fulfill his divine destiny.

In *Gerusalemme Liberata*, Tasso draws on Dante and Ariosto's use of Ovid's Narcissus to explore the power and danger of art. Like the heroes Dante and Ruggiero, Tasso's Rinaldo is bewitched by the earthly beauty and sensual pleasures of the sorceress Armida and forgets his duty to his fellow crusaders. Only when he is rescued by two of his companions and brought to his senses, as a 'corrected' Narcissus, does he rejoin his camp and fulfill his divine duty in the crusade.[36]

---

[36] The present discussion is part of a larger forthcoming work on Tasso and his aesthetic theory in *Gerusalemme Liberata*. The text of Tasso is taken from B. T. Sozzi (Turin 1968) and the translation from R. Nash (Detroit 1987) unless otherwise stated.

Armida's exceptional beauty (*GL* 4.29-31) and siren-like allure (*GL* 4.86) inveigle many crusaders to depart from the camp of Goffredo and the siege of Jerusalem (*GL* 4.8596, 5.60-61, 66-85). Like the victims of Alcina and the sinners in *Inferno* 30, the crusaders who are deceived by the charms of Armida are turned into animals to reflect their loss of reason to lustful passion (*GL* 10.66-67). After Rinaldo frees his companions (*GL* 10.71), he himself succumbs to the temptation of Armida's entrapment. Armida entices Rinaldo to travel on a small skiff to her enchanted isle using a work of art.[37] Like Narcissus and the heroes Dante and Ruggiero, he 'fixes' (*fisa*) his eyes on the beautiful workmanship of the white marble (*Fisa egli tosto gli occhi al bel lavoro/ del bianco marmo, GL* 14.57), whose inscription tells of the magnificent marvels on Armida's island. When he lands, he hears the song of an artificial siren and, like Dante, is lulled into a dangerous sleep (*GL* 14.61-65). The siren sings of the fleeting nature of fame and virtue, and argues instead for a life of pleasure, free from care (*GL* 14.62-64). The siren's song *si fa donno/ sovra i sensi di lui possente e forte:/ né i tuoni omai destar, non ch'altri, il ponno/ da quella queta imagine di morte*, 'makes itself the strong and powerful master of his senses; and now not even thunderbolts – not to speak of anything else – have power to wake him from that quiet imaging of death' (*GL* 14.65).[38] Like Narcissus, Rinaldo has lost all connection with reality and is trapped in a death-like trance. Armida transports Rinaldo to a magical garden, set atop a snow-covered mountain on a faraway island. Armida's paradise itself is an elaborate illusion, a work of art so real it belies its artifice:

> e, quel che 'l bello e 'l caro accresce a l'opre,
> l'arte, che tutto fa, nulla si scopre.
> Stimi (sì misto il culto è co 'l negletto)
> sol naturali e gli ornamenti e i siti.
> Di natura arte par, che per diletto
> l'imitatrice sua scherzando imiti. (*Gerusalemme Liberata* 16.9-10)

> and (what increases the beauty and price of the work) the art that makes it all is nowhere revealed./ You would judge (so mingled is negligence with care) both the grounds and their improvements only natural. It seems an art of nature, that for her own pleasure playfully imitates her imitator. (trans. R. Nash)

Like a work of art, Armida's garden attempts to capture Nature at the height of its beauty, defying the passing of time and the change of season with its perpetual spring.[39]

---

[37] Just as Astolfo is lured onto the back of the whale by the promises of Alcina, leaving his companions behind (*OF* 6.39-43), so also is Rinaldo tempted by the promises inscribed in the marble to board the skiff alone (*GL* 14.58). For the importance of the skiff and Fortune, see D. Quint, 'Tasso, Milton, and the boat of romance', in *Epic and Empire* (Princeton 1993) 248-67.

[38] Falaschi rightly sees Armida's isle as a reworking of the classical underworld, see G. Falaschi, *La favola di Rinaldo: il codice fiabesco e la Gerusalemme Liberata* (Florence 1994).

[39] See Gough's interesting article on Armida's seduction and conversion as Tasso's struggle with aesthetic theory: M. J. Gough, 'Tasso's enchantress, Tasso's captive woman', *Renaissance Quarterly* 54 (2001) 523-52.

To describe the love affair of Rinaldo and Armida, Tasso turns both lovers into Narcissus.40 As Armida gazes at herself in the mirror, which Rinaldo holds in his hands, so Rinaldo gazes at himself reflected in Armida's eyes. The lovers are in love with themselves in love (*GL* 16.20-22). Like Dante and Ariosto, Tasso depicts his hero bewitched by the sensual pleasure of the illusion in front of him, but Tasso departs from Dante and Ariosto in Rinaldo's moment of self-realization as Narcissus. In Tasso, what shatters the trance is not a voice or ring of 'reason', but the self-corrective use of a mirror.

While Armida is away,41 two of Rinaldo's companions rouse him from his dreamlike stupor by showing him his transformed reflection in a polished shield of adamant. Like Columella's marred horse, Rinaldo sees how effeminate, perfumed, and adorned he has become:

> **Egli al lucido scudo il guardo gira;**
> **onde si specchia in lui qual siasi,** e quanto
> con delicato culto adorno: spira
> tutto odori e lascivie il crine e 'l manto;
> e il ferro, il ferro aver, non ch'altro, mira
> dal troppo lusso effeminato a canto;
> guernito è sì ch'inutile ornamento
> sembra, non militar fèro instrumento.
>   **Qual uom, da cupo e grave sonno oppresso**
> **dopo vaneggiar lungo in sé riviene,**
> **tale ei tornò nel rimirar sé stesso:**
> **ma sé stesso mirar già non sostiene;**
> **giù cade il guardo; e timido e dimesso,**
> **guardando a terra, la vergogna il tiene**.
> Si chiuderebbe e sotto il mare, e dentro
> il foco, per celarsi, e giù nel centro. (Tasso *Gerusalemme Liberata* 16.30-31, *cf.* 14.77)

He turns his gaze upon the shining shield, in which is mirrored for him what manner of man he is become, and how much adorned with delicate elegance: he breathes forth all perfumed, his hair and mantle wanton; **and his sword, he marvels at his sword,** (not to speak of other things) **made effeminate** at his side by too much luxury; it is so trimmed that it seems a useless ornament, not the fierce instrument of war. / **As a man by deep and heavy sleep oppressed returns to himself after long**

---

[40] Tasso makes several allusions to Armida as Narcissus, besides the overt reference at 14.66, *e 'n su la vaga fronte/ pende omai sì, che par Narciso al fonte*, 'and now she bends so above his handsome face that she seems Narcissus at the spring': the pride in her supernatural beauty, her scorn of would-be lovers, and even the melting of her cold heart at the sight of Rinaldo (*GL* 4.27, 14.67, 16.38). In a playful turn of the story in Ovid, Tasso transforms the narcissistic Armida into Echo at the moment of Rinaldo's departure as a 'corrected' Narcissus, who is impervious to her pleas (*GL* 16.36, 39).

[41] As Melissa approached Ruggiero in Alcina's absence (*OF* 7.52), so Rinaldo's companions, Carlo and Ubaldo, carefully hidden in the underbrush, await the opportune moment of Armida's departure to rescue their spellbound hero. See also Corrigan, 'opposing mirrors' (n. 34, above) 169-78, who sees the mirror of the shield and its penitential effect in opposition to the lovers' mirror, which reflects their vanity and lust.

delirious raving, so he returned by gazing upon himself; but truly he cannot bear to admire himself; his gaze sinks low; and dejected and abashed, staring at the ground, he is possessed by shame. He would have shut himself under the sea and within the flame, to be concealed, and deep within earth's core. (trans. based on R. Nash)

Rinaldo's reflection not only destroys the illusion of Armida's charms, but it also reveals the effects of a life of dissipation and pleasure. From being one of the fiercest warriors, Rinaldo has become emasculated by Armida's sensual delights. In recognizing his disfigured reflection in the shield, Rinaldo realizes his mistake. Tasso combines Narcissus' moment of self-realization with its error. As a 'corrected' Narcissus, Rinaldo sees the truth about himself and is filled with shame.[42] His humiliation and selfknowledge not only restore him to reason but also stir him to action: he rejoins his companions and fulfills his divine duty.

Dante, Ariosto, and Tasso appropriate Ovid's story of Narcissus to explore both the power and danger of art. All of the qualities that Alberti praised in a painting that, like Narcissus' reflection, successfully blur the distinction between reality and illusion, that is, perfect beauty, semblance of movement, conveyance of emotion, and its transfixing effect, are placed under scrutiny in Renaissance epic. Each of the heroes fall victim to Narcissus' *error* and forgets the purpose of his journey: Dante, in his dream of the Siren, Ruggiero in the magical beauty of Alcina, and Rinaldo in the enchantment of Armida. The pleasure of the aesthetic experience is so dangerous and all-consuming that the heroes are only restored to reason by supernatural intervention: Dante by the angel of zeal, Ruggiero by the ring of 'reason', and Rinaldo by the shield of adamant. Only when each hero repents of his pursuit of false images and pleasures in the self-reflective use of a mirror, as a 'corrected' Narcissus, is he able to fulfill his divine destiny. In Dante's *La Divina Commedia*, Ariosto's *Orlando Furioso*, and Tasso's *Gerusalemme Liberata*, the myth of Narcissus becomes a reminder to reject sensory pleasure in favour of the rational reflection that leads to a transcendent aesthetic experience.

The valence of Narcissus as a metapoetic figure in the later tradition not only makes us more careful readers of Ovid but it also demonstrates how the story of the beautiful boy at the spring continues to resonate in aesthetic concerns today. As Heidegger laments in *The Age of the World Picture* (1938), art seems to have divorced the aesthetic experience from divine transcendence. It is only when we see art again as a process, instead of narcissistic self-indulgence, will we again attempt to transcend ourselves.

Howard University

---

[42] Tasso draws upon Dante's awakening and shame in *Inf.* 30 and *Purg.* 30 both in this passage and in Ubaldo's comment to the newly 'restored' Rinaldo that he should test himself against Armida's charms: *Qual più forte di te se le sirene / vedendo ed ascoltando, a vincer t'usi?* 'What man is stronger than you if by seeing and hearing the Sirens you accustom yourself to overmaster them?' (*GL* 16.41). I will discuss this further in my forthcoming book (n. 36 above).

BERNARDO MORETTI: A NEWLY DISCOVERED COMMENTATOR ON OVID'S *IBIS*[1]

FRANK T. COULSON

In his magisterial study of the medieval and humanistic glosses on Ovid's *Ibis,* La Penna references a commentary transmitted in a manuscript now housed at the Biblioteca Apostolica Vaticana with the shelf mark Reg. lat. 1801, containing a full commentary on the poem that he describes as independent of Calderini's commentary published in 1474.[2] La Penna, who knew of this commentary solely from the Vatican manuscript, makes very little use of it in his edition of select *scholia* to the *Ibis*.[3] My own research on the humanistic tradition of Ovid commentaries, undertaken for a projected *fascicle* of the *Catalogus translationum et commentariorum*, has revealed that this commentary was authored by Bernardo Moretti, a Bolognese rhetorician working around 1460. In addition to his commentary on the *Ibis*, Moretti was also the author of two prose and one versified lives of Ovid.[4] His work seems to have been relatively influential in the late fifteenth century, since I have been able to identify a large number of hitherto unknown manuscript copies of the commentary, increasing the number from one to some eight known witnesses. In this article, I survey Moretti as a commentator on Ovid, briefly discussing his biographies of the poet and then focusing my attention more selectively on the commentary on the *Ibis*.

Moretti was first identified as a commentator on the *Ibis* by Philippe Labbe who noted: 'Bernardo Moretti, who taught rhetoric at Bologna in 1459 and wrote a commentary on the *Ibis* of Ovid'.[5] Moretti is also alluded to very briefly by G. Fantuzzi.[6] La Penna touched upon Moretti in his overview of the *scholia*, and Luca Carlo Rossi discusses very briefly Moretti as a possible source for Calderini's commentary in the introduction to his recently published edition of Calderini's commentary on the *Ibis*.[7]

---

[1] I cite line numbers to the *Ibis* following the text of S. G. Owen (ed.), *P. Ovidi Nasonis Tristium quinque Ibis ex Ponto Libri quattuor Halieutica fragmenta* (Oxford 1915).

[2] A. La Penna, *Scholia in P. Ovidii Nasonis Ibin* (Florence 1959) XLV-XLVI.

[3] He notes *scholia* only on pages 174, 179, and 185.

[4] The prose lives have been discussed and edited in F. T. Coulson, 'Hitherto unedited Medieval and Renaissance lives of Ovid', *Mediaeval Studies* 49 (1987) 152-207.

[5] Philippe Labbe, *Nova bibliotheca manuscriptorum librorum sive specimen antiquarum lectionum Latinarum et Graecarum* (Paris 1653) 46.

[6] G. Fantuzzi in *Notizie degli scrittori bolognesi* 9 vols (Bologna 1781-94) IX (1794) 158.

[7] L. C. Rossi, *Commentarioli in Ibyn Ovidii* (Florence 2011) 20.

44   THE AFTERLIFE OF OVID

My own research on the commentary tradition on Ovid has allowed me to uncover numerous other manuscript witnesses to the works of Moretti.[8] In an earlier article,[9] I surveyed the manuscript evidence, and therefore I shall provide here only a brief and quick overview of the manuscripts, taking into account the one new witness discovered since the publication of the earlier article.

The manuscripts transmitting the works of Moretti may be classified into three major categories:

1. Those manuscripts transmitting the commentary on the *Ibis* and the longer prose life of Ovid.

> Vatican City, BAV, Reg. lat. 1801, saec. XV
> Paris, BnF, lat. 8257, saec. XV
> Florence, Biblioteca Riccardiana, 1202, saec. XV
> Rome, Biblioteca Nazionale Centrale, Varia 37 (commentary to vv. 23-197 only), saec. XV, found on fols. 14r-21v. This manuscript was not catalogued in Coulson, 'Bernardo Moretti' (see above, n. 9).

2. Those manuscripts containing only the prose lives of Ovid written by Moretti and transmitted separately from the commentary on the *Ibis*.

> Naples, Biblioteca Nazionale, V C 39, fols. 393r-395v, saec. XV
> Champaign-Urbana, Spurlock Museum, CMA 8, fols. 81r-87r. saec. XV[10]
> Florence, Biblioteca Fondazione Horne, N. 4/11, fol. 1r-v (short life of Ovid only), saec. XV.

3. Those manuscripts which transmit the verse life of Ovid composed by Moretti.

> Vatican City, BAV, Reg. lat. 1826, fol. 9r-v, saec. XV

The four manuscripts which transmit the complete text of the commentary are to be found, as one might expect, in humanist miscellanies. Paris, BnF, lat. 8257 has a commentary on the *Carmina Priapea* by Bernardinus Cyllenius,[11] while Florence 1202 contains a

---

[8] There is no evidence that Moretti's glosses were ever printed during the late fifteenth or sixteenth century.

[9] F. T. Coulson, 'Bernardo Moretti, Biographer and Commentator on Ovid: the Manuscripts', *Studi medievali* 3rd series 39 (1998) 449-59.

[10] S. de Ricci and W. J. Wilson, *Census of Medieval and Renaissance manuscripts in the United States and Canada* 2 vols (New York 1935-40), I.1076 list a manuscript (current whereabouts unknown) owned by the late Professor Blanche B. Boyer, Mt. Holyoke College which contains on fols. 81r-87r Moretti's life of Ovid. A comparison of the manuscript description with Spurlock Museum CMA 8 revealed the two manuscripts are identical in nearly every aspect, and I suspect the two manuscripts are indeed the same codex inadvertently catalogued twice over the space of the project.

[11] See F.-R. Hausmann, 'Carmina Priapea' in *Catalogus translationum et commentariorum* 9 vols. (Washington, DC, 1960) IV (1980) 423-50.

commentary on Columella by Pomponio Leto.[12] Reg. lat. 1801 contains *scholia* to the *Aratea* of Germanicus.[13]

The two prose lives of Ovid are found detached from the commentary on the *Ibis* in several manuscripts which often contain either humanistic miscellanies or other works of Ovid, most notably the *Epistula Sapphus* and the *Tristia*.[14]

The verse life of Moretti is known from a single manuscript witness, Reg. lat. 1826,[15] which also transmits a number of other poems from the *Anthologia latina* and humanist verses on Ovid (specifically an *Oratio in Ovidium* of Laurentius Rubeus,[16] and verses on Ovid by Franciscus de Magistris[17]).

Moretti's major work of Ovidian biography[18] reflects the new, critical approach applied to Ovidian biography in the later Renaissance. Fausto Ghisalberti, in a seminal article on the tradition of Ovidian biography,[19] underlined the movement of humanistic scholars away from the traditional classifications of the medieval *accessus*[20] to focus more exclusively on the life of Ovid. Humanists founded their life of Ovid on an intimate knowledge of the primary and secondary sources.

Moretti begins his life of Ovid by discussing the traditional events in Ovid's life, his birth at Sulmona, his equestrian background, his early legal training and love of poetry leading to the abandonment of a legal career, his exile and burial at Tomi.[21] Moretti properly interprets the two verses from *Tr.* 4.14.5-6 as a reference to the battle of Mutina in 43 BC where the consuls Hirtius and Pansa lost their lives; and he alludes to Ovid's year in Athens and his facility in Greek. Moretti does repeat the causes for the exile which had circulated in the Middle Ages,[22] but with a degree of skepticism. He concludes that the *Ars amatoria* was in all likelihood the real cause of banishment, while frankly confessing that some of the

---

[12] V. Brown, 'Columella' in *Catalogus translationum et commentariorum* III (1976) 173-93.

[13] The manuscript is catalogued in E. Pellegrin, *Les manuscrits classiques latins de la Bibliothèque Vaticane* 3 vols (Paris 1976-) II.1 (1978) 420-22.

[14] See Coulson, 'Bernardo Moretti', 454-56 for fuller descriptions.

[15] See Pellegrin, *Les manuscrits classiques*, II.1 432-35.

[16] Now edited in F. T. Coulson, 'Hitherto unedited Medieval and Renaissance lives of Ovid (II): humanistic lives', *Mediaeval Studies* 59 (1997) 111-53.

[17] Edited in V. Zappacosta, 'Cantalycii in Ibin Ovidianum Labyrinthum Interpretatio', *Latinitas* 21 (1973) 269-85.

[18] In this article, I treat only the longer prose life. An evaluation of the shorter prose life can be found in Coulson, 'Hitherto unedited Medieval and Renaissance lives of Ovid', 1987.

[19] F. Ghisalberti, 'Mediaeval biographies of Ovid', *Journal of the Warburg and Courtauld Institutes* 9 (1946) 10-59.

[20] For the medieval *accessus*, see Coulson, 'Hitherto unedited lives of Ovid', 1987.

[21] Moretti's two prose lives of Ovid are discussed and edited in Coulson, 'Hitherto unedited lives of Ovid', 1987.

[22] For detailed discussion of these causes, see R. Hexter, *Ovid and Medieval schooling: studies in Medieval school commentaries on Ovid's Ars Amatoria, Epistulae ex Ponto, and Epistulae Heroidum* (Munich 1986).

other reasons advanced, such as Ovid's affair with Livia, or his unwitting view of Augustus engaged in pederasty, are pure guesswork.

Moretti in general draws a highly sympathetic portrayal of the poet, emphasizing Ovid's prodigious talents and congenial mores. He establishes a complete and accurate list of Ovidian works. Only those works that can without doubt be considered part of the canon are admitted: *Heroides, Amores, Ars Amatoria, Remedia Amoris, Fasti, Medea, Metamorphoses, Tristia, Epistulae ex Ponto*. As the life introduced the commentary on the *Ibis*, that work itself is not referenced. Minor works, now lost, which can be deduced from references in the poetry of exile are listed, including a wedding song for Ovid's friend Maximus (*Ex Ponto* 1.2), a triumphal ode for Tiberius Caesar (*Ex Ponto* 3.4), and a work in the Getic tongue in praise of Augustus (*Ex Ponto* 4.13).

The versified life of Ovid written by Moretti, referred to in the manuscript witness (BAV, Reg. lat. 1826) by the title *Carmen de Ovidio*, will receive its *editio princeps* in this article.[23] It is a 36-verse poem, written in elegiac couplets, and falls within a recognized genre of humanist writing, namely verse lives of the Latin poets. Other humanists who wrote verse lives of Ovid include Martino Filetico and Giovanni Battista Cantalicio.[24] The poems of Ovid are not named by title; rather Moretti skillfully uses a paraphrase to designate them, and he alludes specifically to poems which may have been written during Ovid's youth, such as the *De cuculo* and the *De pulice*, as well as the fragmentary *Medicamina faciei femineae*.

Let us now turn to Moretti's major Ovidian work, his commentary to the *Ibis*, and begin by drawing a few general conclusions about its approach to elucidating the poem and its intended audience. One may say at the outset that Moretti has an extensive and commanding overview of the major Latin authors, less so Greek authors, as well as the historians necessary to help explain the arcane allusions in the poem. In addition to the works of Ovid, Moretti's far-ranging references to Latin authors include Virgil, Horace, Propertius, Tibullus, Lucan, Martial, Statius, Juvenal, Persius, Varro, Cicero, Livy, Justinus, Valerius Maximus, Pliny the Elder, Silius Italicus, Aulus Gellius, Macrobius, Sallust, the late-antique grammarian Priscian, the Latin translation and abridgment of Homer by Dictys Cretensis, as well as roughly contemporary authors such as Boccaccio, Mussato, Leonardo Bruni, and Maffeo Vegio. The list of Greek authors is, as one might expect, more restricted, but he does seem to know Hesiod, Herodotus, Plutarch, Homer, Archilochus, and Callimachus in Latin translation. Servius's commentary is extensively used, and he also draws upon the work of the thirteenth-century Swiss mythographer, Conradus de Mure, for at least some information on myth.[25]

The commentary, in general, is aimed at the more elementary reader of the poem. We find, for example, many glosses specifically geared to elucidating grammatical points: the accusative form *Ibida* (59) is a Greek accusative; deponents such as *sequor* and *loquor* (238), which have a 'q' in the present tense, change to a 'c' in the perfect participle passive and its derivatives; there is much paraphrasing of difficult or contorted word order in the poem; and sometimes rather complicated concepts are reduced to their simplest expression.

---

[23] See below, Appendix 1.

[24] Edited in E. Dell'Oro, 'Il de poetis antiquis di Martino Filetico', *Orpheus* n.s. 4 (1983) 427-43 and Zappacosta, 'Cantalycii in Ibin Ovidianum Labyrinthum Interpretatio'.

[25] T. van de Loo, ed., *Conradus de Mure Fabularius* (Turnhout 2006).

Subtle differences in meaning between similar sounding words are also explained, for example how does *ferrugo* differ from *aerugo* (231).

Since much of the poem is taken up with somewhat *abstruse* and *recherché* references to mythological figures and events, usually expressed indirectly through paraphrase, the commentary is largely devoted to providing background for the reader. There are places, it must be admitted, that Moretti concedes defeat and cannot identify an allusion, and the commentary is replete with such phrases as 'de hoc nihil habeo' and 'de hoc nihil aliud invenio'. We also have clear evidence that the poem allows the commentator to branch off into ancillary topics and terms: What are the major rivers of Europe? What are the months of the year, *etc.*? Such digressions are very much in keeping with the pedagogical intent of the commentary.

There are also some places where the commentary works on a higher plane, attempting to show the reader how Ovid has cleverly structured the poem so motifs in a later section pick up those from an earlier section; or the commentator concentrates on Ovid's extensive use of metaphor. Finally, there are a few sections of the commentary, but only a few, where Moretti ventures to give his opinion on a textual reading. Let us look at these categories more closely with examples taken from Moretti's commentary.

1. Allusions to other writers

Moretti frequently references classical Latin authors both to itemize and to discuss other treatments of the same topic, individual or myth. For example, at verse 35 Ovid alludes to the smoke that arose at the funeral pyres of Eteocles and Polynices, and the commentator both explicates the allusion and alludes to Statius and Lucan as writers who provide alternative versions:

> [comment to l. 35]. ... Et prius rogus Etheoclis et Polinicis ostendet concordiam inter ipsos quam mihi sit tecum gratia. Etheocles et Polinices fratres fuere ex Edipo et Iocasta geniti. Iocasta mater fuit Edipi qui cum cognouisset suum scelus se excecauit. Hi de regno contendentes maxima odia inter se exercuerunt in vita et cum comburerentur eorum corpora, rogus eorum et fumus in duas partes se diuisit ut etiam in morte cognosceretur discordia eorum; quod ostendit Lucanus in primo cum ait: 'Vestali raptus ab ara ignis, et ostendens confectas fla<m>ma Latinas scinditur in partes geminoque cacumine surgit Thebanos imitata (mutatua MS) rogos, *etc.*' (*B.C.* 1. 549-52). Et Statius in ultimo *Thebaidos* (12.429-32): 'Ecce iterum fratres! primos ut contigit artus ignis edax, tremuere rogi et nouus advena busto pellitur; exundant diverso *(sic)* vertice flamme alternosque apices abrupta luce coruscant.' Ideo ait hic 'Quam uetus accensa separat ira pyra' (36). De his qui plura cupit legat Statium fere per totum de bello Thebano ubi etiam inueniet hos apud inferos pugnis certare. (Reg. lat. 1801, fol. 146r)

> ... And sooner will the funeral pyre of Eteocles and Polynices be in agreement before there will be accord between you and me. Eteocles and Polynices were brothers born from Oedipus and Jocasta. Jocasta was the mother of Oedipus, who, when he found out this crime, blinded himself. These brothers fought each other for the kingdom; in life there was the greatest strife between them, and when their bodies were burned the smoke from the pyre divided into two streams so that even in death their discord

might be known. Lucan shows this in Book One: 'The fire was snatched from the Vestal altar, and the flame which marked the end of the Latin Festival split into two and rose, like the Theban funeral pyre, with double crest'. And Statius in the last book of the *Thebaid*: 'See once more the brothers! As soon as the consuming fire touched the limbs, the pyre shook and the new arrival is driven from the pyre; the flames rise up with diverse top and they flash twin peaks in the broken light'. So Ovid says: 'The smoke was divided by the ancient wrath as the pyre burned'. Those who wish to know more should read Statius throughout the Theban War where you will find that they battle each other even in the Underworld.

At verse 171 and following, Ovid describes the punishments that await Ibis in the Underworld. Ovid begins with an allusion to the Elysian Fields where Ibis will most definitely not reside, and then moves on to the punishments that await him, referencing Ixion, the Danaids, Tantalus, and lastly Tityos:

> 179-80. *Iugeribus nouem summus* (summum MS) *qui distat ab imo uisceraque assidue debita prebet aui*: Titium intelligit de quo Virgilius in sexto (*Aen.* VI.595), et Servius ibidem, et omnes fere autores. Hic fuit Iouis filius ex Ciara (*sic*), filia Orchomeni, quam Iupiter, Iunonis iram extimescens, in specu sub terra abscondit, ob quod ex terra natus Titius dicitur a poetis. Virgilius in sexto (595): 'Terrae omnipotentis alumnum'. Hic cum Latonae uim inferre uellet, ab Apolline sagittis confossus est; de hoc Seneca in *Hercule furente* multa et Ovidius in primo *de Ponto*. Hic assidue prebet uiscera uulturi et distenditur per nouem iugera, ut ait Tibullus: 'Porrectusqe nouem Titius per iugera terrae assiduas atro sanguine pascit aues'. (1.3.75-76) (Reg. lat. 1801, fol. 153r)

> *Stretched out nine iugera, he shows his innards to the ever-present bird*: He means Tityos, and Virgil speaks of him in the Sixth Book, and Servius in his commentary on the passage and nearly every author. This man was the son of Jove from Ciara, the daughter of Orchomenus. Jupiter, fearing the wrath of Juno, hid her in a cave beneath the earth, and so Tityos is said by the poets to spring from the earth. Virgil in Book Six: 'The offspring of the all-powerful earth'. When he wished to attack Latona, he was pierced by the arrows of Apollo. Seneca says a lot about this in the *Hercules Furens* and Ovid in the First Book of the *Ex Ponto*. He showed his liver always to a vulture and he was stretched through nine *iugera*, as Tibullus relates: 'Stretched through nine *iugera* he constantly fed the birds on his black blood'.

What historical sources does Moretti know in order to answer many of the questions a reader might have concerning events in Roman history? Livy is perhaps the most important historian used by Moretti and is frequently cited as an authority:

> 387. *Et quos dux Pen[eu]us....*De hoc nihil inueni apud Liuium quamuis legerim totum de secundo bello Punico. Legi in quibusdam glosulis satis antiquis quod **Ha<n>nibal** legatos Romanos in puteum demersit, postea iecit super eos puluerem, et cum quererentur ipsi legati a Romanis, iurauit non esse supra terram suam. Nihil aliud habeo. (Reg. lat. 1810, fol. 169v)

And those whom the Punic leader: I have found nothing about this in Livy, though I read all about the second Punic war. I have read in some old glosses that Hannibal put the Roman legates down a well and covered them with dust, and when the Romans asked after these legates, Hannibal said that they were not on top of his land. I have found nothing further.

Justin is also frequently cited, and the works of Cicero are plumbed for their historical anecdotes. For example, Moretti's comments to verses 299-300, wherein Ovid alludes to king Pyrrhus, incorporate information from Cicero, Justin, and Plutarch:

299-300. *Aut, ut Achylidem, cognato nomine clarum, opprimat hostili tegula iacta manu*: Pyrrhus rex Epyrhotarum ex genere Achillis (Eutrop. *Brev.* 2.11.1) ut ipse predicabat, de quo meminit Cicero in primo *Officiorum* afferens Ennii uersus (1.39). Hic uenit in auxilium Tarentinorum contra Romanos temporibus Marci Curii <et> C. Fabritii. Nam Curius, ut ait Cicero in libro *de Senectute*, de eo triumphauit (*Sen.* 55). C. Fabritius partem regni ab eo oblatam repudiauit. Hic reuersus in Graeciam cum Argos oppugnaret iactu tegulae occisus est, ut ait poeta et Plutarchus in fine uitae ipsius Pyrrhi (Plutarch, *Life of Pyrrhus*, 34). Iustinus uero libro XXVo dixit cum saxo occisum (Justinus 25.5)... (Reg. lat. 1801, fols. 162v-163r)

May a tile cast by a hostile hand catch him unawares, just like Pyrrhus who gained renown in the name of his forbearer Achilles: Pyrrhus king of the region of Epirus, was descended from Achilles as he used to relate. Cicero recalls this in Book One of the *Duties*, relating verses of Ennius. He came to assist the people of Tarentum against the Romans in the time of Marcus Curius and Gaius Fabricius. For Curius, as Cicero says in *On Old Age*, triumphed over him. Fabricius rejected part of the kingdom handed over by him. Pyrrhus returned to Greece and was killed by a tile while attacking Argos, as Ovid says, and Plutarch relates in the end of his life of Pyrrhus. Justin in book 25 said that he was killed with a stone....

When Moretti references Greek authors, it is difficult to know if he has access to the original Greek or if he is getting his reference from a secondary source. His references to Homer, for example, are nearly always generic, as the following examples illustrate:

270. *Et Thamire Demo<do>tique caput*: Thamira fuit citharedus Tracius, ut est apud Homerum in secundo *Iliados* (2.595). (Reg. lat. 1801, fol. 160r)

Like the head of Thamyris and Demodocus: Thamyris was a Thracian bard, as one finds in Homer in the second book of the *Iliad*.

274-75. *Frater et uxor solertique uiro*: Vlixem intelligit qui fuit ualde solers. Hic fuit filius Laertae, regis Itace, ex Autolia (*sic*) quam, ut fama refert, Sysiphus, filius Eoli, regis Corinthi, uitiauit cum ad maritum duceretur. Vnde aliquando dicitur ipse Vlixes filius Eoli, de quo meminit Oratius in *Epistolis* et in *Sermonibus*, et Homerus in tota *Odissea*, Virgilius et Iuvenalis, et Ouidius in XIIIo *Metamorphoseos* (13.25-26). (Reg. lat. 1801, fol. 160v)

Brother and wife and to the clever man: He means Ulysses who was very clever. He was the son of Laertes, king of Ithaca, from Anticlea whom, as legend relates,

Sisyphus the son of Aeolus, king of Corinth, raped while he was taking her to her husband. And so sometimes Ulysses is called the son of Aeolus, and Horace mentions this in his *Epistles* and *Satires*, and Homer throughout the *Odyssey*, Virgil, and Juvenal, and Ovid in Book Thirteen of the *Metamorphoses*.

There are also a few places where we find tantalizing allusions to a Latin translation of Callimachus, but to date I have not been able to track down any more details on the probable source for this.[26] For example at verse 315 one finds:

313. *Utque necatorum Darei fraude secundi*: Dareus secundus, nepos primo: De hoc sunt carmina **Ca<l>limachi** traducta: 'Sic tu dispereas sicut periere secundus quos multos Dareus obruerat cinere'. (Reg. lat. 1801, fol. 164r)

Of those killed by the treachery of Dareus the second: Dareus the second, grandson of the first. He is spoken of in the poems of Callimachus translated into Latin: 'May you perish like all those whom Dareus the second overwhelmed with ash'.

Finally, there is every indication that Moretti is abreast of contemporary treatments of myth. Boccaccio's *Genealogia deorum* serves as a source material for our knowledge of mythology at several points; Albertino Mussato is alluded to at least once in the commentary at verse 133, where Thrace is referenced, causing Moretti to go on a long digression about the various rivers called Timauus:

133. Est alius Thimauus Patauinus qui hodie Brenta dicitur de quo Musatus poeta Patauinus: 'In mare fert Patauas unde Thimauus aquas'. (Reg. lat. 1801, fol. 150v)

There is another Paduan Timavo river, today called Brenta, which the Paduan poet Mussato speaks of: 'From where Timavo bears Paduan waters to the sea'.

And we have a tantalizing reference to the poem on Meleager published by the NeoLatin poet Basinio Basini (1425-1457) only a few years before the composition of Moretti's own commentary.[27]

599. Lege hanc fabulam (*i.e.* of Meleager) in octavo *Met.* et diffusus apud Basinium Parmensem qui de hac uenatione opus egraegium conscripsit. (Reg. lat. 1801, fol. 183v)

Read about this story in the eighth book of the *Metamorphoses* and throughout the work of Basinio of Parma who wrote an exceptional poem about this hunt.

---

[26] I am most grateful to Prof. Luigi Lehnus for sharing with me his expertise on the Renaissance reception of Callimachus.

[27] M. S. Jensen and A. Berger, *Die Meleagris des Basinio Basini: Einleitung, kritische Edition, Übersetzung, Kommentar* (Trier 2002).

Finally, in the gloss to verse 496, we find a reference to Maffeo Vegio's poem on Astyanax, written in 1430:[28]

494. *Et Iliaca missus ab arce puer*: Astianas, filius Hectoris, de quadam Troiana turri precipitatus est ab Vlixe, quam rem optime prosecutus est Mafeus Vegius poeta Laudensis in quodam opusculo de morte Astianattis et Ouidius XIIIo *Metamorphoseos*. (Reg. lat. 1801, fol. 177v)

And the boy cast from the Trojan tower: Astyanax, the son of Hector, was cast from a certain tower at Troy by Ulysses. Maffeo Vegio, the poet from Lodi, developed this theme in a certain little work on the death of Astyanax, and Ovid did so in the thirteenth book of the *Metamorphoses*.

2. Points of Grammar and comments of a pedagogical nature

There are many comments in Moretti's commentary which are of a purely grammatical nature and seem to indicate the commentary was used by schoolboys who had to grapple with the basics of syntax and forms. For example, at verse 13 Ovid uses the form *requiem*, and Moretti mentions that the form *requietem* is found in Cicero:

13. *Requiem*: *Legimus etiam apud Ciceronem* in *Catone maiore 'requietem' (Sen.* 65). (Reg. lat. 1801, fol. 145r)

Rest: We also read in Cicero *On Old Age* <the form> *requietem*.

At verse 233, the difference in meaning between the two nouns *ferrugo* and *(a)erugo* is discussed:

231. *T[r]actis (*sic*) ferrugine*: Ferrugo est ferri rugbigo, erugo aeris, vt Iuuenalis: 'Cum tota erugine follem (tollem MS)' *(Sat*. 13.60). Alii putant ferruginem colorem esse eum quem birtinum uocamus qui quidem non differt a colore rubiginis ferri. (Reg. lat. 1801, fol. 155v)

Touched with rust: 'Ferrugo' is the redness of iron, 'aerugo' that of bronze, as Juvenal says: 'Your purse with all its redness'. Others say the color of 'ferrugo' is what we call 'britinus', which indeed does not differ from the color or the redness of iron.

At verse 238, Moretti points out that while the present tense of *loquor* is written with a 'q', the supine and its derivatives are written with a 'c':

238. *Locuta*: 'Loquor' uerbum per q scribitur, tamen supinum et a supino deriuata per c scribuntur, eodem modo 'sequor'. (Reg. lat. 1801, fol. 155v)

Spoke: *Loquor* is a verb written with a q, but in the supine and its derivatives it is written with a c, and in the same way the verb *sequor*.

---

[28] Vegio was one of the outstanding Latin poets of the Quattrocento. His most famous work was his supplement to the *Aeneid.* His works are most easily accessible in Maffeo Vegio, *Short Epics*, tr. and ed. by Michael C. J. Putnam (with James Hankins) (Cambridge, MA 2009).

52 THE AFTERLIFE OF OVID

At verse 225, the masculine and feminine forms of the Latin word for snake are duly noted:

> 225. *Pectoraque unxerunt Erebeae <felle> colubrae*: id est infernalis serpentis, nam Herebus infernus est. Colubra est serpens; dicitur etiam coluber de masculo. (Reg. lat. 1801, fol. 155r)

> *They smeared his breast with the poison of the snake of Erebus*: that is of the snake of the lower world, for Erebus is the underworld. 'Colubra' is a snake. In the masculine it is written 'coluber'.

There are also innumerable places where unusual word usages are explained for the student. Ovid begins the *Ibis* with a reference to a five-year period, a *lustrum*, and Moretti not only explains its meaning in context in the *Ibis*, but also provides its various possible meanings:

> 1-2. *Lustris bis quinque*: id est decem, id est quinquaginta annis; est enim lustrum spatium quinquenale, sicut apud Graecos Olympias. Lustrum interdum lupanar significat, unde Plautus in *Cassina* (768): 'Uxor te ex lustris rapit'. Lustrum <dicitur> quandoque cubile ferarum, et lustrum appellabatur cum populus Romanus censebatur. Hoc frequens est apud Liuium,. Et lustrum est purgatio circum moenia facta. Lucanus in primo *(B.C.* 1.592-94): 'Mox iubet attonitam (*sic*) pauidis a ciuibus vrbem ambire et festo purgare moenia lustro longe per extremos pomeria cingere fines'. (Reg. lat. 1801, fols. 143v-144r)

> *Two times five lustra*: that is to say, ten, that is fifty years. A 'lustrum' is a space of five years, just as is the term Olympiad among the Greeks. It can also mean a brothel, whence Plautus in the *Casina*: 'Your wife snatched you from the brothel'. Sometimes a 'lustrum' means the bed of wild animals, and it also indicates when the Roman people were counted in the census. We find this often in Livy. 'Lustrum' also means a purification around the walls. Lucan in Book One: 'Next he ordered the citizens to march around the astonished city, to purify the walls with long lustration and to encircle the outer boundary of the long pomerium'.

A similar treatment is given to explicating the noun *forum* at verse 14:

> 14. *Foro*: Forum dicitur, teste Varrone, quod illic ferantur res ad uendendum uel cause agitantur (agitandum MS). Nam duplex est forum, scilicet causarum et rerum uenalium, et hoc multiplex, scilicet boarium, piscarium et olitorium. Et forum est locus in prouincia in quo magistratus audit legatos ciuitatum provinciae suae. Cicero in tertio *Epistolarum familiarium* ad Appium Pulcrum sic ait (*ad Fam.* III.6): 'Erant qui dicerent te agere forum Tarsi'. Multa loca a magistratibus sunt appellata, ut Forum Iulii, Forum Cornelii, Forum Sempronii. Quidam putant per 'ph' esse scribendum forum et dici a Ph<o>roneo, Argivorum rege, qui primus dicitur forum instituisse. (Reg. lat. 1801, fol. 145r)

> *Forum*: Forum, as Varro attests, is derived from the fact that things are brought there for sale or legal cases are tried. There are two types of fora: legal or for selling things, and the latter may be of many types, for cattle, fish, vegetables. And the forum is the place in the province where the magistrates hear the legates of the states of their

province. Cicero in the third book of the *Letters to his Friends* to Appius Pulcher says thus: 'There were those who said you were pleading in the forum at Tarsus'. Many places are called after the magistrates, such as the Julian forum, the Cornelian forum, the Sempronian forum. Some think it should be written 'ph' and comes from Phoroneus, king of the Argives, who is said to have first established them.

One other technique very favored by Moretti, and one that again seems to point to the pedagogical purposes of the commentary, is the prose paraphrase, whereby Ovid's verse is broken down into its component parts and explicated. For example, at verses 119-20 Ovid writes: *Sitque quod est rarum solito defecta favore fortunae facies invidiosa tuae, And what's rare, devoid of common charity, the face of your misfortune will be a source of envy,* and Moretti explicates thus:

> 119-20. Sensus est: *facies,* id est qualitas uel status, *tuae fortunae,* id est tuae miseriae, *defecta,* id est uacua, *solito fauore.* Nam solent miseri et calamitosi habere magnum fauorem apud misericordes. *Inuidiosa,* id est odiosa omnibus, *quod est rarum*, id est tot mala feras ut ipsa mala sint odio omnibus uidentibus, *quod est rarum*, id est vix contingit. (Reg. lat. 1801, fols. 149v-150r)

> Here is the sense: *face*, that is quality or state, *of your fortune*, that is of your misery, *be bereft*, that is empty, *of usual favor*. For the wretched and those who suffer have great sympathy with those who show pity. *A source of envy*, that is hated by all, *which is rare*, that is to say, may you bear so many evils and may they be a source of hatred to all who see you, *which is rare*, that is to say, that scarcely happens.

3. Textual interests, sources for myth and literary concerns

Moretti also shows an interest in questions of a textual nature, though such comments are admittedly somewhat rare. At verse 208, Moretti is confronted with the two readings, *levis* or *lenis;*

> 208. Et legas 'levis' non autem 'lenis'. Nam si 'lenis' legas, non stat versus. (Reg. lat. 1801, fol. 154r)

> Read 'levis', light and not 'lenis', mild. For if you read 'lenis', mild, the verse cannot stand.

At verse 176, Moretti enjoins the reader to read '*Aegypti*' and not '*Aegisthi*':

> 176. *Nurus Egypti,* fratris Danai. *Turba cruenta*, appositiue. Vbi est 'Egypti', non legas 'Egysti', nam Egystus est alius. Ne te inducat in errorem quod ubique pro Egypto Egistus scribitur, qui Egystus fuit post Egyptum annis circiter CCCXL. (Reg. lat. 1801, fol. 153r)

> *The daughters-in-law of Aegyptus,* the brother of Danaus. *Blood-stained crowd,* in apposition. Where we have 'Aegyptus', don't read 'Aegisthus', for Aegisthus is someone else. And don't be led into error by the fact that everywhere Aegisthus is written for Aegyptus. That Aegisthus lived about 340 years after Aegyptus.

54   THE AFTERLIFE OF OVID

Of course, the bulk of the commentary is taken up with explicating *abstruse* and *recherché* references to myth, and one naturally asks what specific handbooks and sources lay behind Moretti's explanations. Often, he will send the reader to the appropriate fable in the *Metamorphoses* or to the tragedies of Seneca, or to Servius, without further comment. Moretti also seems to know the *Fabularius* of Conradus de Mure. At verse 537, Moretti confronts two textual readings: '*cognitor*' and '*conditor*', and his explanations are taken almost verbatim from Conrad:[29]

> 537. *Conditor ut tardae:* Blesus conditor Myrrae ciuitatis in Arabia, tardus in construendis moenibus ab hostibus captus est et eius membra sparsa sunt per diuersa loca. De hoc nihil aliud inuenio. Si legitur 'cognitor', potest intelligi de Cynara rege Cypriorum qui cum filia Myrra concubuit; postea eam cognovit sed tarde. Nam post illatam uim eam cognouit. Hic uocatus est Blesus cognomine; de Cynara melius intelligitur. (Reg. lat. 1801, fol. 180r)

> *Just as he who lately*: Blaesus, who established Mura, a state in Arabia, *late* in constructing walls, and he was captured by the enemy and his limbs were dispersed through various places. I cannot find anything else about him. If we read 'cognitor', we can understand Cinyras, the Cyprian king, who slept with his daughter Myrrha. Aterwards, he found her out but too late, for he had already had intercourse before he recognized her. And his cognomen was Blaesus. It is better understood about Cinyras.

But lest our reader be left with a sense that Moretti always operates on a more pedestrian level, let me conclude this section with some comments on what might be termed his 'literary' interests: Is he interested in the structure of the poem? Does he have a sense of imagery and metaphor? What were Ovid's debts to his literary predecessors, particularly his Greek predecessors?

Moretti is quite scrupulous at delineating the large compositional structures of the poem. He notes the introduction to the invective proper, verses 1-64, in which Ovid introduces his enemy, refusing to name him but labeling him with the title *Ibis*. At verse 65, where the invective proper begins, Moretti comments:

> 65. *Dii maris et terrae.....:* Post propositionem more Latinorum poetarum inuocat Ouidius et generaliter omnes deos marinos, terrest<r>es et celestes. (Reg. lat. 1801, fol. 147v)

> *Gods of the sea and land...*After the *propositio*, in the manner of Latin poets Ovid invokes and he addresses generally all the gods, of sea, land and sky.

In addition, Moretti effectively shows how smaller units of the poem are given structural cohesion, as well as highlighting how certain cross references may serve to connect the various strands of the invective. For example, verses 85-104 are primarily taken up with developing the sacrifice of Ibis on the altars of vengeance, and Ovid piles on references taken from sacrifice: *annuite* (85), *precor* (87), *devoveo* (93), *vota* (95), *nulla mora est in*

---

[29] See Conradus de Mure, *Fabularius* (Leius).

me (95)*; ominibus malis* (99)*; da iugulum cultris* (104). Throughout this section, Moretti illustrates how these motifs serve to interconnect the larger passage:

93. *Illum ego deuoueo: deuoueo* id est ad sacrificandum arae exibeo. (Reg. lat. 1801, fol. 149r)

I curse him: I curse, that is I exhibit him at the altar for sacrifice.

95. *Nulla mora est in me:* id est sum paratus. Morem exprimit sacrific[i]orum. *Sacerdos* id est ego tanquam sacerdos; ponit rem ante oculos ut uideatur res ipsa geri. (Reg. lat. 1801, fol. 149r)

There is no delay in me, that is I am ready. He expresses the habit of those performing sacrifices. *A priest*, namely me, as though I were a priest. He places the thing before one's eyes as though it were actually happening.

104. *Da iugulum cultris hostia dira meis:* Seruat in hac re ficta more<m> sacrificantium et iugulantium uictimas et hostias. *Iugulum* pars anterior colli, *cultris* magnis cultellis. (Reg. lat. fol. 149r-v)

Harsh victim, give your throat to my knife: He maintains in the fiction the character of those sacrificing and slaying their victims and sacrificial animals. *The throat*, the front part of the neck, *to my knife*, my big knife.

In several places, Moretti underlines Ovid's explicit use of imagery or metaphor. For example, at v. 43, Ovid writes: *Prima quidem cepto committam proelia versu*, I shall commence the first warfare in the verse I have begun, and Moretti comments:

43. *Prima quidem cepto committam prelia uersu*: Perstat in metaphora more suo. Nam supra dixit armis pro maledic<t>is, nunc prelia pro eodem. (Reg. lat. 1801, fol. 146r)

He continues the metaphor as is his wont. For above he said arms for curses, now battle for the same.

Further, Moretti frequently attempts to underline Ovid's debt to his literary predecessors in the genre of invective, particularly Callimachus and a so-called Battus. In his comments to v. 297, Ovid alludes to the fate of the Lydian seer Achaeus, and Moretti draws the reader to the verses of a certain 'Battus':[30]

297. Acheus uates Lydius intelligitur de quo Bacchus poeta ait: 'Anciacus raptum uictum suspendit Acheum, vnda (vnde MS), nisi hoc credas, aurea testis adest'. Hic dixit 'aurea', Ouidius dixit 'aurifera', aquam Pactoli fluuii in Lydia intelligentes quae arenas aureas producit per Lydiam, sicut Tagus in Hyspania. (Reg. lat. 1801, fol. 162v)

---

[30] Battus is also referenced in Moretti's gloss to v. 257. See La Penna, *Scholia, ad loc.* Housman intimated as early as 1921 that Battus may be a ghost premised on the erroneous manuscript reading found in *Tr.* IV.10.47. See A. E. Housman, 'Review: A. Rostagni, *Ibis*' in *The Classical Papers of A. E. Housman*, ed. J. Diggle and F. R. D. Goodyear 3 vols (Cambridge 1972) III. 1915-36 104951.

He means Achaeus, the Lydian seer, about whom Battus speaks: 'Antiochus captured, seized, and suspended Achaeus, and if you don't believe me, the golden water stands as witness'. He says 'golden' while Ovid says "gold-bearing', both understand the water of the river Pactolus in Lydia which produces golden sand through Lydia, just as the Tagus in Spain.

4. Moretti and Calderini

Finally, let us make a few comments on how Moretti differs from the major commentary on the *Ibis* which circulated in the Renaissance, namely that authored by Domizio Calderini and published in Venice in 1474.[31]

La Penna, in his introduction to the edition of the *scholia* to the poem, notes that Moretti's commentary is essentially independent of Calderini's, and I am in the main in agreement with this assessment. There is some overlap in interests in comments: both commentators are interested in making sure that the reader understands what he is reading; and both provide extended explanations of myth. But in the main, Calderini is less interested in explicating in detail the exact interconnections of the syntax of the Latin, and his comments often remain uniformly laconic. So his commentary is less given over to prose paraphrase and reworking of the Ovidian verses. Calderini also often seems to show less interest in providing background information for the reader, certainly not to the degree that Moretti does. Verse 52 is perhaps a good illustration of these differences:

52. Calderini: *Tincta Lycambeo*: quibus telis vitam Lycambes finivit.

Tinged with <the blood> of Lycambes: with those weapons with which Lycambes ended his life.

51-2. Moretti: *Postmodo, si perges, in te mihi liber iambus tincta Licambeo sanguine tela dabit*: Translatione utitur, id est deinceps si perseueraueris, pingam te carmine iambico, et forte cogam te ad suspendium, sicut Archilocus poeta Lacedemonius cogit Licambem iambicis carminibus que ipse primus inuenit, ut ait Oratius in *Arte poetica* (179): 'Archilocum proprio rabies armauit iambo'. Licambes huic promiserat filiam nomine Neobolem, postea negavit. At Archilocus <indignatus> iambicis tunc primum inventis ita eum momordit et infamia aspersit, quod ille cupiens uitare iambos laqueo uitam finiuit et filia idem fecit. (Reg. lat. 1801, fol. 146v)

If you persist, my invective will direct weapons against you tinged with the blood of Lycambes: He uses a *translatio*, a shift of context, that is to say, if you persist further, I shall paint you with an iambic poem and I shall compel you to hang yourself, just as the Spartan poet Archilochus forced Lycambes to do. According to Horace in the *Ars poetica* he was the founder of the genre. Lycambes had promised his daughter Neobule in marriage to him but later refused, and Archilochus furious attacked him with the newly invented iambic poetry and covered him with infamy, and Lycambes, wanting to avoid the attack, hanged himself, and his daughter did the same.

---

[31] Now edited in L. C. Rossi, *Commentarioli in Ibyn Ovidii* (Florence 2011).

There are also several places where Calderini appears to reference specifically Moretti's earlier commentary and to chastise his interpretation:

403. Calderini: *Ut pronepos*: Male sunt interpetati meo iudicio qui hoc de Hippolito scriptum putant.

In my view those who interpret this as referring to Hippolytus are wrong.

Calderini also takes up Moretti's interpretation of verse 177 (which is found on fol. 153r of Reg. lat. 1801):

177. Calderini: *Poma pater*: Tantalus Paphlagoniam tenuit imperio, ditissimus fertilitate regionis et ob multa metalla quae illuc erant, ut scribit Strabo (cf. XII.8.2). In pugna fuit adversus Troem quoniam Ganymedem rapuerat ut Eusebius scribit (Eusebius of Caesaea, *Praeparatio Evangelica* V.34). Dignatus deorum mensa, Iovis mystica protulit mortalibus, unde apud inferos esse meruit, siciens in aquis ori allabentibus, ut scribit Homerus (*Od.* XI.582). **Quod nonnulli dixerunt** hoc supplicium datum quoniam Pelopen filium diis hospitibus epulandum apposuisset, falsum est.

Tantalus held power in Paphlagonia, rich because of the fertility of the region and because of the many metals found there, as Strabo says. He was in a war against king Tros because he had snatched Ganymede, as Eusebius relates. Worthy of the table of the gods, he related the secrets of Jove to mortals, whence he was rightly placed in the underworld, thirsty, though water lapped round about his mouth, as Homer relates. **Some say** that he received this punishment because he served up his son Pelops to the gods who were guests, but this is false.

Conclusion

Though Ovid's great curse poem, the *Ibis*, written from his exile at Tomi, was known from the twelfth to the fourteenth century, it was in the Renaissance period when one particularly saw a burgeoning interest in explicating this poem.[32] Commentaries proliferate, both anonymously and from the pen of such renowned humanists as Christoforo Zaroto, Pietro Marso and Domizio Calderini. Our research for a forthcoming volume of the *Catalogus translationum et commentariorum,* dealing with the medieval and humanistic school tradition on Ovid, has allowed us to identify some forty anonymous and named commentaries on the *Ibis* dating from the fifteenth and sixteenth centuries, in addition to references to some 12 commentaries no longer extant. No doubt, for these humanists the popularity of the work resided in the extremely *abstruse* and *recherché* mythological references which allowed them to show off their own erudition. In this article, we have examined more closely one such humanist commentator on the *Ibis*. Bernardo Moretti may not be considered the most sophisticated or illuminating commentator on the invective – certainly his skills seem to lag behind those of Calderini – but he is of interest as a newly identified humanist commentator, one who was working at Bologna in the mid fifteenth century where there is a great deal of interest on the *Ibis* and Ovid generally. Until more commentaries on the poem have been

---

[32] For an overview of the commentaries in print from the Renaissance, see R. Ortega, *Los comentarios al 'Ibis' de Ovidio: El largo recorrido de una exégesis* (Frankfurt am Main 1999).

edited and made available in print, it will be difficult to make definitive judgments about Moretti's place in the tradition. Nevertheless, this brief foray has perhaps given the reader a window onto the writings and interests of this hitherto unknown humanist scholar.

The Ohio State University

*I am grateful to Tom Hawkins for his comments on an earlier draft of this article.

APPENDIX

Edition of Moretti's Versified Life of Ovid: *Carmen de Ovidio*

Vatican City, BAV, Reg. lat. 1826, fols. 9r-10r

Nasonem iuuenes hortor celebrare poetam,
  Quo duce Pierides Itala rura colunt.
Hic Bocio genitus, Pelligno in colle virenti,
  Dilexit Musas Castaliamque domum.
Nam cuculum et pulices cecinit puerilibus annis,   5
  Et flammas cecinit Naso poeta suas.
Et iuuenis scripsit diuina poemata Naso,
  Essetque longus connumerare labor.
At maior uarias sumentia corpora formas
  Cecinit et Veneris tela benigna canit.   10
At Cupidineo prebet medicamen amori,
  Annales condit maxima Roma tuos.
Penelope atque alie Peligno carmine uatis
  Et Sulmo resonat cuncta per ora uirum.
Mittitur in Pontum fatis agitatus iniquis   15
  Vnde eius casus tristiciamque legis.
Ibidis inuidiam domat numenque precatur
  Incitata seuo premia digna uiro.
Et Ponto missas relegat pia turba Camenas,
  Que possent seua flectere corda uirum.   20
Fastorum dolor est sex amisisse libellos
  Impia quos rapuit barbara turba Gotum.
Sex tamen his reliquis si multa requirere curas,
  Multa potes multis +orta+ referre bonis.
Hic ritus Latii Romanaque festa leguntur,   25
  Siderii cursus sydera Naso canit.
Hic causas disces sacrorum Musa docebit
  Narrabit causas ille uel ille deus.
Quinquaginta octo uates compleuerat annos
  Naso Tomitana cum cadit exul humo.   30
Non ego pro tantis auderem reddere grates,
  Pierii iuuenes, Pieriique patres;
Ipse deus reddat qui cuncta uidet auditque
  Premia digna precor, premia digna bonis.
Ast ego si quicquam potero dum uita manebit,   35
  Vester ero, patres, vester ero, iuuenes.

23 si multa *scripsi*: simulata *MS* 34 bonis *scripsi*: *quid MS, incertum, fort.* bois.

FROM OVID TO PONTANO:
MYTH, A *FORMA MENTIS*? ELABORATING *HUMANITAS* THROUGH MYTHOLOGICAL *INVENTIO*[1]

HÉLÈNE CASANOVA-ROBIN

In the cultural effervescence of the Italian Quattrocento, Ovid benefitted from a prime position: his texts, widely diffused for centuries and scrutinized in many an allegorical exegesis, inspired new interest under the stimulation of philology and the diversification of schools of thought.[2] Giovanni Pontano (1429-1503), philologer, statesman, patron of Neapolitan culture, and above all an immensely erudite and prolific poet, manifested a deep fascination for the genius of Sulmone. This fascination is evident both in the tales Pontano discovered in the *Metamorphoses* and in the inspiration frequently derived from, and at times even explicitly credited to, Ovid's elegiac writing.[3] The humanist's writings reveal his predilection for Ovidian language, for the ceaseless porosity between the worlds of nature and imagination, for a dynamic universe depicted in action, inhabited by souls whose contours poetry alone may express – a concept familiar since the time of Petrarch. As such, Pontano's use of myth seems indissociable from the notions both of poetic creation and of foundation, two processes that attracted the humanist's profound interest.[4] Such a position, original with regard to his contemporaries, invites further exploration.

Indeed, myth is omnipresent in the Pontanian corpus: it infuses the Campanian countryside and the banks of the Eridan; it accompanies daily scenes of the poet's domestic life; it furnishes a legendary origin for those dearest to him and for the fruits of his

---

[1]   English translation revised with the help of Alexander Paulson.

[2]   The bibliography is very rich on this point: one might look first at: *Aetates ovidianae: lettori di Ovidio dall'Antichità al Rinascimento*, ed. I. Gallo and L. Nicastri (Napoli, 1995), A. Moss, *Latin commentaries on Ovid from the Renaissance* (Summertown, 1998), *Le Metamorfosi di Ovidio nella letteratura tra Medioevo e Rinascimento*, ed. G. M. Anselmi and M. Guerra (Bologna, 2006), C. Burrow, 'Re-embodying Ovid: Renaissance Afterlives', in *Cambridge Companion to Ovid*, ed. P. Hardie (Cambridge, 2002), 301-19, and J. Richmond for the history of his manuscripts: 'Manuscript tradition and the transmission of Ovid's works', in *Brill's Companion to Ovid*, ed. B. Weiden Boyd (Leiden, 2002), 443-83.

[3]   See Elegy 3, 1 of *De Amore Coniugali*, in *Ioannis Ioviani Pontani Carmina*, ed. J. Œschger (Bari, 1948), 172.

[4]   G. Pontano seems to confirm ahead of time the famous sentence of P. Valéry: 'Au commencement était la Fable ! Ce qui veut dire que toute origine, toute aurore des choses est de la même substance que les chansons et que les contes qui environnent les berceaux…' ('In the beginning was the Fable! This is to say that every origin, every dawn of things is of the same substance as the songs and tales which surround the shepherds', in 'Petite lettre sur les mythes', *Variétés* II, Paris, 1957).

phantasia. Ovid's imprint here is predominant: it is particularly evident in the descriptions of metamorphoses composed with equal care to reestablish coherence between the elements of a being in its initial and final forms. However, beyond merely delighting his readers, for Pontano, as for Ovid, myth takes part in a representation of the world as universal *continuum*, a notion Pontano additionally explores in his didactic poems (*Urania, De Hortis Hesperidum*). Here the humanist no doubt perceived the extent to which he could find in myth a kind of first language, protean and infinitely seductive, to transmit a profound and well-formed cosmology.

Ovid's legacy in Pontano has been explored in several studies concerning the reformulation of Ovidian references in the humanist's poems and the allusive and subtle poetry which resulted therefrom.[5] I have myself attempted from time to time to examine the arboreal metamorphoses in Ovid's and in Pontano's writings, as well as the innumerable metamorphoses and enticing mythological figures encountered in their works.[6]

And yet the subject is immense. In this paper I will endeavour therefore to re-examine the strong presence of Ovid in Pontano's works, reflecting not only upon the methods employed in reinterpreting myth, but also on how myth nourished the humanist's mission in its entirety. Pervasive rather than ornamental, myth appears indeed as a veritable *forma mentis*, a way to apprehend nature, a hermeneutical device through which poets sing the world from its creation, and a foundational language for a society in flux, seeking to recover its bearings.

---

[5] See F. Tateo, 'Ovidio nell'*Urania* di Pontano', in *Aetates ovidianae* (Napoli, 1995, *cf.* supra n. 1), 279-91; D Coppini, 'Metamorfosi, metafora, arte allusive nella poesia di Giovanni Pontano', in *Per Giovanni Parenti, una giornata di studio,*ed. A. Bruni e C. Molinari, (Roma, 2009), 93-109; D. Coppini, 'Le metamorfosi del Pontano', in *Le Metamorfosi di Ovidio nella letteratura tra Medioevo e Rinascimento*, (*cf.* supra n. 1), 75-108.

[6] H. Casanova-Robin, 'Dendrophories d'Ovide à Pontano: la nécessité de l'hypotypose, in *Ovide, Figures de l'hybride. Illustrations littéraires et figurées de l'esthétique ovidienne à travers les âges*, ed. H. Casanova-Robin, (Paris, 2009) 103-24; 'Des métamorphoses végétales dans les poésies de Pontano: *Mirabilia* et lieux de mémoire'. in *La mythologie classique dans la littérature néo-latine*, ed. V. Leroux, (Clermont-Ferrand, 2011), 247-68; 'Metamorphosen und intime Fabel: Pontanos Ovidrezeption in den *Eclogen*, in den *Tumuli* und im *De Hortis Hesperidum*', in *Carmen Perpetuum. Ovids Metamorphosen in der Weltliteratur*, ed. H. Harich-Scharwtzbauer and Alexander Honold (Basel, 2013), 67-89; '*Dulcidia et leuamen*: le prisme de la douceur chez Giovanni Pontano, entre idéal poétique et visée éthique', international colloquium on 'Douceur' ('Gentleness') organized by the Société Interdisciplinaire de Recherches sur la Renaissance by F. Malhomme and M. Jones-Davies, Paris-Sorbonne, December 15-17 2011, publication by Brepols expected 2015; 'La place de la Méditerranée dans la construction identitaire de Naples chez les Humanistes du XVe siècle', International colloquium organized by A. Dan and J. Trinquier, *L'invention de la Méditerranée - Repères antiques et médiévaux, héritages renaissants* - Université Paris-Sorbonne / ENS October 26-27, 2012, forthcoming (Paris, 2015); 'Splendeur et magnificence de l'ornement dans l'œuvre de Giovanni Pontano: entre jubilation esthétique et idéal éthique', in *Aux origines de la théorie et de la littérature artistiques: les sources antiques et leur transmission à l'âge humaniste et classique*, dir. L. Boulègue, P. Caye, F. Furlan, F. Malhomme, Proceedings of international colloquium held at the Sorbonne from 29/11/12 to 1/12/12, publication by Paris, Garnier, expected 2015.

I will examine first the methods of Pontano's poetic re-appropriation of Ovidian myth, methods consonant with the ancient principles of *variatio* so well illustrated in the *Metamorphoses* itself. As an example, I will consider the re-imagination of the tale of Phaeton inserted in Pontano's elegiac love-poetry and several new issues raised therein. Following this, I will turn my attention to the pre-eminence accorded to myth's etiological purpose in relation to the celebration of Campania. Finally, I will attempt to show the ethical function of myth which, in contrast to Ovid, becomes in Pontano the means of a conversion to temperance and a device to foster harmony.

I. Ovid's imprint on Pontano's mythmaking: the conversion of Phaeton in his 'auto biographical' love poetry

Pontano borrows several famous characters from the repertoire of the *Metamorphoses* – most notably Phaeton, Adonis, and Polyphemus[7] – whom he refashions according to his pleasure, presenting them alongside characters of his own invention, linked most often to vegetal[8] or aquatic themes. This 'naturalist' orientation of myth goes hand in hand with the choice to portray these Ovidian heroes in a romantic scenario, taking place most often in a *locus amoenus* – a recurring conjunction of myth, pastoralism, and romance.

The example of Phaeton, a hero of monumental importance in Ovid, enriched by a long exegetical tradition ancient and medieval,[9] constitutes a tall order for the poet: how to reinterpret a hero of such complexity, whom Ovid had already so luminously brought to life?[10] Nonetheless, Pontano evokes the hero in two of his major poetic works: in the fifth song of his long astrological poem and in his final collection of elegies, the *Eridanus*.[11] This second occurrence is without any doubt the most original, in that here the myth constitutes a matrix figure of the work. The poet disperses the elements of the tale into several fragments and invents an epilogue to the Ovidian account following Petrarch, who himself had endlessly recreated the myth of Daphne in the *Canzoniere*.[12] Pontano proposes his work as the continuation of Ovid's: Eridan has just received the body of Phaeton, an act immortalized by Ovid in his epitaph (2.327-8). The humanist chooses this scene as the point of departure for his own variations and, recalling in a certain sense the memorializing function of an epitaph, he endeavours to show how Ovid's myth remains inscribed in the memory of

---

[7] V.Tufano, 'Il Polifemo del Pontano. Riscritture teocritee nella *Lyra* e nell'*Antonius*', *Bolletino di Studi latini*, 2010.

[8] H. Casanova-Robin, 'Métamorphoses végétales', supra n. 5.

[9] See, *e.g.*, Lucretius, the Stoics, Fulgentius, Isidore of Seville, Bernard Silvestre, Boccacio.

[10] For the retelling of myth in Pontano, see the rich analysis of D. Coppini, 'La metamorfosi del Pontano',(supra, n. 4): the author describes here the mannerist orientation of Pontano's reading, the usage of fire and water to express romantic ardour and the solar dimension of the girl called Stella. I adhere to this interpretation which, however, does not exclude other readings, by virtue of the semantic plurality that Pontano claims.

[11] Pontano's *Eridanus* is cited in Œschger's edition (supra n. 2).

[12] See P. Hardie's study, 'Ovid into Laura: Absent Presences in the Metamorphoses and Petrarch's *Rime sparse*', in *Ovidian transformations. essays on Ovid's Metamorphoses and its reception*, ed. P. Hardie, A. Barchiesi, S. Hinds, (Cambridge, 1999), 254-70.

the place, a phenomenon well known in antiquity. To sing of his Ferrarese loves, he infuses his verses with the same mythical themes – conflagration, amber, regenerative water – which prevail in the tale of Phaeton, converting them to the purposes of romantic elegy or making of them a crucible for fables of his own imagining.

Phaeton's fall into the river is characterized by Ovid as the encounter of two primordial elements, fire and water: *Excipit Eridanus fumantia abluit ora*, 2, 324. The scene furnishes Pontano with a poetic substrate to mould in the tradition of the *hydropyriques*, in which one finds (with Petrarchan accent) the memory of Plautus, one of his favourite authors.[13] (*Mercator*, 591, 'See my heart and my breast aflame with love: without these tears from my eyes I would be consumed'.) Further, the humanist peppers his poem with allusions to several other Ovidian characters, playing out the creative emulation that he maintains towards his predecessor while inventing his own Ovidesque narrative. The romantic evocation, an autobiographical fiction, places itself narrowly within Ovid's mythological universe, in the course of a conversion from epic to elegy, and in a manner which the author of the *Heroides* would surely not have disavowed.

In the first poem, the river is surrounded by the Heliades who honour it according to their cult, bubbling with the fire that has consumed Phaeton, mirroring the constellation which will bear his name. Pontano, a keen student of astrology,[14] imbues the antique tale with diverse references borrowed from Greek sources (*e.g.* Hesiod, Apollonius of Rhodes, and Aratos):

> Coeruleis generose Vadis, rex diuitis agri,
> Gallica qui medio flumine regna secas,
> Heliades cui serta parant, uenerantur et amnes,
> Nereus et placidis accipit hospes aquis,
> [...]
> Tum tibi per tacitas serpit noua flamma medullas,
> Ureris, et medio feruet in amne calor),
> Salue, amnis, salue, Hesperidum regnator aquarum,
> Cuius et in coelo flumina nota micant. (Erid. 1, 1, 1-12)

> O noble king of Cerulean tides, lord of prosperous fields,
> Who cleaves by water the Gallic lands in two,
> For whom the Heliades prepare garlands, the streams their worship,
> And Nereus a welcome in his peaceable sea.
> [...]
> Thus for you, a new flame slips silently into your marrow
> You scorch and a burning churns your course,
> Greetings, river, greetings, sovereign of Hesperidean waters,
> Whose famed waves sparkle in the sky.[15]

---

[13] See R. Cappelletto, *La 'Lectura Plauti' del Pontano*, (Urbino, 1988).

[14] See B. Soldati, *La poesia astrologica nel 400,* presentazione di C. Vasoli (Firenze, 1986), and G. Pontano, *De rebus caelestibus; De luna fragmentum; Commentationum in centum sententiis Ptolemaei Libri duo; De Meteoribus; Urania.*

[15] My French translation was translated into English with the great help of Lex Paulson. I thank him.

The river, in turn, becomes a propitious site for a bathing scene in the pure Ovidian tradition, dedicated here to the goddess of love:

Siccabat madidos Venus aurea forte capillos
Nuda quidem, si non parte tegatur aquis;
Pectus aquis tegitur, ceruix humerique superstant,
Sulleuat effusas sedula dextra comas, 20
Ima papillarum tegitur pars, eminet illa,
Punicea Charites quam coluere rosa;
Candorem referunt undae, micat aura capillo,
Singula sub uitrea membra notantur aqua. (Erid. 1, 1, 17-24)

She dried her dripping locks, golden Venus
Naked withal, if water had hid no part of her;
Her chest now covered, shoulder and neck emerge,
With right hand she raises with care the undone tresses,
The lesser part of her breast covered, greater still than that
Which the Charities honoured by a purple rose;
The waves renew their sparkle, breeze quivers her hair,
Under clear water each single strand may be seen.

One notices here an interest in the gracefulness of the body as well as the *ekphrastic* character of the depicted scene, with particular care given to the goddess's hair. One notices as well the choice of the *aqua uitrea* which recalls the tale of the encounter between Salmacis and Hermaphrodite (Met. 4.297-300 and 354-5). The verb *siccabat* in the opening line, in turn, inspires a recollection of the scene Ovid briefly recounts in the *Fasti* (4.141: *Litore siccabat...*). The ancient poet had set the figure of Venus on the riverbank, naked and drying her dripping locks, in a tale designed to explain the origin of rituals pertaining to the goddess's cult. Pontano thus chooses to broaden the depiction of the bathing female nude which corresponds with the amorous theme of the collection. However, in sharp contrast with Ovid, there is no mention here of violence nor of transgression: all is peaceful, calm, and pleasing to the senses.

The motif of amber, a substance born of the tears of Phaeton's sisters, is introduced in the second elegy during a sketch with an Alexandrian flavour, in which Love, solitary, seeks the precious item:

Eridani circum ripas alnosque uirentes
Quaerit Amor tenera succina lecta manu;
Quaerenti) assurgunt ripae, Phaetontias arbor
Fundit rore nouo, quae legat ipse puer. (Erid. 1, 2, 1-4)

On the banks of the Eridan, among the blooming alders
Love seeks and gathers amber with delicate hand;
To the searcher the banks give homage, the tree of Phaeton
Yielding his sap anew for the youth himself to harvest.

The memorial embodied in this substance, attested since Antiquity and underscored in this verse by the Hellenizing *Phaetontias* applied to the tree, justifies the special attention Pontano gives to it. Here, though, resin is no longer tied to a mournful memory.

It is henceforth part of Eros' domain, perhaps thanks to its confluence with an epigram of Martial (3.65) in which resin is compared to the delicious kisses of Ismene – a derivation whose novelty is denoted here, in verse 4, by *rore nouo*. In addition, the description of divine gestures as *succina **lecta***, then ***lunauit*** (v. 11), recalls an appearance of Cupid in the first poem of Ovid's *Amores* where the two verbs are identically conjoined (*Am.* 1.1.22, '***legit*** *spicula... **lunauit**que...*'). The Ovidianism of the play is further confirmed by the irruption of a nymph from the bark of a tree, a renewal of antique metamorphosis, here the occasion for a light-hearted game:

> Dumque legit guttaeque manum puer admouet, ora
>   Exerit e tenui cortice nympha sua,
> Quotque puer gemmas, totidem legit oscula uirgo;
>   Ridet Amor, ridet conscia nympha sibi. (Erid. 1, 2, 5-8)

> While the youth seeks and brings his hand toward the drops,
>   The tree-nymph pokes out her face from the delicate bark,
> As many gems as the boy takes, the nymph exacts this many kisses;
>   Love laughs, and the nymph too, knowing her mischief.

In poem 1.12, the lover-poet addresses the crying Heliades (*Adloquitur Heliades sorores*), to register his complaint in the wake of these emblematic figures, revealing the fertility therein:

> Quid moestae, quid coerulea sub fronde, sorores,
>   Lugetis, miseros amne iuuante modos?
> An fratrem Phaetonta, uagis quod tractus habenis,
>   Ah miser, externis exulet ipse locis?
> Hinc electra fluunt, lacrimosaque gutta rigescit,   5
>   Hae lacrimae, hi luctus succina lenta ferunt.
> Flete, piae, lugete, piae Phaetontides, et me
>   Vel socium uestris luctibus accipite.
> Si desint uobis lacrimae, si desit et imber,
>   Ipse quidem lacrimae, luctus, et imber ero;   10
> Per me etiam Eridanus crescet stagnantibus agris,
>   Finis enim lacrimis nulla futura meis;
> Per me etiam ripae mittent incendia, flagret
>   Amnis, et in medias ignis iturus aquas.
> Cedite, cultores; ripas et flumina iam iam   15
>   Usta dabo, in flammas ibit et omne nemus.

> Why, afflicted sisters, why in your azure foliage
>   Do you weep, as the river joins your sad complaint?
> Is it for your brother Phaeton, carried off by restless reins,
>   O unfortunate one, and exiled here in a strange land?
> From whom the amber seeps and whose tear then hardens,   5
>   These tears, these cries, bear at last an amber finery.
> Cry, holy ones, lament, holy Phaetontiads,

>   And receive me as ally to your grief.
> If your tears are wanting, if rain is wanting,
>   I will myself be your grief, rain, and tears;   10
> For me as well the Eridan swells and floods its fields,
>   And my tears shall know no limit;
> For me as well the banks kindle and the river burns,
>   And the fire spreads to midstream.
> Depart, holy mourners; I shall now ignite the banks and waves,   15
>   And now the whole forest shall erupt in holy fire.

The formulation *ad unum*, proper to elegiac idiom, operates here upon the motif of tears, fundamental to this poetic genre.[16] Throughout the poem, the humanist amplifies this motif by way of a new variation on the *hydropyrique*, developed in parallel to his descriptions of self.[17] As for Phaeton, he is elaborated in similarly genre-appropriate fashion as an *exclusus*, relegated to foreign soil – as emphasized by the alliteration '*externis exulet ipse locis*' (v. 4)[18] – thus offering a correspondence with the suffering lover. This shifting of myth toward the representation of the lover-poet, in turn, introduces a new semantic network: a tear-induced fertility symbolizing the renewal of Ovidian material and its perpetuation, of which the phoenix – subject of the previous poem (1.11) – serves as similarly eloquent emblem.

II. Campania though the lens of myth: forma mentis and founding purpose

The retelling of the tale of Phaeton, rooted firmly on the soil of Ferrara, reveals the closeness of the tie between myth and countryside in Pontano's poetry. A panoramic look at the humanist's works reveals that his representation of space in general is constantly informed by myth, a transfiguration that proceeds as much from an aesthetic choice, in Ovid's wake, as from a novel ambition to celebrate the Campanian countryside by ascribing to it a fabulous origin.[19]

---

[16] *Am.* 3, 9; *Her.* 15; but also Horace, *Odes*, 2, 9

[17] Verse 5, *Hinc electra fluunt, lacrimosaque gutta rigescit,* is a near exact reprise of Ovid's *Met.* 2.364 (*inde fluunt lacrimae stillataque sole rigescunt*), but in its substance echoes a wellknown metamorphosis; the metaphorical qualifier *lacrimosaque* alone, striking in its length, revives the mutation process. Pontano is content to suggest synthetically, in the *succina lenta ferunt* of the following verse, the ornamental fate of amber that Ovid had mentioned (*de ramis electra nouis, quae lucidus amnis / excipit et nuribus mittit gestanda Latinis*).

[18] The characterization evoked by the alliterative echo between the prefixes of the two first terms, a phonic device Pontano himself employs with rich expressivity. *Cf.* Pontano's *Actius*, in *Giovanni Pontano I Dialoghi*, ed. C. Previtera (Firenze, 1943), Sec. 1 *De numeris poeticis.*

[19] *Cf.* H. Casanova-Robin, 'La place de la Méditerranée dans la construction identitaire de Naples chez les Humanistes du XVe siècle', supra, n. 5.

68 THE AFTERLIFE OF OVID

II.1. A myth-transfigured countryside

This invasion of mythic representation is at work in Pontano's *Eclogues*, as I have previously endeavoured to show,[20] where every corner of the Neapolitan region is paraded in mythological finery.[21] In bucolic terms associated with the genre of origins, the countryside is depicted here through archaizing mythical figures. Just as Ovid had made myth consubstantial with the pre-Roman Italian countryside (*Met.* 14), for Pontano myth exerts a primary force: it pre-exists the configuration of places, a constitutive principle of birth and creation but also of permanence. The sovereigns of the Campanian hillsides who parade through the first poem, *Lepidina*, embody the traits of a geography animated by primitive forces that the poet seeks to evoke, commingled with more contemporary figures. Thus appears a *Capreone* (a type of faun invented by Pontano) hybridized in gardener's costume, evoking the fertility of the earth:

> Hircosum Capreonem hirco nymphaque creatum
> Succinctum rapis et amictum tempora porro. (Ecl. 1, Lep. 5, 217-218)

> The hirsute Capreone born of goat and nymph,
> His garment embroidered with turnips and a leek-crown on his temples.

The entire Neapolitan urban throng is thus enriched by mythological personifications who reveal Ovid's imprint, embodied in the array of characters who exuberantly display the diverse items which tradition has attached to them. Enter the Siren Parthenope, whose nuptials Pontano will sing, meandering in shape-shifting fashion through the island villages of Capri, Ischia, and Procida, where the rocks and flora take human form and bear a thousand fruits, shells, and fragrant herbs.[22] Other metamorphoses on display include Nape in a turnip (Ecl. 4), rescued *in extremis* by the intervention of Vertumne after falling victim to the *inuidia* of the other nymphs:

> [...] Illa repente
> in bulbum conuersa solo radicibus haesit;
> uestit eam foliis deus et frondescere iussit: (Ecl. 4.12-14)

> [...] She immediately
> changed to a bulb, a plant with roots deep in soil;
> the god dresses it with leaves and calls forth the blooming:

---

[20] H. Casanova-Robin, *Pontano, Églogues/Eclogae*, introductory study, annotated French translation of the Latin text, (Paris, 2011).

[21] Still further, the humanist mythically represents his own estates: his villas on the Pausilippe and in Vomero are equally recalled by the traits of sumptuous nymphs, Antiniana and Patulcis, inspirational deities and guardians who patrol the private universe of Pontano's prose writings (*Aegidius*).

[22] The cerulean nymph Pausilippe wears her hair in tresses of ivy (*implexis hedera frondente capillis,* Lep. 2, 4); Capri stupefies onlookers with his gigantism (*Lepidina*, 2, 84-5 [...] *ingentemque umero ingentemque lacertis /Atque utero et toto retinentem corpore formam.*) and by the black hairs which bristle on his chest and legs (v. 86 *Horrebant sed crura nigris et pectora saetis*).

Alongside this example is that of Coryle in the hazelnut tree (Ecl. 5), both modelled according to characteristics borrowed from Ovid, including the continuance of sensation beyond the moment of mutation:

> Sed quo non penetrat liuor? Dum fessa lauaret
> Ad fontem, dum membra fouet Sebethide in unda,
> Vertit eam cantu in stirpem Circeis Abelle
> Ac densis circum ramis et cortice saepsit.
> Illa nouo latitans sub stipite fleuit et ipsos,
> Ah miseram, audita est poenam deposcere diuos. (Egl. 5. 16-19)

> Yet how far may jealousy reach? To refresh her frame,
> She then bathed in a lively stream and floated on Sebethus' wave,
> When Abelle Circean[23] transformed and rooted her,
> Imprisoning her in an enclosure of thick boughs and bark.
> Coryle began to weep, enclosed in this unknown trunk
> And was heard, O unfortunate one, calling vengeance upon the gods themselves.

II.2. Aquatic metamorphosis

Like Ovid, Pontano puts a special emphasis upon aquatic mythology, singing of the source of the Casis (*Parth.* 2.6) and of the waters of Baïes (*Hendec.* 2.37, 76 et. seq.), which he peoples with fabulous creatures taken both from Ovid's repertoire and from his own powers of invention.[24] The Sebethus, a Neapolitan waterway, is given particular attention, to the point of becoming one of Campania's most eloquent metonyms: Pontano elevates the stream to the status of a reservoir, guarantor of Parthenopean fertility, the poet as one with the Siren of Naples in the proem to *Urania*, where he situates his own Campanian-inspired song. He thus renders the stream as the point of attachment to the Muse Urania in the *Meteors* as well as to his own domain, a place of serene *otium* (at the end of *Meteors*, and at the beginning of *De Hortis Hesperidum*), the critical landmark of the Neapolitan countryside embroidered by the wife figure Ariadna (Ecl. 2.104), and diverse mythological scenes of his own invention are similarly associated (Ecl. 5, 17); he ultimately celebrates his marriage to the Siren in the ample eclogue entitled *Lepidina*; and, in an elegy of the *Parthenopeus* collection (2.14), he relates the mortal origin and metamorphosis of this character. The humanist thus sustains the hybridized essence of the Sebethus, at times a river in its own right, at times a fabulous creature: this choice reveals his profound affiliation to the Ovidian spirit which recovers, beyond aesthetics, a deeper conception of nature and its constitutive elements,[25] the very principle of *continuum*.

---

[23] As a new Circe.

[24] *Hendecasyllabi sive Baiae*, can be read in R. G. Dennis's translation (Harvard, 2006); I used Œschger's edition (supra n.2) for all the poems, except for *De Hortis Hesperidum*: ed. B. Soldati (Bari, 1902) and for the Eclogues, supra n. 20.

[25] See H. Casanova-Robin, introduction to *Ovide, figures de l'hybride* and study infra, 'Dendrophories, d'Ovide à Pontano', supra n. 5.

70 THE AFTERLIFE OF OVID

To recount the metamorphosis of Sebethus, the poet-narrator first adopts an etiological approach, demarcated by the temporal antithesis *nunc/ante*:

Quis tua tam riguo mutauit membra liquore?
Nunc amnis, certe candidus ante puer. (Parth. 2. 14, 15-16)

Who transformed your body into running water?
A river now, surely you were once a beaming youth.

In the following couplet he reaches the outcome, revealing the cause of the transformation, returning to the device of chiasmus, dear to Ovid, who emphasizes in the heart of the verse, in redoubled form, the funereal and premonitory overtones (*nocuit*). His subject, the young man's beauty, source of Doris's passion, is placed in the framework of hexameter, before the reference to the jealousy of the god Nereus in pentameter:

Forma tibi nocuit, nocuit placuisse puellae,
Iraque coerulei quam male nota dei. (Parth. 2. 14, 17-18)

Your beauty was a wound, a wound which pleased young girls,
And which met, so sorrowfully, the rage of the cerulean god.

Following these lines, a detail of the narrative depicts a most unexpected scene: an idyll of a couple intertwined under the dense foliage of myrtle trees, asleep under the zephyrs' caresses and lulled by birdsong and the murmuring stream. Herein is found a recurring theme in Pontano's poetic imagination, that of an amorous couple, a paradigm of harmonious conjugal union, immersed in sensual satisfaction and culminating in a blissful slumber:[26]

Litore constiteras; illuc quoque coerula nymphè
Currit in amplexus nympha decora tuos.   20
Alcyones testes, testes vineta Vesevi,
Vos pariter socio secubuisse toro.
Lectus erat frondes et opaci gramina campi,
Umbra erat antiquis myrtea silua comis;
Silua comas frondosa dabat, quae lenibus auris   25
Spirabat, Zephyro sollicitante, nemus;
Tum uolucres laetis concentibus aera miscent,
Et raucum illisis murmurat aequor aquis. (Parth. 2. 14, 19-28)

You had stopped along the shore; there as well the cerulean nymph
Ran and threw her magnificent self into your arms,   20
The Alcyones were witness, witnesses too the Vesuvian vines,
You partook both of a single bed.
This bed was fashioned of greenery and thick country grass,
Shaded by a myrtle forest of ancient mane.
The forest shook out its mighty mane, tousled by the breath of   25
Gentle breezes, upon Zephyr's whisper;
To which the birds re-joined their joyous melody,
And the waves murmured huskily against the shore.

---

[26] In Egl. 2, *Lyra* 9 and in *De Hortis Hesperidum*, but also *Urania*, 2. 591: *optatos somnos.*

The scene, situated on the foothills of Vesuvius, is described in a weaving together of literary reminiscences, endowing the descriptive *antiquis* with an added metapoetical force: the halcyon birds recall the myth of Ceyx and Alcyone as related by Ovid,[27] and the foliage-tresses evoke the Laura of Petrarch as well as Daphne. The myrtles add a Venusian tone to the scene, and the husky murmur of the sea – a defining detail of this *locus amoenus* after the mention of the birdsong – completes the synesthetic tableau, a tableau Pontano prefigures through acoustic wordplay in his dialogue *Actius*.[28] To this rich intertextuality is added a final element borrowed from Lucretius' *De rerum natura* (Book 5), a text which Pontano read assiduously. The humanist affiliates himself with the Roman poet's notion of *satietas*, prevalent in Epicureanism, suggested here by a state of deep sleep. But the scene's synesthetic soundtrack is not without dramatic purpose, since it permits the introduction of a chatty Nereid, called *loquaci ore* (v. 29-30). Pontano thus renews an Ovidian narrative scheme, or rather, mixes the denunciation theme within the story of Clytie (*Met.* 4.234) with the story of Lara in the *Fasti* (2.599 *et seq.*). As for the topographical disposition, more than a mere picturesque trait, it responds very precisely, as confirmed in verses 29-40, to the conception illustrated in Ovid's *Metamorphoses* of a *muthos* strictly tied to a site in nature, by virtue of a permeability which justifies the unwavering coexistence of humanity and geography. As Ovid described Campania in Book 14 of the *Metamorphoses* in the prevalent references to primitive mythical creatures, Pontano personifies the waterways, the volcano Vesuvius and other Campanian sites without dispossessing them of their original morphology. The deification of the protagonists serves the etiological aim of the poem, helping to reframe the poetic language as a foundation discourse that confers an identity upon each element of nature and yields a principle of harmony. Here, the death of Sebethus by a violent blow from Neptune – similar to that by which Jupiter punishes Lara, or Apollo punishes Coronis – finds a counterpart in his deification by way of a separate creative principle, the rage of Vesuvius:

> At postquam in rabiem dolor hic se uertit acerbam,
>> Vindex ex antris prosilit ipse cauis
> Eructansque uomit fumantis pectoris ignes
>> Ignibus et latos undique uastat agros;
> Iamque insurgebat ponto tumidumque per aequor
>> Iactat ab incensis saxa liquata iugis,
> Cum subito ex alto uox reddita: - Numen aquarum
>> Sebethos, fonti est nomen honosque suo. (Parth. 2.14, 47-53)

> But when his grief gave way to sudden rage,
>> He bounded, vengeful, out of his dark cave
> And hurling fire from his blazing chest, he let his fury loose.
>> With this blaze, he laid waste to wide plains;
> He surged then from deep under the swollen sea,
>> And heaved liquid rock from his firy summit,
> When suddenly a voice rang out: 'Aquatic divinity,
>> Sebethus, a spring and cult shall bear thy name'.

---

[27] See also Prop. 1, 17, 2 *nunc ego desertas alloquor alcyonas.*

[28] *Actius,* in *Giovanni Pontano Dialoghi,* ed C. Previtera, supra n. 17.

If one identifies here a charming *aition* in the volcano's eruption, one can additionally detect echoes of Empedocles' theory connecting cosmogony and erotic passion as Ovid does: the principle of discordance, illustrated here by rage (*eris*), is added to the description of the generative fire which deifies Sebethus. He is thus confronted as well by the principle of love (*eros*), represented by the liaison between Sebethus and his nymph. Through this alliance of fire and water, Pontano renews the *hydropyrique* dear to love poetry, investing a generative purpose therein. This conjunction of elements in turn engenders the metamorphosis, sacralising the volcano's voice in terms which recall the birth of the Canente spring in Book 14 of the *Metamorphoses*.

Nevertheless, in contrast with Ovid, Pontano employs myth in a peaceful setting, seeking to re-establish interrupted harmony and illustrating an ideal of concord.

III. Inflecting myth toward voluptas and concordia

The humanist strips myth of any violent tendency and, to the contrary, makes of it an instrument to serve his ideal of *humanitas*. Pontano emphasizes, as his ancient predecessor did, the sensual possibilities of myth. Nevertheless, he fits these possibilities strictly within the notion of universal concordance, a notion which proceeds only from the taming of excessive passion.

III.1. Alleviation of Mourning

Pontano conceives an original genre that departs from the funereal epigram in his collection of Tombs (*De Tumulis*), in which he inserts pieces designed to celebrate the memory of fictional characters – for the most part, subjects of floral metamorphosis.[29] Here the poet exercises his taste for Ovid's poetry of mutation in short form, verbal virtuosity contending with mythological invention. The jubilant representation of *continuum* among the different species of the natural world share an aesthetic of *leuitas* designed to soothe as much as entertain the reader of these funereal poems. As a result, the fear of death which so preoccupied the philosophers finds here a sort of resolution in the elaboration of myths which correspond to the idea of *facetudo* defined by Pontano in his treatise *De Sermone*.[30] The metamorphoses thus depicted bring a kind of solace to the pain of loss: the humanist eases considerably the pathetic dimension of mortality, underscoring instead the undying link between the world of the living and the world of the dead. This link is one perceptible through the senses, and in particular by the permanent fragrance exhaled by the flowers, a memory of the departed. This process rests, as does the one above, upon the *interpretatio nominis* which the humanist practices with skill.

---

[29]   Famous studies on *De Tumulis* (ed. by J. Œschger, *supra* n. 4): G. Parenti, *Poeta Proteus alter. Forma e storia di tre libri di Pontano* (Firenze, 1985); *Id.* 'L'invenzione di un genere, Il *tumulus* pontaniano', *Interpres* 7 (1987) 125-58; E. Giannarelli, 'I giovanni, la morte e le rose. Appunti di poesia latina', *Interpres* 19 (2000) 188-204; H. Casanova-Robin, 'Métamorphoses végétales', *supra* n. 5; D. Coppini, 'La metamorfosi del Pontano', *supra* n.4.

[30]   *De Sermone*, ed. A. Mantovani (Roma, 2002).

Thus *Laurina* is rendered naturally as a laurel, the product of a double nature, a hybridity depicted time and again in Ovid. The expression of verbal metaphors, (*tegor, uestit*), bear the sign of metamorphosis in the play of the lines' initial words:

Laurina […]
Sub lauru Laurina tegor, mea uestit et ossa
    Laurus, et ipsa meo uescitur e cinere. (De Tum., 1. 23, 3-4)

Under laurel leaves, Laurine hides: he dresses my bones,
        Laurus, and himself lives on my ashes.

Pontano strips the process of all its tragic inflection: the marvellous, emphasized by *elocutio*, is in service to *leuamen*, and is designed to leaven and soothe the mind. The simplicity of language and the synthetic character of the couplet suggests a sublimation of *Laurina*'s death by sweetness, the essence of man and flower mirroring one another through paronymy (*uestit, uescitur*).

The choice of the *leuitas* concept is illustrated more strikingly still in *De Tum.* 1.44. Here one discovers a girl in the bloom of youth, *Candida*, victim of a kidnapping: thus, by way of the skilful representation of an ethereal metamorphosis consisting only of white roses, the poet erases the pathetic aspect of her sudden disappearance. The narrative schema recalls that of Ovid on the subject of Narcissus[31] or of Hyacinth:[32]

Tumulus Candidae Virginis
Ipsa loquitur, Vates respondet
Candida
Nec me marmor habet, nec me tegit urna sepultam;   1
    In niueas abii candida uersa rosas.
Forte interque rosas interque ligustra quieram,
    Aura fouet flatu, mater at ipsa sinu,
Pallida cum coelo nubes delapsa repente   5
    Me rapit, inque auras dissipor ipsa leues;
Dum natam mater gremio, dum quaerit in ulnis,
    Pro nata niueas reperit ecce rosas.
Ne mihi, ne lacrimas quisquam, ne munera donet,
    Ad tumulos; horti sunt mihi nam tumuli.   10

---

[31] *Nusquam corpus erat; croceum pro corpore florem/ Inueniunt foliis medium cingentibus albis* (Mét. 3, 509-10), 'The body was not there at all; in place of the body one finds a flower/ Saffron coloured at the heart, surrounded by white petals'.

[32] Met. 10, 209-12, recalled here by the *ecce* also employed by the Augustan poet (*Ecce cruor… qui desinit esse cruor…nitentior flos oritur…*).

Vates

O felix, cui uere rosae atque aestate sepulcrum
    Sunt aurae, hinc flores fundis et hinc33 Zephyros.

Candida

Neither marble possesses nor urn encloses me in death;
    I passed on, remade in roses snow-white.
I slept amidst roses, amidst privet-bushes,
    Warmed by the breeze's whisper as at my mother's breast,
Until a pale cloud, having slipped from the sky,
    Absconds with me, and I dissipate myself into gentle air;
Then mother seeks out daughter: on her breast, beneath alders,
    For daughter instead are snow-white roses found.
May no one lay offerings, neither tears nor gifts,
    Upon my tomb; for my tomb is this garden hereafter.

Poet

O fortunate one! In spring the roses are your sepulchre,
    In summer, you send blossoms here and Zephyrs there.

The rejection of imprisonment, doubly expressed in the poem's opening lines, surpasses the generic expression of consolation (*sit tibi terra leuis*), hinting rather at the unprecedented nature of this creature whom the marble edifice cannot entirely contain. The participle *uersa* in the pentameter designates, by the ritual character invested in it by Ovidian readers, the phenomenon of metamorphosis. The conjuncture between human and flower lies here in this *candor*, bright marker of returned purity, impossible to hold. The phonic modulation of 'a' eases the coherence of the metamorphic process; the chiasmus *niueas... rosas* testifies to the completion of the now-visible transformation; the twosyllable *abii*, however, tends to swallow itself in this floral invasion, the poet retaining by euphemism the meaning of a departure which is that of perpetual freedom.

The echo effect brought by the paronomasias of *delapsa/dissipor* underscores the link between cause and effect: the speed of disappearance is coupled with the evanescent character of a creature whose volatile existence is portrayed by the bright light which foretells her name. Still more echoes of Ovidian narratives may be observed here: the character of the mother recalls Ceres in search of Persephone and the realization of metamorphosis by substitution (*pro nata... reperit*) is similar to that of Narcissus. Nevertheless, the final couplet dissipates any pathetic inflexion: only vitality remains, expressed by the fertility of writing which transmutes into poetic object the celebratory funeral rites and lends permanence to the ephemeral. By a kind of paradox, inverse of the topographical transformations described in Ovid, the sepulchral site has become a *locus amoenus*. The metamorphosis, finally, is sacralized by the poet's own voice, as Pontano confirms the demiurgic power, in Ficino's words, of the *poeta diuinus artifex*.

---

[33] I adopt here the correction of L. Monti Sabia: *hinc* in place of *hic* (ed. Summonte and in the Aldine edition of 1518, followed by B. Soldati and J. Œschger), a choice which appears more coherent.

III.2. The retelling of Ovidian myths: a lesson in temperance (toward the expression of redemption and the taming of passion)

The reprise of Phaeton's story, given eminent place in Pontano's final collection of elegies, provides him a favourable means to illustrate the questions of *prudentia* and *fortuna*, two notions developed in two concomitant and eponymous treatises near the end of his life. The most eloquent passage on this point is Elegy 2.18 of the *Eridanus*, where a new expression of heroism is found, read as redemption, or rather as a wisdom acquired from trials endured.

According to the humanist's conception, nature offers the spectacle of a perfected universe, at once a principle of order and beauty and a source of irrational catastrophe, disorder and confusion. *Fortuna*[34] is explored as a means of interpreting the irrational forces that seem to dominate human life. All of these elements existed, in more or less significant measure, in the Ovidian fable of Phaeton: Pontano, prolonging via *retractatio*, raises and integrates them into an ethical-philosophical reflection he ceaselessly nourishes, until his final hour, through meditation on his public and private acts.

Here the failure of Phaeton, fallen into the river after having committed an act of *hybris* with inevitable consequences, finds a contented resolution in which one can detect the result of the famous association of *uirtus*, *impetus* and *kairos* central to the Quattrocento.[35] The choice of the elegy's dedicatee, whom appears in the second part of the poem, confirms the philosophical aim of the myth's retelling: Girolamo Carbone[36] was a disciple of the Neapolitan Academy particularly esteemed by Pontano, who elsewhere dedicates several poems to him,[37] as well as a philosophical treatise entitled *De immanitate*.[38] Pontano additionally makes Carbone one of the protagonists of his final dialogue *Aegidius*,[39] dedicated to a reflection upon rhetoric and philosophy. Certainly the humanist avoids all austere didacticism, as evidenced by the passage near the end of the text end which describes a scene whose temperance is only matched by its sensuality. However, he renews the tradition of allegorical exegesis according

---

[34] On *Fortuna* in Renaissance humanism, see Don Cameron Allen, 'Renaissance Remedies for Fortune: Marlowe and the *Fortunati*', *Studies in Philology* 38 (1941) 188-97; the treatise is now edited by F. Tateo with a rich introduction and an Italian translation: *Giovanni Pontano, La Fortuna* (Napoli, 2012). See also: Id., 'La prefazione originaria e le ragioni del *De Fortuna* di Giovanni Pontano', *Rinascimento* 47 (2007) 125-63; F. Buttay-Jutier, *Fortuna. Usages politiques d'une allégorie morale à la Renaissance* (Paris, 2008); M. Santoro, *Fortuna, ragione e prudenza nella civiltà letteraria del Cinquecento* (Napoli, 1978), (first chapter on Pontano).

[35] See P. Caye, '*Ars, Virtus* et *Fortuna*. Le différend Pétrarque/Alberti sur le sens des arts plastiques et sur leur capacité à surmonter la fortune', in *Hasard et Providence XIVe-XVIIe siècles*, ed. M.L. Demonet (Tours, 2007), 1-12.

[36] On Girolamo Carbone, see the work of P. de Montera, *L'humaniste napolitain Girolamo Carbone et ses poésies inédites* (Napoli, 1935).

[37] *Eridanus*,1, 40: see H. Casanova-Robin, 'L'adresse de Giovanni Pontano à Girolamo Carbone dans l'élégie I, 40 de l'*Eridanus*: un idéal d'*humanitas*?', in *Pratiques latines de la dédicace,* ed. J.C. Julhe (Paris, 2014), 445-64.

[38] *Giovanni Pontano, De immanitate liber*, ed. L. Monti Sabia (Napoli, 1970).

[39] See dialogue *Aegidius*, and the famous study: G. Toffanin, *Giovanni Pontano fra l'uomo e la natura* (Bologna, 1938), now edited and translated by F. Tateo (Rome, 2013).

to his own fashion. For Pontano, Phaeton is a *proficiens* who must draw a lesson (*docent, iure timendum*) from this *labor*, as Ovid required, and then must follow his own progression toward wisdom. Eridan offers him a rebirth, as suggested by the verb *suscipit*, describing the ritual of paternal recognition, and the participle *fotum*, implying a vital emotionality. The restorative purpose of this gesture is emphasized by the paronomasias *solaris/solatur*, as well as the homoteleutons *ambustum/fotum*, which create a harmonious thread of complementarity between wound and remedy. The consolation given by Eridan, symmetric to Apollo's warning in Ovid, begins by recalling the immutable character of destiny:[40]

> Cuique suis stant fata locis; mihi uoluitur amnis,
> Amnis inexhaustis non rediturus aquis; (Erid., 2, 18, 7-8)

> Fate fixes for each his place; and so for me in this riverine gyre,
> This river whose waters neither return nor run dry;

The following verses deliver a commentary on Phaeton's transgression and fall, with the assistance of the Stoic doctrine of fate:

> Terra tibi est genitrix. Coelum tamen inde petisti;
> Ipse docet casus, quid ferat hora sequens. (Erid., 2, 18, 9-10)

> Earth was your mother; yet you ventured to rich sky:
> Your overthrow reveals what must happen after.

One finds traces here of the description of Chrysippus which Cicero gives in the *De Fato*,[41] a work which seeks to reconcile fate with individual freedom. Eridan, *magister sapientiae*, instructs Phaeton that he must hereafter re-join the path which is properly his own, Fortune thereby offering him a second chance. Returning, the young man confesses to the impassioned *impetus* (*studium*, v. 26) which had caused his downfall, a pathetic scene rich in Ovidian echoes:

> Exul agor coelo pulsus patriisque quadrigis,
> Eiicit et tellus, ustaque pellit aqua,
> Solaque in Eridano superat spes. Haec ubi dixit,
> Illius madidos concidit ante pedes.   (Erid., 2.18, 27-30)

> I am exiled, banished from sky and my father's chariot,
> Repellent to the land, outlaw to the scorched waters,
> In you alone, Eridan, rest my hopes. Thus he spoke,
> And cast himself before the river's sodden feet.

---

[40] Echo of the astrological concepts developed elsewhere by Pontano (see supra) with reference to Manilius, *Astronomica*: *Fata regunt orbem, certa stant omnia lege /Longaque per certos signantur tempora casus*. (4, 14-15).

[41] Cicero, *De fato*, 18 (41-42).

Exul no longer connotes the *exclusus amator*, but rather the penitent man, whereas *pulsus* recalls the memory of Ovidian verse.[42] From verse 31 onward, Pontano presents the coronation of the young man, whom Eridan offers royal rank and a spouse, this a reference to the famous episode of Evander installing Aeneas on his maple throne (*Aen.* 8.178). In the following verses, the restoration of equilibrium is underlined in harmonious rhythm through binary cadences and a melodious use of sonorities arranged with expressivity and refinement. The dual syntax serves as well the theme of 'two fortunes'[43] which alternatively instruct Phateon in a conclusive couplet linking the hero to an emblematic figure of recovered *uirtus*:

> Nunc alto positus solio, nunc pressus ad imum,
> Fortunae instabiles edocet esse uices. (Erid., 2. 18, 41-42)

> Once exalted to a high throne, now sunken to the depths,
> His lesson is Fortune's most unstable skew.

Thus, the lesson which the poet draws, as it appears in the elegy's final verses, is less one of sober austerity than one of *uoluptas* tempered this time with Aristotelian accents.[44] The mythic universe and one of autobiographical fiction are bound together once again into harmonious union, a source of pleasure, inner tranquillity, and creative fertility:

> Nos quoque, fatorum leges per utrumque secuti,
> Solamur cantu tempora nostra senes;
> Hinc Amor, inde Venus mulcent, dulcissime Carbo,   45
> Ut mihi sint senii taedia nulla mei.
> Stella mihi solamen adest, mihi molle leuamen
> Eridanus, niueas dum canit inter aues:
> Ipse canit, recinunt cygni, iuuat aura canentis,
> Hos inter cantus en mea nympha uenit,   50
> Amplexuque senem dignatur et oscula iungit,
> Et nostra in tenero collocat ora sinu.
> Exitus hic uitae, post bella grauisque labores,
> Siue senecta leuis, seu iuuenilis amor.   (Erid. 2.18, 43-54)

> I too have traced fate's shifting laws, forth and back again,
> And I assuage my aging years in verses;
> First Love, now Venus caress me, my sweetest Carbo,
> Till the torments of age become to me as nothing.
> Stella still my solace, and my gentle comfort
> Eridan, he who chants among snow-white birds:
> He sings to answer the swans, and breezes aid the song,
> So amidst this music my nymph now arrives,

---

[42] *Met.* 2, 97 *nullam patiere repulsam* (Apollo speaks); 155 *pulsant* (horses); 313 *expulit* (Jupiter).

[43] Petrarch, *De remediis utriusque fortunae*, a work which inspired considerable interest in the Quattrocento; its themes were carried forward by Coluccio Salutati, in the *De fato.*

[44] Aristotle, *Nicomachean Ethics.*

Judging the old man worthy of embrace and clasping kiss,
  She guides my face to her tender breast,
And thus my life ends, after battles and hard toil,
  In peaceful senescence or, better, in youthful love.

III.3. Finding a principle of harmony in the language of myth

Although metamorphosis, if not myth itself, often tends in Ovid to signify the intrusion of discord, the totality of Pontano's mythic material expresses a gentle reconstruction of harmony through the reestablishment of *continuum*. The humanist-poet delights in the trampling of boundaries (as did Ovid himself), toward his chosen end of pacification, concordance, and aesthetic ornamentation – elements which constituted the ideal of *humanitas* such as Pontano understood it, from his reading of Cicero in particular,45 and which he developed over the course of his dialogues and treatises.46 In his verses, Pontano repairs the disjunctions that Ovid had wrought: Phaeton recovers his *dignitas*, in the moral and aesthetic sense of the term, in the *Eridanus*; in *Urania*, he is presented henceforth as the protector of a well-regulated order (2.1). In the *De Hortis Hesperidum*, Adonis heralds the return of perennial fertility by metamorphizing into a citron, a symbol of a golden age reborn47 (if not for the kingdom of Naples, at least for Pontano's *villa*). As for Sebethus, another matrix figure of the work, he harbours no bitterness for the loss of his human form, but as the waterway is sought, he is endowed equally with a beneficial purpose, paradigmatic of the humanist's myth-making.48

Peopling his literary space with mythological creatures arrayed in Ovidian finery, Pontano underscores the necessity of *ficta* – a term which in this context distinguishes the fables of poets from historical accounts. *Ficta* are the sole drivers, according to the humanist, of a tranquillity of soul that is nevertheless closely affiliated with worldly pleasure:

Ficta iuuant; quae nostra tamen patientia fatum
  Aut fugit, aut mollit, si superare nequit.   (Erid. 2. 31, 69-70)

Poems delight me; they are my talisman warding off fate,
  Stalling, softening, though it may not be overcome.

The humanist thus draws an original lesson from his reading of Ovid, sustained equally in the *Tristia* and the *Epistulae ex Ponto*: the poetic fiction participates in the first instance

---

45 Cic., *De off.*, 31, 111: *aequabilitas uniuersae uitae, tum singularum actionum.*

46 Pontano's treatises on the 'social virtues' as named by F. Tateo (G. Pontano, I libri delle virtu sociali, ed. By F. Tateo, Roma, 1999), and see also others as *De magnanimitate*, *De sermone*, *De prudentia*, *Aegidius*, and *De immanitate*.

47 H. Casanova-Robin, 'Métamorphoses végétales' and 'L'ornement', supra n. 5.

48 *De Hortis Hesperidum*, 1, 15-22: En ipso de fonte et arundine cinctus et alno /Frondenti caput, ac vitreo Sebethus ab antro /Rorantis latices muscoque virentia tecta /Ostentans, placidas de vertice suscitat auras, /Quis solem fugat et salices defendit ab aestu./ Ergo agite, et virides mecum secedite in umbras, / Naiades, simul et sociae properate, Napaeae, / Quaeque latus tyrio munitis, Oreades, arcu.

in this strength of soul or, rather, in the endurance required to surmount adversity. In his verses, *ficta* ring out with *patientia*. Poetry is not merely for relaxation, but inspires a special kind of philosophical progression conceived as a propaedeutic to the gentleness illustrated in the verse itself, a veritable metonym of the art of living with a large place reserved for exalted aesthetic pleasures. His praise of *ficta* elevates the *ars* capable of producing such a language and such pleasing mental images, rich in stimulating cultural reminiscences – *ficta* formed of archetypes – and properly conferring another dimension to thinking through the stimulation of *phantasia*. This conception, which Ovid had illustrated so well, is further enriched by the optimism of a humanist who seemed to have made Cicero's famous formula his own:

Cic, *Tusc.* 5. 23, 66 *cum Musis, id est cum humanitate et doctrina.*

Université Paris-Sorbonne
E.A. 4081 Rome et ses renaissances

OVID'S JANUS AND THE START OF THE YEAR IN RENAISSANCE *FASTI SACRI*

JOHN F. MILLER

During the past twenty years or so Ovid's *Fasti* has undergone major reappraisal by classical scholars, but we have only begun to understand the complex reception of this elegiac calendar-poem. The work's reception in Latin extends at least from the *Peristephanon* of Prudentius in the fourth century, which versified a number of martyrs' feast days in what was then the emerging Christian calendar,[1] to the Frenchman Claude-Barthélemy Morisot's ambitious composition in the seventeenth century of the missing six books of Ovid's versified year, July through December in 3,964 original elegiac verses.[2] It was during the Renaissance that the *Fasti* exercised its most substantial and diverse influence. A period of intense activity centered in Rome and in Florence during the late Quattrocento. In 1481 Poliziano lectured on the *Fasti* at the Studio of Lorenzo de' Medici, and his collected notes, *Collectanea in enarrationem Fastorum*, testify to his extensive work in elucidating the customs and myths mentioned by Ovid.[3] Within the same Florentine *milieu* painters turned to some apparently original stories from the *Fasti* as well as, of course, the myriad tales from the more famous *Metamorphoses*. In fact, Botticelli in *Primavera* brilliantly refashioned Ovid's brief account of the goddess Flora's identity in May (*Fasti* 5.195-206) *as* a metamorphosis – simultaneously depicting, à la Daphne, the transformation of the nymph Chloris into the floral deity as she is chased by Zephyr.[4] A decade or so later Piero di Cosimo rendered the *Fasti*'s two-stage narrative of Bacchus inventing honey (3.737-60) in a lively seriocomic diptych that features the drunken, mischievous Silenus.[5] Meanwhile in Venice Giovanni Bellini memorably reoriented Ovid's story of Priapus and Lotis in his *Feast of the Gods*, later modified by Titian.

In Rome, the focal point – again, starting in the 1480's – was the so-called Roman Academy of Pomponio Leto, under whose influence, as Angela Fritsen has shown, first Paolo Marsi (1482) and then Antonio Costanzi (1489) produced commentaries on Ovid's

---

[1] Anne-Marie Palmer, *Prudentius on the martyrs* (Oxford 1989) 111-21.

[2] P. Ovidii *Nasonis Fastorum libri duodecim, quorum sex posteriores a Claudio Bartholomaeo Morisoto Divionensi substituti sunt* (Dijon 1649). See Paul G. Schmidt, 'Transformation und Substitution von Ovids *Fasten* im 16. und 17. Jahrhundert', in *Acta Conventus Neo-Latini Hafniensis. Proceedings of the Eighth International Congress of Neo-Latin Studies,* ed. Ann Moss *et al.*, Medieval & Renaissance Texts & Studies 120 (Binghamton NY 1994) 895-98.

[3] *Commento inedito ai Fasti di Ovidio,* ed. F. Lo Monaco (Florence 1991).

[4] Paul Barolsky, 'Botticelli's *Primavera* and the poetic imagination of Italian Renaissance art', *Arion* 3.8.2 (2000) 5-35.

[5] John F. Miller, 'Piero di Cosimo's Ovidian diptych', *Arion* 15.2 (2007) 1-13.

Fasti.[6] These were later combined into a joint edition (1497), which was often reprinted during the next thirty years. Both commentators' special interest was antiquarianism but both also acknowledged a political significance of Ovid's elegy in arguing for the supremacy of the Christian Church. At the same time, Leto's Academy seems to have given rise to a humanist poetic genre conspicuously based on Ovid's *Fasti,* the Christian calendar poem.[7] The first *Fasti sacri* came from the hand of Lodovico Lazzarelli around 1484,[8] followed a few years later by Lorenzo Bonincontri's *Fasti* (1491) written in a mixture of meters. Poets with other affiliations continued the genre in the *Cinquecento*. The celebrated Carmelite Baptista Mantuanus published a *Fasti* near the end of his life, in 1516, which saw eleven re-printings later in the century. Perhaps to be expected of the one whom Erasmus called 'Christian Virgil', Mantuan eschewed Ovid's elegiacs for continuous dactylic hexameters. In 1547 appeared Ambrogio Fracco's exuberant *Sacrorum fastorum libri duodecim*, followed in 1554 by the *Fastorum libri duodecim* of Girolamo Chiaravacci. Both of these adhered to the Ovidian precedent of elegiacs and both were dedicated to Pope Paul III. Thereafter neo-Latin calendrical poetry emerged in France – the Benedictine Hugues Vaillant's *Fasti sacri* in 1674 – and even in the Protestant north, where the *Fasti Ecclesiae Christianae* by a professor in Rostock named Nathan Chytraeus reacted critically to the Catholic perspective of Mantuan as well as to Ovid's pagan antiquity.[9] In the vernacular literatures, too, Ovid's *Fasti* made an impact – invoked in England by Spenser, Herrick, and Milton, in Spanish by Cervantes' *Don Quixote*,[10] and in Italian by Sforza Pallavicino, whose *Fasti Sacri* aimed to rival the modern Latin poetic calendars but remained unfinished just like Ovid's *Fasti*.[11]

This paper examines how a cross-section of the Latin poetic calendars present the first day of the year, especially in response to Ovid's own account of the first day of the Roman year, which features the first month's eponymous god Janus. In a vivid display of his access to divine inspiration, Ovid imagines the two-faced Janus appearing before him at home in order to answer his questions about both the deity himself and the first day's ritual ceremonies (1.63-288). In a long sequence of responses to the curious antiquarian poet Janus discourses on matters ranging from his own double form, his function, and name to the reason for various sacral customs on January 1 to why the Romans closed the shrine of Janus when at peace but opened it during war time. As the god of beginnings in

---

[6]   A. Fritsen, 'Renaissance commentaries on Ovid's *Fasti*', diss. Yale 1995.

[7]   Overview: John F. Miller, 'Ovid's *Fasti* and the Neo-Latin Christian calendar poem', *International Journal of the Classical Tradition* 10 (2003) 173-86.

[8]   *Fasti christianae religionis*, ed. M. Bertolini (Naples 1991).

[9]   See Paul G. Schmidt, 'Antike Kalendardichtung in nationalgeprägter Umformung des 16. Jahrhunderts. Die *Fasti ecclesiae christianae* des Nathan Chytraeus', in *Antike-Rezeption und Nationale Identität in der Renaissance, insbesondere in Deutschland und in Ungarn,* ed. Tibor Klaniczay *et al.* (Budapest 1993) 111-17.

[10] See Maggie Kilgour, 'The Poetics of time: The *Fasti* in the Renaissance', and Frederick De Armas, '*Don Quixote* as Ovidian text', both in *A Handbook to the reception of Ovid*, ed. J. F. Miller and C. Newlands (Wiley-Blackwell: Malden MA 2014).

[11] See Silvia Apollonio, 'Prime ricerche sui *Fasti sacri* di Svorza Pallavicino', *Aevum* 84 (2010) 76793.

various ways – prayers, entrances, and even the cosmos – Ovid's Janus stepping forth on the year's first day is fittingly encoded with the poetic agenda of the *Fasti*.[12] The encounter sets the pattern for the many interviews to come between the calendrical poet and divinities. Abiding themes, such as peace and Augustan empire, are forcefully announced, as is the poem's deep engagement with the *Aitia* of Callimachus. The first day of the year is no less an important programmatic moment for the Christian calendar-poets. The very choice of which day to put at the head of a poetic calendar might be making a statement while that issue was contested on the continent before Pope Gregory reformed the calendar in 1582.[13] Bonincontri, for instance, both reflects a regional variant and initiates a chain of associations when he begins his calendar poem with 25 December, Christmas. The day's first day is otherwise heavily charged poetically for all the humanist calendar-poets, not least for the way it forcefully demonstrates the meaning of Ovid's ancient, pagan *Fasti* for the project of a Christian *Fasti sacri*.

When after various preliminaries Lazzarelli takes up the year's first day in his *Fasti Christianae religionis* (1.219), it is not January 1 but Advent Sunday, the first day of the ecclesiastical year. Among the Latin poetic calendars Lazzarelli's has a unique structure, comprising as it does not the usual 12 books (one for each month) but 16, the first three dedicated to the moveable feasts like Advent Sunday, Easter, and Ascension, then twelve devoted to the Church's celebrations of fixed date from March through February, and a final book on the Last Judgment. Nonetheless, on the first day of his year, Advent Sunday, Lazzarelli does follow Ovidian procedure by conjuring up a holy interlocutor (1.227-66). He delivers a general petition for information about the day's ritual to whomever the Omnipotent one will allow to descend from the sky (1.227-29 *o quem permittet ab alto / Omnipotens labi ... / dic ritus causam*) – Lazzarelli explicitly does not dare (*non audeo*) to summon the divine messenger Mercury because of his pagan status, although he does apostrophize that now purely mythical divinity – (1.231 *(fore quod quereris) nil nunc nisi fabula restat*, 'you complain about it but nothing but the myth now remains'). St. Peter immediately appears to the poet, and from the start we realize he is replacing not so much Mercury as the divinity who manifests himself to Ovid on the first day of the ancient Roman year. Both the description and phraseology put us in mind of Janus' epiphany in Book 1 of Ovid's poem.[14] Peter's beard and keys are singled out (1.234-36, 240-41), which are conspicuous attributes of Ovid's Janus (*Fasti* 1.99, 228, 253-54, 259). The epithet *claviger* ('key-bearer') applied to the saint's hand and then to Peter himself was invented by Ovid to describe Janus (*Fasti* 1.228 *clavigerum ... deum*);[15] Peter's characterization of the keys as his *arma* (1.236 *me promunt dextrae scilicet arma meae*, 'the arms of my right hand

---

[12] Philip Hardie, 'The Janus episode in Ovid's *Fasti*', *Materiali e Discussioni* 26 (1991) 47-64 and Mario Labate, 'Tempo delle origini e tempo della storia in Ovidio', in *La representation du temps dans la poésie augustéenne*, ed. J. P. Schwindt (Heidelberg 2005) 177-201.

[13] For the range of possibilities see *The Catholic Encyclopedia* vol. 3 (New York 1908) 739 s.v. 'Chronology'.

[14] Compare the introduction of the two speeches: Peter *clavigeram tenensque manum simul edidit ore* (1.235) and Janus *tenens ... clavem ... / edidit ... ore* (Ovid, *Fasti* 1.99-100).

[15] Elsewhere in Ovid the adjective signifies 'wielder of the club (*clava*)', usually applied to Hercules (*Fasti* 1.544, 4.68, *Met.* 15.22 and 284, *Ibis* 253) and once also to Periphetes (*Met.* 1.437).

clearly show who I am') likewise reproduces the pointedly peaceful Janus' own metaphor for his single key (*Fasti* 1.253–54 '*nil mihi cum bello ... et*', / *clavem ostendens, 'haec' ait 'arma gero'*, '"I have nothing to do with war ... and' – showing his key, he said – 'these are the arms I bear"'). Just like his pagan counterpart, too, the saint claims to be the *caelestis ianitor aulae* (1.241; *Fasti* 1.139) through whom (*per me*) humanity gains access to the celestial divine (*Fasti* 1.119 *me penes est unum vasti custodia mundi*) – in Janus' case it is the gods whom he admits to the sky (*Fasti* 1.121-22, 126). Peter thus emerges as a Christian equivalent to Janus, who is never mentioned. In Peter's explanations that follow, however – for the origin of Advent and its four weeks – Ovid's Janus is no longer evoked. After Lazzarelli allusively sets up St. Peter as a Janus-figure, or perhaps the rival of Ovid's holy interlocutor on January 1, the purely Christian aetiology proceeds without further reference to Ovid's divine encounter on the year's first day. As if to punctuate that difference, while Janus genially entertains multiple questions from Ovid, Peter abruptly vanishes just when Lazzarelli is about to continue the conversation.

Mantuan meditates on the same Ovidian text quite differently in unfolding the inaugural feast day of his Christian calendar-poem. For him that day is January 1, traditionally the feast of Christ's Circumcision: *Prima dies nostri (salvete) renascitur anni*, / *quae tamen est octava Dei lactentis ab ortu*, 'The first day of *our* year is reborn (all hail), which however is the eighth day after the birth of the infant God'. Even while he introduces his sacral year, Mantuan dates that start from Christ's Nativity; the emergence of God into human form is itself a beginning of monumental significance, and *ortus* can mean both 'birth' and 'beginning'. After he explains the Christian holy day, Mantuan turns to the name of January and thus to Janus. 'The first day of Janus' (*Prima dies Iani*), he says in concluding the Circumcision with a ring-compositional echo, 'gleams with such great splendor' (*tanto splendore coruscat*) from the feast. This leads him to gloss Janus in what is logically an appendix but surpasses the festal depiction in length. Here Mantuan treats the subjects of Janus' first long speech to Ovid – the god's identity, name, and peculiar form (*Fasti* 1.101-44) – but does so *in propria persona*, that is without conjuring up any sacred interlocutor. The poet reinterprets Janus' words from a Biblical perspective: 'this Janus was in fact that Noah' (*Ianus hic... ille fuit Noë*) who after the Deluge traveled to the site that would be Rome, where a month and a hill (the Janiculum) memorialize his sojourn there.[16] The name *Ianus* is actually a corrupted form of the Latinized Assyrian word for wine, *Iainus*[17] – Noah is said to have invented the vine and wine (*cf.* Genesis 9:20). Correspondingly, the idea of his two-faced form arose from the fact that he saw the two eras of the Flood and its aftermath: *fingitur esse biceps, quoniam duo secula vidit.*

---

[16] *Et post facta sui collem mensemque reliquit* / *nominis haeredes, quod non abolebitur unquam.* Mantuan adds the month January to the commemorations of himself stated by Ovid's Janus, even as the humanist poet intensifies with reference to the future; *cf.* Ovid, *Fasti* 1.145-46 *arx mea collis erat, quem volgo nomine nostro* / *nuncupat haec aetas Ianiculumque vocat.* A story like Mantuan's that links Janus with Noah dates to the Middle Ages. In the 12th/13th-century guidebook *Graphia aurea Urbis Romae* (secs. 1-2) one reads that Noah traveled to the site that would be Rome – *ubi nunc Roma est* (Janus' phrase at *Fasti* 1.243) – where after his death Noah's son Ianus inherited his Italian kingdom and gave his own name to the Ianiculum.

[17] Ovid in the *Fasti* four times explains a current name as arising from the loss or corruption of one letter (1.326, 5.195-96, 481-82, 536).

JOHN F. MILLER: OVID'S JANUS AND RENAISSANCE *FASTI SACRI*   85

All this Mantuan develops in language and style much less extensively indebted to Ovid's First of January than is Lazzarelli. There is some Ovidian colour, to be sure. The movement's opening verse, for instance (quoted above), is a pastiche of Ovidian phrases.[18] The tale of Noah/Iain's trip to the place *ubi nunc Roma est* clearly refashions the story of Saturn's arrival witnessed by Ovid's Janus and marked by the same phrase (*Fasti* 1.243). There is no doubt, however, that Mantuan is correcting Ovid point by point: Janus' previous identity was *not* primeval Chaos – the explanation found in Ovid's *Fasti* (1.103) – but Noah/Iain; and Janus' name and form are to be connected with that Biblical identity, not with his classical function as celestial doorkeeper (or *ianitor* – *cf. Fasti* 1.115-44). Mantuan perversely twists Ovidian Janus' explanation of the nautical image on Roman coinage as a memorial of Saturn into proof that it was the ship of the one later called Janus that survived the Deluge. This critique of Ovid's pagan calendrical aetiology is cast in terms of illuminating the ignorance and misperception of antiquity in general. At the close, Mantuan notes that the ancient Greeks and Romans were deceived (*falluntur*) because they did not know the annals of the first ancestors (*quia non novere parentum / primorum annales*) – these would be the Bible. The word *annales*, however, also glances at Ovid, who at the start of the *Fasti* claims that he has unearthed sacred rites from the ancient annals, *sacra ... annalibus eruta priscis* (1.7).

Next, among the Italian poetic calendars, comes Ambrogio Novidio Fracco's *Sacri Fasti* of 1547.[19] Fracco combines the approaches to Ovid of both Mantuan and Lazzarelli in producing perhaps the most thoroughgoing imitation of Ovid's *Fasti*, as his adopted name Novidius (New Ovid) would lead one to suggest. Like Mantuan, on 1 January he treats both the feast of the Circumcision and the identity of Janus, but in reverse order, so that the Ovidian content is pushed to the forefront, where this poet more directly applies his Christian critique. On the other hand, like Lazzarelli, Fracco adopts the dialog scenario and language of Ovid but – again – does so much more extensively. In place of the Ovidian epiphany of Janus, Fracco enjoys a visitation from the Trinity – a triple divinity to trump the double pagan god. In both cases the luminous apparition occurs when the poet has just taken up his writing tablet – a key moment that Ovid borrows from the proem to his Callimachean model, the *Aitia* (*fr.* 1.21-22): compare Fracco 1.129–30[20] *hoc ego sic sumpta dicebam forte tabella, / undique quum fundi lumine visa domus,* 'I was saying this, having taken up my tablet, when on all sides the house seemed to be flooded with light'; Ovid 1.93-94 *haec*

---

[18] *Prima dies Iani tanto splendore coruscat*: *prima dies* initial at *Fasti* 1.166 & 6.140; *Iani* only at third-foot caesura in Ovid (1.257, 586, etc.); *corusc** always ends a verse in Ovid (*Fasti* 6.635, *Met.* 1.768, 4.494, 12.288). Mantuan's introductory verse is echoed after a direct polemical reference to Ovid's pagan *Fasti* in the opening elegy of a sequence on the months by the fifteenth-century Croatian poet Giorgio Sisgoreo: *Carmina* 3.11.11-12 *prima dies Iani toto celeberrima mundo est, / qua deus incisa carne puellus erat;* the poem begins *Nil mihi cum veteri Romane gentis honore, / quam canit in fastis Naso poeta suis. / Vana superstitio ...*

[19] My discussion of Fracco adapts J. F. Miller, 'I *Sacri Fasti* di Ambrogio Novidio Fracco in conversazione con i *Fasti* di Ovidio,' in *Vates operose dierum. Studi sui Fasti di Ovidio,* ed. Giuseppe LaBua (Rome 2010) 198-209.

[20] My own numeration of the edition of *Ambrosii Novidii Fracci Ferentinatis Sacrorum fastorum libri XII* (Rome 1547).

ego cum sumptis agitarem mente tabellis, / lucidior visa est quam fuit ante domus, 'When I was pondering these matters, having taken up my tablets, the house seemed brighter than it was beforehand'. Moreover, Fracco engages in a long conversation with the Trinity, which exactly matches in number the ten exchanges between Ovid and his divine interlocutor.[21]

We see from the start that Fracco simultaneously presents his ecclesiastical material in distinctly Ovidian terms and critiques Ovid's pagan religious perspective. Take the opening address to the Trinity (1.115-28):

Interea, aeternus quia coeli limina servas,
  ad superosque aditum tu mihi primus habes,
Trine parens rerum, Ianum qui denique formis
  antiquum ut superes, nunc tria colla geris,
quod sacra cum causis paro dicere vera per annum
  signaque iam coelo reddita certa tuo,
est homini si fas voces audire deorum,
  vatibus ut castis ante fuisse putant,
Ipse refer Ianus, de quo sunt nomina mensi,
  unde biceps (lateat cum deus ille suos)
quisve sit. atque tibi cur est nunc forma triformis,
  quam modo nos templo cernimus esse tuo?
adde simul triplicem cur non coluere priores:
  credibile est veterum te prius esse deis.

And so, since you guard the threshold of the sky for eternity, and you first of all provide access to the divine for me, o Triune parent of the universe, who now have three heads so that you finally surpass ancient Janus in form, because I am preparing to tell of the true feasts throughout the year along with their explanations, and the constellations now made fixed in your sky, if it is right for a mortal to hear the voices of the gods, as they think was the case previously for pure poets, you yourself tell why Janus is two-headed, he from whom the month's name derives (since that god is obscure to his people), and who he is. And why do you now have a triple form, which we see nowadays in your shrine? Add as well why the ancients did not worship a triple being. It is believable that you antedate the gods of the ancients.

As the Christian poet turns to the present guardian of the heavenly threshold, the opening distich reorients a comment by Janus, namely *Fasti* 1.173-74 *ut possis aditum per me, qui limina servo, / ad quoscumque voles ... habere deos*, 'so that through me, who guard the threshold, you have access to whichever deities you want'. We can take the reversal of human and divine addressees as simple variation rather than polemical in force, but the adjectives *aeternus* and *primus* suggest a rivalry with Janus. Then Fracco openly specifies

---

[21] For details see Miller, 'I *Sacri Fasti* di Ambrogio Novidio Fracco' (above n. 19) 203-04.

that, as he puts it – mildly flirting with heresy[22] – his three-headed addressee surpasses ancient Janus in aspect (*superes*). The poet himself likewise, in the next distich, is implicitly claiming to outstrip the poetic project announced in the opening verse of Ovid's *Fasti* (1.1-2): *Tempora cum causis Latium digesta per annum, / lapsaque sub terras ortaque signa canam,* 'I sing of the times arranged throughout the Latin year, along with their explanations, and the constellations that fall beneath the earth and then rise'. Fracco's subject is the *true* festivals (*sacra ... vera*)[23] along with their aetiologies, and the constellations now *fixed* – not rising and falling – in *God's* sky (*caelo ... tuo*).[24] Most remarkable of all, Fracco's ensuing initial queries to the Trinity not only match, but actually repeat Ovid's first questions to Janus (*Fasti* 1.89-92 *quem tamen esse deum te dicam, Iane biforme? ... / ede simul causam, cur de caelestibus unus / sitque quod a tergo sitque quod ante vides,* 'Yet which god am I to say you are, double Janus? ... And give as well the reason why you alone of the heavenly ones sees what is in front and behind you'). The Christian god is asked to explain his own triple form, as was Janus his unique bifrontal shape – *triformis* matches *biforme* at verse-end to drive home the parallel – but also (and first of all) to elucidate the origin and identity of the month's two-headed eponymous divinity. It is as if Fracco is not satisfied with the classical god's own explanation of himself, so for the truth he invites the perspective of the deity who replaces Janus at the head of a proper calendar-poem. 'That god', he says, 'is obscure to his own people'.

This blend of close structural imitation and theological correction of Ovid continues throughout the conversation. Again at the start of the exchange, for instance (*Sacri Fasti* 1.139-40), note Trinity's first words to Fracco: *pone metum vates, melioris conditor anni, / dictaque percipias, me referente, mea,* 'Set aside your fear, o poet, you the writer of a better year, and take in my words as I pronounce them'. This replays Janus' encouragement to the frightened poet as he begins to address Ovid: *Fasti* 1.101-02 *disce metu posito, vates operose dierum, / quod petis, et voces percipe mente meas,* 'Put down your fear and learn what you seek, o hard-working poet of the days, and take my words into your mind'. But at the same time the appellation pointedly revises Juno's later address to Ovid as the *vates, Romani conditor anni* (*Fasti* 6.21). Fracco is said to write 'of a better year' as the *vates, melioris conditor anni.* Likewise, Trinity's countering selfassertions about his own identity repeatedly allude polemically to the start of Janus' account of himself. The latter begins (*Fasti* 1.103-04): *me Chaos antiqui (nam sum res prisca) vocabant, / aspice quam longi temporis acta canam,* 'The ancients used to call me Chaos (for I am a primeval being); see of what great antiquity are the deeds of which I sing'. In a cutting one-upmanship the Trinity starts with the fact that he is *before* Chaos (*Sacri Fasti* 1.145 *ante Chaos cum sim ...*). A few couplets later comes his sharp rejoinder to the Ovidian pentameter: 1.155-56 *sic ea quae longi sibi sumpsit temporis acta / omnia iam senis nostra diebus erant.* The primeval events

---

[22] On iconographical experiments in representing the Trinity, see F. Boespflug and Y. Zaluska, 'Le dogme trinitaire et l'essor de son iconographie en Occident de l'époque carolingienne au IVe Concile du Latran (1215),' *Cahiers de civilisation médiévale* 37 (1994) 181-240.

[23] Another intertext is *Fasti* 2.7 *idem sacra cano.*

[24] The qualification at 1.121-22 both picks up Ovid's qualification at *Fasti* 3.167-68 as he turns to Mars, *si licet occultos monitus audire deorum / vatibus, ut certe fama licere putat,* and responds to Ovid's proud pronouncement at *Fasti* 6.7–8 *fas mihi praecipue voltus vidisse deorum, / vel quia sum vates, vel quia sacra cano.*

or *longi ... temporis acta* which Janus 'claimed for himself' – this language distorts Janus' words for rhetorical effect – were in fact God's own six-day cosmogonic works known from Genesis' account of Creation.

Fracco's Trinity voices the idea found in Mantuan that Janus is a fictitious corruption of Noah/Iain. In addition, like Lazzarelli, he highlights St. Peter as a Christian counterpart to Janus. But in both cases Fracco makes clear that he is reading Ovid's Janus allegorically. Janus' shape is taken to arise from ignorant antiquity's (*rudis ... vetustas)* mistaken construal of the double aspect of God's Creation (*Sacri Fasti* 1.145-50). In the case of St. Peter, Janus is said to be a *rerum ... figura,* just as in this respect was Noah before him (1.197-98). These two prefigured 'the heavenly ship' (*sydeream ... ratem*) of Peter, symbolizing the Church (as in the common iconography), and his keys to heaven.[25] Again, the Ovidian Janus' description of himself is arrogated for the sanctified apostle. The double deity proudly declared *praesideo foribus caeli,* 'I preside over the doors of heaven' (*Fasti* 1.125), which Trinity pointedly applies to the Christian celestial doorkeeper, *praesidet hic foribus caeli* (*Sacri Fasti* 1.209). The demonstrative pronoun furthers the intertextual dialectic. It is *this* one, not Janus, who guards the heavenly doorway. A few couplets later Ovidian phrasing is appropriated for a similar effect, in the picture of St. Peter's vast bilateral range of vision – taking in both East and West – where the play on Janus' name, too, underscores that the pagan divinity has been supplanted by the saint: *Sacri Fasti* 1.215-16 *colleque de Iani, coeli dum Ianitor adstat, / Eoasque domos hesperiasque videt,* 'and while the Doorkeeper of Heaven stands at his post, from the hill of Janus he sees the countries of the East and West'; *cf. Fasti* 1.139-40 *sic ego perspicio caelestis ianitor aulae / Eoas partes Hesperiasque simul,* 'Thus I, the doorkeeper of the heavenly hall, look over the eastern and western regions at once'. And St. Peter's vantage point – or rather vantage points – doubly trump Janus, who has been made to surrender not only his heavenly superintendence as *caeli ianitor* but also his eponymous hill, whence we are no doubt to imagine the apostle gazing out from the church of San Pietro in Montorio on the Gianicolo. At the same time, the saint's farreaching view over the earth echoes the Trinity's own three-fold perspective claimed earlier, which in turn rivals Janus' claim to look in two (but only two) directions without moving (*Fasti Sacri* 1.189-90):

> oraque quas domui tres aspicientia partes
> in loca non moto vertice terna fero.

> Without moving my neck I point in three directions my faces which behold the three regions I have subdued.

> ora vides Hecates in tres vertentia partes,
> servet ut in ternas compita secta vias:
> et mihi, ne flexu cervicis tempora perdam,
> cernere non moto corpore bina licet.
> (*Fasti* 1.141-44)

---

[25] *Sacri Fasti* 1.204 *huic tribui clavem sydereamque ratem; cf.* 1.206 *cum rate dat claves imperiumque seni.* Matthew 16:19 *et tibi dabo claves regni caelorum.*

JOHN F. MILLER: OVID'S JANUS AND RENAISSANCE *FASTI SACRI* 89

You see the faces of Hecate turned in three directions so that she may guard the crossroads split into three roads: I too may look in two directions without moving my body so that I don't lose time by bending my neck.

Actually, the Trinity's assertion also mischievously alludes to Janus' own divine *comparandum* for his peculiar form, namely Hecate, who turns her faces in three directions at once. The true triple deity has transvaluated that comparison, in effect turning it on its head.

As in Ovid's *Fasti*, the Trinity's epiphany to Fracco on the first day of the year is but the first of several holy apparitions to the poet, for which the initial encounter serves as a kind of template. To come will be meetings with the Blessed Virgin (in March), a trio of Muses (in April), and the Holy Spirit (in June).[26] Such entrance upon Fracco's stage by both pagan and Christian authorities finds an even more complex form in my final example of the Christian calendar-poem, namely the Cremonan Girolamo Chiaravacci's *Fasti* of 1554, where pagan and Christian authorities appear alongside one another. That conjunction is emblematic, I think, of Chiaravacci's stance towards Ovid and pagan antiquity.

In the poem's opening movement,[27] Chiaravacci asks the Muses to inspire his poem about the sacred days, noting, by the by, that an unnamed *ille* (namely Ovid) left his work only begun when he died.[28] One of the Muses straightaway appears, saying first of all that the poet should really consult the divine Moses, widely revered as lawgiver and who will reveal the celestial regions: 17-18 *consule divini coelestia pectora Mosis, / quem legum auctorem mundus uterque colit.* The Muse casts some inspirational stuff upon the poet's head, which he internalizes, and – *ecce* – Moses appears before him, brilliantly arrayed and accompanied by what look to be the personified year, days, and hours, and with Pallas Athena, too, at his side.[29] This rather busy scene is loosely modelled on Janus' simpler

---

[26] Fracco likewise imitates Ovid's technique of conversing on aetiological matters with people he meets. For instance, on April 4 he encounters in Rome a man from Lombardy who discourses on the feast of Ambrose, patron saint of his native Milan.

[27] References follow my own numeration of the copy of *Hieronymi Claravacaei Cremonensis ad Paulum III Pont. Max. Fastorum libri* XII (Milan 1554) in the Rare Book and Manuscript Library at Columbia University.

[28] 1.11-12 *Vos quoque Seriades vestro date vela poetae, / incoeptum moerens ille reliquit opus.* The 'daughters of Serius' were nymphs of a tributary of the Po near Chiaravacci's native Cremona; *cf.* verse 5 of the *Scacchia, Ludus* by Vida, Chiaravacci's contemporary and fellow Cremonan, *dicite Seriades nymphae certamina tanta.* The allusion to Ovid and his *Fasti* left incomplete at death recalls what Ovid himself said about both his *Metamorphoses* and *Fasti* at the time of his exile (*Tr.* 2.63 *opus ... reliqui*; *cf.* 552. The phrasing even more strongly echoes *Ars* 2.73 *inceptum ... reliquit opus,* the fisherman agape at the crashing Icarus). Interestingly, Chiaravacci goes on apparently to characterize the project of Ovid's elegiac (and peaceful) *Fasti* in terms of a *recusatio*-scene like that which began the *Amores*: 1.13-14 *barbara tentabat Romano dicere versu / proelia, surripuit Calliopea pedem; cf. Am.* 1.1-2 *Arma gravi numero violenta bella parabam / edere ... risisse Cupido / dicitur atque unum surripuisse pedem.* The conflation amounts to an insightful reading of the *Fasti* in the elegiac tradition.

[29] 1.23-30 *Quumque ego divinas agitarem pectore flammas, / ad vultus Moses adstitit ecce meos. / candida vestis erat, radiabant tempora mitra, / ibat ab aerio plurimus ore lepos. / Annus erat dextra, laevaque a parte dierum / Saecula, fixae horae limitibusque suis. / sol erat in vultu, medioque vertice Phoebe, / contigerat felix Pallas utrumque latus.*

apparition to Ovid when he was taking up his writing tablets to begin the *Fasti* (an Ovidian moment to which Fracco also referred).[30] Here it is Pallas rather than Moses, the Janus-figure suddenly appearing, who first instructs Chiaravacci: 1.31 *illa regit vatem* 'she guides the poet'. She reveals to him the stars and explains the zodiac's signs for 150 verses. The scene is not explicitly set on the first day of the year, as in the other calendars, but is nonetheless similarly obsessed with beginnings, including the start of the year. Eventually Moses himself speaks; he takes up the matter of the year, again, in phraseology that echoes Janus addressing aetiologies to Ovid: 1.191-92 *accipe quaesiti vates tibi tempora mensis, / tempora non uno carmine nota tibi,* 'listen, poet, to the times of the month that you ask about, times known to you not only from one poem' (*cf.* Janus at *Fasti* 1.115 *accipe quaesitae quae causa sit altera formae,* 'listen to what is the second cause of my form that you ask about'). We have not actually heard the poet ask about the month (*quaesiti ... mensis*). Moreover, Moses' capacious knowledge extends to what Chiaravacci has read! His reference to more than one poem points beyond Ovid's *Fasti* to the *Metamorphoses*, whose account of creation and early human life provides the narrative structure for Moses' aition. This acknowledges the relationship between the two Ovidian poems long before Richard Heinze's pioneering *Ovids elegische Erzählung* (1919), even as the two texts are here being revised. Moses opens by characterizing primeval matter just as Janus did when he started to explain his own origin as Chaos:

> terra, mare, et coelum, et quantum complectitur axis,
> ante Dei vultus <u>unus acervus erat</u>.
>
> (*Chiaravacci* 1.193-94)

The earth, sea, and sky, and however much the axis embraces was all one heap before the face of God.

> lucidus hic aer et quae tria corpora restant,
> ignis, aquae, tellus, <u>unus acervus erat</u>.
>
> (Ovid 1.105-06)

This clear air and the three other elements,
fire, water, and earth, were all one heap.

On the other hand, the Hebrew prophet thinks of the ingredients more closely in terms of the *Metamorphoses*' account of creation (*Met.* 1.15 *utque erat et tellus illic et pontus et aer,* 'though there was earth, and sea, and air'; *cf.* 23 *caelum,* 24 *caeco ... acervo*). It is a Biblical version of the latter narrative that Moses then expounds. There was a golden age (*cf. Met.* 1.89-150), whose end was marked by Cain's slaughter of Abel (Chiaravacci 1.241-42 *tum primum fratris gladio percussus Abelus,* 'then for the first time was Abel struck down by the sword of a brother'; *cf. Met.* 145 *fratrum quoque gratia rara est,* 'and also among brothers goodwill was rare'). God called a divine council, as did Ovid's Jupiter, once again

---

[30] Ovid, *Fasti* 1.93-100 *haec ego cum sumptis agitarem mente tabellis, / lucidior visa est quam fuit ante domus. / tum sacer ancipiti mirandus imagine Ianus / bina repens oculis obtulit ora meis. / extimui sensique metu riguisse capillos, / et gelidum subito frigore pectus erat. / ille tenens baculum dextra clavemque sinistra / edidit hos nobis ore priore sonos:*

to announce a flood as punishment for evil humanity. This brings us once more to Noah, who, however, does not turn out to be Janus as in other Christian *Fasti.* Here we are told that, among his inventions after the Deluge – wine, for instance – Noah divided the year according to the movements of the sun (1.297): *ille tibi ad solis cursus diviserat annum.* There is only a vague parallel for this in Genesis (8.13) in that Noah beheld dry land again on the first day of the first month of the new year. According to Chiaravacci's Moses, Noah is responsible for establishing the months of the year, an achievement that for the Romans Ovid's *Fasti* attributes to Romulus (1.27-28).

Next the poet asks what the first day signifies or means (1.313-14): *dic mihi magne pater, dic rerum maxime vates, / quid vult prima sibi mense recepta dies*? Note that here Moses is the one called *vates,* and as such is kindred to the poet, albeit 'greatest' and 'prophet'. Note, too, that his upward gaze (1.315 *ille oculos tollens ad coeli sydera, dixit*) recalls both the posture of the Muse as she inspired Chiaravacci (1.21 *dixerat et toto suspexit lumine coelum*) and the global gaze of Janus at the close of his conversation with Ovid (*Fasti* 283-84 *dixit et attollens oculos diversa videntes / aspexit toto quicquid in orbe fuit,* 'he spoke and raising up his eyes that looked in different directions, he surveyed all contained in the whole world'). After reviewing some items in Jewish history and culture, Moses focuses on a custom addressed also by Ovid's Janus, namely the gift of money on the year's first day. His aetiology for the practice is not unlike that given by Janus for gifts at Rome on 1 January – so that the rest of the year may follow in a joyful spirit (1.336 *annus ut hoc solo munere laetus eat; cf.* Ovid, *Fasti* 1.188 (said of the gift of dates and honey, right before explaining cash gifts) *et peragat coeptum dulcis ut annus iter,* 'and so that the year may run through its course sweetly, as it began'; *cf.* 1.26 *felix totus annus eat,* 'may the whole year proceed happily'). But in this case a second aition is appended (1.337-38): *aut quia syderea stellatus fronde capillos / de pura Chistus virgine natus erat,* 'or because Christ, whose hair is adorned with a heavenly crown of stars, was born from the pure virgin' – presumably this means that the cash gifts commemorate the Nativity celebrated a few days ago. Moses soon modulates into the Lord's Circumcision, the traditional ecclesiastical feast of 1 January, and Jesus is said thus to claim the day, and the year, for himself (1.349): *vendicat ille diem, primus sibi vendicat annum.* The Jewish *vates* then enthusiastically apostrophizes the day (1.355-56): *salve, festa dies toto celeberrima mundo, / et niteas vultu, quo meliore nites,* 'Hail, feast day renowned through the whole world, and may you gleam with an ever happier aspect'. This echoes Ovid's address to January 1 at the installation day of Rome's consuls (1.87-88 *salve, laeta dies, meliorque revertere semper, / a populo rerum digna potente coli,* 'Hail, joyful day, and always return happier, day worthy of worship by the people ruling the world'). The worldwide power of Rome encoded in the pagan occasion has been transmuted to the celebrated status of the corresponding Christian feast day throughout the entire world.

Eventually the curious poet inquires after the source of the first month's name (1.404 *unde sibi primus nomina mensis habet*), which brings Moses to Janus and to Roman history. As do the other humanistic *Fasti,* he highlights the story of the exiled Saturn's arrival in Latium by ship which Janus tells Ovid (*Fasti* 1.233-54) in order to explain the boat inscribed on some Roman coinage. Chiaravacci elevates the status of Janus above what the god claimed for himself, making him a seemingly greater power in Latium in those days, the very one who installed Saturn in a new kingdom, as well as himself producing the

92   THE AFTERLIFE OF OVID

commemorative coinage[31] – Mantuan gives a similar version.[32] Ovid's Janus rather follows up his reminiscence of Saturn's arrival in Italy with reflection on how he resided in those primitive times on the hill now called Janiculum from his name (1.241-48). Moses instead links the memorialization of Saturn in the *Saturnia tellus* with that of Janus in the name of the year's first month. Adapting another passage in *Fasti* 1, Chiaravacci has Moses state that the early *patres* called the first month after Janus but that Romulus instead gave that honour to his own father Mars, when he divided the year into ten months[33] – in that apportionment Rome's first king was 'ignorant of his error' (1.424 *Romulus erroris necius ipse sui*). Early on in his poem (at *Fasti* 1.27-4) Ovid describes Romulus' mistaken ten-month year, with his father Mars' month at the head, and the poet speculates on the reasons for this *error* in an apostrophe to Caesar (surely we think here of the reformer of the calendar, Julius Caesar, as well as of Augustus or Tiberius or Germanicus): *scilicet arma magis quam sidera, Romule, noras, / curaque finitimos vincere maior erat. / est tamen et ratio, Caesar, quae moverit illum, / erroremque suum quo tueatur habet,* 'To be sure, Romulus, you knew warfare better than the stars, and your greater concern was to conquer neighbours. Yet, Caesar, there is also a reason which motivated him, and he has a way to defend his error' (1.29-32). King Numa, Ovid goes on to say (1.43-44), prefixed to the ten an additional two months, with Janus honoured at the start. Moses, however, attributes the correction of this calendrical problem not to Numa but to Caesar (Chiaravacci 1.425 *hunc Caesar veniens errorem movit ab anno*), who is said to have named the first month after Janus as the beginning for Romulus' institution (1.427-28 *et primum Iani dixit de nomine mensem / principium rebus Romule magne tuis*). Capping the substitution, the Ovidian address to Caesar becomes an apostrophe to Romulus.

All in all, like Fracco and to a lesser extent Lazzarelli, Chiaravacci is deeply engaged with the language, techniques, and content of the Ovidian Janus' epiphany to the poet on the first day of the year. Unlike his humanistic confrères, however – and that includes Mantuan – Chiaravacci is not really polemical vis-à-vis Ovid's *Fasti* as an embodiment of pagan antiquity's account of sacred time. Here the Greek goddesses Pallas Athena and an unnamed Muse share the stage with Moses as the poet's revered authorities. Moses is cast in the mould of Ovid's Janus without dissonance. Biblical episodes from Genesis and elsewhere – Noah, Abel, Moses' own Decalogue[34] – are integrated into the Ovidian narratives of earth's

---

[31]   Janus remembers Saturn's reception in Latium after he had been expelled from the sky by Jupiter (Ovid 1.235-36 *Saturnum ... receptum: / caelitibus regnis a Iove pulsus erat*), and says that posterity commemorated his coming with the numismatic emblem (1.239-40). Moses ascribes both the welcome and memorialization to Janus (Chiaravacci 1.411-14 *ille dedit regi Saturno regna domosque: / nam pater imperiis ab Iove pulsus erat ... quin etiam nummis vela ratemque dedit*).

[32]   *Memorant etenim sub principe Iano / aequorea primum signata numismata puppi.*

[33]   Chiaravacci 1.419-24 *hinc etiam patres Iani de nomine mensem / dixerunt primum, non tamen ille fuit. / nam pater Iliades Romani conditor anni / hunc dixit mensem de genitore suo, / inque decem menses totum diviserat annum / Romulus erroris nescius ipse sui.* The final measure echoes that attributed by Chiaravacci earlier to Noah, *ille tibi ad solis cursus diviserat annum* (1.297). Striking examples of Ovidian phrasing are *pater Iliades* (*Fasti* 4.23) and *Romani conditor anni* (of Ovid himself at 6.21).

[34]   See 1.223-32 for the Commandments in elegiac couplets.

prehistory. The alternative aitia for cash gifts on 1 January – to ensure a happy year, as in Ovid, and to commemorate Christ's birth – do not seem to conflict with one another. The one explicit reference to calendrical error – by Romulus – is said to have been corrected by Caesar, not by Catholic doctrine – again, in contradistinction with the other *Fasti sacri*. Fracco everywhere juxtaposes Christian and Ovidian antiquities but always with an edge of theological critique. In his blending of traditions Chiaravacci may have been influenced by Hermeticism, which much occupied the thinkers of the age – Lazzarelli, for instance, translated the Hermetic texts into Latin, as had Ficino more famously before him. Cosmology and astrology as well as the authority of Moses also loom large in the Hermetic tradition.[35] Whatever its source, at least to judge from this long rambling episode, the relative lack of Christian contestation of pagan religion seems to be a hallmark of Chiaravacci's *Fasti*. My survey of the neo-Latin calendar poem in Italy, then, perhaps fittingly ends with a text that for once exudes a harmony between Ovid as progenitor of the genre of calendrical poetry and Ovid as the source of lore about ancient Rome's religious calendar.[36]

University of Virginia

---

[35] See D. P. Walker, *The Ancient theology* (Ithaca, NY 1972) Index s.v. 'Moses'; A. Grafton, *Joseph Scaliger. A study of the history of classical scholarship.* Vol. 2 (Oxford 1993) 67-70.

[36] Many thanks for the reactions to my paper at the Warburg Institute's Afterlife of Ovid conference, which have improved this revised version. Some of the same material was presented at the August 2009 FIEC convention in Berlin, where I benefited from the comments of Fritz Graf. I am also grateful to John Dillery, Blaire French, Nicholas Geller, and Mathias Hanses for their help.

LETTER-WRITING AFTER OVID:
HIS IMPACT ON NEO-LATIN VERSE EPISTLES

GESINE MANUWALD

In the international Republic of Letters of the Renaissance period letters were a vital medium for humanists to stay in touch and to discuss various matters of mutual interest. These letters are mostly written in prose and could fulfil practical purposes (despite their literary and rhetorical shaping). At the same time the composition of fictional letters or letters in poetry flourished; for this literary genre Ovid's metrical epistles provided a challenging precedent.

In Ovid's verse epistles (as in the earlier ones by Horace) the standard definition of letters had already been surpassed; these texts are not simply written messages from one person (or group of people) to another, set down in a tangible medium, physically conveyed from sender(s) to recipient(s), who are separated from each other, and overtly addressed from sender(s) to recipient(s) by conventional formulae of salutations at the beginning and the end.[1] While the ancient authors keep some of these elements to mark their poems as letters, many were never intended to be sent (or could not be sent) and were written with a secondary, wider audience in mind, beyond the named addressee. Besides, due to their format, these pieces share similarities with other poetic genres, particularly epigrams, elegies, and satires, which may make it difficult to describe verse epistles precisely and to distinguish them from other forms of poetry.

Due to the fluidity of the ancient basis, Renaissance letter writing in verse provided an enormous potential of showing intriguing ways of creatively engaging with ancient models and of developing them further. Yet, except for a few famous examples, NeoLatin verse epistles have been less studied than other types of poetry or letters in prose from the same

---

[1] See M. Trapp (ed.), *Greek and Latin letters: an anthology, with translation*, Cambridge Greek and Latin Classics (Cambridge 2003) 1. – On the genre of 'letter', with reference to antiquity, see *e.g.* I. Sykutris, 'Epistolographie', *RE Suppl.* V (1931) 185-220; K. Thraede, *Grundzüge griechischrömischer Brieftopik*, Zetemata 48 (München 1970); J. T. Reed, 'The epistle', in *Handbook of classical rhetoric in the Hellenistic period 330 BC-AD 400*, ed. S. E. Porter (Leiden / New York / Köln 1997) 171-93; Trapp 3-34; C. Edwards, 'Epistolography', in *A companion to Latin literature*, ed. S. Harrison (Malden (MA) / Oxford 2005) 270-83; R. K. Gibson / A. D. Morrison, 'Introduction: what is a letter?', in *Ancient letters: classical and Late Antique epistolography*, ed. R. Morello / A. D. Morrison (Oxford / New York 2007) 1-16; J. Ebbeler, 'Letters', in *The Oxford Handbook of Roman Studies*, ed. A. Barchiesi / W. Scheidel (Oxford 2010) 464-76; on the problems of defining 'genre' see *e.g.* M. Depew / D. Obbink (eds), *Matrices of genre. authors, canons, and society*, Center for Hellenic Studies Colloquia 4 (Cambridge (MA) / London 2000). – No distinction between the terms 'letter' and 'epistle' (*i.e.* identifying pieces of different literary status) is intended here (for a summary of the earlier discussion on this issue see *e.g.* Thraede 1-4; S. K. Stowers, *Letter writing in Greco-Roman antiquity*, Library of Early Christianity (Philadelphia 1986) 17-20).

THE AFTERLIFE OF OVID

period.[2] At least, the last few years have seen the appearance of two studies on a selection of epistles from heroines.[3] A comprehensive treatment of the entire genre of verse letters cannot be attempted in the present context either. Instead, the possibilities of developing the structure introduced by Ovid will be demonstrated paradigmatically by a closer look at two Neo-Latin letters from heroines. The two poets who have written these letters, Helius Eobanus Hessus in Germany and the Scot Mark Alexander Boyd, have developed the genre differently in their own specific ways.

The humanist and scholar Helius Eobanus Hessus (1488-1540) is an obvious choice: for if one tries to think of an early modern author who writes verse epistles in Ovid's style, the 'German Ovid' or 'Christian Ovid' will immediately come to mind: Hessus was called the 'German Ovid', initially by Erasmus,[4] after the first publication of *Heroidum*

---

[2] See J. IJsewijn / D. Sacré, *Companion to Neo-Latin studies: part II: literary, linguistic, philological and editorial questions. Second entirely rewritten edition*, Suppl. Hum. Lov. XIV (Leuven 1998) 77: 'To the best of our knowledge no comprehensive study of the Neo-Latin metrical epistles exists except for the subgenre of the so-called heroical letters (*Heroides*), an off-spring of Ovid's letters purportedly sent by famous mythical women and men to their absent or unfaithful lovers.' – For an overview of the heroic letter see H. Dörrie, *Der heroische Brief: Bestandsaufnahme, Geschichte, Kritik einer humanistisch-barocken Literaturgattung* (Berlin 1968), and now (among the Jesuits) J. Eickmeyer, *Der jesuitische Heroidenbrief. Zur Christianisierung und Kontextualisierung einer antiken Gattung in der Frühen Neuzeit*, Frühe Neuzeit 162 (Berlin / Boston 2012); for a brief survey of the genre of the Neo-Latin verse epistle see G. Manuwald, 'NeoLatin verse epistles', in *A handbook of Neo-Latin literature*, ed. V. Moul (Cambridge forthcoming).

[3] C. Ritter, *Ovidius redivivus: Die Epistulae Heroides des Mark Alexander Boyd. Edition, Übersetzung und Kommentar der Briefe Atalanta Meleagro (1), Eurydice Orpheo (6), Philomela Tereo (9), Venus Adoni (15)*, Noctes Neolatinae 13 (Hildesheim / Zürich / New York 2010); Eickmeyer, *Der jesuitische Heroidenbrief* (n. 2, above).

[4] For the term 'Christian Ovid' see Erasmus, *Ep.* 874 / 30.6 (19 Oct. 1518): 'Jam arbitrabar mihi probè cognitam *Germaniam*, & quicquid esset insignium ingeniorum pervestigatum. Adamabam ingenium *Beati Rhenani*: exosculabar indolem *Philippi Melanchthonis*: suspiciebam *Capnionis* majestatem: capiebar *Hutteni* deliciis. Et ecce derepente *Hessus*, quod antehac in singulis vel amabam, vel mirabar, unus universum exhibuit. Quid enim aliud Heroides tuæ quàm *Christianum Ovidianum* referunt? Cui vel in oratione soluta contingit ea facilitas, quæ tibi in omni carminis genere? Eloquentiam æquat eruditio; & utrumque decorat *Christiana* pietas. Jam in oratione prosa talis es, ut alienus à carmine videri possis. O venam ingenii verè auream! Nec à stylo mores abhorrent, quibus nihil candidius, nihil simplicius, nihil potest esse purius. ... Bene vale, *Germaniæ* nostræ vel præcipium decus.' – 'I thought I knew my Germany well and had sought out all its distinguished minds. I was devoted to the abilities of Beatus Rhenanus, found Philippus Melanchthon's character delightful, admired Reuchlin's dignity, and was much taken with Hutten's charming conversation. And here is Hessus all of a sudden, uniting in himself all I had previously loved or admired in others separately. What does one think of in your *Heroides* but a Christian Ovid? Who is so happy in plain prose as you are in verse of every kind? Your learning balances your gifts of expression, and your Christian piety enhances both. In prose you are already so successful that one would think you had no poetry in you. Yours is a truly golden vein of talent. And your character matches your style: nothing could be more frank, more simple, more unspoilt. ... Farewell, chief ornament of our native Germany' (trans. R. A. B. Mynors / D. F. S. Thomson).

Christianarum Epistolae (1514).[5] As the title indicates, this work is a collection of letters by Christian heroines: Ovid's women in *Heroides* (taken from myth with the exception of the poetess Sappho) have been replaced with Christian women who are mentioned in the Bible or have been recognized as saints. Moreover, despite its title, the collection includes two

---

[5] The collection was first published in 1514 (*Helii Eobani Hessi Heroidum Christianarum Epistolae. Opus novitium, nuper œditum*, Anno M.D.XIIII (Leipzig)), followed by a second revised edition published in 1539 (*Helii Eobani Hessi Farragines Duae, Nuper ab eodem qua fieri potuit diligentia contractœ, et in hanc, qum uides formam coactœ, quibus etiam non parum multa acceßerunt nunc primum et nata & œdita. Catalogum operum ipsorum uersa pagella ostendet. Acceßit unicuiq; farragini suus etiam index, explicãs quid in singulis libris contineatur, & ad quos potißimum autor scribat*, Halae Suevorum, Anno XXXIX). For the second edition the epistles were rearranged and organized into three books (see below with n. 13); besides, passages that might be problematic in the changed religious environment were modified. – A modern edition of the Latin text of the first edition with English translation and notes is available in H. Vredeveld (ed.), *The Poetic Works of Helius Eobanus Hessus. Edited, translated, and annotated*, 2 vols, Medieval and Renaissance Texts and Studies 215 / 333 (Tempe (Ariz.) 2004 / 2008) II (2008) 126-431, whose Latin text and English translation have been used throughout (with occasional slight modifications). A modern edition of the Latin text of the second edition with German translation is provided by H. Vredeveld (ed.), *Helius Eobanus Hessus. Dichtungen. Lateinisch und Deutsch. Herausgegeben und übersetzt. Dritter Band. Dichtungen der Jahre 1528-1537*, Mittlere deutsche Literatur in Neu- und Nachdrucken 39 (Bern / Frankfurt a.M. / New York / Paris 1990) 269-483. For the text of Hessus' works see also www. uni-mannheim.de/mateo/camena/AUTBIO/hessus.html. – On Hessus' life and works see (in addition to several older studies) *e.g.* G. Ellinger, *Geschichte der neulateinischen Literatur Deutschlands in der ersten Hälfte des 16. Jahrhunderts II: Die neulateinische Lyrik Deutschlands in der ersten Hälfte des sechzehnten Jahrhunderts* (Berlin / Leipzig 1929) 3-23 (8-10 on *Heroides*); I. Gräßer-Eberbach, *Helius Eobanus Hessus. Der Poet des Erfurter Humanistenkreises* (Erfurt 1993) (52-55 on *Heroides*). On *Heroides* see also A. Budzisz, 'Helius Eobanus Hessus' *Heroides* as an example of Renaissance religious elegy', in *Ad litteras. Latin Studies in Honour of J. H. Brouwers*, ed. A. P. Orbán / M. G. M. van der Poel (Nijmegen 2001) 273-81; Eickmeyer, *Der jesuitische Heroidenbrief* (n. 2, above) 151-92; on Hessus' letter *Elisabeth Ludovico marito suo* (with Latin text and German translation) see R. Rener, 'Helius Eobanus Hessus, Heroides IV: "Elisabeth Ludovico marito suo" oder: Die wundersame Einbürgerung des thüringischen Landgrafen in Hessen', in: *Hundert Jahre Historische Kommission für Hessen 1897-1997. Festgabe dargebracht von Autorinnen und Autoren der Historischen Kommission. Erster Teil*, ed. W. Heinemeyer, Veröffentlichungen der Historischen Kommission für Hessen 61 (Marburg 1997) 437-61; on the position of Hessus' letters in their time and with relation to medieval traditions see A. Suerbaum, '"Ovidius christianus": Helius Eobanus Hessus in der Tradition der "Heroides"-Rezeption seit dem Mittelalter', in *Humanismus in der deutschen Literatur des Mittelalters und der Frühen Neuzeit. XVIII. Anglo-German Colloquium Hofgeismar 2003*, ed. N. McLelland / H.-J. Schiewer / S. Schmitt (Tübingen 2008) 89-103.

letters by men, which the poet justifies in the dedicatory letter by Ovid's precedent (16.1).[6] These are the first letter, a letter from Emmanuel to Mary (*Emmanuel Mariae*),[7] answered immediately by the Virgin Mary, and the last letter, from Hessus himself to Posterity (*Eobanus Posteritati*). Hessus thus adopts not only the model of Ovid's single *Heroides*, but also that of the paired ones (moving the pair to the front). He also includes the motif of a personal *sphragis* in the style of Ovid's exile letters in *Tristia* into a collection inspired by *Heroides*; in this final poem Hessus reflects upon his relationship to the current emperor, as Ovid does in his exile poetry.

The full title of *Heroidum Christianarum Epistolae* describes Hessus' work as an *Opus novitium*, and in the dedicatory letter Hessus explains that he has written these poems since he did not see any other poet exerting himself in this genre (9.1).[8] He thereby continues a claim of Ovid, who describes his epistles as something novel in *Ars amatoria* (Ov. *Ars* 3.345-46).[9] However, due to Ovid's work, the 'novelty' in Hessus' case is of a different

---

[6] Hessus, *Her. Chr.*, dedicatory letter 16.1: *Hoc quoque pium lectorem admonitum volo, mirum nec esse nec videri debere, si prima et ultima epistolae non heroidum sed heroum potius denominationem sibi vendicare videntur, nihil iccirco principaliori heroidum appellationi officere, cum etiam (ut philosophi dicunt) a principaliori soleat fieri denominatio, et Ovidium idem in Paride, Leandro, et Acontio fecisse constet.* – 'There is one other thing to which I wish to draw the gentle reader's attention: namely, that it ought neither to be nor to seem strange if the first and last letters do not appear to fit the category "letters from heroines" but rather "letters from heroes". But that is no reason to stop me from using the predominant designation "letters from heroines", since (as the philosophers say) denomination is customarily based on preponderance. Besides, it is common knowledge that Ovid did the same thing with respect to Paris, Leander, and Acontius' (trans. Vredeveld, slightly adapted).

[7] In the second edition 'Emmanuel' has been changed to 'God the Father' (*Her. Chr.* 1.1 *Deus pater Mariae virgini*; 1.2 *Maria virgo Deo patri*). – Letters from Heaven constituted a popular genre since late antiquity throughout the Middle Ages and into the early modern period, though these seem to have been more concerned with theological doctrines (see B. Schnell, 'Himmelsbrief', in *Die deutsche Literatur des Mittelalters. Verfasserlexikon. Band 4*. 2nd ed. (Berlin / New York 1983) 28-33).

[8] Hessus, *Her. Chr.*, dedicatory letter 9.1: *Causa scribendarum epistolarum ea potissimum fuit, quod videbam ea in re nullum hactenus poetarum admodum elaboravisse, indignum ratus omnem ingenii florem in prophanis quibusdam ac frivolis occupationibus desumere* – 'What moved me in particular to write heroic epistles was the realization that none of our poets thus far had bothered with this material to any extent. Frankly, I was shocked to see all the choicest talent squandered on certain profane and frivolous subjects' (trans. Vredeveld).

[9] Ov. *Ars* 3.345-46: *vel tibi composita cantetur 'Epistula' voce;* | *ignotum hoc aliis ille novavit opus.* – 'or let some Letter be read by you with practised utterance; he first invented this art, unknown to others' (trans. J. H. Mozley / G. P. Goold).

nature, apart from the fact that there were previous experiments in Italian NeoLatin poetry, though they do not amount to an entire book of such epistles.[10]

The claim to novelty does not mean Hessus ignores Ovid; on the contrary, he acknowledges him as a model, stating that in the Christian letters he has not so much imitated as admired Ovid (7.1),[11] which suggests a flexible relationship to the classical poet. Since out of Hessus' two letters by male writers only one is part of a pair and the other, the 'Letter to Posterity', is not an ordinary letter between lovers, he has deviated from the paradigm adduced for justification. But what Hessus stresses as a feature distinguishing his work from classical poetry is its Christian character (9; 12). In an opening epigram, entitled *Hessi de se eulogium*, he even asserts that the classical poets should give way to him who is presenting a 'nobler theme'.[12]

While these letters established Hessus' renown as a poet, there was apparently also criticism that they included matters not attested in the Bible, which can be inferred from the introduction to the second edition, published in 1539. For this edition Hessus omitted three

---

[10] The writings by Giovanni Antonio de' Pandoni, called Porcellius (*c.* 1405-85?) and Basinio da Parma (*c.* 1425-57) included poetic letters; however, these were only printed in 1539 (*Trium poetarum elegantissimorum, Porcellij, Basinij, & Trebani opuscula, nunc primùm diligentia eruditissimi viri Christophori Preudhomme Barroducani in lucem œdita*, Paris 1539 (http://reader.digitale-sammlungen. de/de/fs1/object/display/bsb10190444_00013.html)) and could therefore have only reached Germany in manuscript form by the time Hessus was starting on the *Heroides* (see Ellinger, *Geschichte* (n. 5, above) 8; Dörrie, *Der heroische Brief* (n. 2, above) 371). Before Hessus there were, however, examples in prose such as Petrarch's *Epistola Posteritati*. Equally, Baptista Spagnuolo Mantuanus (1447-1516), with *Parthenice*, describing the lives of Mary and Christian saints in epic style, and Jakob of Gouda or Jacobus Magdalius Gaudensis (*c.* 14501520) could be regarded as forerunners in terms of poetic subject matter. Verbal similarities (in the letters by Emmanuel and Mary) to phrases in Mantuanus' *Parthenice* and also Venantius Fortunatus' poems, which include a letter by a nun to her groom Christ (*Carm.* 8.3), suggest that Hessus was familiar with some of these works. In fact, Hessus mentions Baptista Mantuanus in the dedicatory letter, but insists that this poet did not use the same genre and style as himself (*Her. Chr.*, dedicatory letter 15.5). Hessus remains the first to have published a collection of letters by Christian heroines, and he was the first to do so in Germany.

[11] Hessus, *Her. Chr.*, dedicatory letter 7.1-2: *Ut igitur redeam unde digressus sum, Praesul optime: scripsi Heroidas has Christianas numero omnino vigintiquattuor, in quibus scribendis Ovidium Nasonem non tam imitatus quam admiratus sum. Illud enim assequi, hoc praetermittere nunquam potui.* – 'Well then, to return to the point from which I digressed, best of bishops: I have written twenty-four of these Christian heroides all told. In composing them I did not so much imitate Ovidius Naso as admire him. For the former is something I could achieve; the latter is something I could never neglect' (trans. Vredeveld, slightly adapted) – See also below on *Her. Chr.* 24.133-34.

[12] Hessus, *Her. Chr.*, *Hessi de se eulogium*: *Sunt quibus omne iocis teritur iuvenilibus aevum | Musaque servandos perdit inepta dies. | At mea, cui debet, Christo devota iuventa est. | Huic ero devotus, si volet ipse, senex. | Cedite gentiles meritis, non arte poetae. | Materia vates nos meliore sumus.* – 'There are poets who fritter away their whole life in puerile trifles, while their fatuous Muse squanders the days that ought to be put to good use. As for me, my youth is devoted to Christ, to whom it belongs. To him, if he so wishes, I'll remain devoted in my old age. Give place, heathen poets, in merit, not art. I am a bard with a nobler theme' (trans. Vredeveld, slightly adapted) – The notion that a Christian version is 'nobler' (*melior*) than the Ovidian text also appears in Neo-Latin versions of *Fasti*, for instance in Ambrogio Novidio Fracco, *Sacrorum fastorum libri duodecim* (1547) (1.139-40: *pone metum vates, melioris conditor anni, | Dictaque percipias, me referente, mea.*; on this piece see Miller in this volume).

letters and arranged the others in three books according to the level of 'fiction': a first book of 'historical' letters, *i.e.* of those whose contents were based on the Bible, a second one of 'mixed' letters, in which letters of that type were combined with others whose substance was taken from other sources, and a third one of 'fictional' letters, whose stories do not have a direct connection with the Bible. Still, Hessus emphasizes in the introductory piece that even the stories in the letters of that category are not so 'false' that they could not appear to be true or even be true if some details were removed.[13]

Besides, although the Christian content was important to Hessus, the collection is still a literary endeavour, which also includes, in line with Ovid's precedent, play with unusual

---

[13] See dedicatory letter (1539), vv. 45-64: *Responsura habiles contraximus omnia ad artus | Forma prior castis non satis apta fuit | Ordine deinde alio discretas ire puellas | Iussimus, et proprium quamque tenere locum | Namque ita confuse prius et sine legibus ibant | Ut foret incerti gratia nulla chori | At mea nunc triplici discrimine turba puellae | Audaces populo plena theatra petunt | Prima loco positas vulgo subsellia praebent | Quas Evangelii littera testis habet | Alter habet mistas vero falsoque sorores | Tertius (ut fama est) omnia falsa locus. | Non ita falsa tamen nequeant ut vera videri | Veraque si quaedam dempseris esse queant. | Nam rudis historiae mala somnia miscuit aetas | Diraque pro vero corpore monstra tulit | Sic mihi mista tamen genus hoc sunt omnia veris | Ut prodesse magis quàm nocuisse queant | Qui prius ergo vagi fuerant et in ordine nullo | Iam fiunt ista tres <–> ratione libri.* – 'I condensed everything that agreed with one another into a structure easy to handle. The earlier format was not sufficiently suitable for the chaste <maidens>. Then I ordered the girls to move in a different order, separated from one another, and each to occupy her own place. For previously they moved in such a confused manner and without any rules that there was no charm for this vague group. But now my group, divided into three, the girls boldly rush to the theatres full of people. The first benches offer the people <maidens> located there for whom the gospel is a witness. The second place houses sisters mixed with respect to what is true and false. The third place (as rumour has it) has only falsehoods. Yet they are not so false that they cannot appear to be true and can be true if you take away some details. For raw antiquity has mixed bad dream appearances with historical truth and brought forth terrible monsters instead of true bodies. But I have mixed everything with regard to this genre with truth in such a way that it can benefit more than do harm. Thus, those <books> that had been without purpose and with no order, thereby have now become three books.' – Yet adherence to 'Christian truth' is already emphasized in the introduction to the first edition (Hessus, *Her. Chr.*, dedicatory letter 14.1-3: *..., si hoc unum addidero, argumenta videlicet epistolarum omnino me ad sacrae historiae veritatem composuisse. Qua in re Gregorium, Hieronymum, Augustinum, Eusebium, et alios quam plures Christianae veritatis verissimos adsertores imitatus sum, quibus non minorem fidem habere Christianum quemque decet quam Graecos Herodoto, Philostrato, Thucididi, et Latinos Livio, Salustio, Valerio, et aliis. Quod si quis futurus est qui dicet in Halcione, Catharina, Elisabetha, et aliis quibusdam historiam intervertisse, meminerit is, queso, nihil tam esse alienum a bono poemate quam nudum historiae filum et rei gestae sine poeticis quibusdam velut parergis additis, contextum simplicem quod ipsum Lucano, non incelebri alioqui Civilium bellorum scriptori, pene poetici nominis palmam abstulisse quidam adserunt.* – '..., if I may add only this one point: namely, that in working out the storylines for these letters I have faithfully adhered to the truth of sacred history. In this matter I have followed the example of Gregory, Jerome, Augustine, Eusebius, and a great many other thoroughly reliable champions of Christian truth, in whom every Christian ought to place no less trust than the Greeks did in Herodotus, Philostratus, and Thucydides, and the Romans in Livy, Sallust, Valerius, among others. But if some future reader objects that in "Alcyone", "Catherine", "Elizabeth", and a few other letters I have tempered with the story, he should please remember that nothing is so alien to a good poem as the bare thread of historical events, without the addition, so to speak, of some poetic embroideries – a plain style of writing that in the opinion of certain critics is almost enough by itself to strip Lucan, the otherwise not undistinguished chronicler of the Civil Wars, of the honorable title of poet' (trans. Vredeveld, slightly adapted).

writing situations and conscious references to other classical writers. Ovid's status as a model does not lead to a large number of direct verbal reminiscences of Ovid's *Heroides*; instead similarities more frequently consist in shared motifs and structures. Nevertheless, it is clear throughout that Hessus makes use of Ovid's works at key points, often with telling twists, so that allusions acquire a changed meaning in a new context.[14]

For instance, the second letter of the collection in the first edition, Mary's reply to the letter from Emmanuel, begins with a verbal reference to Ovid's *Heroides*. The opening couplet *Quam sine te non est tellus habitura salutem,* | *Ut partam per me possit habere, veni.* – 'The salvation that the world cannot have without you, so that it can have it born by me, come!' (2.1-2) is structurally reminiscent of the beginning of *Heroides* 4 (Phaedra to Hippolytus) and 19 (Hero to Leander).[15] The first line of both these Ovidian poems begins with *quam* and ends with *salutem*, and in the second case the second line also ends with *veni*. Ovid, as he often does, employs *salutem* as part of the conventional greeting formula and creates a pun on this basis; in the context it means 'greeting' or 'welfare'. In Hessus it could seem at first glance as if *salutem* was just part of a conventional greeting formula; however it turns out that the word has the Christian spiritual meaning 'salvation' and thereby indicates the letter's religious tone. This is emphasized by the introductory line of Mary's letter which refers back to the similarly structured opening of the preceding letter from Emmanuel to her (1.1).[16] Against this background, Mary's wish that the addressee should come takes on a special meaning: it is not intended that the lover should come back, as in the Ovidian epistle, but that Christ may come into the world.[17]

While a woman answering a man, as Mary replies to a letter from Emmanuel, has a precedent in Ovid, there is a significant difference: the two correspondents are not separated, and their relationship is not characterized by heterosexual love.[18] Instead a (future) mother

---

[14] For a collection of passages from classical poets Hessus might be alluding to see the notes in Vredeveld, *The Poetic Works* (n. 5, above).

[15] Ov. *Her.* 4.1-2: *quam nisi tu dederis, caritura est ipsa, salutem* | *mittit Amazonio Cressa puella viro.* – 'With wishes for the welfare which she herself, unless you give it her, will ever lack, the Cretan maid greets the hero whose mother was an Amazon'; 19.1-2: *quam mihi misisti verbis, Leandre, salutem* | *ut possim missam rebus habere, veni!* – 'That I may enjoy in very truth the greeting you have sent in words, Leander, O come!' (trans. (here and in what follows) G. Showerman / G. P. Goold).

[16] Hessus, *Her. Chr.* 1.1-2: *Quam legis, aeternam rebus paritura salutem,* | *Non est mortali littera facta manu.* – 'The letter you are reading, O you who are about to give birth to eternal salvation for the world, this letter was not written by a mortal hand' (trans. Vredeveld, slightly adapted).

[17] On these connections see also Eickmeyer, *Der jesuitische Heroidenbrief* (n. 2, above) 162, 167-68. – A similar modification of meaning in a play with conventional epistolary formulae can be found at the end of the two letters (Hessus, *Her. Chr.* 1.207-08; 2.127-28; *cf.* also Budzisz, 'Helius Eobanus Hessus' (n. 5, above) 279). – That *nuncius ales* – 'winged messenger' (2.54) has become an angel, rather than Ovid's Mercury (Ov. *Her.* 16.68: *nuntius ales* – 'winged herald'; 16.62: *Atlantis magni Pleionesque nepos* – 'grandchild of mighty Atlas and Pleione') is a common transposition of classical concepts into a Christian world. The reaction is the same in both cases (2.63: *obstupui* – 'I felt paralyzed'; Ov. *Her.* 16.67: *obstipui* – 'I was mute').

[18] The mention of *thalamus* in Emmanuel's letter carries a different meaning in this religious context (1.147-48: *"Hic meus ardor erit," dixi, "meus ignis in illa.* | *Haec est in thalamos digna venire meos."* – ' 'She will be my true flame', I said. 'My fire will burn in her. She is worthy of coming into my chamber' (trans. Vredeveld, slightly adapted)).

answers a letter by her son who is not yet born. The non-reality of this situation can only be explained on a religious level, which assumes that the son has a higher status than (the human) Mary despite her own saintly position.

In Hessus the respective positions of mother and son are clear from the start by means of a motif from the letter by the Ovidian Briseis to Achilles: Briseis excuses the clumsiness of her letter due to her barbarian background and her limited knowledge of Greek, and the stains on the letter due to her tears (Ov. *Her.* 3.1-4).[19] Mary excuses the substandard writing because the letter is written by a mortal with a shaky hand (2.3-5). This explanation at the beginning corresponds with Emmanuel's opening statement that this letter was not written by a mortal hand (1.2).

Taken as a whole, Emmanuel's opening letter sets out the parameters: even prior to the appearance of the angel Gabriel, whose impending arrival he announces (1.161-62). Hessus has Emmanuel tell Mary that she, a virgin, will give birth to a child who is already inside her. He has Emmanuel predict the birth in cold winter under a humble roof amid hay and straw, as well as the adoration of the magi and the flight to Egypt (1.95-128). With respect to the particular form of conception, Emmanuel distances himself from *imprudens ... vetustas* (1.151), which created stories such as those of Danae and Leda; he insists that 'we are better minded' (1.149-52).[20] Still the framework within which Hessus has Emmanuel argue remains based on the ancient world: for instance, the souls of miserable people are located in Tartarus (1.38), or Satan is referred to as 'Stygian Jupiter' (1.180). At the same time Emmanuel has a historical distance, when he makes a comprehensive judgement on the period of Augustus, during which he will be born (1.169-74). Potential doubts from Mary on what will happen to her are brushed away with the comment that with him, who has all the power, everything can be done easily (1.3334).[21] With a distinct reference to Virgil's *Eclogue* 4 (4.4), Emmanuel promises that with his birth the last of the ages prophesied by the Cumaean Sibyl will arrive (1.19798).[22]

---

[19] Ov. *Her.* 3.1-4: *quam legis, a rapta Briseide littera venit, | vix bene barbarica Graeca notata manu. | quascumque adspicies, lacrimae fecere lituras; | sed tamen et lacrimae pondera vocis habent.* – 'From stolen Briseis is the writing you read, scarce charactered in Greek by her barbarian hand. Whatever blots you shall see, her tears have made; but tears, too, have none the less the weight of words'.

[20] Hessus, *Her. Chr.* 1.149-52: *Sed neque caelesti descendam tectus in auro | Nec mihi mentitus suscipietur olor. | Qualiter imprudens mentita est cunque vetustas | Viderit, ingenio nos meliore sumus.* – 'But when I come into the world, I will neither conceal myself in a shower of gold nor will I disguise myself in the form of a swan. For whatever it is that foolish antiquity may have seen, it played fast and loose with the truth. We are better minded.' (trans. Vredeveld) (*cf.* 2.49-50) – See also Budzisz, 'Helius Eobanus Hessus' (n. 5, above) 279; Eickmeyer, *Der jesuitische Heroidenbrief* (n. 2, above) 164-65.

[21] Hessus, *Her. Chr.* 1.33-34: *Nec dubita. Qui cuncta potest, id posse necesse est, | Et facile est nasci virgine matre Deo.* – 'Do not doubt it. He who can do everything, necessarily can do this. And for God it is easy to be born of a virgin mother' (trans. Vredeveld, slightly adapted).

[22] Hessus, *Her. Chr.* 1.197-98: *Ultima tunc veniet Cumaei carminis aetas, | Verus ut incauto spiritus ore canit.* – 'Then will arrive "the last era of Cumaean prophecy," as the true spirit sings from an unsuspecting mouth' (trans. Vredeveld, slightly adapted – *cf.* Virg. *Ecl.* 4.4: *ultima Cumaei venit iam carminis aetas* – 'Now is come the last age of the song of Cumae' (trans. H. Rushton Fairclough).

While it has often been remarked in respect to Ovid's *Heroides* that in the situations of those women letters do not make sense, a letter to Christ as an answer is even more useless, practically speaking, since he is envisaged as omniscient and has just informed Mary of the events she reflects upon in her letter. Accordingly, Mary voices the futility of her efforts towards the end: *Sed tibi quid refero, quae me prior omnia nosti?* – 'But why I am reciting this to you, all this that you knew long before I did?' (2.113 (trans. Vredeveld, slightly adapted)). This picks up the exclamation of the Ovidian Deianira in her letter to Hercules: *sed quid ego haec refero? scribenti nuntia venit | fama, virum tunicae tabe periere meae.* – 'But why I am reciting things like these? Even as I write comes rumour to me saying my lord is dying of the poison from my cloak'. (Ov. *Her.* 9.143-44). In Ovid Deianira's consideration means there is no point in recalling past events, since it is too late; it does not indicate a difference in abilities. In Hessus, as Mary explicitly states, the issue is that it is not possible for human beings to write letters to Emmanuel telling him something he does not already know (2.119-22). Still, Mary writes to him, and the remarkable fact that the addressee is within her womb is reinterpreted as an advantage, since he can thus receive the letter immediately (2.123-24).

Nevertheless, Hessus makes Mary react as an 'ordinary' human being when she describes her feelings, after she has read Emmanuel's letter; she uses the words of the Ovidian Medea in her letter to Jason (Ov. *Her.* 12.61),[23] when Medea characterizes her situation prior to her decision to support Jason against her father: *hinc amor, inde timor* (2.10). Yet Mary is sure that Emmanuel will understand her (2.15: *Et facis*), as she is made to say, alluding to a phrase used by Ovid in *Tristia* towards Augustus (Ov. *Tr.* 2.41: *idque facis*). Trusting Christ's forgiveness Mary dares to be audacious: *Audaces venia cogimur esse tua* – 'By your very forgiveness you compel me to be bold'. (2.16 (trans. Vredeveld, slightly adapted)). The value relevant in this context is particularly highlighted by a reference to the Ovidian phrase *audaces facie cogimur esse tua* – 'tis by your charms I am driven to be bold' (Ov. *Her.* 20.54) from Acontius' letter to Cydippe. The change from *facie* to *venia* illustrates it is not physical beauty which Mary later rejects as a factor motivating Christ to be interested in her (2.84-86), but 'forgiveness' which is the essential characteristic of Christ.

After Mary has announced her decision to get rid of all fear in view of God's omnipotence (2.29), she tells Emmanuel about the annunciation by the angel Gabriel and her reaction to the incident (2.33-88). The chronological relationship between Mary receiving Emmanuel's letter and the annunciation it predicted remains open; at any rate Gabriel seems to deliver a separate oral message. Mary gives a self-contained account of events: in the evening she had locked herself into her room and was reading Isaiah's prophecy that a virgin will bear a son (7.14).[24] This made her praise the unknown virgin, and ask God that he should show, as the true God, that he alone could be born of a virgin, in contrast to the stories about Jupiter, who takes on various appearances (2.39-52; *cf.* Ov. *Her.* 17.55-56). At this point the angel Gabriel had appeared, entering through the locked door, clad in white, with golden locks and carrying an olive branch (2.53-74).

---

[23] Ov. *Her.* 12.61: *hinc amor, hinc timor est; ipsum timor auget amorem.* – 'On the one hand was love, on the other, fear; and fear increased my very love.'

[24] In this passage the son is given the name 'Emmanuel' (see also Mt 1.23).

This version of the story includes significant elements of the veneration of Mary in Hessus' time. Whereas in the gospel according to Luke (1.26-38) only few details about the annunciation are given, Hessus elaborates on it in line with traditions developed in texts and works of art depicting the life of the Virgin Mary, on the basis of apocryphal texts. They include (2.35-36; 2.63–64) the locked room as a symbol of virginity, the bolt on the door (first in Bernard of Clairvaux) or Mary's reading of Isaiah out of all Biblical texts (first in Ambrose).[25] In Hessus the Biblical words of the annunciation are reported briefly (2.65-66); since Mary has already been informed by Emmanuel's letter, details are no longer necessary.

Mary's key quality is that she as a virgin gives birth to Christ, which she expresses thus: *Dum loquor, ecce levi velut auctior effluit alvus | Pondere, nec laesi damna pudoris habet!* – 'As I speak, lo, my womb has grown fuller, as if with a slight burden, and yet suffers no damage from violated chastity!' (2.73-74 (trans. Vredeveld, slightly adapted)). The phrase *laesi ... pudoris* recalls the words of Ovid's Dido in connection with her selfreproaches because of the unfaithfulness towards her former husband Sychaeus: *exige, laese pudor, poenas! violate Sychaei* – 'Exact the penalty of me, O purity undone! – the penalty due Sychaeus'. (Ov. *Her.* 7.97). Here the violation of *pudor* refers to disloyalty towards the dead husband rather than to the state of virginity; nevertheless, the reference underlines the significance of *pudor* for Mary.

That qualities other than physical beauty determine the relationship between Emmanuel and Mary is highlighted by another verbal allusion in *Te mea virginitas, tua me claementia movit* – 'My virginity has moved you, your merciful grace has moved me'. (2.83 (trans. Vredeveld, slightly adapted)), where *virginitas* and *claementia* replace *forma* in the (differently structured) line *inque vicem tua me, te mea forma capit* – 'and your beauty takes me, and mine in turn you' (Ov. *Her.* 17.180) from Helen's letter to Paris.[26] Hessus' verse is part of Mary's considerations after the annunciation, when she ponders why it is she who has been called upon to be the mother of God (2.75-88). Initially she was embarrassed that she herself is the virgin whom she praised. But then she feels justified to take on the task assigned to her since God has selected her (an argument corresponding with Emmanuel's letter, 1.129-48).

In this context Mary calls herself beautiful, but not in the sense of external beauty: *Pulchra tibi mentis facie, pulcherrime rerum, | Quod placui, sed non qualibet arte, iuvat.* – 'To you I am beautiful in the countenance of my soul, O most beautiful of beings. That I pleased you like this, and not by some artifice, is a profound joy'. (2.85-86 (trans. Vredeveld)). Therefore it is a happy union, emphasized by the contrast with Ovid's presentation of the disastrous relationship between (the stepmother) Phaedra and (her stepson) Hippolytus, from where the address *pulcherrime rerum* for the male addressee derives, but where it marks the reason for the writing mother's distress: *o utinam nocitura tibi, pulcherrime rerum, | in medio nisu viscera rupta forent!* – 'Ah, would that the bosom which was to work you wrong, fairest of men, had been rent in the midst of its throes!' (Ov. *Her.* 4.125-26).[27]

---

[25] On the textual tradition of details of the annunciation scene see S. Lüken, *Die Verkündigung an Maria im 15. und frühen 16. Jahrhundert. Historische und kunsthistorische Untersuchungen.* Rekonstruktion der Künste 2 (Göttingen 2000) 32-40.

[26] See also Eickmeyer, *Der jesuitische Heroidenbrief* (n. 2, above) 169.

[27] For Mary looking back the addressee personifies qualities (2.100: *Tu mihi tuta quies, tu mihi somnus eras.* – 'You were my safe repose, you my sleep' (trans. Vredeveld)) rather than actual relationships, as Achilles for Briseis (Ov. *Her.* 3.52: *tu dominus, tu vir, tu mihi frater eras* – 'you were my master, you my husband, you my brother').

Mary explicitly refers to Emmanuel's statement in his letter (2.89: *scribis*) that he has always been with her (1.139-48): she has sensed this from an early age (2.89-112). Hence she adorned herself for him, not for the eyes of men: *tibi, non oculis hominum, gestamina sumpsi* – 'for you, not for the eyes of men, I put on ornaments' (2.93 (trans. Vredeveld, slightly adapted)). By contrast, Helen in Ovid, with reference to the judgement of Paris, is content with the eyes of men and is sceptical of divine praise: *contenta est oculis hominum mea forma probari;* | *laudatrix Venus est invidiosa mihi.* – 'My beauty is content to be approved in the eyes of men; the praise of Venus would bring envy on me' (Ov. *Her.* 17.125-26).

By her attention to God Mary says she differed from other girls (presumably alluding to her time as a virgin at the temple) and that God strengthened her intention to remain a virgin even against the wishes of her parents Anna and Joachim. Directly addressing her mother, Mary now promises a powerful grandson and glory for the entire family (2.11112). The details about Mary's childhood, the naming of the parents, the reverence for her mother and the holy family are details of her life which entered mainstream church beliefs from apocryphal notices. For instance, in 1472 Pope Sixtus IV ratified the feast of the Presentation of the Virgin Mary for the Catholic Church, and in 1481 he established a day of remembrance for Saint Anne.

This means that Hessus has Mary mention elements of her life which are linked to sacred events in contemporary church rituals. When in the collection's second edition Hessus includes this letter among those that are 'historical', *i.e.* contain Biblical truths (1.2 *Maria virgo Deo patri*), this agrees with contemporary doctrines of the (Catholic) church. Hessus had engaged closely with Martin Luther's views in the meantime (*cf.* Hessus' *Afflictae Ecclesiae epistola ad Lutherum*), but the emphasis on the Bible as a key source is in line with Luther's tenets. For Hessus there does not seem to be a contradiction between Protestant doctrines and the cult of Mary or between the veneration of saints and humanism.

The problem in transferring the Ovidian model of a correspondence between a pair of separated lovers to an exchange of letters between the mother and the (unborn) child of the Holy Family is addressed by Hessus' Mary at the end of the letter: she justifies her writing to the omniscient Christ by claiming that he enjoys having his deeds praised just as much as receiving sacrifices and that he listens to prayers as well (2.113-22).[28] This functions as a Christian explanation for the kind of correspondence conceived by Hessus, in addition to the fact that the basis is spiritual love.

For educated (humanist) readers Hessus has adopted the set-up as well as words and verse structures from Ovid's *Heroides*, thus indicating the connection to the literary paradigm. The examples discussed show that the allusions, where they occur, are not instances of convenient phrases reused, but that elements are rather re-employed and reinterpreted at important points in the argument to turn these letters into well-crafted religious statements.

---

[28] God's preferences (2.115-16: *Cuncta licet videas, semper licet omnia noris,* | *Saepe tamen dici te tua facta iuvat.* – 'Even though you are all-seeing, even though you are all-knowing, you nevertheless delight in often having your deeds recounted' (trans. Vredeveld)) are described in terms reminiscent of Ovid's remarks on Jupiter (Ov. *Tr.* 2.69-70: *fama Iovi superest: tamen hunc sua facta referri* | *et se materiam carminis esse iuvat* – 'Jupiter has more than enough of glory: yet is he pleased to have his deeds related and himself become the theme of song' (trans. (here and in what follows) A. L. Wheeler / G. P. Goold)).

By means of this poetic technique, for instance, the term *mystica sacra*, which the Ovidian Phyllis applies to the cult of Ceres, by which Demophoon has sworn (Ov. *Her.* 2.42: *et per taediferae mystica sacra deae*), is transferred to Isaiah's prophecies (2.38: *Docta prius tanti mystica sacra viri.*).

Hessus, aware of his innovative achievement, places his own 'Letter to Posterity'[29] at the end of the book with the corresponding self-confidence.[30] The first couplet: *Quam legis, hanc Hessus quondam tibi, diva, reliquit,* | *Ipsa tuo ut legeres tempore, Posteritas.* – 'The letter you are reading, goddess Posterity, Hessus left it to you in days past, so you could read it in your own good time' (24.1-2 (trans. Vredeveld)) looks back to Ovid's opening of this 'autobiography': *ille ego qui fuerim, tenerorum lusor amorum,* | *quem legis, ut noris, accipe posteritas* – 'That thou mayst know who I was, I that playful poet of tender love whom thou readest, hear my words, thou of the after time' (Ov. *Tr.* 4.10.1-2). Both couplets end with the word *posteritas*; however, in Ovid this refers to later generations, while in Hessus' it is an address to personified Posterity.[31] Posterity seems to have fulfilled Hessus' wish for being read!

---

[29] On Hessus' 'Letter to Posterity' see *e.g.* Rener, 'Helius Eobanus Hessus' (n. 5, above) 440-45; K. Enenkel, 'Autobiographisches Ethos und Ovid-Überbietung: Die Dichterautobiographie des Eobanus Hessus', *Neulateinisches Jahrbuch* 2 (2000) 25-38; K. Enenkel, 'In search of fame: selfrepresentation in Neo-Latin humanism', in *Medieval and Renaissance humanism. Rhetoric, representation and reform*, ed. S. Gersh / B. Roest, Brill's Studies in Intellectual History 115 (Leiden / Boston 2003) 93-113 (esp. 104-09); R. J. Weinczyk, *Eoban und Ovid. Helius Eobanus Hessus' Brief an die Nachwelt und Ovids Tristien – Spurensuche in einer Dichterwerkstatt. Mit Abbildungen Joan Mirós*, Kalliope 9 (Heidelberg 2008). Latin text of *Eobanus Posteritati* with German translation and some notes also in H. C. Schnur (ed.), *Lateinische Gedichte deutscher Humanisten. Lateinisch und deutsch. Ausgewählt, übersetzt und erläutert*, RUB 8739-45 (Stuttgart 1966) 210-19, and in W. Kühlmann / R. Seidel / H. Wiegand (eds), *Humanistische Lyrik des 16. Jahrhunderts. Lateinisch und Deutsch*, Bibliothek deutscher Klassiker 146 / Bibliothek der frühen Neuzeit 5 (Frankfurt a.M. 1997) 328-38, 1140-43.

[30] Enenkel ('Autobiographisches Ethos' (n. 29, above) *passim*; 'In Search of Fame' (n. 29, above) 107-08) points out how two different agendas at work in the poem, expressing one's love to the addressed female and surpassing the model in the description of one's life, explain the particular character and chronology of this letter; they both ask for positive presentation, and together they make it possible to include autobiography in a collection of letters to and from heroines.

[31] Because Hessus' letter is part of the collection of *Heroides*, which consists of letters between individuals, a single defined addressee is needed; elevating Posterity to the status of a kind of goddess puts her in line with the Christian heroines, though Hessus is at pains to point out that he does not value her as highly as the Christian God (24.37-46). The beginning of Ovid's second line *quem legis* appears as *quam legis* at the start of Hessus' first line, and the seemingly small change is significant: the emphasis of the first few lines in Ovid is on the writer and his character, whereas in Hessus it is on the letter. The notion of the writer's playfulness in poetry is taken up later in Hessus' letter with the phrase *iuvenilia carmina lusi* (24.113), but the emphasis is different since the activity is connected with age rather than with a subject matter or genre. Towards the end of the letter Hessus confirms that Ovid (with no work specified) has been his model, but, as in the dedicatory letter, he reiterates that he admires Ovid rather than tries to be like him (24.133-34: *His mea Peligni mirari Musa poetae* | *Ingenium potius quam sapere ausa fuit.* – 'In writing these letters, my Muse presumed more to admire the genius of the Pelignian poet than to smack of it' (trans. Vredeveld)).

Eobanus Hessus was not the only humanist who developed variations of Ovid's *Heroides* by introducing new themes. Even before Hessus, the Scottish-born poet Marcus Alexander Bodius (Mark Alexander Boyd, 1562-1601) composed a book of verse epistles based on Ovid's *Heroides*. Nowadays Boyd is mainly remembered for his Scottish sonnet 'Fra bank to bank, fra wood to wood I rin', but in his lifetime and shortly afterwards he was known for his Neo-Latin poetry, and a seventeenth-century scholar even called him 'Naso redivivus'.[32] Over the course of his adventurous life, which took him to France (as a law student and soldier) at a young age, Boyd developed a sound knowledge of the ancient languages and a substantial literary competence. In 1590 Boyd wrote replies to all the single letters in Ovid's *Heroides*, which turns this work into the only complete collection of reply epistles in Latin.[33] Shortly afterwards, in 1592, Boyd produced another work inspired by Ovid's *Heroides*, in which he no longer had himself guided by the figures presented in Ovid and reacted to his poetry, but was inspired just by the form:[34] in *Epistolae Heroides, et Hymni* he wrote, in free imitation, 15 letters by Greek heroines (*e.g.* Atalanta, Antigone, Eurydice, Philomela), the goddess Venus and heroines from early Rome and Rome's subsequent history, such as Rhea Silvia, Lavinia, Sophonisba, Paulina, Julia (daughter of Augustus) and Octavia; none of these women appear in Ovid.[35] As he explains in the preface to the first collection, Boyd believes that Ovid, his preferred elegiac writer, cannot be equalled, hence he does not wish

---

[32] See O. Borrichius (Borch), *Dissertationes academicae de poetis, publicis disputationibus in Regio Hafniensi Lyceo assertae ab anno 1676 ad annum 1681*, Frankfurt 1683: *In Marco Alexandro Bodio Scoto redivivum spectamus Nasonem, ea est in ejusdem epistolis Heroidum lux, candor, dexteritas.* – 'In the Scot Mark Alexander Boyd we see a reborn Naso; such is the light, candour and dexterity in his epistles of Heroines'; see also R. Sibbald, *Scotia Illustrata sive Prodromus Historiae Naturalis*, Edinburgh 1684: *Dein Vir Epistolas Argumento Ovidianis pares. Felix hæc, tenuis, Latina et legitima Elegia.* – 'Then a man with letters equal to those of Ovid as regards content. Happy this slender elegy, in Latin, and as prescribed by the rules of the art' (quoted from Ritter, *Ovidius redivivus* (n. 3, above) 5).

[33] See *e.g.* Dörrie, *Der heroische Brief* (n. 2, above) 104-05, 108. – On Boyd's reply epistles see P. White, *Renaissance postscripts: responding to Ovid's Heroides in sixteenth-century France* (Columbus (Ohio) 2009) 207-15 (Latin text in *Marci Alexandri Bodii Epistolæ Quindecim, quibus totidem Ouidij respondent* (Bordeaux 1590)).

[34] On Boyd's *Heroides* see E. Paleit, 'Sexual and political liberty and neo-Latin poetics: the *Heroides* of Mark Alexander Boyd', *Renaissance Studies* 22.3 (2008) 351-67; Ritter, *Ovidius redivivus* (n. 3, above) (observations on the relationship to Ovid's *Heroides* on 29-55). – For an overview of Boyd's life and works see I. C. Cunningham, 'Marcus Alexander Bodius, Scotus', in *A palace in the wild. Essays on vernacular culture and humanism in Late-Medieval and Renaissance Scotland*, ed. L. A. J. R. Houwen / A. A. MacDonald / S. L. Mapsone, Mediaevalia Groningana (Leuven 2000) 161-74.

[35] For Ovid it would have been difficult to present contemporary women in this fashion (see Cunningham 'Marcus Alexander Bodius, Scotus' (n. 34, above) 163); when Boyd selects women from the Augustan period among others, he creates another link to Ovid on a different level.

108   THE AFTERLIFE OF OVID

to claim to 'bring back' Ovid. At the same time, having 'Ovid before his eyes', Boyd does not intend to write any kind of Latin, rather a kind of Latin based on Ovidian eloquence.[36]

One of the most striking differences between Ovid's *Heroides* and Boyd's second collection is the integration of historical women (in the broadest sense). Among the letters by these women the letter from Julia to her father Augustus (*Her.* 13) is particularly interesting because it also touches on the issue of Ovid's exile.[37] The letter from Julia to Augustus is indebted to Ovid's *Heroides*, since it is a letter from a woman to a man, albeit with the significant difference that the addressee is not the lover, but the father of the writer. Julia sends a letter from her place of exile, where her father, as she narrates, has sent her, cruelly and unjustly. Thus her letter alludes to Ovid's exile poetry, *Tristia* and *Epistulae ex Ponto*, since Julia, like Ovid, laments her exile and suffers from Augustus' wrath. Significantly she uses the words *Cæsaris ira* (13.4), which recall Ovid's words in his exile poetry, where he refers to Augustus' wrath a number of times (*e.g.* Ov. *Tr.* 5.1.41; *Pont.* 1.4.29; also *Pont.* 1.2.87; 1.2.96; 1.8.69-70).

[36] Boyd (n. 33, above) 8: *Sed a te veniam facilius vt impetrem, Lector, si quod imprimis expetebam, Nasonem non refero, & si hoc meum studium nec meo merito obtrectatores invenerit, quasi ego plurium Poëtarum huius sæculi iudicium aspernatus, veteribus me coniunxerim, pernoscant non mihi fas fuisse, qui Ovidium præ oculis ferrem, linguæ Latinæ phrases, quas isti vocant, in Epistolas congerere; nec me in eo totum fuisse, vt quid præter puram, & communem dicendi formam quempiam edocerem; summo vero studio ne aliter, quàm Latinè scriberem præcavisse, & æquabilem hanc Ouidianæ eloquentiæ formam æmulatum feriò; nec aliter licuisse imitari.* – 'But so that I will obtain pardon from you more easily, Reader, if there is anything that I was seeking especially: I do not bring back Naso. And if my endeavour should find detractors without my fault, as if I – scorning the judgement of the majority of poets of this age – was associating myself with the ancients, they shall know that it was not right for me, who was having Ovid before my eyes, to collect any phrases of the Latin language, as they call them, for the Epistles. And that I did not identify with him to such an extent that I put forward anything other than some pure and common way of speaking; but that I took care that I did not write in any other way but in Latin, and I claim that I emulated this style consistent with Ovidian eloquence, and that it was not allowed to imitate in any other way'.

[37] Latin text of all epistles in *M. Alexandri Bodii Epistolæ Heroides, et Hymni. Ad Iacobum sextum Regem. Addita est eiusdem Literularum prima curia.* Antverpae (*i.e.* La Rochelle). M. D. [XC]II. The title page says that the volume was printed in Antwerp; actually it was published in La Rochelle, printed by Jérôme Haultin (for data on the printing house L. Desgraves, *Les Haultin, 1571-1623*, L'Imprimerie à La Rochelle 2 / Travaux d'humanisme et renaissance XXXIV (Genève 1960), including examples of books from 1591 (nos 121, 122) printed in two versions at La Rochelle and at 'Anvers'). Apparently, this was a common practice used by this printing house and a clever way of enabling the publication of non-religious books or books clashing with current religious beliefs at La Rochelle (on the difficulties of publishing non-conformist material at La Rochelle see *e.g.* K. C. Robbins, *City on the ocean sea. La Rochelle, 1530-1650. Urban society, religion, and politics on the French Atlantic frontier*, Studies in medieval and reformation thought 64 (Leiden / New York / Köln 1997) 178-83). Boyd's *Heroides* were reprinted (without the preceding summaries) in *Delitiæ poetarum Scotorum hujus ævi illustrium.* Amsterdami apud Iuhannem Blaev. CIↃ IↃ CXXXVII (Julia's letter on pp. 173-75, with minor differences in spelling and punctuation). – The four letters by Atalanta, Eurydice, Philomela and Venus are available in a modern edition by Ritter, *Ovidius redivivus* (n. 3, above), with German translation and commentary.

Yet in Ovid's *Heroides* too there are complaints about unjust treatment by a cruel father: Canace complains about Aeolus, who sent her a sword as a hint to commit suicide, since she had had a child with her beloved brother (Ov. *Her.* 11); Hypermnestra complains about her father Danaus, who has thrown her into jail after she opposed his order to kill her husband Lynceus, the only one of his daughters to do so (Ov. *Her.* 14). Like Julia in Boyd (13.91-94), both Ovidian women end their letters in resignation,[38] but their letters are sent to the men with whom they have been in a relationship. Boyd, however, has Julia address her father and accuse Augustus from the start.

Just as Ovid has his letter-writing women explain the situation in which they write these epistles, *i.e.* their background story, so does Boyd in Julia's case: she intends to make public what was going on with reference to her alleged crimes, so as to perish with better feelings, as she says at the beginning (13.5-6). Such a starting point to the letter contradicts the fiction that Augustus is the addressee. However, analogous contradictions can be found in Ovid's *Heroides*, for instance, when Dido, in her letter to Aeneas, also addresses Sychaeus (Ov. *Her.* 7.103-11); Hessus too adopts this technique when Mary, in her letter to Emmanuel, turns to her mother Anna (2.111-12). Further, Julia's wish for publicity in Boyd may suggest an underlying political intention. The charges against her, irresponsible way of life and rumours of adultery (13.7-10; *cf.* Tac. *Ann.* 3.24.2; Suet. *Tib.* 11.4; Cass. Dio 55.10.12-13)[39] are explained away as fictions created by a tyrannical ruler. That Augustus was such a tyrant is proved with reference to his abolition of the early Republican order and his behaviour towards Cicero (13.15-20). Boyd has Julia merely indicate these historical events; he apparently presupposes the relevant knowledge among his readers, *i.e.* information derived from the historiographical accounts by Tacitus,

---

[38] Ov. *Her.* 11.127-28: *tu, rogo, dilectae nimium mandata sororis | perfice; mandatis obsequar ipsa patris!* – 'Do thou, I pray, fulfil the behests of the sister thou didst love too well; the behest of my father I shall myself perform!'; 14.123-30: *at tu, siqua piae, Lynceu, tibi cura sororis, | quaeque tibi tribui munera, dignus habes, | vel fer opem, vel dede neci defunctaque vita | corpora furtivis insuper adde rogis, | et sepeli lacrimis perfusa fidelibus ossa, | sculptaque sint titulo nostra sepulcra brevi: | 'exul Hypermestra, pretium pietatis iniquum, | quam mortem fratri depulit, ipsa tulit.'* – 'But do thou, O Lynceus, if thou carest aught for thy sister, and art worthy of the gift I rendered thee, come bear me aid; or, if it please thee, abandon me to death, and, when my body is done with life, lay it in secret on the funeral pile, and bury my bones moistened with faithful tears, and let my sepulchre be graved with this brief epitaph: 'Exiled Hypermnestra, as the unjust price of her wifely deed, has herself endured the death she warded from her brother!'

[39] Tac. *Ann.* 3.24.2: *ut valida divo Augusto in rem publicam fortuna, ita domi improspera fuit ob impudicitiam filiae ac neptis, quas urbe depulit adulterosque earum morte aut fuga punivit. nam culpam inter viros ac feminas vulgatam gravi nomine laesarum religionum ac violatae maiestatis appellando clementiam maiorum suasque ipse leges egrediebatur.* – 'Though the fortunes of Divine Augustus prospered in matters of state, at home they were unfavorable owing to the immorality of the daughter and granddaughter whom he drove from the City, and punished their adulterers with death or banishment. (For in calling their fault – widespread though it is between men and women – by the weighty name of "infringed obligations and violated sovereignty" he thereby exceeded the clemency of our ancestors and his own laws)' (trans. A. J. Woodman); Suet. *Tib.* 11.4: *comperit deinde Iuliam uxorem ob libidines atque adulteria damnatam* ... –'Shortly after this he learned that his wife Julia had been banished because of her immorality and adulteries …' (trans. J. C. Rolfe).

Suetonius, Plutarch and/or Cassius Dio (*e.g.* 13.15-16 vs. Plut. *Cic.* 46.5; 13.5152 vs. Suet. *Aug.* 69.1; see below).

Julia's argument concerning Augustus' tyrannical wrath, which may be caused even by trivial details and was known not only in Rome, but also among the far-away Sauromatae (13.23-24), brings her to Ovid's fate. Since Ovid often talks about being among the Sauromatae in his exile poetry (*e.g.* Ov. *Tr.* 2.197-98; 5.1.74), the geographical designation is a clear signal. When Julia laments Ovid's unjustified exile and the strictness of her father, who was not even mollified by the poem Ovid sent from Tomis (13.25-34), this remark includes a reference to the beginning of Ovid's *Epistulae ex Ponto*: the comment *Quodq; Tomitano mittit tibi litore carmen,* | *Mulceret Stygios lactea vena Deos.* – 'The poem that he sends to you from the shore of Tomis could placate the Stygian Gods with its milky stream' (13.31-32) takes up *Naso Tomitanae iam non novus incola terrae* | *hoc tibi de Getico litore mittit opus* – 'Naso, no recent dweller now in the land of Tomis, sends to you this work from the Getic shore' (Ov. *Pont.* 1.1.1-2; *cf.* also *Tr.* 2.27-28), with an emphasis on the poetry's potential effect. In contrast to Augustus' neglect of Ovid's writings, Julia is made to admit she admired Ovid (13.37-38), whereby her praise of Ovid's poetic art functions as an indirect praise of Ovid by Boyd.

From Ovid's poetic standing the argument moves to his social status: Julia goes on to state that in earlier (Republican) times Ovid would not have been inferior to the rank of her own family (13.39-40). Perhaps this is meant to hint at Suetonius' comment that Augustus initially considered men from the equestrian order as husbands for Julia (Suet. *Aug.* 63.2).[40] Ovid has just been called an 'equestrian poet' in this letter (13.25: *equitis ... poëtæ*), and Ovid mentions this status in his own works (Ov. *Tr.* 2.89-90; 2.11014; 4.10.7-8). However, Julia's words do not imply that the adultery she is accused of is connected with a relationship with Ovid.

Julia even stresses that nobody in the city was more decent than Ovid (13.42), just as Ovid himself distinguishes between life and poetry (Ov. *Tr.* 2.345-58). Nevertheless, this fact seems useless to her, because her father's wrath makes the law disappear (13.43-44). She goes on to mention the charge reported by Ovid that he is a teacher of adultery (Ov. *Tr.* 2.212: *arguor obsceni doctor adulterii*), with the added twist that Julia, following his doctrines, is an adulteress (13.45-46: *Doctor adulterij Naso, cui mœcha volenti* | *Iulia, ...* – 'A teacher of adultery is Naso, for whom, as he wants, Julia is an adulteress, ...'). The general criticism Ovid refers to in *Tristia* is thus exemplified.

Boyd does not make Julia refute any of these reproaches directly. On the contrary, Julia's letter to her father becomes an invective, when she focuses on the contrast between her father's alleged decency (which prompted his actions against Ovid) and his licentious sexual life: Augustus as well as his wife Livia are accused of a lack of chastity (13.4760). In this context Boyd alludes to elements taken from Suetonius, such as the detail that for the purposes of homosexual intercourse Augustus singed the hair on his legs with hot nuts

---

[40] Suet. *Aug.* 63.2: *multis ac diu, etiam ex equestri ordine, circumspectis condicionibus* – 'after considering various alliances for a long time, even in the equestrian order' (trans. J. C. Rolfe).

(13.57-60; *cf.* Suet. *Aug.* 68)[41] or that at a dinner party, in the presence of her husband, he led the wife of an ex-consul away from the dining room and returned her after a sexual encounter (13.51-52; *cf.* Suet. *Aug.* 69.1).[42]

Julia slurs Livia as a partner in Augustus' sexual life in so far as she claims that Livia leads young boys to him (13.47-48). Perhaps for this detail Boyd developed the note in Suetonius (Suet. *Aug.* 71.1) that Livia brought young women to Augustus. In line with the negative picture of Livia sketched by Julia, she juxtaposes the sadness of the aging Livia with her own easy way of dealing with the vicissitudes of life, the only reference to the charge of light-hearted lifestyle and presented as a reason for the exile (13.53-55).

The most personal aspect of the invective follows, when Julia is made to comment bitterly that the (Augustan) *Lex Iulia de adulteriis coercendis* (on the basis of which she was sent into exile) does not apply to the 'king' (13.61-62: *Non tamen exilium metues, lex Iulia regem | Legibus exemit, liber ut unus eat* – 'Yet you will not fear exile; the Julian Law exempts the king from laws, so that he is the only one to walk free'). The term 'king', politically sensitive in ancient Rome, marks the culmination of the view that Julia conveys of her father. Accordingly she laments the disappearance of the old Roman heroism of men like Cassius or the two Bruti (13.63-64). Her defamation of Augustus is enhanced by a comparison between Augustus and Caesar: Augustus is presented as the unjustly honoured pederast and Caesar as the true master, an outstanding politician and general (13.67-80). While Julia initially complains that Rome, the city of Mars, no longer has men such as Cassius and Brutus (13.63-64), Caesar is now singled out with reference to Augustus; with a direct address to personified Rome she notes the inconsistency of Caesar's murder (13.73-74), so that someone as morally depraved as Augustus came to power as a single ruler, since this was a disgrace for the entire nation descended from the Trojans (13.80).

Boyd makes Julia phrase this conclusion to the long lament of her father's moral depravation in a way as if the addressee of the letter was not her father; a few lines earlier Julia has addressed Rome (13.73). Accordingly, in view of the subsequent justification against possible objections that one should not challenge one's father (13.81-82), a broader audience beyond the two correspondents seems to be envisaged. The reason that Julia adduces as an excuse for her procedure is because the father has exiled his daughter: he therefore is no longer a father for her. The wording, *nec / non pater ille mihi*, highlighted by repetition at the beginning and end of a couplet, suggests a public audience (13.83-84: *Nec pater ille mihi, qui me temerauit, & almae | Eripuit patriæ, non pater ille mihi* – 'And he is not a father for me, he who has polluted me and snatched me away from my nourishing country, he is not a father for me').

---

[41] Suet. *Aug.* 68: *solitusque sit crura suburere nuce ardenti, quo mollior pilus surgeret* – 'he used to singe his legs with red-hot nutshells, to make the hair grow softer' (trans. J. C. Rolfe).

[42] Suet. *Aug.* 69.1: *feminam consularem e triclinio viri coram in cubiculum abductam, rursus in convivium rubentibus auriculis incomptiore capillo reductam* – 'taking the wife of an ex-consul from her husband's dining room before his very eyes into a bed-chamber, and bringing her back to the table with her hair in disorder and her ears glowing' (trans. J. C. Rolfe).

Fittingly, Julia moves on to interventions of Roman citizens on her behalf (13.85-86), a historical detail from Cassius Dio's report (Cass. Dio 55.13.1; *cf.* also Suet. *Aug.* 65.3; *Tib.* 11.4): Augustus is said to have answered that fire should sooner mix with water than he would recall Julia, and the inhabitants of Rome threw firebrands into the river. But this was without effect, as Julia states: her father will not surrender his wrath and let her come home (13.87-92).[43] Hence the letter ends with Julia accepting her fate in resignation (13.93-94: *I modo quid lubeat peragas durissime, nos nos | Ibimus immiti quò vocat ira manu* – 'Just carry out what you wish, you very harsh man, we will go wherever your wrath calls us with merciless hand'), in contrast to Ovid, who, in his exile poetry, constantly hopes to assuage the emperor's wrath by his poetry (*e.g.* Ov. *Tr.* 2.27-28: *his precor exemplis tua nunc, mitissime Caesar, | fiat ab ingenio mollior ira meo* – 'Such precedents now form the basis of my prayer, O merciful Caesar, that my poetic gift may assuage thy wrath').

Boyd has clearly taken details from ancient historiographers to flesh out the particular tension between Julia and her father. Yet the strictness of paternal wrath is also a motif in the Ovidian letters by Canace and by Hypermnestra: Canace calls her father *ferus* (Ov. *Her.* 11.9) and considers his unbound wrath (11.15). Hypermnestra characterizes her father as *violentus* (Ov. *Her.* 14.43) and *saevus* (14.53), and she compares his unending wrath with that of Juno towards Io (14.85-108). Such mythological references are lacking in Boyd: he has Julia talk about the father's wrath as a motivation for action, but his wrath and cruelty are placed into the context of Roman politics.

At the same time the revelation of personal mistakes on the father's part calls into question the moral basis for the daughter's punishment. Augustus' sexual behaviour, to which Boyd has Julia allude and which must seem plausible to educated readers of the basis of their knowledge of ancient historiography, gives her entire exposition an air of credibility, while the charges raised against her remain rather general and are not refuted in detail, which agrees with the lack of clarity in the ancient sources. The more general statement that a ruler always finds a reason to act against the weak (13.11-14), the charge that the 'king' can exempt himself from his own laws (13.61-62) and the broader perspective beyond the nominal addressee allow the assumption that Boyd not only has a historical woman from ancient Rome write a letter inspired by Ovid and ancient history, but also makes a political statement.[44] Such a political interest agrees with other writings by Boyd: he produced a work in French entitled *Discours civiles sur le Royaume d'Ecosse*, of which the first book exists, and a short treatise entitled *Politicus* on the qualities of a statesman.[45]

---

[43] Boyd seems to presuppose that Julia's place of banishment is Rhegium on the Italian mainland opposite Sicily (13.55), to where she was moved from Pandataria, the original place of exile (Cass. Dio 55.13.1; Suet. *Aug.* 65.3). According to Cassius Dio this was due to pressure from the people.

[44] Paleit, 'Sexual and political liberty' (n. 34, above) sees a reflection of Boyd's own life in this letter, including his 'exile' in France and criticism of the Scottish king James VI; however, this cannot be verified from what is known about Boyd's life (contra also Ritter, *Ovidius redivivus* (n. 3, above) 56-57 n. 185).

[45] See Cunningham 'Marcus Alexander Bodius, Scotus' (n. 34, above) 164-65.

While the poetic form of the letter and the precise content are the result of the poet's invention, the idea of having Julia write a letter is not as fictional and far-fetched as it may sound, since Tacitus reports in *Annales* that Julia wrote a letter to her father Augustus, full of hatred against Tiberius, her second husband, though Tacitus also mentions that this letter was thought to have been written by Sempronius Gracchus (Tac. *Ann.* 1.53.1-3).[46] At any rate various details to which Boyd has Julia refer show he knew the texts of ancient historians very well.[47] Adaptations of individual Ovidian motifs beyond the overall set-up and general ideas are perhaps found more rarely.

What is dominant is the generic assignment as a letter from a heroine. The nonmythical content may surprise educated readers, but the psychological situation of a desperate woman, who feels that she has been treated unjustly by her father, finds parallels in Ovid's epistles by Canace and Hypermnestra (Ov. *Her.* 11; 14). The transfer of their situations to a prominent historical daughter makes readers view the historical facts, and also Ovid's exile, in a new light. The adaptation to the historical situation means that the letter can no longer be addressed to a loving man. Since love is not relevant in Julia's letter and because of the clear allusions to Ovid's exile poetry, it has been suggested that Boyd intended this letter to be seen as an exile poem like those of Ovid.[48] Even though there are reminiscences of those Ovidian works, due to the similarity of the situation, Boyd has included this piece in a collection of letters from heroines and hence clearly intended it to be set against Ovid's *Heroides* as the main framework of reference.

---

[46] Tac. *Ann.* 1.53.1-3: *eodem anno Iulia supremum diem obiit, ob impudicitiam olim a patre Augusto Pandateria insula, mox oppido Reginorum, qui Siculum fretum accolunt, clausa. fuerat in matrimonio Tiberii florentibus Gaio et Lucio Caesaribus spreveratque ut imparem; nec alia tam intima Tiberio causa cur Rhodum abscederet. imperium adeptus extorrem, infamem et post interfectum Postumum Agrippam omnis spei egenam inopia ac tabe longa peremit, obscuram fore necem longinquitate exilii ratus. par causa saevitiae in Sempronium Gracchum, qui familia nobili, sollers ingenio et prave facundus, eandem Iuliam in matrimonio Marci Agrippae temeraverat. nec is libidini finis: traditam Tiberio pervicax adulter contumacia et odiis in maritum accendebat; litteraeque, quas Iulia patri Augusto cum insectatione Tiberii scripsit, a Graccho compositae credebantur.* – 'In the same year Julia passed her final day, who for her immorality had formerly been shut away by her father Augustus on the island of Pandateria, then subsequently in the town of the Regini who live near the Sicilian strait. She had been in a marriage to Tiberius while Gaius and Lucius Caesar flourished, and had spurned him as her inferior; and no other reason was so close to Tiberius' heart for his withdrawal to Rhodes. Once he acquired command, he ensured the annihilation of the outcast by deprivation and protracted atrophy, disgraced as she was and (after the killing of Postumus Agrippa) destitute of all hope, deeming that her execution would be obscured by the length of her exile. There was a similar reason for his savagery against Sempronius Gracchus, who, from a noble family, skillful in intellect and prevaricatingly fluent, had defiled the same Julia during her marriage to Marcus Agrippa. Nor was that the limit of the man's lust: when she was passed to Tiberius, the persistent adulterer inflamed her with a truculent hatred for her husband; and the letter which Julia wrote to her father Augustus, with its assault on Tiberius, was believed to have been composed by Gracchus' (trans. A. J. Woodman).

[47] From Boyd's instruction for teaching and aspiring poets it is clear that he was familiar with a wide range of ancient authors and that he regarded knowledge of ancient literature as an important precondition (see Cunningham 'Marcus Alexander Bodius, Scotus' (n. 34, above) 166; Ritter, *Ovidius redivivus* (n. 3, above) 76-77; for a list of ancient authors mentioned in Boyd's works see Cunningham 'Marcus Alexander Bodius, Scotus' (n. 34, above) 173-74).

[48] Thus Ritter, *Ovidius redivivus* (n. 3, above) 56.

If one compares the two letters by heroines, by Mary and by Julia, it is obvious that in these epistles Hessus and Boyd have imitated and developed the Ovidian model each in their own and thus different ways. Despite the changes, just like Hessus' direct comments in the paratexts to his collection, Boyd's letter implies admiration for Ovid when he makes Julia praise Ovid's poetry. Not all the letters by Hessus and by Boyd share exactly the same characteristics, but those from Mary and from Julia show how humanist poets were able to exploit the potential and the structures found in Ovid's epistles. The combination of Ovidian letters from heroines with new content has found successors in both areas explored by the two poets: Hessus' introduction of religious elements was taken up in Jesuit poetry,[49] and further letters by historical women followed after Boyd's example.[50]

While Hessus presents Mary's letter as a literary immersion in faith, Julia in Boyd voices political beliefs going beyond her personal fate. At the same time both poets present their topics in a very detailed and sophisticated form, and because many aspects are only hinted at, the same command of material is expected from readers: in the letters that he has Emmanuel and Mary write, Hessus assumes familiarity with the complex theological construction of the virgin birth as well as of circumstantial details at the birth of Christ (with the cold night clearly based on conventions in his home country); Boyd expects historical knowledge, often evoking the entire context by mere allusions. In some ways the Neo-Latin poets thus adopt poetic techniques of Ovid, who demands extensive mythological knowledge of his readers. However, in contrast to *Heroides*, the insertion of Christian or historical material into the Ovidian form of a letter, written by a woman in love and/or in despair to a beloved male, makes the feelings of the woman as a topic recede into the background. Hence in both letters the basic emotions of the writers remain relatively straightforward.

That the addressees of the letters are no longer the lovers of the women and thus a basic component of Ovid's structure has been given up is a precondition or a result of the novel combination. This can be seen as a depravation of the Ovidian basis or as an artistic and imaginative further development, which might have delighted Ovid.

University College London

---

[49] For examples see Eickmeyer, *Der jesuitische Heroidenbrief* (n. 2, above).

[50] For examples see Ritter, *Ovidius redivivus* (n. 3, above) 66-67.

ET PER OMNIA SAECULA IMAGINE VIVAM:
THE COMPLETION OF A FIGURATIVE CORPUS
FOR OVID'S *METAMORPHOSES* IN FIFTEENTH- AND
SIXTEENTH-CENTURY BOOK ILLUSTRATIONS*

FÁTIMA DÍEZ-PLATAS

1. Introduction

Almost in the same way as the consideration of Ovid himself as a poet has been subjected to several changes through time, Ovid's *Metamorphoses* has suffered several transformations since it was written. It is clear that before the restoration of the philological purity of the text, *Metamorphoses* has rarely been considered as an autonomous and unitary poem, because it incorporated multiple stories and episodes whose intertwined structure had been deliberately conceived by the poet. Despite the *carmen perpetuum*, an awareness of the individuality of the stories and the necessary functional division of the long poem in separate books has become evident in the constant tendency to subsume unity to multiplicity, whereby the unitary poem is reduced to episodes, moments and figures.[1] This tendency, while revealing the deep structure of the composition of Ovid's work, transformed the poem into an enormous archive into which hundreds of separate elements of world knowledge, antiquity, and myth could be deposited and ordered.[2] If Ovid's poetry may be reduced to episodes, moments, or even atomized into figures, as has been shown in the kind of transformation-explanation that entails the *Argumenta* attributed to Lactantius,[3] the image responds adequately by establishing a meaningful relationship with the text and with the knowledge of the readers. It can be

---

I wish to thank Peter Mack and John North for inviting me to share my approaches on the illustration of Ovid, the Warburg Institute for the immense opportunity for the research, and Patricia Meilán for all the shared study on Ovid editions. This article is part of the results of the research project BIBLIOTECA DIGITAL OVIDIANA: Las ediciones ilustradas de Ovidio. Siglos XV al XIX (III): Las bibliotecas de Castilla y León (HAR2011-25853) funded by the Spanish Ministry of Economy and Competitiveness. Finally, I ought to apologize to Ovid himself for having manipulated the last two lines of the *Metamorphoses*, changing the *fama* to *imago*, to express my intention of exploring his survival through the figurative corpus created to illustrate his works.

[1] H. Cazes, 'Les bonnes fortunes d'Ovide au XVIème siècle', in *Lectures d'Ovide, publiées à la mémoire de Jean-Pierre Néraudau*, ed. E. Bury, M. Néraudau (Paris, 2003) 239-64 (263-64).

[2] B. Ribémont, 'L'*Ovide moralisé* et la tradition encyclopédique médiévale', *Cahiers de recherches médiévales* 9, *Lectures et usages d'Ovide* (2002) (Online edition. Accessed: 03/01/2013: URL: http://crm.revues.org/907), L. Bolzoni, *La stanza della memoria. Modelli letterari e iconografici nell'età della stampa* (Torino, 1995) specially the chapter on the illustrated book.

[3] A. Cameron, *Greek Mythography in the Roman World* (Oxford, 2004) chapters 1-4.

argued, then, that the sets of images which have accompanied, since the Middle Ages, the various editions and versions of *Metamorphoses* have reacted to the value assigned to the poem at each particular time.[4]

Certainly, one of the clearest responses to the significance of the Ovidian text is represented by the figurative explosion which took place in the fourteenth century in the allegorized and moralized Ovidian versions, namely in the first French *Ovide moralisé* manuscripts.[5] It has often been noted that the diffusion of Ovid's work was facilitated by the accessibility of the translated and moralized text, which was transformed into a compendium of cases with figures shaped into the mould of stories, safely Christianized and closely related to the equally moralized Bible. Thus its transformation brought on the creation of a *corpus* of 'transvestite' images concealing the Ovidian stories and figures. The evident benefits of this process for the knowledge and diffusion of the figure and the work of Ovid had its counterpart in the acquisition of a handful of non-Ovidian inputs,

---

[4] On the illustration of the *Metamorphoses* in the Middle Ages, *cf.* G. Orofino, 'Ovidio nel Medioevo: l'iconografia delle *Metamorfosi*', in *Aetates Ovidianae. Lettori di Ovidio dall'Antichità al Rinascimento*, ed. I. Gallo, L. Nicastri (Salerno, 1995) 189-208, and C. Lord, 'A survey of imagery in medieval manuscripts of Ovid's *Metamorphoses* and related commentaries', in *Ovid in the Middle Ages*, ed. J. G. Clark, F. T. Coulson, K. L. McKinley (Cambridge, 2011) 257-83. For the study of the illustrated editions of Ovid the starting point are still G. Duplessis, *Essai bibliographique sur les différentes éditions des oeuvres d'Ovide ornées de planches publiées aux XVe et XVIe siècles* (Paris, 1889) and M. D. Henkel, 'Illustrierte Ausgaben von Ovids Metamorphosen im XV, XVI und XVII Jahrhundert', *Vorträge der Bibliothek Warburg* (19261927) 53-144. On the illustration of Ovid see also N. Llewellyn, 'Illustrating Ovid', in *Ovid renewed: Ovidian influences on literature and art from the Middle Ages on the twentieth century*, ed. C. Martindale (Cambridge, 1988); *Der verblümte Sinn: Illustrationen zu den Metamorphosen des Ovid*, ed. Kräubig, G. Bickendorf (Kornwestheim, 1997); G. Huber-Rebenich, *Metamorphosen der 'Metamorphosen': Ovids Verwandlungssagen in der textbegleitenden Druckgraphik.* (Rudolstadt, 1999), and F. Díez-Platas, 'Tres maneras de ilustrar a Ovidio: una aproximación al estudio iconográfico de las *Metamorfosis* figuradas del XVI' in *Memoria Artis*, ed. Mª C. Folgar, A. Goy, J. M. López, 2 vols (Santiago de Compostela, 2003) I 247-67. Two projects on the illustration of Ovid in the Internet are also to be taken in consideration: *Ovid Illustrated: The Reception of Ovid's Metamorphoses in Image* and *Text* (http://ovid.lib.virginia.edu/about.html) and *Biblioteca Digital Ovidiana. Ediciones ilustradas de Ovidio (Siglos XV al XIX)* (www.ovidiuspictus.eu).

[5] Eleven of the 23 manuscripts of the *Ovide moralisé* in verse are illuminated, and the so-called *Ovide moralisé* in prose is also in four illuminated manuscripts (C. Lord, 'Three manuscripts of the *Ovide Moralisé*', *The Art Bulletin* 57, 2 (1975) 161-75). The Latin moralization of the poem by Pierre Bersuire (*Petrus Berchorius*) known as *Ovidius moralizatus* is preserved in some 60 manuscripts, only three of which are illuminated (C. Lord, 'Illustrated manuscripts of Berchorius before the age of printing', in *Die Rezeption der 'Metamorphosen' des Ovid in der Neuzeit: der antike Mythos in Text und Bild*, ed. H. Walter, H.-J. Horn, Ikonographische Repertorien zur Rezeption des antiken Mythos in Europa 1 (Berlin, 1995) 1-11). See also *Ovide métamorphosé. Les lecteurs médiévaux d'Ovide, études réunies*, ed. L. Harf-Lancner, L. Mathey-Maille, M. Szkilnik (Paris, 2009) and the contributions of M. Cavagna, S. Cerrito, F. Clier-Colombani, I. FabryTehranchi, W. Göbbels at *Les Archives de littérature du Moyen Âge* (*ARLIMA*, www.arlima.net/index.html).

overlapping additions, and allegorical senses which stuck in a lasting way to Ovid's works and offered a different vision of the myths.[6]

The response of the image, then, was subsumed under the hypertrophic development of the text, and consequently the sets of images created for these illuminated texts reached more than three hundred illustrations, among which can be found, apart from the Biblical images, a complete set of representations of the episodes, moments, and figures of the poem, presented under a more restrained and contemporary raiment.[7] Undoubtedly, it was this profuse response of the image to the transformation which moralization entailed, which gave to the Ovid illustrations a history worth telling. Furthermore, this response resulted in the completion of the first repertoire of images of the mythical stories contained in *Metamorphoses*; a set of images which will be transformed in later figurative interventions.

2. Selecting images for Ovid in the age of printing: the illustrated incunabula of Metamorphosis *and the relationship between the image and the book*

Certainly, this visual corpus generated in the Middle Ages in the context of the enlarged and altered texts of the moralizations, experienced a significant redefinition with the introduction of the printing press, due to the changes in the structure of the books as well as to the obvious effect of multiplication and diffusion of texts.[8] In the last quarter of the fifteenth century Ovid was extensively published,[9] but not illustrated, with the sole

---

[6] R. Blumenfeld-Kosinski, 'Illustrations et interprétations dans un manuscrit de l'*Ovide Moralisé* (Arsenal 5069)', *Cahiers de recherches médiévales*, 9, 2002, 71-82, J. Drobinsky, 'La narration iconographique dans l'*Ovide Moralisé* de Lyon (BM MS 742)', in *Ovide métamorphosé* (n. 5, above) 223-38.

[7] The two oldest manuscripts from the *Ovide Moralisé* in verse show a profuse set of images including several religious and allegorical scenes: Rouen, Bibliothèque municipale (BMR), MS 0.4 (1044) 453 miniatures, and Paris, Bibliothèque nationale de France (BnF), MS Arsenal 5069, 302 miniatures (Lord 'Three Manuscripts' (n. 5, above) 171-75); a manuscript containing a prose version (Paris, BnF, fonds français. 137) features 73 historiated initials, 15 large miniatures at the beginning of each book and 33 small miniatures on the episodes of the poem, and one of the three illuminated manuscripts of the *Ovidius Moralizatus* (Bergamo, Biblioteca Angelo Mai, MS Casaff. 3. 4) is illustrated with two hundred and nine miniatures including scenes of the episodes and the images of the gods corresponding to the descriptions from the *De formis figurisque deorum*, the first chapter of the Bersuire's work. Lord 'Illustrated manuscripts' (n. 5, above) 4-9, Lord 'A survey of imagery' (n. 4, above) 270-75.

[8] R. Brun, *Le livre français,* (Paris, 1969) 20-36; L. Armstrong, *Reinaissance Miniature Painters and Classical Imagery. The Master of the Putti and his Venetian Workshop* (London, 1981) esp 18; A. Labarte 'Les incunables: la presentation du livre', in *Histoire de l'édition française,* ed. H.J. Martin, R. Chartier, J.-P. Vivet, 3 vols (Paris, 1983) I *Le livre conquérant. Du Moyen Âge au milieu du XVII*[e], 207-15; *Printing the written word. The social history of books,* ed. S. Hindman, (Cornell, 1991); D. Sansy, 'Texte and image dans les incunables français' in *Medievales* 22-23, (1992) 47-70.

[9] The most published Ovidian work was the *Heroides*, with 35 editions, followed by the 22 editions of the *Metamorphoses* out of which 16 are Latin and six are vernacular versions: O. Mazal, *Die Überlieferung der antiken Literatur im Buchdruck des 15. Jahrhunderts*, 4 vols (Stuttgart, 2003) II, 372-75.

118

exception of the *Heroides*.[10] On one hand, classical Latin texts were usually not illustrated due to their use in classrooms; on the other hand, the percentage of illustrated books in relation to texts without images was significantly smaller.[11] Therefore, Ovid came out in the new era of illustration in his former medieval personality, since the illustrated incunabula of *Metamorphoses* are printings of moralizations and vulgarizations from previous centuries, and, moreover, can be counted on the fingers of one hand.

In the Franco-Flemish area, the famous bookseller, publisher, and printer Colard Mansion of Bruges published in May 1484[12] a French version of a moralized *Metamorphoses* text of disputed authorship,[13] which was reprinted in Paris by Antoine Verard in 1493 with slight differences in the text and illustrations, under the new title *Bible des poëtes*.[14] In Italy, the only fifteenth-century illustrated edition of Ovid preserved is the well-known *Ovidio Metamophoseos vulgare*, printed in Venice 1497 by Zoane Rosso for Lucantonio Giunta, which features the allegorized text of an old fourteenth-century Italian vulgarization by Giovanni dei Bonsignori.[15] These first printed products represent, however, the point of departure for two models of constructing sets of illustrations for the Ovidian poem; two different series which display a different response to the structure and significance of the texts.

The Flemish edition of the allegorized text of the poem came out accompanied by a rich corpus of 34 xylographies that included seventeen small format illustrations which

[10]   The earliest illustrated printed Ovid was the *Heroides* which appeared in Naples in 1474 printed by Sixtus Riessinger: Mazal, *Die Überlieferung der antiken Literatur* (n. 9, above) 377-78.

[11]   M. Pastoreau, 'L'illustration du livre: comprendre ou rever?', in *Histoire de l'édition française* (n. 8, above) I 501-29 (501-02).

[12]   Duplessis no. 5 and Henkel 61-64 (n. 4, above). *Cf.* the facsimile edition of the illustrations: D. Henkel, *De houtsneden van Mansion's Ovide Moralisé, Bruges 1484* (Amsterdam, 1922).

[13]   On the text and the sources *cf.* A. Moss, *Ovid in Renaissance France. A survey of the Latin editions of Ovid and commentaries printed in France before 1600* (London, 1982) 23; S. Vervacke, *Forme et fonction des traductions moralisées des Métamorphoses d'Ovide,* (Québec, 1999); J. C. Moissan y S. Vervacke, 'Les *Métamorphoses* d'Ovide et le monde de l'imprimé: la *Bible des poëtes*, Bruges, Colard Mansion, 1484', in *Lectures d'Ovide* (n. 1, above) 217-37; M.-F. Viel, 'La *Bible des poëtes*: une réécriture rhétorique des Métamorphoses d'Ovide', *Tangence*, 74 (2004), 25-44.

[14]   Henkel 64-65; G. Amielle, *Recherches sur des traductions françaises des 'Metamorphoses' d'Ovide illustrées et publiées en France à la fin du xve siècle et au xvie siècle* (Paris, 1989) 31-76; M. B. Winn, *Anthoine Vérard, Parisian Publisher, 1485-1512: Prologues, poems and presentations,* (Geneva, 1997) particularly 269-80.

[15]   Duplessis no. 9; Prince D'Essling, *Les livres à figures Vénetiens de la fin du XVe siècle et du commencement du XVIe,* 4 vols (Florence-Paris, 1907-1914), I (1907) no. 223; M. Sander, *Le livre à figures italien depuis 1467 jusqu'en 1530: essai de sa bibliographie et de son histoire*, 6 vols (Milan, 1969) II no. 5330; Henkel 65-68. On the text and on this particular edition *cf.* B. Guthmüller, '*Ovidio metamorphoseos vulgare'. Forme e funzioni della trasposizione in volgare della poesia classica nel Rinascimento italiano* (Fiesole, 2008) 62-86 and 185-203 (Italian trans. from the original in German: *Ovidio Metamorphoseos vulgare. Formen und Funktionen der volkssprachlichen Wiedergabe klassischer Dichtung in der italienischen Renaissance,* (Boppard am Rhein, 1981)).

accompanied descriptions of the ancient gods inserted at the beginning of the book,[16] and a set of seventeen larger woodcuts, in an almost full-page format, featuring complex narrative scenes from the episodes and stories of the poem.[17] Although the number of scenes represented exceeds the number of the fifteen books in which the text is divided in the Colard edition,[18] the association of one large illustration to each of the books becomes clear (Figure 1); the image is closely attached to the beginning of a new book, and visually connected with the often rubricated titles.[19] This feature, which seems obviously related to the development of the French full-page miniature[20] suggests, however, that the image helps with the structure of the book itself, as a form of punctuation, which has been explored mostly for the sixteenth-century book illustration.[21]

The set of images constructed for the Colard edition show what Ovid's text can inform readers about the image of the ancient gods, and it displays an emerging awareness of the original structure and unity of the *Metamorphoses* text itself. The setting-up of the series of the fifteen images, designed to match the division of the text into books, is traceable

---

[16] The 1484 edition includes the description of 16 figures considered as gods, translated from the *De formis figurisque deorum* (see n. 7, above): Jupiter, Mars, Apollo, Venus, Mercurius, Diana, Minerva, Juno, Cybele, Neptunus, Pan, Bacchus, Pluto, Vulcanus, Hercules and Esculapius. Each description is accompanied by a corresponding woodcut, and in addition, there is a small woodcut representing Laomedon, Apollo and Neptunus in the construction of the walls of Troy, which inserted in Book VI. *Cf.* Henkel, *De houtsneden* (n. 12, above) 39-42.

[17] The book and the chapter on the gods is introduced by a large cut representing the gods gathered around the figure of Saturn being emasculated by Jupiter; the second preface authored by Colard is introduced also by large cut representing the allegory of the felled oak of Antwerp, a parable used to explain the value of the Ovidian text, but not related at all to the contents of the poem. The remaining 15 large woodcuts each introduce one of the 15 books. The illustrations start with the representation of the episode of Deucalion and Pyrrha, combined with the Christian scene of the fallen angels. The rest of the illustrations feature an scene from a story or episode of the following book: Phaeton at the Palace of Sun (II), Cadmus and the founding of Boeotia (III), Pyramus and Thisbe (IV), Pluto and Proserpine (V), Minerva and Arachne (VI) (Figure 1), Jason, the firebreathing Bulls and the Golden Fleece (VII), Minos and Scylla (VIII), Hercules and Achelous (IX), Orpheus and Euridyce (X), The death of Orpheus (XI), The rape of Helen (XII), The arms of Achilles (XIII), Dido and Aeneas or Glaucus and Circe (XIV) and the Founding of Crotona (XV). *Cf.* Henkel, *De houtsneden* (n. 12, above) 35-37.

[18] The feature is clearly stated in the title: *Cy commence Ovide de Salmones son livre intitule Methamorphose, Contenant. Xv. Livres particuliers (...).*

[19] This can be confirmed in the copies by Verard, which lack the woodcut for the second preface (see n. 17, above) and, in some cases, also the first woodcut of the castration of Saturn, reducing to 15 the illustrations to introduce the books. On this, *cf.* Winn, *Anthoine Vérard*, (n. 14, above) 27073.

[20] F. Avril, N. Reynaud, *Les manuscrits à peinture en France 1440-1520*, (Paris, 1995) and *Miniatures flamandes 1404-1482*, ed. B. Bousmann, T. Delcourt (Anvers, 2011).

[21] J.-M. Chatelain, L. Pinon, 'Genres et fonctions de l'illustration au XVIe siècle', in *Mise en page et mise en texte du livre français. La Naissance du livre moderne (XIVe-XVIIe siècles),* ed. H-J. Martin (Tours, 2000) 236-69 (244-48).

Ey commence le .vj. liure ouide dont la premiere fable est du debat entre Pallas et Pranes.

Prebuerat dictis tritonia. Palas escoutoit la merueille que la muse lui racontoit des .ix. pies nouuellement muees. et bi-

en loa leur disputation.
Puis dist en basse voix. Et q me vault ce q pour los me lasse. trop suis pzee de ce que pranes par son ozgueil ne me daigne obeyz. pour ce quelle est belle ouuriere et bien tissant aler le vueil enua pz et lui feray gparer son ozgueil se reuerêce ne me pozte

Figure 1 Minerva and Arachne. Mansion, Bruges 1484. Bibliothèque nationale de France, département Réserve des livres rares, RES G-YC-1002 (Photo: Gallica Bibliothèque Numérique)

already in fourteenth-century manuscripts in the verse version of the *Ovide Moralisé*[22] and, especially, in some fifteenth-century Flemish manuscripts of the prose version and related to the Colard edition as potential antecedents, where the scenes selected to build the series are, with slight divergences, basically the same.[23] On the other hand, the choice of subjects – namely the episodes narrated within the first verses of each book – insists on the function of the image as an echo of the structure of the text, recalling the transitions between stories and episodes which is a characteristic feature of Ovid's poem; also, at the same time, punctuates the separation of the books, marking the beginnings of each unity, as a development of the function of the capital letters. The selection of this particular group of scenes and the visual privilege assigned to them results in the completion of a 'sort of' significant corpus in which the content of the books could be summarily recalled and anticipated in the images.

Turning now to the Italian context, the *Ovidio Metamophoseos vulgare*, a luxury edition which has been compared to the *Poliphilo*,[24] is the only surviving illustrated incunable produced by the city of Venice.[25] The Venetian vulgarization displays a series of 53 woodcuts of a certain quality to illustrate as many episodes in the text,[26] showing – like the Flemish and French productions – a similar tendency to reduce the figurative apparatus of the former moralizations. The edition, however, does not adhere to the fifteen illustrations scheme that echoes the structure of the text, probably due to the different structure of Bonsignori's allegorized version, broken up into books, chapters, and paragraphs with independent titles. Thus, the illustrations, arranged alongside the multitude of separate

[22] Paris, BnF, fonds français 373; Geneva, Bibliothèque Publique et Universitaire (BPUG), MS fonds français 176, and Vaticano, Reg. Lat. 1480. It is to be noted in these manuscripts the structure of the 15 books was marked by the association of a single image of one god (see above n. 7). Lord 'A survey of imagery' (n. 4, above) 273.

[23] London, British Library, Royal 17 E IV and Norfolk, Holkham Hall, Library of the Earl of Leicester, MS 324 illustrated with 15 miniatures, one per book, could be considered as iconographic models for Colard's edition. Two other manuscripts (Copenhaguen, Kongelige Bibliotek (KB), Thott 399, and Paris, BnF, f. fr. 137) despite having more than 15 miniatures, feature also the use of larger and framed illuminations to introduce the books. Lord 'A survey of imagery' (n. 4, above) 281, n. 49. *Cf.* also Henkel, *De houtsneden* (n. 12, above) 7-15. A. Vogel, 'Iconografische context van de illustraties in de *Ovide Moralisé*' (Online edition. Accessed: 3/06/2013. URL: www.historischebronnenbrugge. be/ index.php?option=com_content&task=view&id=37&Itemid=77).

[24] G. D. Painter *The ,Hypnerotomachia Poliphili' of 1499: an introduction on the dream, the dreamer, the artist, and the printer* (London, 1963).

[25] Out of the 25 XVth century editions of the *Metamorphoses*, 12 were produced in Venice: Mazal, *Die Überlieferung* (n. 9, above) 373.

[26] On the illustration *cf.* E. Huber-Rebenich, 'Die Holzschnitte zum *Ovidio Methamorphoseos vulgare* in ihrem Textbezug' in *Die Rezeption der 'Metamorphosen'* (n. 5, above) 48-57; E. Blattner, *Holzschnittfolgen zu den Metamorphoses des Ovid, Venedig 1497 und Mainz 1545,* (Munich, 1998), and G. Huber-Rebenich, 'Kontinuität und Wandel in der frühen italienischen Ovid-Illustration. Die Tradition der Holzschnitte zu Giovanni dei Bonsignoris. *Ovidio metamorphoseos vulgare*', in *Metamorphosen: Wandlungen und Verwandlungen in Literatur, Sprache und Kunst von der Antike bis zur Gegenwar Festschrift für Bodo Guthmüller zum 65. Geburtstag*, ed. H. Marek, A. Neuschäfer, S. Tichy (Wiesbaden, 2002), 63-79.

stories, which stand as autonomous pieces of information, punctuate the text in a different manner (Figure 2), interspersing among the stories as alternative figurative versions.

These facts lead us to the issue of the choice of the figured episodes. The corpus of 53 scenes, most of them of narrative character, includes the formulation of stories never represented before, but, nevertheless, lacks illustrations for well-known and iconographically established episodes such as the tale of Piramus and Thisbe, as well as the highly visual episode of the contest between Pallas and Arachne.[27] These absences are especially striking from the textual and iconographical viewpoint since both receive ample treatment in the Bonsignori's text, and have iconographical antecedents (Figure 1). Nevertheless, the most relevant characteristics of the newly made illustrations are their dependence on Bonsignori's text – several details in the images represent elements which were not present in Ovid's poem – and their distinct Venetian flavour, as many of the scenes seem like a parade of Venetian life: views of the city, heroes as *condottieri*, snapshots of quotidian scenes, as well as dresses and hairstyles that show the new clothes the classical figures have adopted.[28] The woodcuts of this Venetian edition were intended to illustrate this particular version of the Ovidian work, providing both instruction and enjoyable images.

Thus, the figurative series of the Venetian edition represents a new paradigm for the visual presentation of the contents of the poem, which will continue to influence illustrated Ovids until the second part of the sixteenth century. The model conceived for the illustration of the Ovidian content entailed the designing of a whole set of full scenes, predominantly narrative, which covered a significant number of the stories of each book of *Metamorphoses*, seeking to display a balance between text and image. The choice of the stories to be represented aimed to establish a first definite corpus which could eventually grow with the addition of new scenes. Nevertheless, this definite corpus of mythological figured motives imitated and reworked, both in the Italian and Lyonnais printing tradition during the sixteenth century, as we will see, does not correspond exactly to the set of illustrations of the 1497 Venetian edition.

3. A significant shift: the 1505 Parma edition and the corpus of illustrations for Metamorphoses *in the sixteenth century*

Lucantonio Giunta, the editor of the 1497 volume, promoted in 1501 a reprint of Bonsignori's *Ovidio Metamorphoseos vulgare* with the same set of woodcuts, slightly modified due to the moral issues which had affected the first issue of the illustrations.[29]

---

[27] Both episodes have a long iconographic tradition in the figurative corpus of the *Ovide Moralisé* and, as stories narrated at the beginning of a book (IV and VI, respectively), they also appeared in the 15 illustrations scheme. (See n. 17, above).

[28] G. Huber-Rebenich, 'L'iconografia della mitologia antica fra Quattro e Cinquecento. Edizioni illustrate delle *Metamorfosi* di Ovidio.' *Studi Umanistici Piceni* 12 (1992) 123-133 (126 f.).

[29] Duplessis no.10; Essling no. 225; Henkel 69; Sander no. 5331. B. Guthmüller, 'Un curioso caso di censura d'immagini: le illustrazioni ovidiane del 1497', in B. Guthmüller, *Mito, poesia, arte: Saggi sulla tradizione ovidiana nel Rinascimento* (Roma, 1997) 237-50. (Italian trans. of the original in German: *Literatur, Musik und Kunst im Übergang von Mittelalter zur Neuzeit* (Gottingen, 1995)).

. **Ⅲ.**   xxi

Hermone coftei fo figliola di Marte: elquale puoi fo adorato pdio : ela fua matre fo uenere:che anche fu adora/ ta p dea:de cui Cadmo hebe quatro fi gliole cioe Autonoe,Semele, Agaze uicem, Madōna Autonoe fe marito a mifier Aurifto de cui ingenero Ate/ on,Semele che fo la feconda giaque cō Ioue:de cui naque Baccho, Agaze

giaque con Ioue decui generoe Pen/ theo,ben fe poteua adunque ralegra/ re Cadmo effendo fuocero de fi fati dei cōe fono Marte e Venus,Ma aue gna che li foffe tanto alegro : nonde/ meno non de effer dito felice per ca/ gione di quatro aduerfitade che gli auenero,   Cap,   **VI.**

Afteon mutato in ceruo:

A prima aduerfita di Cadmo fo Ateon figliolo de' Auto/ noe fua figliola , percio che gli una uolta andando ad caciare con molte compagnie e fameglie e cō piu de,xxxiiii. cani , Dice Ouidio che ēlli cani ucifero tante fiere che tuta la fel/ ua era fanguinata & effendo nel mezo di,Comādo a tuti che laffafero el cazā p cafon dil grāde caldo, Et ceffandofe coftoro de la cacia:Ateon andaua fo/ lo per una felua nelaquale era una bel/ la fpelonca : laqual fe chiama Sarga/ phie:e foto quella fpelunca:era una fō te molto bella:alaquale fe foleua anda re Diana alauare con le compagne, Et effendo Diana nuda nela fonte e tute

laltre nimphe cō lei : Ateō dicio igno rante foprauene ala fonte ne non ue/ deua coftoro,Ma como le nimphe lo uide cominciaro a cridare:e tute circō daro Diana acio che non foffe ueduta da homo,Ma Diana era fi grande che auāzaua fo pra le altre fi che poteua be ne effere ueduta,

Cap,   **VII.**

Siendo Diana nuda nela fon te nō hauea le faete appechia te , Ma geto laqua nel uolto ad Ateon dicendo, ua e fe tu puoi di fecuramente ad ogni perfona che tu mai ueduta nuda , E ftato un pocho Ateon fo conuertito in ceruo: e fo fa/ to tuto paurofo fi cōe lo ceruo E co/

Figure 2 Diana and Acteon. Giunta, Venice 1497. Bibliothèque nationale de France, département Réserve des livres rares, Rés. g-Yc-439, f. XXIr. (Photo: Gallica Bibliothèque Numérique)

Figure 3 The mission of Cadmus. Mazzali, Parma 1505i. Biblioteca del Seminario Diocesano de Mondoñedo. Lugo, Spain (Photo: Biblioteca Digital Ovidiana. Courtesy of the Seminario Diocesano del Mondoñedo. Lugo, Spain)

This 1501 copy, virtually identical to the 1497 original, constitutes the starting point of the wandering of the series of 53 illustrations of Ovidian episodes, which were created for the vernacular version and seemed to fit this particular text.[30] However, in 1505, a beautiful Latin edition of the *Metamorphoses* with the commentary of Raphael Regius[31] came out in Parma in the house of Francesco Mazzali.[32] Despite being a Latin edition, the book is fully illustrated with 59 woodcuts, 52 of which seem to correspond to the blocks of the Venetian edition of 1497 or, even more, to the modified blocks of 1501.[33] The seven remaining images are completely new, but are similar in their figurative layout and style to the Venetian originals.

---

[30] Giunta promoted a new reprint of 1501 in 1508 (Essling no. 227; Henkel 69; Sander no. 5332), but copies of the same set of illustrations appeared also in the 1517 edition of the text of Bonsignori by Rusconi (Essling no. 231, Sander no. 5333). Huber-Rebenich, 'Kontinuität' (n. 26, above) 78 Abb.1 (5), Abb. 7 (2).

[31] Duplessis no. 11; W. Pollard and C. W. Dyson Perrins, *Italian book-illustrations and early printing. A catalogue of early Italian books in the library of C. W. Dyson Perrins*, (London, 1914) no. 171; Henkel 69; Sander no. 5315. F. Díez-Platas, 'Una presencia excepcional de Ovidio en Mondoñedo: la edición de Parma 1505', *Estudios Mindonienses* 28 (2012) 543-60. Woodcuts of a copy of this edition is accessible at *Biblioteca Digital Ovidiana* (www.ovidiuspictus.eu/listadoediciones.php).

[32] Mazzali was a printer active in Reggio Emilia until 1505, when he moved to Parma, printed some works including this Ovid and died in the same year: F. J. Norton, *Italian printers, 1501–1520* (Cambridge, 1958) 69-70.

[33] See n. 30, above.

They were almost certainly by the same artist, on the basis of the monograms that appear on some of the woodcuts in both editions.[34]

Six new stories are illustrated in the Parma edition: the mission of Cadmus in search of his sister Europa and the founding of Boeotia (Figure 3), which are narrated in the first verses of Book III (vv. 1-137); the story of Narcissus, narrated in Book III (vv. 339-510); the episode of the Minyas' daughters, who refused to attend the mysteries of Bacchus at Thebes, told in the opening lines of Book IV (vv. 1-54); the irruption of Phineus at the wedding of Perseus and Andromeda (Figure 4), told in the opening lines of Book V (vv. 1-235); the Pallas and Arachne story, told in the first verses of Book VI (vv. 1-145). As well as the story of Phrixus and Helle (Figure 5), which, although it does not appear in Ovid's poem, is included in Bonsignori's work as the first story of Book VII, explains the origin of the Golden Fleece and contextualizes the entire story of Jason and Medea in Colchis and its disastrous consequences. The seventh divergence in the Parma edition from the Venetian model is the insertion of a different woodcut for the first illustration of Book I, the Creation of the world, which features a new version of the scene with the figure of a God creator of animals and nature.

The additions to the *corpus* of figured stories from the Parma edition supply what was missing in the Venetian version, where relevant episodes, such as the stories of Narcissus or Arachne, were not illustrated. The addition of these woodcuts not only completes an ideal *corpus* of images for the Ovidian stories, but also raises the question of the possible existence of an older and more complete set of illustrated episodes, which served as a model for these two different editions. The presence of the illustration for the story of Phrixus and Helle, related to the mythical material added by Bonsignori, could argue the case for the existence of a lost illustrated edition featuring the same vernacular text with a more complete set of woodcuts, as was proposed a long time ago.[35] In any case, it still remains an enigma whether the 1497 edition omitted some of the new woodcuts specifically created for the occasion, or whether at least six of the originals may have been lost. Since we lack a complete archaeological reconstruction of the potential source edition of these two publications, it must be considered that the Parma edition's set of images constitutes the most complete *corpus*, which becomes the model for the long list of Venetian and French illustrated editions of the poem that follow,[36] as we will examine later.

A new controversial element comes to join this complex issue: the existence of another Latin edition from 1505,[37] apparently published in Parma on the very same day and in the same house of Francesco Mazzali. Despite its seemingly being a kind of 'twin sister' of

---

[34] The new cut for the illustration of the irruption of Phineus at the wedding of Perseus and Andromeda (Book V) is signed with the same monogram ia as 15 woodcuts from the 1497 edition, *cf.* Díez-Platas 'Una presencia' (n. 31, above) 546 and 548.

[35] L. Donati, 'Edizioni quattrocentesche non pervenuteci delle *Metamorfosi*', in *Atti del Convegno internazionale ovidiano di Sulmona del 1958*, (Roma, 1959). The argument received no endorsement from scholars, Guthmüller «Ovidio metamorphoseos vulgare» (n. 15, above) 194 ff.

[36] Huber-Rebenich, 'Kontinuität' (n. 26, above).

[37] Essling no. 226 ; Pollard-Dyson Perrins no. 172 ; Henkel 69 ; Sander no. 5315.

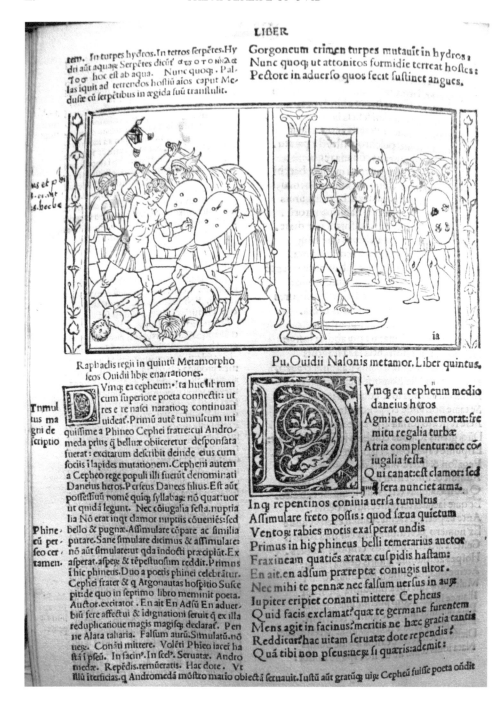

Figure 4 The irruption of Phineus at the wedding of Perseus and Andromeda. Mazzali, Parma 1505i. Biblioteca del Seminario Diocesano de Mondoñedo. Lugo, Spain (Photo: Biblioteca Digital Ovidiana. Courtesy of the Seminario Diocesano del Mondoñedo. Lugo, Spain)

Figure 5 The story of Phrixus and Helle. Mazzali, Parma 1505i. Biblioteca del Seminario Diocesano de Mondoñedo. Lugo, Spain (Photo: Biblioteca Digital Ovidiana. Courtesy of the Seminario Diocesano del Mondoñedo. Lugo, Spain)

the already examined copy, this 'second' edition[38] – which from now on now will be referred at as 1505ii – has a different title, different typography, and a different set of illustrations, despite having an identical colophon and the same number (59) of woodcuts. Only four of the six woodcuts for the new illustrated episodes of the 'first' edition of Parma – from now on 1505i – appear in 1505ii: the story of Narcissus, the daughters of Minyas, the story of Arachne, and Phrixus and Helle. To illustrate the two remaining episodes, the mission of Cadmus in Book III and the episode of the struggle between Phineus and Perseus in Book V, 1505ii uses, instead, two repeated woodcuts. Thus, among the illustrations for Book III in the position where 1505i displayed the new woodcut on the mission of Cadmus, 1505ii uses the woodcut representing the episode of Thetis and Peleus, which appears also in its correct position in Book XI; furthermore, in the position where 1505i displayed the new illustration of the irruption of Phineus at the wedding of Perseus, 1505ii repeats the woodcut of the battle of Hercules and the Amazons (Figure 6), which appears in its correct position also in Book IX.[39]

The misuse of these images recalls a kind of iconographic *concordantia ad sensum*: the use of the image of the Amazonomachy to illustrate the Phineus and Perseus confrontation involves replacing one battle scene with another. The Peleus *pro* Cadmo substitution constitutes, instead, a real *tour de force*, where the only common element in

---

[38] Pollard-Dyson Perrins no. 172 ; U. Hoepli, *Vendita all'asta della preziosa collezione proveniente della cessata libreria de Marinis,* 3 vols (Milan, 1925-26) II (1925) no. 271; Sander no. 5315, and Díez-Platas 'Una presencia' (n. 31, above), 548-50.

[39] See tables of the whole series of the illustrations from 1497, 1505i and 1505ii editions and their placement in Díez-Platas 'Una presencia' (n. 31, above) 551-56.

Liber

ē. In turpes hydros.In tetros serpētes. Hy/ dri autē aquæ serpētes dñr αποτοηιιαα Τοσ. hoc eſt ab aqua. Nunc quoq; pallas inquit ad terrēdos hoſtiū ɔios caput Meduſæ cum ſerpētibus in ægida ſuū tranſtulit.

Gorgoneum crimen turpes mutauit in hydros
Nunc quoq; ut attonitos formidie terreat hoſteis
Pectore in aduerſo quos fecit suſtinet angues

Tumultus magni deſcriptio

Phineū cū perſeo certamen

❡Raphaelis regii in quintū Metamorphoſeos Ouidii Librū enarrationes.
Vmq; ea cepheū. Ita hūc librū cū ſupiore poeta ɔnectit: ut res e re naſci narratioq; ɔtinuari uideaſ.
Primū āt tumultum iniqſſime a Phineo Cephei fratre: cui Andromeda pri⁹ q̃ belluæ obiiceret̃ deſponſata fuerat: excitarū deſcribit deide eī⁹ cū ſociis ī lapides mutatiōe. Cepheni āt a Cepheo rege pp̃r illi fuerūt denoſati. Daneius heros. Perſe⁹ Danees fili⁹. Eſt āt poſſeſſiuū nomē qnq; ſylla bæ: nō q̃tuor ut qdā legūt. Nec cōiugalia feſta: nuptialia: Nō erat inqt clamor nuptiis ɔueniēs ſed bello & pugnæ. Aſſimulare cō / pare ac ſimilia putare. Sæ ſimulare dicius & aſſimulare: nō āt ſimulare: ut qdā idocti p̃cipiūt. Exaſperat: aſpeg̃ & tēpeſtuoſū reddit. Prius i hic phine⁹. Duo a poetis phinei celebrat̃. Cephei frater & q argonautas hoſpitio ſuſcepit: de quo in. vii. li. meminit poeta. Auctor: excitator En ait. En Adſū. En aduerbiū fere affectui & idignatiōi ſerunt q̃ ex illa reduplicatiōe magis magiſq; declaratur. Pēne: Alata talaria. Falſū auię ſimula tu: nō neg̃. Conatu: mittere. Voleti phineo iacet̃ haſtā ī pſeū. In facin⁹. In ſcel⁹. Serua tæ: Andrōedæ. Repēdis: remūeratis. Hac doɐe. Vt illū iterficias: q Andromedā monſtro mario obiectā ſeruauit. Iuſtū āt gratūq;

❡P. Ouidii Naſonis metamor. Liber Quintus

Vmq; ea cepheum med daneius heros
Agmine cōmemorat/frmitu regalia turbæ
Atria complentur/nec cō iugalia feſta
Qui canat / eſt clamor ſed q̃ fera nunciet arma
Inq; repentinos conuiuia uerſa tumultus
Aſſimulare freto poſſis quod ſæua quietum
Ventorum rabies motis exaſperat undis
Primus in hic phineus belli temerarius auctor
Fraxineā quatiens æratæ cuſpidis haſtam/
En ait. en adſum præreptæ coniugis ultor
Nec mihi te pennæ nec falſum uerſus'in aurum
Iuppiter eripiet conanti mittere Cepheus
Quid facis exclamat? quæ te germane furentem
Mens agit in facinus? meritis ne hæc grā tantis
Redditur? hac uitam ſeruatæ dote rependis?
Quam tibi non perſeus/ uerū ſi quæris ademit

Figure 6 The Amazonomachy. (Parma) 1505ii. Biblioteca General de la Universidad de Murcia, Fondo antiguo, S-B-1786 (1), f. 53v. (Photo: InterClassica Biblioteca Digital Séneca)

both stories is the spurious presence of a dragon-snake. The comparison between both Parma editions leads to the conclusion that one of them seems to have been constructed on the model of the other, and that the careful structure of the original edition was intended

FÁTIMA DÍEZ-PLATAS: A FIGURATIVE CORPUS FOR OVID'S *METAMORPHOSES* 129

to be reproduced in the second version, but, because it lacked two of the new woodcuts it had to draw upon the existing materials. It is more than probable that Parma 1505ii is just a 'pirate' Venetian edition by an unidentified and obscure printer.[40] However, it seems *Fortuna* who decided to diffuse the error in the illustration of *Metamorphoses*,[41] because the edition that became the source for the illustrations of both the Latin and the vernacular editions of *Metamorphoses* up to the mid-sixteenth century was not the beautiful and carefully organized Parma 1505i, but the defective and incomplete Parma 1505ii.

4. Coda: errors, choices, corrections, and the fortune of the Venetian illustration series

The Italian and French tradition of the illustration of *Metamorphoses* in the first half of the sixteenth century was built upon some inconsistencies, partly caused by the assumption of a flawed model, the most complete series from 1497-1505ii, that, with some additions and slight modifications, mostly technical, became the visual corpus which were fitted to different types of editions. On one hand, reprints of the Bonsignori text, as well as Latin editions with the Regius commentary edited in Italy, started to employ the set of 59 illustrations, which were copied and modified.[42] On the other hand, there occurred a substantial modification in the model of illustration which took place in Lyon, France, where due to its close connections with Venice, the models of the 14971505ii corpus were imported and adapted for the illustration of a series of Latin editions with commentary by Raphael Regius.[43]

The Lyonnais printing opted for the punctuated model of a single image per book, the 15 woodcuts scheme that went back to Colard Mansion, making a choice of subjects that did not differ much from the fifteenth-century selection.[44] Nevertheless, this selection of the images of the first episodes narrated in each book was impaired by the inconsistencies of the 1497-1505ii corpus. Thus, the French editions incorporated the erroneous use of Peleus *pro* Cadmo (Figure 7) and of the cut of the Amazonomachy for the story of Phineus fight for the illustration of Book III and V respectively. In addition, to introduce

---

[40] The typography of 1505ii is similar to a probably Venetian Juvenal edition from 1503 (*cf.* Norton, *Italian printers* (n. 32, above) 69). The use and the placement of the woodcuts also supports the conclusion that 1505ii was made up on the model of 1505i, faking consequently its date, place and printer.

[41] To the best of my knowledge, there are only five extant copies of 1505i *vs.* the twenty copies of 1505ii. CIAS A PARMA Y A MONDOÑEDO Y MI ARTENDE?. CONSIDERA SOLO LA MALA, PERRINS, SANDERS CREEN QUE LA MALA ES LA SEGUNDA?

[42] Huber-Rebenich, 'Kontinuität' (n. 26, above) 78 Abb.1 (6), Abb. 4.

[43] The tradition began in the 1510 Lyonnais edition printed by Davost for Gueynard (Duplessis no. 25; Henkel 70). F. Saby, 'L'illustration des *Métamorphoses* d'Ovide à Lyon (1510-1512): la circulation des images entre France et Italie à la Renaissance', *Bibliothèque de l'École des Chartes*, 158 1 (2000) 11-26, and Huber-Rebenich, 'Kontinuität' (n. 26, above) 78 Abb. 2, 3 and 6.

[44] The set includes Creation (I), Phaeton at the Palace of Sun (II), Tetis and Peleus *pro* Cadmus and the founding of Boeotia (III), Myniades sisters (IV), the Amazonomachy *pro* the fight between Peleus and Phineus (V), Minerva and Arachne (VI), the story of Phrixus and Helle *pro* Jason, the fire-breathing Bulls and the Golden Fleece (VII), Minos and Scylla (VIII), Hercules and Acheloos (IX), Orpheus and Euridyce (X), The death of Orpheus (XI), The prodigy at Aulis (XII), The arms of Achilles (XIII), Glaucus and Circe (XIV) and Numa Crowned King (XV). See n. 17, above.

Figure 7 The episode of Thetis and Peleus. Gueynard, Lyon 1510. Bibliothèque nationale de France, RES P-YC-1408, f. xlvii v. (Photo: Patricia Meilán)

Book VII, the French editions made a new choice and used the Phrixus and Helle woodcut to illustrate the tale of the deeds of Jason in Colchis, which resulted in the perpetuation of the image of the wedding of Ino and Athamas – and the story which lies behind it – as the image of the love story of Jason and Medea (Figure 10).[45]

The image of this tale – which appears in Bonsignori and not in Ovid – reflects a different kind of inconsistency regarding the relationship of the image with the text. The apparently spurious use of this particular image relates directly to the issue of the use of illustrations in Latin editions of *Metamorphoses*. Despite the absence of the cited story in the Ovidian text, the Regius commentary recalls the story at the end of the sixth book to explain the origin of the Golden Fleece sought by Jason, the protagonist of the first verses of the next book. The use of the Phrixus and Helle woodcut in the Parma edition, where it does not appear inserted at the beginning of the seventh book as expected, but at the end of the sixth just below the lines of the commentary on the story, perfectly reflects the relationship established between the image and the text.

Following the usage established by the Parma model, the Latin commented editions, printed in Italy up to the middle of the century, adopted the ample figurative apparatus outlined above, but the series of illustrations experienced an increase in number and in

[45] Huber-Rebenich, 'L'iconografia' (n. 28, above) 127-28.

Figure 8 The mission of Cadmus. Tacuinus, Venice, 1513. Bayerische Staats Bibliothek, Res/4 A.lat.a. 421, f. xlii v. (Photo: Müncher Digitalisierungszentrum (MDZ). Digitale Bibliothek)

Figure 9 The fight between Perseus and Phineus, Bindoni, Venice 1540. Private Collection. (Photo: Fátima Díez-Platas)

Figure 10 The story of Jason and Medea. H. Ravani, Venice, 1548-1549. Private Collection. (Photo: Fátima Díez-Platas)

correction. The change took place in the famous Venetian printing house of Tacuinus, who, for the first time, illustrated a Latin edition of 1513[46] with an augmented set of woodcuts of uneven quality, inspired probably by the 1505i set of images. In this new corpus, the misuse of the woodcuts of the Amazonomachy and of the Thetis and Peleus episode was corrected, and coherent illustrations of the episode of Cadmo in Boeotia (Figure 8) and the fight between Perseus and Phineus entered the series (Figure 9).[47] Henceforth, the illustration of the Latin editions of the works of Ovid started to make more sense. The ample commentaries to the different works, which obviously refer to Ovid's text, also seek, however, to become a 'sort of' amplification, not of the original text, but of the information contained in Ovid's work. Functioning as explanatory notes, intended to inform the readers about the history, identity, or denominations of certain figures, the text of the commentaries together with the original text also becomes an important source for understanding the illustration. The image, in turn, aside from its role in beautifying the text, appears to function as an added device which reaffirms the contents and enlarges the range of Ovidian materials available in each edition (Figure 10). Furthermore, the Latin editions displayed a new concept of the book and of the page. As well as from the visual viewpoint, repeating the feature of presenting the classical work in portions surrounded by the commentary establishes an evident distinction and a visual hierarchy between the original text and its additions and supplements. The image fits this new organic structure and qualifies as a different supplement to the original text, becoming part of the content of the text.

In the second half of the sixteenth century, the increased and corrected Venetian corpus of illustrations continued to inspire the development of sets of engravings created for new versions of *Metamorphoses*. Following the two different models of illustration, the series of images for books which consecrated the 15 images scheme,[48] and the series of images for stories that reached an extraordinary development in number,[49] confirmed

---

[46] Duplessis no. 30; Essling no. 229 ; Henkel 70 ; Sander no. 5319.

[47] The edition features 61 illustrations for the stories, two more than 1505i, with other significant changes. Huber-Rebenich, 'Die Holzschnitte' (n. 26, above) 56; Huber-Rebenich, 'Kontinuität' (n. 26, above) 78-79 Abb. 8, 9, 10 and 11.

[48] The model reappeared in Italy in the set of woodcuts created for the first edition of the verse translation of the *Metamorphoses* by G. A. dell'Anguillara, published in Venice in 1561 (Henkel 8485), which were reused in a Spanish verse translation in 1589 (Díez-Platas 'Tres maneras' (n. 4, above) 261-64), and provided a model for later Anguillara editions (Henkel 86-87). The edition of the translation that came out in Venice in 1584 featured a set of 15 magnificent full-page copperplates by Giacomo Franco. Henkel 96-99; Díez-Platas 'Tres maneras' (n. 4, above) 26467; G. Huber-Rebenich, S. Lütkemeyer, H. Walter, *Ikonographisches Repertorium zu den Metamorphosen des Ovid. Die textbegleitende Druckgraphik, II: Sammeldarstellungen*, (Berlin, 2004).

[49] The illustrations for the stories emerged in Italy in the set of woodcuts created for the Italian translation of the poem by Ludovico Dolce, first published in Venice in 1553 (Henkel 82-84; B. Guthmüller, 'Imagine e testo nelle *Transformationi* di Ludovico Dolce', in *Mito* (n. 29, above) 251-74, and Huber-Rebenich, 'Kontinuität' (n. 26, above) 79 Abb. 12.), and later on, in France, in the extraordinary *La Metamorphoses d'Ovide figurée* published in Lyon in 1557 with by the set of one hundred and seventy eight woodcuts by the outstanding Lyonnais engraver Bernard Salomon. Henkel 77-81, and Díez-Platas 'Tres maneras' (n. 4, above) 255-61.

the role of the image, either in uniting the poem of *Metamorphoses*, or fully disintegrating it. These two styles emphasized the strong textual structure or displayed the autonomy of the stories, masterfully gathered and weaved by Ovid, who, thereby, reached an 'imaged' afterlife.

University of Santiago de Compostela

THE IO IN CORREGGIO: OVID AND THE METAMORPHOSIS OF A RENAISSANCE PAINTER*

HÉRICA VALLADARES

Antonio Allegri da Correggio (1489?-1534) is one of the most enigmatic painters of the Italian Renaissance. Traditionally seen as a provincial artist with little direct knowledge of classical antiquity, he has often been set in opposition to the worldly, erudite Titian.[1] But the erudition of Correggio's sensuous and delicate oeuvre has in fact been greatly underestimated. Particularly intriguing is the small corpus of mythological paintings executed in the last decade of the artist's life, whose subjects radically deviate from the religious images he produced for most of his career. Within this small mythological corpus, the *Io* (1530-31, Figure 1) merits special attention. As a number of scholars have noted, Correggio's *Io* breaks with earlier iconographies of this myth: instead of depicting the nymph in the guise of a cow, as she commonly appears in numerous other

---

* I would like to thank Philip Hardie, Peter Mack, and John North for giving me this opportunity to share my research on Correggio. I am also grateful to Marden Nichols, Giancarla Periti, Michael Sullivan, and Sara Switzer for their insightful comments on earlier iterations of this article. Unless otherwise noted, all translations are my own.

[1] See, for instance, L. Barkan, *The gods made flesh: metamorphosis and the pursuit of paganism* (New Haven and London 1986) 175-76. The image of Correggio as a naïve, provincial painter can be traced back to Giorgio Vasari's biography of the artist. See G. Vasari, *Le vite de' più eccellenti pittori, scultori e architettori nelle redazioni del 1550 e 1568*, ed. R. Bettarini with commentary by P. Barrochi, 6 vols (Florence 1966) IV (part 1) 49-50. Against this view, see E. Panofsky, *The iconography of Correggio's Camera di San Paolo* (London 1961) 35; E. Knauer, 'Zu Correggios Io und Ganymed. Ernst Zinn zum 60. Geburtstag', *Zeitschrift für Kunstgeschichte* 33 (1970) 64; D. Ekserdjian, *Correggio* (New Haven and London 1997) 291; F. Tonelli, 'Il chiostro ionico dei cassinesi di San Pietro a Modena, una proposta per Correggio, una per Girolamo Bedoli, e alcuni spunti per Cristoforo Solari', in *Su questa pietra…Nuovi studi e ricerche sull'abbazzia benedittina di San Pietro in Modena*, eds. S. Cavicchioli and V. Vandelli (Mondena 2014) 89-106. For a sensitive critique of Vasari's biography of Correggio, see M. Spagnolo, 'Allegri, Lieto, Lucente: note per la biografia del Correggio', in *Correggio e l'antico*, ed. A. Coliva (Milan 2008) 31-46. Carlo Ginzburg has eloquently argued against the general view of Titian as an erudite, humanist painter. According to him, Titian did not read Latin and was, therefore, acquainted with Ovid's *Metamorphoses* solely through modern 'translations' (*volgarizzamenti*) of this poem. Ginzburg further demonstrates that Titian's iconographic innovations in depicting Ovidian mythological narratives draw largely from to the work of early modern engravers, whose illustrations were commonly found in fifteenth and sixteenth-century editions of Ovid's works. See C. Ginzburg, 'Tiziano, Ovidio e i codici della figurazione erotica nel Cinquecento', in *Miti, emblemi, spie: morfologia e storia* (Turin 1986), 140 ff.

Figure 1 Correggio, *Io* (1530-31), Kunsthistorisches Museum, Vienna. Photo: Art Resource, NY

Figure 2 Ovid, *Metamorphoses*, trans. C. Marot (early 16th century), MS. Douce 117, fol. 34r. Bodleian Library, Oxford. Photo: Bodleian Library

representations (*e.g.*, Figure 2), the painter presents us with an innovative reimagining of the story in which pleasure and metamorphosis are fused into one emblematic moment.[2]

Although Correggio's debt to Ovid's *Metamorphoses* has been generally regarded as unproblematic,[3] his composition in fact reverses the poet's account of Io's transformation

---

[2] Eksderjian, *Correggio* (n.1, above) 284; M. Fabianski, *Correggio: le mitologie d'amore* (Milan 2000) 73-83; L. Freedman, 'Correggio's *Io* as Reflective of Cinquecento Aesthetic Norms', *Jahrbuch der kunsthistorischen Sammlungen in Wien* 84 (1988) 101.

[3] Eksderjian, *Correggio* (n. 1, above) 284; Fabianski, *Correggio* (n. 2, above) 154; Freedman, 'Correggio's *Io*' (n. 2, above) 98.

140 THE AFTERLIFE OF OVID

by changing Jupiter into a cloud, while preserving the nymph's human form. Ovid's version of the tale reads as follows (*Met*.1.588-612):

Viderat a patrio redeuntem Iuppiter illam
flumine et 'o virgo Iove digna tuoque beatum
nescio quem factura toro, pete' dixerat 'umbras
altorum nemorum' (et nemorum monstraverat umbras)
'dum calet et medio sol est altissimus orbe.
quod si sola times latebras intrare ferarum,
praeside tuta deo nemorum secreta subibis,
nec de plebe deo, sed qui caelestia magna
sceptra manu teneo, sed qui vaga fulmina mitto.
ne fuge me!' (fugiebat enim.) iam pascua Lernae
consitaque arboribus Lyrcea reliquerat arva,
cum deus inducta latas caligine terras
occuluit tenuitque fugam rapuitque pudorem.
Interea medios Iuno despexit in Argos,
et noctis faciem nebulas fecisse volucres
sub nitido mirata die, non fluminis illas
esse, nec umenti sensit tellure remitti;
atque suus coniunx ubi sit circumspicit, ut quae
deprensi totiens iam nosset furta mariti.
quem postquam caelo non repperit, 'aut ego fallor
aut ego laedor' ait delapsaque ab aethere summo
constitit in terris nebulasque recedere iussit.
coniugis adventum praesenserat inque nitentem
Inachidos vultus mutaverat ille iuvencam;
bos quoque formosa est.

Jupiter had seen the girl returning from her father's stream and said, 'O Maiden worthy of Jove, destined to make some lucky husband happy in bed, seek the shade of these deep groves while the Sun is at its highest point and grows warm in the middle of the sky'. (And he pointed to the shady woods.) 'But if you fear to go into the wild beasts' den alone, you will safely enter this secluded grove under the guidance of a god – and not just a minor god. For I hold the heavenly scepter in my mighty hand and hurl the roaming thunderbolt. Oh, do not flee me'! (But she was already in flight.) And already she had left behind Lerna's pastures and the Lyrcean fields dense with trees, when the god conjured up a thick, dark cloud that concealed the broad earth, put a stop to her flight, and ravished her.

Meanwhile, Juno looked down upon the middle part of Argos and marveled that the sudden clouds had created the appearance of night in broad daylight. She knew that these clouds were not made of river mist nor emanated from the earth's dampness. She looked around to see where her husband might be, as a wife long since accustomed to the deceits of a spouse caught in the act. And when she could not find him in heaven she said, 'I am either deceived or betrayed', and gliding down from heaven's dome, she stood upon the earth and commanded the clouds to part. But Jupiter had foreseen his wife's arrival and had transformed Inachus' daughter into a shiny white heifer. Even as a cow she was still beautiful.

In Correggio's ardently sensual painting, the cloud that, according to Ovid, was conjured by Jupiter to stop the nymph's flight and conceal his dalliance from Juno (*Met*.1.597-609) becomes the god's body – or at least, his earthly manifestation. He envelops the nymph's luminous form with a dark, anthropomorphic mass that threatens to engulf her and conceal her from our sight. At the same time that Jupiter reaches down for a kiss, Io throws back her head, eager to receive her lover. Instead of the well-known narrative of Io's ravishment, Correggio presents us with an image of mutual desire and pleasure.

The intense eroticism of this scene is, however, tempered by a certain tenderness which is communicated through the nymph's pose and gestures: by showing us her back, Correggio uses Io's body to block our visual access to the lovers' embrace, presenting us with an obstructed view of the sexual act. Though titillating, this image can hardly be described as pornographic. The nymph's facial expression, her softened gaze and the gentleness with which she wraps her arm around the god's paw-like limb suggest that sexual intimacy is, in this case, interlaced with sentiment.

The tenderness of Correggio's image becomes especially apparent when we compare it to other contemporary erotic representations. For instance, a fresco of Jupiter and Olympia painted after a drawing by Giulio Romano in the Palazzo del Te in Mantua (Figure 3) exemplifies the kind of erotic image *all'antica* popular among artists associated with the school of Raphael.[4] Federico II Gonzaga, who had this pleasure palace built and decorated between 1524 and 1534, was also the patron who commissioned the *Io* and other mythological paintings by Correggio. In fact, Egon Verheyen has argued that the *Io* was originally intended for a specific room in Palazzo del Te, where it would have hung together with Correggio's *Ganymede*, *Danae* and *Leda*.[5] Federico's love of antiquity and his taste for prurient portrayals of the loves of the gods are well attested.[6] And so, it is

[4] On the classical aesthetics of erotic imagery produced by Raphael and his followers, see B. Talvacchia, *Taking positions: on the erotic in Renaissance culture* (Princeton 1999); J. Turner, 'Invention of sexuality in the Raphael workshop: before the *Modi*', *Art History* 36 (2013) 72-99. On Correggio's engagement with 'lascivious' images produced by contemporary artists, see A. Nova, 'Correggio's 'Lascivie'', in *Renaissance Love: Eros, Passion and Friendship in Italian Art around 1500*, eds. J. Kohl, M. Koos, and A. W. B. Randolph (Berlin 2014) 121-30.

[5] In his biography of the artist, Vasari writes that Correggio painted the *Leda* and the *Danae* (which he, following Giulio Romano, identifies as 'Venus'), 'to be sent to the emperor' by Federico II Gonzaga. See Vasari, *Le vite de' più eccellenti pittori* (n. 1, above) 52. The implication here is that these two works were commissioned for Charles V, whose coronation took place in Bologna in 1530. But as Egon Verheyen has shown, Vasari's account of the early history of Correggio's *Amori di Giove* is rather unreliable. See E. Verheyen, 'Correggio's *Amori di Giove*', *Journal of the Warburg and Courtauld Institutes* 29 (1966) 160-65. On the possible location of Correggio's mythological paintings in Palazzo del Te, see Verheyen's detailed analysis of the surviving documentary evidence (165-92).

[6] On Federico II Gonzaga's taste as a collector, see Ekserdjian, *Correggio* (n. 2, above) 284; B. Furlotti and G. Rebecchini, *Il Rinascimento a Mantova* (Florence 2008) 143,170; S. Campbell, *The cabinet of eros: Renaissance mythological painting and the studiolo of Isabella d'Este* (New Haven and London 2004), 227; G. Rebecchini, 'Exchanges of works of art at the court of Federico II Gonzaga with an appendix on Flemish art', *Renaissance Studies* 16 (2002) 381-91.

Figure 3 Attributed to Rinaldo Mantovano after designs by Giulio Romano, *Jupiter and Olympia*, Palazzo del Te, Mantua (1527-30). Photo: Art Resource, NY

striking that, given his patron's taste and his knowledge of Giulio Romano's work, Correggio chose to approach his own *Amori di Giove* in a very different style.

Correggio's unique, intensely sensual representation of the myth of Io has inspired a long-standing search for the artist's visual sources. The so-called Ara Grimani (Figure 4), an ancient monument found in Rome in the early 1500s that Correggio may have known first-hand, has often been advanced as a possible model.[7] The charming depiction of a satyr and a nymph on one of the altar's reliefs certainly resembles Correggio's own portrayal of Io and Jupiter. Furthermore, comparison with the Ara Grimani highlights the sculptural quality of Correggio's painting. The stark contrast between dark and light tones along with the rather shallow pictorial space of his canvas recall the appearance of ancient

---

[7] Knauer, 'Zu Correggios Io' (n. 1, above), 61-64; Fabianski, *Correggio* (n. 2, above) 76; Freedman, 'Correggio's *Io*' (n. 2, above) 101. Knauer also argues that, if we accept that Correggio was in Rome in the early sixteenth century, he may also have seen the Ara Grimani while in the Eternal City, before it was sent to Venice in 1523 (62-64).

Figure 4 *Ara Grimani*, Museo Archeologico Nazionale, Venice (1st century BCE/1st century CE). Photo: Art Resource, NY

reliefs and cameos, turning the *Io* into a large-scale gem,[8] in which a long and complex narrative is compressed into a single electrifying scene.

But the figure of Io also closely resembles one of Raphael's nymphs on the ceiling of the loggia of Cupid and Psyche in the Villa Farnesina in Rome (Figure 5) – a work of art Correggio must have known through Giulio Romano's drawings and may likewise have seen during a possible trip to the Eternal City.[9] Raphael's nymph was, however, herself modeled after antique prototypes, so that Correggio's *Io* must be seen as a self-conscious fusion of ancient and modern designs – an example of the new classical style associated

---

[8] Fabianski, *Correggio* (n. 2, above) 80. On the parallels between ancient sculpture and Correggio's *Io*, see also L. Freedman, *Classical myths in Italian Renaissance painting* (Cambridge 2011) 145.

[9] On the question of Correggio's journey to Rome, see C. Gould, *The paintings of Correggio* (Ithaca 1976) 40-50; Ekserdjian, *Correggio* (n. 1, above) 77; J. Shearman, *Only connect: art and the spectator in the Italian Renaissance* (Princeton 1992) 181.

Figure 5 Workshop of Raphael, *Cupid and the three Graces*, Villa della Farnesina, Rome (1517-19). Photo: Art Resource, NY

with artistic circles in Rome that quarried Greco-Roman art, especially sculpture, for naturalistic, sensual representations of the human body and adapted these models for a variety of religious and secular subjects.[10]

While the iconographic lineage of Correggio's *Io* has been carefully traced and analyzed, the artist's subtle appropriation of Ovid's text remains largely unexplored. Far from being an unprecedented outlier in Correggio's oeuvre, the *Io* is the fruit of almost two decades of experimentation with the process of translating words into images. As such, it marks a turning point in his engagement with classical subjects and reveals him to be a surprisingly sensitive interpreter of ancient visual and literary traditions. In a recent, polemical study of Italian Renaissance art, Alexander Nagel describes the transformation of religious imagery in the sixteenth century as resulting partly from the artists' 'realization that the image had an archaeological structure that one could excavate beneath the top layer'.[11] As our brief discussion of the *Io*'s iconographic sources has shown, Correggio was clearly interested in the visual archaeology of images. But he was also attuned to their *philological* structure, *i.e.*, the way in which images could trigger a search for meaning that went beyond the identification of iconographic types to involve viewers in a dynamic pursuit of literary allusions.[12] Correggio's *Io* thus constitutes a fascinating example of post-antique Ovidian reception that not only calls into question previous perceptions of Correggio as an artist, but also enriches our understanding of the rapport between image and text in the early modern period.

Almost nothing is known about Correggio's training as an artist and a humanist,[13] but between 1517 and 1519, he began to identify himself through a Latinized version of his name, Antonius Laetus, which appears on two of his paintings (the now lost *Madonna of Albinea*

---

[10] Alexander Nagel has argued that, in sixteenth-century art, sculpture was 'a figure for the antique'. See A. Nagel, *The controversy of Renaissance art* (Chicago 2011) 105-06. On the adaptation of ancient iconographic models for a variety of subjects by Renaissance artists, see Fabianski, *Correggio* (n. 2, above) 78-80; Freedman 'Correggio's *Io*' (n. 2, above) 100-01; L. Freedman, 'A nereid from the back: on a motif in Italian Renaissance art', *Storia dell'arte* 70 (1990) 323-36; D. Rosand, 'Titian and the bed of Polyclitus', *The Burlington Magazine* 117 (1975) 242-45; Turner, 'Invention of sexuality' (n. 4, above) 86-98. On the diffusion of Raphael's classicism after his death in 1520, see K. Oberhuber and A. Gnann, *Roma e lo stile classico di Rafaello, 1515-1527* (Milan 1999) 17-58.

[11] Nagel, *The controversy* (n. 10, above) 41.

[12] *Cf.* Charles Dempsey's discussion of how the paintings by Annibale Carraci on the Farnese Gallery (1597-1600) were designed to elicit a literary, poetic response from the viewer. According to Dempsey, a learned courtier 'would have had little trouble in identifying, and appreciating the wit behind the quotation from the opening lines of the *Aeneid* engraved on Venus's footstool in the *Venus and Anchises*. Nor would he have missed the punning reference to Virgil's '*Omnia vincit amor*' in the medallion of Cupid and Pan. And as he looked about him at the wanton display of Love's power over gods and men, he would not have failed to supply the second half of the line – '*Et nos cedamus Amori*', See C. Dempsey, '"*Et nos cedamus Amori*": observations on the Farnese Gallery', *Art Bulletin* 50 (1968) 371. On visual and textual puns in the work of Giulio Romano, see Nova, 'Correggio's '*Lascivie*' (n. 4, above) 127.

[13] Ekserdjian (n. 1, above) 1-19.

and the *Portrait of a Lady*, Figure 6) and on several legal documents.[14] As Giancarla Periti has persuasively argued, the artist's act of re-naming himself represents more than a mere bilingual pun on his patronymic, Allegri (Allegri/Lieto/Laetus): instead it communicates both the artist's unique artistic identity and his understanding of the highly philological discourse on the emotions that informed contemporary aesthetic debates in the learned, courtly *milieu* of his hometown. In the humanistic parlance of sixteenth-century Correggio, *letizia* signified an inner, spiritual joy, while *allegrezza* was defined as a sensual, bodily pleasure.[15] By re-naming himself Laetus, Correggio transformed his patronymic into an indication of his concern with a more elevated, metaphysical form of happiness, and in so doing he proclaimed *lietezza – i.e.* a sense of joy that is both expressed and elicited visually – as his signature style.[16]

But the delight provoked by Correggio's paintings was not meant to be just a visual pleasure. There was also an intellectual aspect to Correggio's *lietezza*. In other words, part of the pleasure derived from Correggio's images was triggered by an interactive exchange between viewer and work of art that was, of course, mediated by the artist himself. Correggio's *Portrait of a Lady* (*c.* 1519, Figure 6) may be taken as an example of the way in which he engaged viewers both visually and intellectually. Although the sitter's identity has long been a matter of debate, she can be identified by her dress as a young, aristocratic widow, belonging to the Third Order of Saint Francis – an affiliation which is indicated by the Franciscan tertiary girdle at her knee. Despite this visible mark of her religious devotion, this beautiful young lady is shown in a seductive three-quarter view. Her alluring, sidelong gaze is directed toward the viewer, to whom she proffers a large silver vessel. She thus entices the beholder to enter into a dialogue with the image. The key to this dialogue lies in the elegant Greek inscription that adorns the lady's bowl.

The inscription's central word, ΝΗΠΕΝΘΕΣ, alludes to Helen's analgesic elixir in the Telemachy (*Odyssey* 4.219-32). Its full text has been reconstructed as follows: ΗΤΟΝ ΝΗΠΕΝΘΕΣ ΑΛΟΧΟ (it was a [remedy] dissolving sorrows and banishing anger) – a modern *sententia* clearly inspired by the well-known Homeric passage.[17] But how should we interpret this literary reference in the context of Correggio's painting? Arguing that the lady in the portrait must be Ginevra Rangone, Periti suggests we read the painter's evocation of the Homeric νηπενθές in relation to her biography. Ginevra was a cultivated young woman from Modena, said to have been well versed in Petrarchan poetry who in 1503 married Galeazzo da Correggio, the son of Niccolò da Correggio, a court poet in Milan and Ferrara known for his translations of classical texts and his adaptations of

---

[14] G. Periti, 'From Allegri to Laetus-Lieto: The shaping of Correggio's artistic distinctiveness', *The Art Bulletin* 86 (2004) 459.

[15] Periti, 'From Allegri to Laetus-Lieto' (n. 14, above) 460-61, 468-70.

[16] Periti 'From Allegri to Laetus-Lieto' (n. 14, above) 460, 470. Vasari was the first to write about the sense of joy conveyed to the beholder by Correggio's paintings. See, for instance, his description of the *Madonna of Saint Jerome*, in which the figure of a smiling *putto* induces all viewers to smile; Vasari, *Le vite de' più eccellenti pittori* (n. 1, above) 52.

[17] Periti 'From Allegri to Laetus-Lieto' (n. 14, above) 468.

Figure 6 Correggio, *Portrait of a Lady* (ca. 1519), The Hermitage, St. Petersburg. Photo: Art Resource, NY

Ovidian mythological episodes for the stage.[18] In 1517 Ginevra was widowed, but she married Luigi Alessandro Gonzaga two years later. In light of these facts, Correggio's portrait ought to be understood as a poetic depiction of this learned gentlewoman. The death of her first husband is the sorrow for which she has sought solace. But the fact that

---

[18] On Niccolò da Correggio, see s.v. 'Niccolò da Correggio', *The Oxford Companion to Italian Literature*, eds. P. Hainsworth and D. Robey (Oxford 2002) 410.

the cup is empty indicates her suffering has been soothed, and that she has found new joy through the prospect of a second marriage.[19]

Yet we might also argue that the sight of this beautiful lady and the pleasure of deciphering the cup's contents likewise offered the viewer a pleasant draught – a form of νηπενθές capable of lifting his or her spirits that was the fruit of the painter's art. After all, the Greek inscription on the lady's bowl was not the only textual fragment featured in this painting: the artist's own signature, Anton.[ius] Laet.[us], was itself 'inscribed' on the trunk of the laurel tree that frames the woman's elegant figure. Thus, Correggio's laurel tree is a similarly polyvalent symbol, evoking Petrarchan notions of poetic triumph and erotic yearning.[20] Indeed, the act of inscribing one's name on a tree was itself rich in poetic resonances. In the work of Virgil, Propertius and Ovid as well as in the writings of their Renaissance followers, Boiardo and Sannazaro, despondent lovers often carve their names and those of their mistresses on trees as an expression of sorrow, loneliness and nostalgia.[21] But as Rensselaer Lee has demonstrated, during the sixteenth century, this *topos* underwent a sea change in the hands of Ariosto. In the *Orlando Furioso*, the lovers' act of jointly carving their names on trees became a symbol of intense, unalloyed happiness.[22] It is clear, then, that the painter's name (Allegri/Laetus) and the painting's theme of *lietezza* were closely intertwined.[23] But even more importantly, it is Correggio's signature that draws these different threads of signification together – a signature that evinces both the artist's humanistic, poetic aspirations and his love of wordplay.

A similarly dialogic method of engaging the viewer also informs Correggio's treatment of mythological subjects in the Camera di San Paolo in Parma (Figure 7). Painted around 1518-19 for the greatly learned abbess Giovanna Piacenza, the frescoes in this room feature a series of lunettes rendered in grisaille whose figures in a number of cases replicate the iconography on ancient Greek and Roman coins.[24] But interspersed with these examples of antiquarian knowledge, we find several images that, though drawn from the texts and monuments of classical antiquity, defy easy categorization and identification. Thus, by combining the emerging science of numismatics with the

---

[19] Periti 'From Allegri to Laetus-Lieto' (n. 14, above) 464-68.

[20] Periti 'From Allegri to Laetus-Lieto' (n. 14, above) 467.

[21] Virgil, *Ecl.* 10.52-54; Propertius 1.18.1-4, 19-22; Ovid, *Her.* 5.21-22, 25-26; Boiardo, Madrigal 2.5 (= *Sonetti e canzone del poeta clarissimo Matteo Maria Boiardo, Conte di Scandiano*, ed. A. Panizzi (Milan 1845), 147). For passages from Sannazaro's *Arcadia* in which he revisits the *topos* of lovers carving their names on trees, see J. Sannazaro, *Arcadia and the Piscatorial Eclogues*, ed. and trans. R. Nash (Detroit 1966) 9, 13, 23, 34, 53-65, 103-06. For a general discussion of this ancient poetic *topos* and its reception in the early modern period, see R. Lee, *Names on trees: Ariosto into art* (Princeton 1977) 9-11.

[22] Lee, *Names on trees* (n. 21, above) 30.

[23] Periti 'From Allegri to Laetus-Lieto' (n. 14, above) 467.

[24] In the early fifteenth century, Parma was an important center for numismatics. For a discussion of local collectors and Correggio's access to ancient coins, see Ekserdjian, *Correggio* (n. 1, above) 7980, 86; Panofsky, *The Iconography of Correggio's Camera* (n. 1, above) 17-18.

Figure 7 Correggio, Camera di San Paolo, Parma (1518-19). Photo: Art Resource, NY

Figure 8 Correggio, *The Punishment of Hera*, Camera di San Paolo, Parma (1518-19). Photo: Art Resource, NY

contemporary passion for emblems, Correggio's lunettes presented viewers with an intriguing display of images that both pleased the eye and challenged one's imagination.[25]

Among the many classical subjects that adorn the walls of the Camera di San Paolo, *The Punishment of Hera* (Figure 8) stands out as an especially erudite, coded image. Zeus' punishment of his wife, recounted in a short passage from Homer (*Iliad* 15.18-24), is rarely represented in the visual arts. In fact, Erwin Panofsky credits Correggio as being the first modern artist to depict accurately the Homeric description of this goddess as she was suspended between heaven and earth.[26] Furthermore, the artist's choice of showing anvils tied to her feet suggests to him that Correggio, in composing this lunette, must have drawn inspiration from a Greek source. For in an early sixteenth-century Latin commentary on Virgil, in which Homer's verses are cited, the word ἄκμονας (anvils;

---

[25] On the relation between numismatics and emblematics in the cultural milieu of fifteenth-century Northern Italy, see Panofsky *The iconography of Correggio's Camera* (n. 1, above) 30-36.

[26] Panofsky, *The iconography of Correggio's Camera* (n. 1, above) 25-26, 85-86.

Iliad 15.19) is translated as *pondera* (weights) instead of *incudes*.[27] But lacking an ancient iconographic model for this unusual subject, Correggio transformed the well-known image of Marsyas bound to a tree into an image of Hera.[28] The resulting portrayal of Zeus' consort is surprising for a number of reasons: not only is she depicted as a very young and beautiful woman, but Correggio's Hera also appears to bear her suffering effortlessly. How then are we to understand the presence of this Olympian deity in this particular guise in Giovanna Piacenza's apartment?

For Panofsky, Correggio's Hera must be interpreted through the lens of several ancient and modern commentaries on Homer as a cosmological allegory equating Zeus' wife with the element Air.[29] In his eyes, the proximity of the lunette featuring Hera to that showing a personification of Tellus, as well as the goddess' 'cheerful equanimity' in a most painful situation prove that she was not meant to be seen as 'a tortured delinquent setting a warning example to other transgressors'.[30] Rather, this figure – along with those in the other lunettes – reflects the abbess' and her peers' taste for classicizing displays of mythological knowledge, their preference for recondite textual sources, and their propensity for cryptic allusion. Beyond this, Panofsky finds it difficult to articulate a precise theological or philosophical principle that might transform this dazzling collection of images into a unified program. At best, Correggio's frescoes appear to allude to an individual creed that extols virtue in the face of adversity, while insisting on fate's inexorable power to determine all outcomes.[31]

More recently, however, Correggio's Hera has been read in light of Giovanna Piacenza's own experiences as a nun.[32] While entrance into an aristocratic convent like San Paolo offered Giovanna the chance to dedicate herself to the pursuit of knowledge and achieve a position of power within her monastic order, life as an abbess was not without its difficulties. Tensions with the male members of the curia over the autonomy of convents like San Paolo in sixteenth-century Italy were a constant reminder of how tenuous the nuns' control over what they considered their property truly was. Thus, Correggio's intriguing representation of *The Punishment of Hera* might be understood as a subversive commentary about general perceptions of a nun's existence. Instead of a painful penance, cloistered life could be far less difficult to bear than others imagined – an interpretation that Giovanna's own 'career' would have invited and borne out. But at the same time, this image could also be read as a bittersweet reflection on the precarious condition of early modern women

---

[27] The commentary cited by Panofsky was traditionally attributed to Valerius Probus. It was appended to Egnatius' edition, published in Venice in 1507. See Panofsky, *The iconography of Correggio's Camera* (n. 1, above) 26, n.1.

[28] Panofsky, *The iconography of Correggio's Camera* (n. 1, above) 88, n.2. On the Pergamene sculptural group showing Apollo ordering Marsyas to be flayed by a Scythian slave, see *s.v.* 'Marsyas', *LIMC* 8 vols, VI (1992) 365-78; F. Haskell and N. Penny, *Taste and the Antique* (New Haven and London 1981), 262-63.

[29] Panofsky, *The iconography of Correggio's Camera* (n. 1, above) 85-88.

[30] Panofsky, *The iconography of Correggio's Camera* (n. 1, above) 88.

[31] Panofsky, *The iconography of Correggio's Camera* (n. 1, above) 98-100.

[32] G. Periti, *In the courts of religious ladies: art, vision, and pleasure in Italian Renaissance convents* (Yale U. P. forthcoming).

inside and outside convents. Such biographical readings of Correggio's Hera in no way detract from Panofsky's earlier interpretations. Rather, the two approaches can be fruitfully combined to demonstrate the semantic richness of Correggio's paintings. As Periti herself observes, in the Camera di San Paolo, each viewer was urged to discover the meaning of Correggio's images subjectively – a process that might have been informed (or not) by the individual's understanding of the monastic, courtly and humanistic traditions that inspired their creation.[33]

Although it is impossible to determine how exactly Correggio's *Punishment of Hera* was interpreted by either Giovanna or those whom she received in her abbatial apartment, it is clear that this fresco, like the contemporaneous *Portrait of a Lady,* was designed to lure the viewer through the beauty of its subject and its erudite reference to classical literature. In both paintings, Homer's words are translated into images whose interpretation hinges on the beholder's knowledge of the original text and, in the case of the *Portrait*, of the original Greek itself. But the *Io* is a different story. In this painting, it is not so much Ovid's poetry, but his poetics that Correggio translates into oil on canvas. In its abbreviated synthetic form, the *Io* dramatizes the interplay between seen and unseen, interior and exterior, and presence and absence that are also recurring motifs in the *Metamorphoses* – not least in the episode of Io itself.[34] Moreover, this dreamlike vision of the god's ephemeral embrace presents metamorphosis as a metaphor for the creative process, setting Correggio's work on a par with Ovid's transformative poem.

In the fifteenth and sixteenth centuries, Italian artists and humanists such as Leon Battista Alberti, Jacopo de' Barbari, and Titian saw the arts of painting and poetry as being intimately connected. In fact, in relation to painting, the term *poesie* came to denote the representation of 'independent mythological inventions'.[35] That this definition of *poesia* was widely diffused and accepted among sixteenth-century Northern Italian artists is clear from Paolo Pino's *Dialogo di pittura*, published in Venice in 1548, where he declares poetry an essential part of the painter's craft. Having divided painting into its three traditional components – *disegno, colorito* and *invenzione* – Pino writes: '[*invenzione*]…means the finding of *poesie* and stories in and of themselves; because Painting is properly speaking *Poesia*, that is, Invention'.[36]

Correggio's *Io* is, then, a *poesia*. More than just an illustration of a mythical narrative, it is both a witty transformation of a rare mythological subject and a sophisticated pictorial invention designed to draw the eyes and minds of spectators through its layers of visual

---

[33] Periti, *In the courts of religious ladies* (n. 32, above).

[34] P. Hardie, *Ovid's poetics of illusion* (Cambridge 2002) 3-7. On the many *double entendres* in Ovid's account of the myth of Io, see A. Feldherr, *Playing gods: Ovid's Metamorphoses and the politics of fiction* (Princeton 2010) 15-24.

[35] C. Dempsey, *The portrayal of love: Botticelli's Primavera and humanist culture at the time of Lorenzo the Magnificent* (Princeton 1992) 27. On Renaissance definitions of *poesie*, see also Freedman, *Classical myths* (n. 8, above) 201-14. P. Barolsky 'Ovidian Wit and erotic play in the painted poetry of Correggio', *Source* 12 (1993) 19-23

[36] P. Pino, *Dialogo di pittura* (Venice 1548), republished in *Trattati d'arte del Cinquecento: fra manierismo e Controriforma,* ed. P. Barocchi 3 vols (Bari, 1960-62) I (1960) 115. Cited and translated by C. Dempsey in Dempsey, *The portrayal of love* (n. 35, above) 28.

and textual references. But unlike *The Portrait of a Lady* and *The Punishment of Hera*, the *Io* is not tied to a key passage or word. Although Ovid's account of this myth in the *Metamorphoses* may be considered Correggio's primary literary source, it here serves as a springboard for the painter's own creation, which inventively deviates from the canonical Ovidian narrative. Explicating the differences between Correggio's image and Ovid's text must have been, from the beginning, one of the painting's hooks – it has certainly proven to be a productive venue for scholarly debate in the past sixty years.

In his now classic study on Correggio's *Amori di Giove*, Verheyen identifies Bernardo Lapini's late fifteenth-century commentary on Petrarch's *Trionfi* as the primary source for the *Io*. In Bernardo's text, the tale of Io appears as the first of twelve amatory narratives involving the father of gods and men, where he is said to have embraced Inachus' daughter while in the form of a cloud (*…e lei comprese in forma di nebula*).[37] If Correggio was indeed following Bernardo's words in creating his composition, the identification of this textual reference helps us reconstruct a possible point of origin for his unusual portrayal of this myth. It does not, however, in any way limit the interpretive possibilities that this image was meant to elicit. Verheyen himself demonstrates this when, immediately after announcing his discovery, he shifts from pinpointing the artist's debt to Bernardo to analyzing the meaning of Correggio's painting. Focusing on the figure of a deer which is shown drinking water from a stream in the lower right corner of the canvas, Verheyen writes:

> In the medieval tradition of painting the presence of deer at a spring or on the river of Paradise symbolizes a longing for God, and this interpretation is borne out by Psalm 41, by Valeriano, and by Cesare Ripa:…*un Cervo che beve l'Acqua di un ruscello secondo il detto di David nel Salmo 41, dove assomiglia Iddio al desiderio che ha un cervo assettato di avvicinarsi a qualche limpida fontana.* The inclusion of a deer in the *Io* painting is an emblem which demonstrates its fundamental idea: *Desiderio verso Iddio.*[38]

But Verheyen's allegorical reading of Correggio's *Io* is not the only Neoplatonic interpretation of this painting to have been put forth. More recently, Luba Freedman expanded Verheyen's brief analysis of this painting by interpreting the *Io* in the light of contemporary debates on the nature of love and desire – debates that would have been very much *au courant* at the court in Mantua during the years when Correggio was working on his mythologies for Federico II Gonzaga.[39] Drawing from the works of numerous authors, including Marsilio Ficino, Pico della Mirandola, Leone Ebreo, Baldassare Castiglione and Pietro Bembo, Freedman sees the *Io* as replete with Neoplatonic references. She begins by proposing that the *Io* illustrates the commonplace notion that to love is to die. As such, this painting may be seen as embodying Ficino's description of love as bitter sweet (*dulce amarum*): 'As death, [love] is bitter, but

---

[37] Verheyen, 'Correggio's *Amori di Giove*' (n. 5, above) 186.

[38] Verheyen, 'Correggio's *Amori di Giove*' (n. 5, above) 186. See also G. D. Wind, 'Sport for Jove: Correggio's *Io* and *Ganymede*', *Gazette des Beaux-Arts* 109 (1987) 106; P. Barolsky, *Ovid and the metamorphoses of modern art from Botticelli to Picasso* (New Haven 2014) 50.

[39] Freedman, 'Correggio's *Io*' (n. 2, above) 93-96.

being voluntary, it is sweet'.[40] At the same time, Io's pose evokes Renaissance definitions of the kiss as the soul's escape from the body to be united with the loved one's spirit.[41] The nymph's S-shaped posture, her *figura serpentinata*, also recalls Bembo's and Castiglione's characterization of love as a fire that consumes one with desire. Thus Io's sinuous form becomes a visual metaphor for the flame of love.[42] Lastly, the deer which was interpreted by Verheyen as an emblem of *desiderio verso Iddio*, is seen as an allegory of insatiable desire and a premonition of death drawn from French *chansons de geste* – a poetic genre well-known at the court in Mantua through the studies of Mario Equicola, the secretary to Federico's mother, Isabella d'Este.[43]

By tracing numerous possible literary 'intertexts' for Correggio's *Io*, Freedman offers a portrait of the intellectual milieu that informed its creation and early interpretation. Like the *Portrait of a Lady* and the *Punishment of Hera*, the *Io* presented viewers with a modernized version of the classics, in which ancient works of literature and art were made to reflect contemporary beliefs and concerns. But although it is quite likely that Correggio was influenced by the then fashionable Neoplatonic debates on the nature of love, it is equally possible that in transforming Ovid's tale of ravishment into a scene of mutual desire and pleasure he drew from far less erudite sources – namely popular sixteenthcentury Italian 'translations' of the *Metamorphoses*. In one such 'vulgarization' of Ovid's poem, Nicolò di Agustini's *Metamorphosi cioè trasmutationi tradotte del latino diligentemente in vulgar verso, con le sue allegorie*, printed in Venice numerous times in the 1520s and 30s, the 'translator' inserts a whole *ottava*, in which Jove is said to court Io like a gallant lover, igniting in the reluctant nymph a reciprocal longing for him.

> Cosi fu vincitor di quella caccia
> Giove, e la vaga nimpha a forza prese
> E tenendola stretta ne le braccia
> Con parlar non da deo, ma d'huom cortese
> Basciandoli la sua vermiglia faccia
> Al fin de l'amor suo tutta l'accese
> E seco giacque in quella nube folta
> Con piacer d'ambe dua piu d'una volta.[44]

---

[40] Freedman, 'Correggio's *Io*' (n. 2, above) 93-94. See also M. Ficino, *Commentary on Plato's Symposium*, ed. and trans. S. R. Jane (Columbia 1944) 143.

[41] Freedman, 'Correggio's *Io*' (n. 2, above) 95. On Renaissance theories of the kiss, see also P. Galand-Hallyn, 'Jean Second et la bête à deux dos dans les *Baisers* (1539-1541)', in *Ovide: figures de l'hybride. Illustrations littéraires et figurées de l'esthétique ovidienne à travers les âges*, ed. H. Casanova-Robin (Paris 2009) 325-39.

[42] Freedman, 'Correggio's *Io*' (n. 2, above) 96-98.

[43] Freedman, 'Correggio's *Io*' (n. 2, above) 94-96. See also Ekserdjian, *Correggio* (n. 1, above) 286. Sara Switzer sees in the image of Correggio's deer a possible Petrarchan reference (*cf.* Petrach's Sonnet CXC). S. Switzer, 'Correggio and the sacred image' (PhD dissertation, Columbia University 2012) 41 n. 111.

[44] N. di Agustini, *Metamorphosi cioè tramutationi tradotte del latino diligentemente in vulgar verso, con le sue allegorie* (Venice 1533) fol. 10v.

Thus Jove was the winner in that hunt, and seized the nymph by force. Holding her tight in his arms, and speaking to her not like a god, but like a gentleman, kissing her on her reddened face, at the end of his love-making he set all of her on fire, and lay with her in that thick cloud, with pleasure felt by both more than once.

Not all scholars, however, see the anthropomorphic cloud representing Jupiter's divine being in Correggio's *Io* as the result of modern literary re-interpretations of this myth. Marcin Fabianski, for instance, has argued for a different kind of textual contamination. According to him, Correggio's choice of depicting the enamored god in this vaporous form resulted from the fusion of two different metamorphic narratives: the myth of Io and that of Ixion, which Correggio may have known not only through Ovid's *Metamorphoses* and the *Ibis*, but also through Lucian's *Dialogue of the Gods* – a text that had been cited by Mario Ecquicola in his own amatory treatise.[45] The idea that, in depicting the tale of Io, Correggio might have been inspired by other passages from Ovid is rather intriguing and opens up a different range of possible interpretations. For instance, Io's languid appearance may be seen as a visual evocation of *Ars* 2.689-92, where Ovid describes the physical signs of female sexual pleasure in great detail.[46] In this Ovidian light, the deer drinking water from a stream might be seen not just as a Neoplatonist emblem, but also as a pictorial allusion to the venatic metaphors that are characteristic of Latin love poetry.[47]

But Correggio's ingenious solution for representing the lovers amidst a thick, dark cloud should not be considered solely through a web of ancient and modern textual references. It must also be understood in the context of Renaissance artistic theory and practice. Leonardo da Vinci, in his *Libro di Pittura*, advises fellow artists to look closely at the forms that naturally appear on the surface of ancient walls and stones, or sometimes amidst ashes, clouds, or muddy pools. For one might find in these most wondrous inventions (*invenzioni mirabilissime*) from which the artist's imagination can create fantastical battle scenes, landscapes and chimerical creatures.[48] For fifteenth and sixteenth-century Italian artists, clouds were, then, both a wonderfully creative medium and a potent catalyst for new

---

[45]   Fabianski, 154. On the popularity of Ovid's *Ibis* in the early modern period, see Frank Coulson's article in this volume. For a catalogue of Latin editions of Ovid's *Metamorphoses* printed in Parma in the fifteenth century, see I. Affó, *Memorie degli scrittori e letterati parmigiani. Tomo terzo* (Parma 1791), lxiii-lxv, lxviii-lxix, lxxvi-lxxvii, xc. Fabianski also points out that Correggio's transformation of Jupiter into a cloud may have been intended as a pictorial evocation of the pun on *nubes* (clouds), *innuba* (unmarried maiden) and *nubere* (to marry) found in Latin Christian authors, see Fabianski, *Correggio* (n. 2, above) 154. On this pun, see also G. Didi-Huberman, *Fra Angelico. Dissemblance et figuration* (Paris 1990) 202. Given Correggio's earlier adaptations of Homeric motifs, it is also possible that his choice of depicting Jupiter as a cloud might have been inspired by the seduction scene in *Iliad* 14, in which Zeus, 'the cloud-gatherer', envelops Hera and himself in a golden cloud so that they may enjoy each other without being seen (341-51).

[46]   Fabianski, *Correggio* (n. 2, above) 155, n.70.

[47]   See, for instance, Virgil, *Aen.* 4.69; Ovid *Ars* 1.45-50, 263-70; *Met.* 1.505-07. See also Wind, 'Sport for Jove' (n. 38) 106 ff.

[48]   Leonardo da Vinci, *Libro di pittura: edizione in facsimile del Codice Urbinate lat. 1270 nella Biblioteca Apostolica Vaticana*, ed. C. Pedretti (Florence 1995) 2 vols I (1995) fol. 35v. See also A. Nagel, 'Leonardo and *sfumato*', *Res* 24 (1993) 7-20.

artistic inventions. So, by transforming Jupiter into a cloud, Correggio was also fashioning himself a worthy peer of other great cloud painters, such as Mantegna and Raphael, whose works may have inspired his own *invenzione*.[49]

In 1530-31 clouds would have been very much on Correggio's mind for yet another reason. From 1530 to 1534, the year of his death, Correggio worked on the largest and most ambitious artistic project of his career: the frescoes for the cupola of the Cathedral in Parma.[50] The subject of this monumental painting was the *Assumption of the Virgin*, shown here as she rises from her tomb toward heaven (Figure 9). Correggio's composition represented a radical reimagining of this traditional religious subject. Painted *di sotto in sù*, Correggio's *Assumption* presents the Virgin's entrance into the heavenly kingdom not as a formal, static moment, but rather as a joyful, rapturous process to which we are made witnesses and, to some extent, participants.

It is clear from Correggio's preparatory drawings for the frescoes in the Cathedral in Parma and the Mantuan mythologies that he was thinking of these two commissions in tandem. It has long been known that Correggio's *Ganymede* is an exact copy of one of the angels in the squinch with Saint Bernard. But the figure of Io herself is closely modeled after a drawing (later rejected) for the *vergine assunta*.[51] It is, of course, not uncommon for artists to reuse their own material in different compositions. But in the case of *Io*, the parallels with the *Assumption* point to Correggio's desire to infuse this intensely sensual and pagan subject with his own signature *lietezza*.

In painting the *Assumption* and the *Io*, Correggio employed several of his earlier pictorial strategies, such as the use of *chiaroscuro* and soft, almost disappearing contours, along with intensely affectionate gestures, to create images that would not only represent ecstasy, but

---

[49]   G. Berra, 'Immagini casuali, figure nascoste e natura antropomorfa nell'immaginario artistico rinascimentale', *Mitteilungen des Kunsthistorischen Institutes in Florenz* 43 (1999) 358, 375-76. On Mantegna's influence on Correggio, see Berra, 'Immagini casuali', 375; Fabianski, *Correggio* (n. 2, above) 80; S. Campbell, 'Mantegna's Triumph: the cultural politics of imitation 'all'antica' at the court of Mantua 1490-1530', in *Artists at court: image-making and identity 1300-1550*, ed. S. Campbell (Boston 2004) 101-05; Campbell, *The cabinet of eros* (n. 6, above) 222, 228. On Correggio's acquaintance with several works by Raphael featuring anthropomorphic clouds, especially the *Sistine Madonna* and the *Disputa,* see Campbell, *The cabinet of eros* (n. 6, above) 229-31; Gould, *The paintings of Correggio* (n. 9, above) 40-46; J. Shearman, 'Raphael's clouds and Correggio's', in *Studi su Raffaello*, ed. M. Hamoud and M. Strocchi (Urbino 1987) 2 vols II (1987) 657-68. On clouds as a recurring element in Correggio's paintings, see H. Damisch, *A theory of / cloud/: toward a history of painting*, trans. J. Lloyd (Stanford 2002), 1-37.

[50]   On the dates for Correggio's frescoes in the Cathedral in Parma, see C. Cecchinelli, 'Il pittore e i ponteggi: nuovi documenti e nuove date per gli affreschi del Correggio nella cupola della cattedrale di Parma (1530-1534)', *Nuovi Studi* 15 (2009) 135-52.

[51]   On Correggio's *Ganymede*, see Ekserdjian, *Correggio* (n. 1, above) 282. On the parallels between *Io* and earlier preparatory drawings for the *Assumption*, see Switzer, 'Correggio and the sacred image' (n. 43, above) 41.

Figure 9 Correggio, *Assumption of the Virgin*, Parma Cathedral, Parma (1530-34). Photo: Art Resource, NY

also trigger a joyful response in his viewers.[52] That the experience of spiritual joy should be a key component of the representation of the Virgin's Assumption is, of course, not surprising. What is truly surprising is the way Correggio transforms the potentially lewd subject of Io's encounter with Jupiter into a delightful contemplation on the nature of love, the pleasures of the imagination, and the rivalry between painting and poetry. In so doing, Correggio changed this violent tale of divine lust into something gentler and sweeter, bringing Ovid's narrative closer to contemporary idealized views of the classical past that tended to filter out the more brutal aspects of Greco-Roman culture.[53]

While the frescoes on the cupola of the Cathedral in Parma constituted Correggio's public apotheosis as an artist, the mythologies he painted for Federico II Gonzaga represented a more private, personal triumph. Although he had painted other classical subjects before, the *Io* constituted an important departure from his earlier treatment of ancient art and literature. With this painting, Correggio declared himself a visual poet – an artist who, like Ovid himself, was capable of updating the classical tradition through a playful, humorous, sensual re-interpretation of well-known myths. Given Correggio's

[52] G. Periti, 'Nota sulla 'maniera moderna' di Correggio a Parma', in *Parmigianino e il manierismo europeo: atti del convegno internazionale di studi, Parma, 13-15 giugno 2002*, eds L. Schianchi and S. Ferino-Pagden (Milan 2003), 298-303; Switzer, 'Correggio and the sacred image' (n. 43, above) *passim*. See also n. 16, above.

[53] *Cf.* Hélene Casanova-Robin's essay on Pontano's treatment of Ovidian themes in this volume.

linguistic sensibility and his appreciation for wordplay, evident in his transformation of his own name, it is possible that the *Io* was intended as a kind of rebus. In Italian, the nymph's name, Io, and the first person singular pronoun are homophones.[54] But Correggio's play on Io and *io* could also have been inspired by Ovid's own account of this myth. In one of the most poignant moments of the Ovidian narrative, the nymph (now in the guise of a cow) reveals her true identity to her father by tracing her name on the sand with her newly acquired hoofs (*Met.* 1.649-50).[55] The act of inscribing one's name was, as we have seen, an important *topos* in the creation of Correggio's artistic identity earlier in his career. It is then likely he would have revisited it on this occasion, challenging the viewer to recognize his 'signature' through a combination of literary, visual and aural cues.

Correggio's *Io* is, then, an elegant fusion of word and image, of antiquity and modernity, which was also a witty statement of the artist's identity: *Io*, Correggio, the painter of *lietezza* who, like Ovid before him, transforms received mythological tradition into an expression of his own personal style. Painted at the height of Correggio's success as a modern, Lombard artist, at a moment when he was poised to become a painter of even greater, 'national' renown, the *Io* heralded a new phase in his career. The *Io* was, although much smaller in scale, in many ways, as ambitious a composition as the *Assumption*. But the great promise latent in both works was never to be fully realized. In 1534, while still in his forties, Correggio died, leaving behind him beautiful, tantalizing suggestions of pleasures that might have been.

Department of Classics,
The University of North Carolina at Chapel Hill

[54] Hubert Damisch remarks that *Io* is 'the mark of subjectivity'. See Damisch, *A theory of /cloud/* (n. 49, above) 23.

[55] Alessandro Barchiesi argues that Ovid's description of Io writing her name on the sand (*Met.* 1.649-50) itself contains a bilingual pun on IΩ/ἰώ (ἰώ = *me miserum*). See *Ovidio Metamorfosi*, ed. A. Barchiesi 3 vols (Rome 2005-) I (2005) 221. On this pun, see also Feldherr, *Playing gods* (n. 34, above) 19. It is also possible that, in devising this scene in the story of Io, Ovid had in mind a visual pun between the shape of a cow's hoof and that of the Greek letter ω.

RUBENS AND OVID

ELIZABETH MCGRATH

In memoriam J. B. Trapp

For artists of Rubens's era Ovid's *Metamorphoses* was an indispensable resource – so much so that Karel van Mander (the Dutch writer on art) could describe the book in 1604 as the Painters' Bible.[1] Despite the advance of Calvinism, to one side, and of the Counter Reformation, to the other, there continued to be a widespread demand in the Netherlands for pictures of love stories from classical mythology,[2] and to most people (then as now) mythological love stories meant tales from Ovid. To make life easy for artists there were plenty of epitomes of the *Metamorphoses* available (van Mander's was one, which conveniently supplied morals to the tales as well, for those who felt the need for them).[3] There were even more 'illustrated Ovids' available: editions, or more often epitomes, of the text, with abundant woodcuts or engravings. One such was the picture book published in convenient pocket-size at the Plantin Press in Antwerp in 1591 (*cf.* Figure 1), in which summaries of the tales (in this case by the late Roman author Lactantius Placidus) appeared side by side with the etchings.[4] These works often specifically advertized themselves as aimed at artists, and in his *approbatio* of the Plantin volume the ecclesiastical censor cited as justification of the publication its 'singular utility' not only to students of poetry, but to

---

[1] K. van Mander, *Wtlegghingh op den Metamorphosis…* (Alkmaar, 1604), sig. Iiiiv: '*het … t'Schilders Bybel gheheeten was om datter veel Historien uyt gheschildert wierden*'. Van Mander wrote this in the introduction to his own 'explanation' of the Ovidian tales.

[2] This is well attested in the inventories not only of princely collections, but, in the Netherlands at least, where the ownership of pictures was relatively widespread, in the households of well-to-do citizens. See notably E. J. Sluijter, *De 'heydensche fabulen' in de schilderkunst van de Gouden Eeuw* (Leiden, 2000); C. Van de Velde. 'Profane historieschilderkunst', in *Antwerpen in de zeventiende eeuw* (Antwerp, 1988) 365-77; N. De Poorter, 'Of Olympian gods, Homeric heroes and an Antwerp Apelles: observations on the function and 'meaning' of mythological themes in the age of Rubens (1600-1650)', in *Greek gods and heroes in the age of Rubens and Rembrandt*, exh. cat., ed. P. Schoon and S. Paarlberg (Dordrecht, 2000) 65-85.

[3] These were mostly derived from the French edition of Natale Conti's *Mythologia*, first published at Paris in 1583. For Van Mander's sources see esp. Sluijter, *De 'heydensche fabulen'* (n. 2 above) 17983.

[4] *P.Ovidii Nasonis Metamorphoses, argumentis brevioribus ex Luctatio Grammatico collectis expositae: una cum vivis singularum Transformationum iconibus in aes incisis* (Antwerp, 1591). Luctatius Grammaticus is usually equated with Lactantius Placidus. On the continuing use of his *argumenta*, see, for example, A. Moss, *Ovid in Renaissance France (Warburg Institute Surveys VIII)* (London, 1982) esp. 41-44. For Rubens's purchase of this book see below, at n. 9.

Figure 1 Pieter van der Borcht, *The Banquet of Tereus* from *Metamorphoses*, Antwerp, 1591

painters.[5] Sometimes indeed the text was reduced to a caption, as in the prints by Antonio Tempesta (*cf.* Figure 2), which were produced in different editions.[6] Artists could leaf through these books for ideas even if they did not then follow the simplified compositions exactly. Some would then go on to read the stories, in a suitable translation – the Latin text was rarely consulted.[7]

Rubens by contrast read Ovid in the original, but he too might on occasion resort to illustrated Ovidian compendia as a point of departure. Towards the end of 1636, four years before he died, he was commissioned to make an enormous series of large mythological pictures for Philip IV's hunting lodge outside Madrid, the Torre de la Parada: over sixty items in all – and to be completed in a short time span.[8] In fact the artist not only employed the members of his studio but took on a team of independent Antwerp painters to help him execute these works, and had his collaborators sign their respective contributions, which were, nonetheless, all based on Rubens's sketches. We know from his accounts with the Plantin-Moretus shop in Antwerp that in January 1637, just after he

---

[5] *Metamorphoses* (as in n. 4), *Approbatio*, unnumbered page, *ad finem*: '... propter singularem utilitatem hoc Poeticarum Fabularum Enchiridion elaboratissimum dignum esse ut et imprimatur, et ab omnibus studiosis Poësios, et pictoribus diligenter legatur et inspectetur, iudico'. For the ownership of illustrated Ovids by artists see E. McGrath, 'Artists, their books and subjects from mythology' in *Classical Mythology in the Netherlands in the age of Renaissance and Baroque*, ed. Carl Van de Velde (Leuven, Paris and Walpole, MA, 2009) 301-32, esp. 306-11.

[6] See *Metamorphoseon sive Transformationum Ovidianarum libri quindecim aeneis formis ab Antonio Tempesta florentino incisi* (Antwerp, 1606). On the impact of this book see E. Leuschner, *Antonio Tempesta. Ein Bahnbrecher des römischen Barok und seine europäische Wirkung* (Petersberg, 2004) 520-61.

[7] Though the Dutch writer on art Gerard de Lairesse complained of painters not reading anything at all but simply following unthinkingly the illustrations in the Ovidian books and compendia: *Groot Schilder-book*, 2 vols (Amsterdam, 1712) I: 123; cited in Sluijter, *De 'heydensche fabulen'* (n. 2 above) 97-98.

[8] On this series see notably S. Alpers, *The decoration of the Torre de la Parada* (*Corpus Rubenianum Ludwig Burchard*, IX) (Brussels, London and New York, 1971).

Figure 2 *Deucalion and Pyrrha*, from Antonio Tempesta's series of Ovid's *Metamorphoses*, Antwerp, 1606 (Photo: Warburg Institute)

had begun working on this project, Rubens bought a small (*sextodecimo*) *Metamorphoses* with engravings or etchings ('*coperen*') – presumably the Plantin volume published in 1591 with etchings by Pieter van der Borcht (*cf.* Figure 1).[9] It is apparent it gave him some suggestions, especially perhaps because he seems to have designed the pictures in corresponding pairs, or groups, for different walls or rooms in the hunting lodge. *Cadmus and Minerva*, for example, with armed men springing from the newly sown dragon's teeth, seems to have been paralleled with *Deucalion and Pyrrha*, in which a race of humans (peaceable, this time) is likewise born of the earth from rocks cast backwards by the old

---

[9] '1 Ovidii metamorphosis 16o cop. f. 4' (14 January 1637). See P. Arents, *De Bibliotheek van Pieter Pauwel Rubens: een reconstructie*, ed. A. K. L. Thijs *et al.* (Antwerp, 2001) 198, E191, identifying the volume, for which see above, n. 4. When I drew attention to the reference to this book in previous publications, I mistakenly supposed that it could not be the Plantin volume of 1591, which I believed was larger in size. For the relevance of the book to Rubens see E. McGrath, *Subjects from History (Corpus Rubenianum Ludwig Burchard, XIII.1)*, 2 vols (London, 1997) I: 65; McGrath, 'Artists, their books…' (n. 5) 309-11.

Figure 3 Rubens, *Deucalion and Pyrrha*, sketch. Madrid, Museo del Prado (Photo: Museum)

couple who alone have survived the Flood.[10] Rubens's sketch for the latter painting (Figure 3) reveals how he adapted a familiar composition from illustrated Ovids (*cf.* Figure 2),[11] but he certainly paid close attention to the text of *Metamorphoses* (I. 313414). With this in mind, he made it clear that not only both husband and wife have their heads piously covered as they throw behind them the stones which will reform themselves into humans, but that Pyrrha's stones will turn into females and Deucalion's produce males. Moreover, departing from the letter of the text, Rubens added, in Ovidian spirit, an allusion to the obvious attraction between the newly created couples destined to repopulate the world after the Flood.[12]

Where the subject particularly engaged him, Rubens executed the large-scale picture himself. Such was the case with the *Banquet of Tereus* (Figure 4), illustrating the terrible revenge enacted on the Thracian king by his wife Procne and her sister Philomela.[13] The

---

[10] Alpers, *Torre* (n. 8) 188-89, no. 9 and 200-01, no. 17; figs 76-77, 95-96; for the argument about correspondences see McGrath 'Artists, their books…' (n. 5 above) 310.

[11] Rubens includes, on the mountain top to the right, the stranded 'ark' of Deucalion; the temple to the left is where the old couple have previously sought advice of the oracle.

[12] On this point, see J. S. Held, *The Oil Sketches of Peter Paul Rubens*, 2 vols (Princeton, N.J., 1980) I: 255, 270-71, no. 184. Held points out that Rubens repositioned Deucalion and Pyrrha so that in the corresponding new-born couple the woman could be in front, making for a more elegant arrangement of the naked figures, drawn one to another.

[13] Alpers, *Torre* (n. 8 above) 262-64, no. 57; figs 182-83, rightly concluding that the sketch is recorded only in copies; also M. Diáz Padrón, *El siglo de Rubens en el Museo del Prado*, 3 vols (Barcelona 1995) II: 918-19.

Figure 4 Rubens, *The Banquet of Tereus*. Madrid, Museo del Prado (Photo: Museum)

artist was perhaps prompted to think of the subject by the print in his illustrated compendium (Figure 1), but Ovid's text was the real inspiration,[14] all the more since, to capture the sense of the story in a way that would be visually compelling, he revises some features of the poet's narrative, as well as adding his own touches. Ovid describes how Procne and Philomela, in mad Bacchic mode, enter the chamber where Tereus has just dined, to reveal to him that it is the body of his son, Itys, which he has unwittingly consumed. Maddened by grief and a desire for vengeance for her sister, whom Tereus had raped and incarcerated after cutting out her tongue, Procne killed the boy, with help from Philomela. When the women burst in to confront Tereus with the horror of his punishment, the poet lets Procne speak words of bitter irony while Philomela presents him with Itys's bloody head. In his wordless version of the story, Rubens, however, exchanges the roles of sisters, to underline that it was the child's mother, not his aunt, who initiated his cruel murder. Philomela, pallid and haggard after her torture and imprisonment, is evidently the woman in the foreground who expresses herself by gesture alone, her open mouth a soundless testimony to her missing tongue.[15] To make the point that Procne had cleared the room so that Tereus would dine alone (VI. 647-51), there is a cowering servant peeping in at the door (his shrinking dismay echoed in the pose of the Cupid carved over the lintel above). The vehemence of

[14] Ovid, *Metamorphoses* VI. 412-676, esp. 587-666.

[15] *Cf.* the comments in Held, *Sketches* (n. 12 above) I: 297.

164   THE AFTERLIFE OF OVID

Tereus's repulsion is expressed in the upturned table, intensifying Ovid's '*ingenti mensas clamore repellit*' (VI. 661; 'with resounding roar he pushed away the table'),[16] while the poet's '*sicut erat sparsis furiali caede capillis*' (VI. 657: 'in disarray, with hair blood-splattered from the wild slaughter') is brilliantly captured in the abandoned state of the women, as is the powerful '*misit in ora patris*' (VI. 659: 'she thrust before [*literally* 'sent into'] the father's face') of the brutally proffered head.

At the same time as he bought the little 'illustrated Ovid' for the Torre de la Parada commission, the artist received two other books he had ordered: a new edition of Servius's commentary on Virgil (in the text of Petrus Daniel published by Chouet at Geneva in 1636), and the three-volume edition of Virgil's works by Ludovicus Cerdanus (de la Cerda) (Cologne, 1628).[17] This highlights the fact that unlike other painters of the period, Rubens not only read ancient texts in the original, but did so from humanist, as well as artistic, interest – if not simply for pleasure. It is important to remember he had been very close to his brother Philip, a distinguished classicist and the favourite pupil of Justus Lipsius, and he may have inherited part of Philip's library when the scholar died prematurely, in 1612. We know quite a lot about the artist's own book purchases, particularly from the accounts he kept with the Plantin Press, from 1610 under the charge of his friend, Balthasar Moretus (the pair had studied at a Latin school together).[18] From these records it is evident Rubens regularly bought scholarly editions of a whole range of classical authors, Greek as well as Latin (though, in all the cases where the edition can be identified, he chose volumes in which the Greek text was provided with a parallel Latin translation).[19]

There is no record, however, of which edition or editions of Ovid Rubens owned or regularly consulted. But since we can be confident that he would have had in his possession a text with all the usual Renaissance commentaries, I have taken as a point of reference the three-volume folio *Opera omnia* published at Frankfurt in 1601, which is furnished with the

[16] Tereus's kicking of the table is echoed, in reverse, in the gesture of Herod in the near contemporary (*c*. 1638) Feast of Herod (Edinburgh, National Gallery of Scotland), painted for a Flemish collector living in Naples with a taste for gory subjects. It is clear that the two pictures, involving severed heads at feasts, were very much associated in Rubens mind, which underlines the fact that the *Banquet of Tereus* was a subject of special interest to him. For the *Feast of Herod* see M. Jaffé, *Rubens: Catalogo Completo* (Milan, 1989) 346, no. 1187; C. Whitfield in *Painting in Naples from Caravaggio to Giordano*, exh. cat. ed. J. Martineau and C. Whitfield (London, 1982) 239-40, no. 138; *cf.* McGrath, *History* (n. 9 above), I: figure 17 and II: 37-39 for a related drawing, with another idea for a gruesome theme of decapitation on the reverse of the sheet (Cyrus's head plunged into a bowl of blood).

[17] See McGrath, *History* (n. 9 above) I: 65; Arents, *Bibliotheek* (n. 9 above) 198-99, E190; 192. 191. For the relevance of Virgil to Rubens's work of this period see McGrath, 'Artists, their books...' (n. 5) 312-39.

[18] For Rubens's relationship with Moretus, the grandson of Christophe Plantin, and their attendance at Rumoldus Verdonck's Latin school, behind Antwerp Cathedral, see M. Rooses, 'Petrus-Paulus Rubens en Balthasar Moretus', *Rubens-Bulletijn*, I (1882) 203-19, esp. 207-12; *cf.* M. Morford, *Stoics and Neo-Stoics: Rubens and the circle of Lipsius* (Princeton, 1991) 187.

[19] See McGrath, *History* (n. 9), I, 62-65. The artist evidently made an effort to improve his Greek and began purchasing bi-lingual texts *c.* 1615, starting with Pausanias; the following year he bought Constantinus's Greek-Latin lexicon, a revision of that of Étienne (Stephanus), and went on to purchase the works of several Greek historians.

commentaries of Raffaelo Regio and Jacobus Micyllus for the *Metamorphoses*, Antonius Constantius Fanensis (Antonio Costanzi) and Paulo Marsi (with scholia by Melanchthon) for the *Fasti*, and Micyllus and Bartholomaeus Merula for the *Ars amatoria*.[20] In fact Rubens was just as familiar with Ovid's other major works as he was with *Metamorphoses*. He quotes from the *Fasti* and the *Heroides* in his surviving letters,[21] and when in 1624 he published an engraving illustrating Susanna and the Elders he pointedly gave it the tag: '*Turpe senilis amor*': 'Amorous old men are disgusting' (*Amores* I.9.4).[22] Moreover, an earlier print of what might seem to be a simple genre scene, showing an old woman letting a boy light his candle from the burning one she holds, was inscribed by Rubens with lines from the *Art of Love* (III. 93 and 90) where the reference is to the capacity of a woman to satisfy multiple lovers: '*Quis vetet apposito lumen de lumine tolli?/ Mille licet capiant; deperit inde nihil*' ('Who will refuse one light be lit from another? Let a thousand be taken; nothing is lost from the first').[23]

Of course citations of familiar, almost proverbial, lines – such as '*adhuc sua messis in herba erat*', adapted from *Heroides* XVII.263, in a letter about the premature death of a friend[24] –might just have been culled from *florilegia* or commonplace books; and in the case of any other artist it would be reasonable to assume that they were. But there are too many examples in Rubens's oeuvre of pictures and details in pictures which were directly prompted by passages in Ovid for it to be a matter of isolated verses. From his youth Rubens probably knew large sections of Ovid's poetry by heart – and not only from works approved for the schoolroom. The *Ars Amatoria* was certainly a constant inspiration. It was this poem which determined the tone and much of the content, for example, of the tapestry series on the life of Achilles that the artist designed in the early 1630s.[25] Here, adapting Homer's theme to Ovidian purpose, he portrayed the hero as a man ruled by

---

[20] *Publii Ovidii Nasonis Sulmonensis poetae operum tomus primus ...[etc]*, 3 vols (Frankfurt, Wechel, 1601).

[21] Arents, *Bibliotheek* (n. 9 above) 310, 313.

[22] See E. McGrath, 'Rubens's *Susanna and the Elders* and moralizing inscriptions on prints' in *Wort und Bild in der Niederländischen Kunst und Literatur des 16. und 17. Jahrhunderts*, ed. H. Vekeman and J. Müller Hofstede (Erftstadt 1984) 73-90, esp. 81-85 and figure 12.

[23] The few variations with the modern text of the *Ars amatoria* (*e.g. tolli* rather than *sumi*) do not affect the basic sense. For this print, executed after Rubens's design by Paulus Pontius, a proof state survives (Bibliothèque Nationale de France, Paris) on which Rubens himself penned the inscription to be used. See E. De Jongh and G. Luijten, *Spiegel van Allergdag: Nederlandse genreprenten 1550-1700* (Amsterdam, Rijksmuseum, 1997), 209-12, no. 40; also N. van Hout, *Copyright Rubens: Rubens en de grafiek/Rubens et la gravure* (Ghent, 2004), 72-73, illustrating the different stages of the printing process.

[24] Letter of 14 January 1611 to Johann Faber, on the death of the painter Adam Elsheimer. See M. Rooses and C. Ruelens, *Correspondance de Rubens et documents épistolaires concernant sa vie et ses oeuvres*, 6 vols (Antwerp, 1887-1909) VI: 327.

[25] For the series see E. Haverkamp Begemann, *The Achilles Series* (*Corpus Rubenianum Ludwig Burchard*, X) (Brussels and London, 1975); F. Lammertse and A. Vergara, *Peter Paul Rubens: The Life of Achilles*, exh. cat. (Rotterdam, 2003).

Figure 5 Rubens, *The Education of Achilles*, sketch. Rotterdam, Museum Boijmans – Van Beuningen (Photo: Google Art Project, WikiCommons)

love.[26] The scene intended to introduce the cycle (Figure 5) already gives us a clue: for Ovid begins his *Art of Love*, in which he is going to provide instruction to Cupid himself, with the analogy of Achilles and Chiron. Even the fearsome hero who would terrify friend and foe alike once trembled before his tutor, the old centaur who tamed his wild nature by teaching him the lyre and made him hold out his hands for punishment (Figure 5); this encourages Ovid to give a poetic lesson to Amor, who though merciless too, is, after all,

---

[26] For this interpretation see McGrath, *History* (n. 9 above) I: 117-20.

Figure 6 Rubens, *The Rape of the Daughters of Leucippus*. Munich, Alte Pinakothek

just a boy.[27] With this passage in mind Rubens teasingly pictured Chiron educating young Achilles in horsemanship by letting him ride on his back while nonetheless keeping him

---

[27] *Ars Amatoria* I.7-17: '*Me Venus artificem tenero praefecit Amori;/ Tiphys et Automedon dicar Amoris ego./ Ille quidem ferus est et qui mihi saepe repugnet:/ Sed puer est, aetas mollis et apta regi./ Phillyrides puerum cithara perfecit Achillem,/ Atque animos placida contudit arte feros./ Qui totiens socios, totiens exterruit hostes,/ Creditur annosum pertimuisse senem./ Quas Hector sensurus erat, poscente magistro/ Verberibus iussas praebuit ille manus./ Aeacidae Chiron, ego sum praeceptor Amoris:...*'.

168 THE AFTERLIFE OF OVID

in order with his rod.[28] And it was with the *Art of Love* in mind that Rubens painted the previously unknown subject of the Rape of the Leucippides (Figure 6), and illustrated it the way he did, extrapolating the scene from the context of the mythological story (which ends badly, with a fight in which Castor is killed). As in the *Art of Love*, the abduction of Phoebe and Hilaira, daughters of Leucippus, provides a classic instance of the Ovidian truism (as Rubens and his like-minded contemporaries would have seen it) of how decent and delicate young women will be shy and at first reluctant to yield to male embraces, and so need to be swept up in the heat of passion. It is this story, after all, which concludes the notorious passage about seduction in the *Ars amatoria*:

> And if she doesn't give [her kisses] freely, just take them anyway, ungiven. Maybe at first she'll fight, and call you 'wicked rogue' (*improbe*); but her wish in fighting is really to be won. Only be sure your clumsy force doesn't bruise her tender lips or that she can complain of roughness. A man who has taken kisses and taken nothing more deserved to lose even what was already granted. After a kiss any failure in the fulfilment of desire – well really, that is not modesty, it is just bad manners (*rusticitas, non pudor fuit ille*)! Call it violence if you like; this is a violence which girls appreciate. They often like to think they have given themselves to pleasure unwillingly. A woman suddenly seized in an impulse of violent passion is happy and counts the outrage a compliment. But when a woman who could be compelled goes off untouched she may put on an appearance of pleasure but will in fact be depressed. Violence was what Phoebe suffered, violence was done to her sister and each ravished girl was happy with her ravisher.[29]

The Cupids here underline the intention of the brothers, and that the abduction is a preliminary to marriage: it should be noted that they are occupied with controlling the horses,

---

[28] Rubens would also have remembered Juvenal's reference to Achilles fearing Chiron's rod even when quite a big boy (*Satires* VII. 210: '... *metuens virgae iam grandis Achilles...*'). This passage is cited in Merula's commentary in the 1601 Ovid, *Opera* (n. 20 above) I: 308. That Rubens was thinking of the Achilles/Cupid comparison is further underlined by the playful allusion he makes in his composition to a famous statue of a Cupid on the back of a centaur (tormented by love) which he had copied in Rome. See McGrath *History* (n. 9 above) I: 117-18.

[29] Ovid, *Ars amatoria* I.664–80: '*Illa licet non det; non data sume tamen./ Pugnabit primo fortassis, et Improbe dicet:/ Pugnando vinci se tamen illa volet./ Tantum, ne noceant teneris male rapta labellis,/ Neve queri possit dura fuisse, cave./ Oscula qui sumpsit, si non et caetera sumpsit:/ Haec quoque, quae data sunt, perdere dignus erat./ Quantum defuerat pleno post oscula voto?/ Hei mihi, rusticitas, non pudor ille fuit./ Vim licet appelles, grata est vis ista puellis:/ Quod iuvat, invitae saepe dedisse volunt./ Quaecunque est Veneris subita violata rapina,/ Gaudet: et improbitas muneris instar habet./ At quae cum cogi posset, non tacta recessit,/ Quum simulet vultu gaudia, tristis erit./ Vim passa est Phoebe; vis est illata sorori:/ Et gratus raptis raptor uterque fuit*'. I cite the text from the 1601 Frankfurt edition (n. 20 above; I: 328). Modern editions introduce minor emendations, mostly in tense, *e.g. sumet* for the second *sumpsit* in l.669. See McGrath *History* (n. 9 above) I: 121-31; also U. Heinen, '"*Con ogni fervore*": Love and Lust in Rubens's Library, Life and Work', in *Munuscula Amicorum: Contributions on Rubens and his Colleagues in Honour of Hans Vlieghe*, ed. K. Van der Stighelen, 2 vols (Turnhout, 2006) I: 79-101, esp. 88-95.

Figure 7 Rubens, *Boreas and Orithyia*. Vienna, Akademie der Bildenden Künste

a familiar symbol of the bridling of sexual passion in epithalamia of the period.[30] A similar idea involving the relationship of marriage and abduction informed the splendid painting of *Boreas and Orithyia* (Figure 7), made a few years earlier, c. 1612.[31] In this work Rubens presents the message of the *Art of Love* through a story from the *Metamorphoses*. Again the subject is the resort to force, exerted in pursuit of love by an impulsive and impatient lover.

---

[30] Heinen, 'Love and Lust' (n. 29 above) 91-92, sees the Cupids more as subjecting the horses to love. Whatever the case, there is a clear association with Rubens's various versions of the *Rape of the Sabines*, which likewise involve Cupids and more obvious marital allusions. Here too the primary inspiration is the interpretation of the subject as an example of forcible abduction that precedes marriage in the *Art of Love*. See McGrath *History* (n. 9 above) I: 120-21; II: 181-225.

[31] N. Lowitzch in J. Kräftner, W. Seipel and R. Trnek eds, *Rubens in Wien: Die Meisterwerke*, Vienna 2004, 106-09, no. 22.

The fierce and cold North Wind is seen acting with the bluster and aggression that comes naturally to him: in the *Metamorphoses*, Ovid relates how, his entreaties to Orithyia's father having failed to win her, Boreas, in furious indignation ('*horridus ira*'), simply caught up with her and carried her off to his snowy home.[32] A passage in the fifth book of the *Fasti* probably encouraged Rubens's interpretation. There, after giving a memorably laconic report of her rape by the wind-god Zephyr, the nymph (now goddess) Flora lays the blame on Boreas: his example in snatching Erechtheus's daughter made his brother feel he had every right to act the same way.[33] At the same time Flora takes it all in good part: Zephyr has made up for things by wedding her, and she has never had cause to complain of her marriage bed.[34] Nor, by implication, has Orithyia. Boreas and Orithyia thus serve as another instance of what, doubtless, was to Rubens and many of his contemporaries, a fact of life, or rather of love: that the natural reluctance of modest women may need to be overcome by more than mere words of persuasion.

The playful *putti* engaged in a game of snowballs in the surrounding sky allude to the North Wind's icy blasts. The two infants with Cupid-like wings are boys; the other pair are girls – one clearly and the other presumably furnished with the sort of dragonfly wings Rubens gives to airborne female babies.[35] It can be noted gendered roles apply even in celestial games: the girls have the job of catching snowflakes and making snowballs for the boys. As with the *amoretti* in the *Rape of the Leucippides*, these infants serve to counteract, even subvert, the harsh impact of the abduction, suggesting a happy outcome for Orithyia. As it happens, the children foreshadow the four, two of either sex, which Pausanias tells us she was to bear to Boreas.[36] But, in addition, they lend a jocular element not present in the Leucippides painting, which, along with the red face and inflated cheeks of Boreas, accords perfectly with the relatively light and ironical tone Ovid takes in his account of this story in the *Metamorphoses*, which brings a change in mood following the terrible episode of the Banquet of Tereus.[37] In fact the tale, which concludes Book VI, is not even one of metamorphosis, except in the sense that Boreas is transformed from pleading suitor to exasperated abductor, moving abruptly from speechmaking to action with the words

---

[32] Ovid, *Metamorphoses*, VI. 682-721, esp. 685-86; 690-93; 705-08; Ovid, *Opera* (n. 20 above) III: 122-23.

[33] Ovid, *Fasti*, V.201-04: '*Ver erat; errabam: Zephyrus conspexit, abibam./ Insequitur; fugio. fortior ille fuit./ Et dederat fratri Boreas ius omne rapinae,/ Ausus Ericthea praemia ferre domo*'. See Ovid, *Opera* (n. 20 above) II: 248.

[34] Ovid, *Fasti*, V.205-06: '*Vim tamen emendat, dando mihi nomina nuptae;/ Inque meo non est ulla querela thoro*'. Ovid, *Opera* (n. 20 above) II: 248.

[35] Rubens never gives the bird wings of amoretti to flying girls. On Rubens's female '*putti*' see E. McGrath, 'Rubens's infant-cornucopia', *Journal of the Warburg and Courtauld Institutes* 50 (1977) 315-18.

[36] The children were two winged, wind-god boys, Zetes and Calais, and a pair of girls, Cleopatra and Chione, goddess of snow. See Pausanias, *Description of Greece*, III.15.2; *cf.* I.38.2 and III.15.4 (on Chione).

[37] It with a hint of sarcasm that Ovid sums up Boreas's bombastic speech which precedes the abduction: '*Haec Boreas aut his non inferiora locutus/ Excussit pennas...*' (VI.702-03).

Figure 8 Rubens and Frans Snyders, *Pythagoras advocating Vegetarianism*. Royal Collection, Buckingham Palace

'I should have forced, not begged, Erechtheus to be my father-in law' (VI. 700-01: '... *socerque/ Non orandus erat mihi, sed faciendus Erichtheus*'). This aspect of the story may have had a particular personal attraction for Rubens too, given the crucial role he seems to have had a few years earlier in pushing his brother Philip to move decisively in his courtship of a much admired Antwerp lady, Maria de Moy. Rubens told a mutual friend in 1609 how he spurred his brother into taking the initiative after Philip had 'pined two years in vain'; matters of love, Rubens says, should not be entered into coolly, but '*con ogni fervore*'.[38] It is clear that he had, as it were, internalized the Ovidian message illustrated so clearly in *Boreas and Orithyia*.

At the same time Rubens found subjects in the *Metamorphoses* that no one else ever did. Such is the case with his splendid *Pythagoras advocating Vegetarianism* (Figure 8), a picture he made in collaboration with his friend, the fruit and vegetable specialist

---

[38] See Rooses and Ruelens, *Correspondance* (n. 24 above) VI: 323-324. *Cf.* Heinen, 'Love and Lust' (n. 29 above) 87. This episode is also known through the letters of one of Maria's disappointed suitors; see C. Ruelens, 'Le mariage des frères Rubens', *Rubens-Bulletijn*, 3 (1888) 145-88, esp. the letters of 11 December 1608 and 1 February 1609 (185-88).

172   THE AFTERLIFE OF OVID

Frans Snyders.[39] Here he was inspired by the impassioned plea Ovid has Pythagoras make to the early Roman king Numa and his followers against the killing of animals at the opening of the fifteenth book. The philosopher eloquently expatiates on how little need there is for slaughter when (as he says):

> We have apples bending the branches with their weight and grapes swelling on the vine. There are plants just ready to eat and others which the heat of a flame will make palatable ... The earth is lavish in supply of riches, of harmless foods, and provides feasts that demand no killing or bloodshed.[40]

Rubens made this picture for his own house, presumably for his dining room. Like Ovid, he turned his subject into a celebration of nature's bounty as well as a defence of vegetarianism (Rubens supposedly ate meat sparingly).[41] A group of friendly nymphs and satyrs take part in the celebration, enthusiastically gathering fruits to add to the succulent pile of earthly produce and thus promote Pythagoras's Ovidian argument – though they seem to remain invisible to the philosopher's listeners, who otherwise surely would be distracted.

That nymphs and satyrs should be seen working as well as frolicking together was a Rubensian innovation. It was, however, in part inspired by Ovid's story of the invention of the cornucopia. At *Metamorphoses* IX (1-92) the river god Achelous tells Theseus and his companions how he lost one of the horns which were his special weapon, when (as sometimes happened: *cf. Metamorphoses* VIII.881-86), he took on the form of a bull. In a contest over the fair Deianira, we learn, Hercules wrenched it from his brow. The river's consolation now is that the Naiads stuffed it with fruits and flowers and 'made it sacred', so that his missing horn enriches Abundance herself (IX. 87-88: '*Naïdes hoc, pomis et odore flore repletum,/ Sacrarunt: divesque meo bona copia cornu est*'). Luckily Achelous still has some benefit from it, since a nymph then enters the scene with the brimming cornucopia to supply harvest fare for his dinner table (IX.89-92). Rubens illustrated this event in a picture made in collaboration with his friend, Jan Breughel, a painter who

---

[39]   See McGrath *History* (n. 9 above), I: 67, 108 and fig 31; II: 47-52; C. White, *The later Flemish pictures in the collection of Her Majesty the Queen* (London, 2007), 230-36. (The recent cleaning of the painting shows its quality still more clearly than before.) In the few cases where the episode of the conversion of Numa features in illustrated Ovids, Numa is shown simply standing listening to a lecture. *Cf.* McGrath, *History* (n. 9 above), II: 48-49. Still, as Fátima Díez Platas pointed out to me, there is a charming illustration of the philosopher gesticulating between a group of farm animals and a clump of nut- and fruit-bearing trees in the illustrated Ovid published at Mainz in 1551: *P. Ovidij Nasonis des aller sinreichsten Poeten Metamorphosis, das ist von der wunderbarlicher Verenderung der Gestalten der Menschen, Thier und anderer Creaturen ... / etwan durch ... Albrechten von Halberstatt inn Reimeweiss verteutscht ... ; gebessert von Georg Wickram ...* ([Mainz], 1551).

[40]   Ovid, *Metamorphoses* XV.75-82: '*Parcite mortales dapibus temerare nefandis/ Corpora; sunt fruges; sunt deducentia ramos/ Pondere poma suo, tumidaeque in vitibus vuae./ Sunt herbae dulces; sunt quae mitescere flamma/ Molliri queant.... / Prodiga divitias alimentaque mitia tellus/ Suggerit atque epulas sine caede et sanguine praebet*'. See Ovid, *Opera* (n. 20 above) III: 276.

[41]   For Rubens's moderate diet see R. de Piles, *Conversations sur la Conaissance de La Peinture* (Paris, 1677) 213-15. It may be noted, though, that, mindful of the philosopher's well-known taboo ('*A fabis abstineto*', in the version of Erasmus's *Adagia*), Rubens showed Pythagoras rejecting (by trampling underfoot) the broad bean (*vicia faba*).

Figure 9 Rubens, *Nymphs and Satyrs filling the cornucopia*. Madrid, Museo del Prado (Photo: Museum)

specialized in the representation of flowers, fruits and natural history.[42] More important, however, were the free variations he composed around Ovid's tale of the Acheloan horn, associating it with an imagery of Bacchic fertility in which pans, satyrs, and old Silenus, fat with autumnal ripeness, become representatives of the life-giving forces of the earth. Enlisting these followers of Dionysus, and their companion nymphs, to help the Ovidian Naiads, Rubens imagined the cornucopia (conveniently expanded from bull-size) as constantly 'topped up' with fresh produce for eternal overflow. This theme culminates in the great painting in the Museo del Prado (Figure 9), in which Silenus and the satyrs, happily fruit-gathering with the nymphs, fulfil their roles as ancient deities of earthly abundance, rather than simple figures of lust and sexuality (though there are some lapses when the individual satyrs are diverted into seduction efforts).[43] Banished too is

---

[42] On this picture (New York, Metropolitan Museum of Art) see A. T. Woollett, A. Van Suchtelen *et al.*, *Rubens and Breughel: a working friendship*, exh. cat. (Zwolle, 2006) 60-63, with figure.

[43] K de Clippel, 'Rubens's 'Nymphs and Satyrs' in the Prado: Observations on its Genesis and Meaning', *The Burlington Magazine*, 149 (2007) 76-81; *cf.* McGrath 'Infant-Cornucopia' (n. 35 above). The urn flowing with water on which one nymph is leaning, determinedly uninterested in the attempt of a nearby satyr to charm her with an apple, provides a reminder of the watery context that is appropriate for Naiads, even if there is no sign of Achelous.

174   THE AFTERLIFE OF OVID

any threatening aspect of Dionysiac riot; the god's tiger lies, tamely inebriated, in the corner.[44] This picture was another work which remained with Rubens until the end of his life. Indeed it has been shown recently, that having been begun in *c.* 1615, it was reworked and considerably enlarged many years later: the artist not only added and altered the figures and their relationships, but placed the pagan gods and woodland spirits within a Flemish landscape setting.[45]

Seventeenth-century painters were often relatively free to choose the mythological themes they depicted: patrons and customers might just ask for a touching love story or a painting with nude figures. In Rubens's case this was particularly true since he was known to be so well versed in the classics. But in the later part of his life he was in the fortunate position of being able to paint large pictures for his own pleasure. One such painting was evidently the wonderful *Feast of Venus* in Vienna (Figure 10), which connects nature and fertility with a celebration of the power of love, with particular reference to Ovid.[46]

Rubens's starting point was *Fasti* IV.133-38, on the April festivities in honour of Venus:

> Come and duly worship of the goddess, you mothers and brides, and you who wear no chaste garlands and long robes [*i.e.* prostitutes]. Remove the golden strands of necklace from the marble neck, take off her rich ornaments; the goddess is to be washed all over. When her neck is dried put the gold necklaces back on; now she is to be given other flowers, new roses.[47]

---

[44]   The motif of the drunken, tamed tiger or panther is a favourite one in Rubens's Bacchic scenes. On the (supposedly) mollifying effect of wine on these animals see notably G. P. Valeriano, *Hieroglyphica* (Basle, 1575) 84-85, *de panthera*, and *de tigride*. This learned handbook was owned and consulted regularly by Rubens (*cf.* McGrath, *History* I: 62-65).

[45]   For the details of the changes see De Clippel, 'Rubens's "Nymphs and Satyrs"' (n. 43 above).

[46]   On this painting see notably P. Fehl, 'Rubens' "Feast of Venus Verticordia"', *The Burlington Magazine* 114 (1972): 159-62; K. Demus in *Peter Paul Rubens, 1577–1640.* exh. cat. (Vienna, 1977) 127-32, no. 55; and M. Geraerts, 'Rubens's *Feast of Venus* reconsidered: the turning of hearts to or from love? Sensuality or virtue?' in *The nude and the norm in the early modern Low Countries*, ed. K. de Clippel, K. Van Cauteren and K. Van der Stighelen (Turnhout, 2011) 159-80. Like the *Nymphs and Satyrs* (Figure 8), this painting was expanded by Rubens in the course of working on it, though in this case, the work extended over a shorter period. See Geraerts, *Feast of Venus* (above) 17375. Unlike Figure 8, the painting was apparently not in Rubens's possession when he died. It is usually said that it is first recorded in the Habsburg collection in Prague in 1718, but Gerlinde Grüber has kindly informed me that it was already present in Prague Castle in 1685, in an inventory as yet unpublished. It was perhaps acquired by Archduke Leopold Wilhelm of Austria, governor of the Spanish Netherlands (1647-56). Probably, however, it was initially made by the artist for an intimate friend or family member, if not for himself.

[47]   '*Rite Deam Latiae colitis matresque nurusque,/ Et vos, quis vittae longaque vestis abest./ Aurea marmoreo redimicula demitte collo:/ Demite divitias: tota lavanda dea est./ Aurea siccato redimicula reddite collo:/ Nunc alii flores, nunc nova danda rosa est*'. See Ovid, *Opera* (n. 20 above) II: 189-90. The modern '*solvite*' for '*demitte*' in l.135 is a later emendation of Nicolaus Heinsius. For '*abest*' in l.134 see below, at n. 56; I have ignored the text's '*adest*' for reasons given there. For the relevance of *Fasti* IV.133-38 to an earlier painting by Rubens see E. McGrath, 'Garlanding the Great Mother: Rubens, Jan Breughel and the celebration of Nature's fertility', in *Munuscula Amicorum* (n. 29 above) I: 103-22, esp. 113-16.

Figure 10 Rubens, *Feast of Venus*. Vienna, Kunsthistorisches Museum (Photo: Google Art Project, WikiCommons)

At the centre of the picture we see women of different status (and degrees of undress) busy around the statue. One is drying the leg of the washed figure, who seems already to have her necklaces back on again, and a new veil; another two have combined to apply their perfume from a convincingly ancient *phial*, while the foremost of the pair, a seductive representative of those untrammelled with chaste garlands, jokingly holds up the mirror she has brought to the scene to let Venus check the effect, and a soberly veiled woman sacrifices to the goddess on a tripod. Along with her necklaces, however, the image of Venus is receiving not only a wreath of spring flowers, the red and white roses being lowered over her head, but is being encircled by an enormous swag of autumnal fruits, borne by trails of airborne *amoretti*, more of whom have descended to the earth to join hands with girl infants and encircle the statue. Cupid himself embraces a baby Psyche in the foreground. All around, nymphs, satyrs, and bacchantes (including an Indian follower of Dionysus with a tambourine) joyfully sport and dance, in a grove near a temple. They are apparently sensed rather than seen by the two well-dressed young women who enter from the right carrying dolls dressed in similar (seventeenth-century) style to their own.

It has long been recognized that the picture embodies a tribute to the great Venetian painter Titian who inspired so much of Rubens's late work.[48] Around 1635 the artist had copied Titian's painting of the *Worship of Venus* (Figure 11), made more than a century earlier for Alfonso d'Este.[49] This work was based closely on the *ekphrastic* description

---

[48] See esp. K. M. Swoboda, 'Das Rubens Venusfest in der Wiener Gemäldegalerie', *Mitteilungen des Instituts fur Öesterreichisches Geschichtsforschung*, 22 (1969) 213-37.

[49] On Rubens's copies of this painting, and the companion *Andrians*, see J. Wood, *Copies and adaptations from Renaissance and earlier artists. Italian artists, II. Titian and North Italian art* (*Corpus Rubenianum Ludwig Burchard, XXVI, 2*) 2 vols (Turnhout, 2010) I: 141-68; II: figs 51-60.

Figure 11 Titian, *Worship of Venus*. Madrid, Museo del Prado (Photo: Museum)

of Cupids gathering apples in the shrine of Venus in the *Imagines* of Philostratus (I. 6), though the reference in the text to nymphs who have left votive gifts was translated by Titian into two young women who bring objects – a mirror and a book or tablet – to dedicate to the goddess, whose statue is also included. Even when he made his full-scale copy (Figure 12) Rubens clearly had been thinking about appropriate dedications to Venus, and he 'corrected' the tablet (or book) to a comb. When he came to adapt this motif to his *Feast of Venus* (Figure 10), Rubens brought the mirror and comb right up to the figure of Venus, and gave the young women entering from the right a pair of dolls to offer. Rubens was greatly interested in the religious customs of the ancients (which was one reason why he knew the *Fasti* so well) – the tripod he illustrated, for example, is modelled on a recent archaeological discovery discussed with his friend, the antiquarian Nicolas-Claude Fabri de

Figure 12 Rubens, Copy after Titian, *Worship of Venus*. Stockholm, Nationalmuseum (Photo: Google Art Project, WikiCommons)

Peiresc.[50] And he had obviously read about the votive practices of ancient Rome. A passage in Persius's *Satires* (II.69-70) talks of girls dedicating dolls to Venus.[51] But Rubens would also have consulted his antiquarian handbooks, in particular the *Dies geniales* by the Italian humanist, Alexander ab Alexandro, for this discusses the custom of dedicating dolls in a

---

[50] Fehl, '*Venus Verticordia*' (n. 46 above) 160; Swoboda, 'Das Rubens Venusfest' (n. 48 above) 221; *cf.* M. Van der Meulen, 'A note on Rubens's letter on tripods', *The Burlington Magazine*, 119 (1977) 646-51.

[51] Persius, *Satires* II.69-70: '... *in sancto quid facit aurum?/ Nempe hoc quod Veneri donatae a virgine pupae*'. *Cf.* Fehl, '*Venus Verticordia*' 160 and n. 9; also McGrath, 'Garlanding the Great Mother' (n. 47 above)) I: 113-14 and 121-22, n. 50, citing the edition of the *Satires* of Persius and Juvenal by E. Lubinus (Hannover, 1603) 620, which Rubens may well have owned; see further below, n. 61. On the dedication of dolls see also Lactantius, *Divinae Institutiones* II.4.13.

passage on the temple of Venus Erycina at the Porta Collina outside the walls of Rome, and associates this temple with the statue of Venus Verticordia.[52]

Nowadays, Rubens's picture usually goes under the title *The Feast of Venus Verticordia* since Philipp Fehl, who first pointed to the relevance of the *Fasti*, considered that Ovid was talking about that feast throughout lines 133-62, and that Rubens in turn must have understood the passage similarly. But this view is incompatible with many features of the text, and still more at odds with the evidence of the painting.[53] It is difficult to disentangle the sequence of references made by Ovid in the verses in question: moving from the annual sprucing up of Venus's statue to the episode with the goddess hiding herself from satyrs with myrtle and to the worship of Fortuna Virilis, before turning to the story of the temple of Venus Verticordia and its construction on the advice of the Cumaean Sibyl to turn licentious Rome back to strict morals. But a Venus concerned with moral probity, as Verticordia should be, seems far from Ovid's thoughts in the passage as a whole. Rather it would appear that the poet deliberately mingles details about different cults related to Venus, appropriate to his different categories of women. As for Rubens, not only does he relish bringing together in his picture respectable matrons, brides and the sort of women who have no use for *vittae* and long dresses in a way that would never have happened in ancient Rome; he surrounds the female worshippers with the joyful licence of rustic and bacchic gods and revellers in a scene that seems more evocative of the uninhibited feast of Venus Erycina.[54] It is all the more interesting, then, that he would have been aware that the commentator Antonio Costanzi, who must have taken lines 13362 to refer to Venus Verticordia, had been sufficiently exercised by the inclusion of the courtesans in l.134 to emend the verse to the tame 'And you who wear chaste garlands and long dresses' ('*Et vos, quis vittae longaque vestis adest*' [rather than *abest*]). This emendation is introduced, with an asterisk, in the text of the 1601 Franfkfurt edition which I cited above,[55] along with Costanzi's argument that *meretrices* belonged only with the festival of Venus Erycina.[56] Paolo Marsi's refutation of the emendation is, however, included in the same volume; he points out that Ovid usually invokes chaste *vittae* only to wish them away, and concludes: 'Thus he now says women of all kinds worship Venus, apart from Vestal Virgins and modest married women'.[57] Clearly Rubens opted for Marsi's reading.

Alexander ab Alexandro reports that Venus Erycina, to whom adolescent girls supposedly offered up their dolls, is said to have had her temple at the Porta Collina outside

---

[52]   Alexander ab Alexandro, *Genialium dierum libri sex* (Lyons, 1616) 52v-53 (book II. chapter 3). Rubens had bought the edition of Frankfurt 1594 in 1615. See Arents, *De Bibliotheek* (n. 9 above) 145, E31. See further n. 58 below.

[53]   As also is argued in Geraerts, '*Feast of Venus*' (n. 46 above) esp. 166-68.

[54]   *Cf.* Geraerts, '*Feast of Venus*' (n. 46 above) 166-68, referring to the April *vinalia* associated with Erycina. In fact Fehl himself sees Rubens as referring to the cult of Venus Erycina as well as Verticordia: Fehl, '*Venus Verticordia*' 160.

[55]   See n. 47.

[56]   Ovid, *Opera* (n. 20 above) II: 189 E-F: '*Cavendum ne pro verbo adest, abest legamus. Matronae enim hoc tempore (teste Macrobio) Venerem colebant, non meretrices, quarum erat festum Veneris Erycinae ...*'.

[57]   Ovid, *Opera* (n. 20 above) II: 190G, concluding: '*Sic nunc omnes mulieres colere Venerem inquit, praeter Vestales virgines et pudicas matrones*'.

the city to keep it safely out of sight of respectable married women.[58] He goes on to talk of the statue of Venus Verticordia being placed there too at some stage, implying that this was to prevent licentious behaviour getting out of hand.[59] Rubens was probably encouraged by this comment to associate the laughter-loving Erycina, Horace's *Erycina ridens* (*Odes* I.2.33), with the sterner Verticordia.[60] Alexander sees the dedication of dolls as a sign that girls reaching adolescence now wish to dispense with the playthings of youth. More tellingly, contemporary commentators on Persius associate the dedication with marriage and add that the young women no longer need the dolls they offer to Venus since they will soon, through her, have children of their own.[61] That this idea was in Rubens mind is very clear: the joyfully riotous, baby-filled, picture is above all a celebration of Venus's power as goddess of the love which leads to happy fruitfulness. The artist is not even concerned to designate the scene as a festival specific to April, given the gigantic garland of succulent fruits that is carried aloft. At any rate the importance to the picture of this symbol of fecundity has overridden any concern to keep the focus on a spring festival. And, while it may be that Ovid's reference to Venus hiding behind myrtle from a band of rampant satyrs (*Fasti* IV.142-43) was relevant to the presence in the painting of the rustic gods of nature, the theme of abundance and fruitfulness in itself would have been enough to summon forth the nymphs and satyrs from Rubens's imagination. As in the *Pythagoras* (Figure 8), the artist presented these sylvan creatures as invisible too, but (like the *putti*) still affect the mood of the mortals who come to this sacred grove. Rubens's imagery of love and fertile nature is brought marvellously to bear on the passage in the *Fasti*. The *Feast of Venus* may be a celebration of the artist's debt to Titian, but it is just as much a tribute to the inspiration he found in the playful poet of tender loves, *tenerorum lusor amorum*.[62] In particular, it is a testimony to the sense of freedom in developing a poetic theme and weaving stories together that Ovid bequeathed to Rubens.

The Warburg Institute

---

[58] Alexander ab Alexandro, *Dies geniales* (n. 52 above) 52v-53: '*Sic Veneris Erycinae templum extra Collinam magna mole constructum ferunt .... ne libido invalesceret. Utque luxuria a matribusfamilias abesset procul, ideo ab urbe remotum extra pomoerium locavere. Ad hanc aedem... ludos Apollinares saepe celebratos comperimus: in quam virgines aetate adolescenti Veneri puppas, velut puerilia rudimenta, offerre tradunt. In ea quoque intercursu temporum, Veneris Verticordia simulachrum, quod homines ab effusa libidine averteret, dedicatum fuit*'.

[59] This idea seems to have been taken up by Vincenzo Cartari, in his *Imagini de i dei*, cited in Fehl, '*Venus Verticordia*' 160, n. 9, in the edition of Padua, 1603 (490).

[60] See above, n. 58.

[61] See I. Casaubon, *Auli Persii Flacci Satirarum liber* (Paris, 1615) 220-21 '*...Pupae a virginibus pubertatem consecutis aut nupturis Veneri solitae dicare, ut ab ephebis bullae: quia in omni mutatione, insignia vel instrumenta vitae anteactae diis consecrare moris erat...*' *Cf.* Juvenal and Persius, *Satires*, ed. E. Lubinus (Hannover, 1603) 620: On *nempe hoc*: '*... solebant autem Virgines nupturae suas pupas, imagunculas puellares vel sigillaria Veneri offerre, tanquam iam puerilibus ineptiis valedicturae*'; on *pupae*: '*Has nupturae Veneri donabant, significantes se brevi veros pupos pupasque Veneris beneficio habituras*'. For the verses of Persius see above, n. 51.

[62] As Ovid famously describes himself in his 'epitaph' (*Tristia* III. 3. 73-74).

IMPORTING THE OVIDIAN MUSE TO ENGLAND

MAGGIE KILGOUR

Like other Renaissance countries, England imitated the story of the *Aeneid* in order to trace its origins to the legendary city of Troy. The myth of the immigration of the Trojan Brute, descendent of Aeneas, was especially popular under Elizabeth, appearing in Spenser's *Faerie Queene* III. 9. 41-53, which tells how Aeneas left Troy and went to Rome from whence his grandson Brutus came to Britain:

> For that same *Brute*, whom much he did aduaunce
>   In all his speach, was *Syluius* his sonne,
>   Whom hauing slain, through luckles arrowes glaunce
>   He fled for feare of that he had misdonne,
>   Or els for shame, so fowle reproch to shonne,
>   And with him ledd to sea an youthly trayne,
>   Where wearie wandring they long time did wonne,
>   And many fortunes prou'd in th'*Ocean* mayne,
> And great aduentures found, that now were long to sayne.
>
> At last by fatall course they driuen were
>   Into an Island spatious and brode,
>   The furthest North, that did to them appeare:
>   Which after rest they seeking farr abrode,
>   Found it the fittest soyle for their abode,
>   Fruitfull of all thinges fitt for liuing foode,
>   But wholy waste, and void of peoples trode,
>   Saue an huge nation of the Geaunts broode,
> That fed on liuing flesh, and dronck mens vitall blood.
>
> Whom he through wearie wars and labours long,
>   Subdewd with losse of many *Britons* bold:
>   In which the great *Goemagot* of strong
>   *Corineus*, and *Coulin* of *Debon* old
>   Were ouerthrowne, and layd on th'earth full cold,
>   Which quaked vnder their so hideous masse,
>   A famous history to bee enrold
>   In euerlasting moniments of brasse,
> That all the antique Worthies merits far did passe. (III. 9. 48-50)[1]

---

[1] All citations are from Edmund Spenser, *The Faerie Queene*, ed. A. C. Hamilton, rev. 2nd edn (London 2007).

In Spenser, the line of Aeneas and Brute ultimately produces the female knight Britomart, Elizabeth's ancestor and prototype, who in this scene is listening eagerly to the story. The narrator of this tale of cultural transmission is, however, the debauched knight Paridell, who uses his skills as a storyteller to seduce his host's wife, Hellenore. While the names, of course, link the lovers to those who began the Trojan War, Helen is now a whore, and Paridell a parody Paris. The scene thus suggests that ancient works may become corrupted as they pass through time, as here the Virgilian *translatio* becomes an Ovidian scene of seduction.[2]

As Mihoko Suzuki first argued, the scene in which Britomart hears of her origins enables Spenser also to mediate on his own classical inheritance. For Suzuki, Ovid is a bad influence, as the Ovidian lover Paridell misuses the story of the Virgilian Britomart. Yet, as Syrithe Pugh especially has shown, Spenser's Britomart is herself shaped through Ovidian myths, and the centre of the canto which describes her quest is occupied by the highly Ovidian Garden of Adonis.[3] Moreover, for a number of Spenser's contemporaries, Ovidian stories, especially those of seduction, offered a counter myth of *translatio* to that of the Virgilian epic. The publication of the first three books of the *Faerie Queene* in 1590 roughly coincided with the emergence of a new English genre which we call the English epyllion: short, usually erotic poems based on Ovidian myths, such as, most famously, Shakespeare's *Venus and Adonis*, *Rape of Lucrece,* and Marlowe's *Hero and Leander*. The brief fad for such poems is framed by two narratives which focus particularly on the movement of Ovidian figures and even dynasties to England: Thomas Lodge's 1589 *Scillaes metamorphosis* and John Weever's 1600 *Faunus and Melliflora.* Both of these works draw specifically on episodes that appear in Ovid's retelling of the *Aeneid* in *Metamorphoses* XIII-XIV, books in which 'the issues of literary continuation, appropriation, and repetition are central'.[4] As often noted, Ovid reworks Aeneas' journey to give it an Ovidian spin, emphasizing the role that desire plays in the *Aeneid*, and turning Virgilian *translatio* into metamorphosis to remind us that the *Aeneid* is at heart the story of the transformation of Trojans into Romans.[5] Above all, he foregrounds the act of storytelling itself, and constructs a genealogy for his own poem by shifting attention from Virgil's *translatio imperii* to scenes which tell of the 'importing of the Muses' to Rome.[6] I suggest here that Ovid's revision of the Virgilian *translatio* provided a model for English writers concerned with transforming the classical inheritance into a new native tradition and creating their

---

[2] See especially Mihoko Suzuki, '"Unfitly yokt together in one teeme": Vergil and Ovid in *Faerie Queene* III.ix'. *English Literary Renaissance* 17.2 (1987) 172-85 (179). Suzuki, however, oversimplifies the relation of the two classical authors as simply one of conflict.

[3] Syrithe Pugh, *Spenser and Ovid* (Aldershot 2005).

[4] K. Sara Myers, *Ovid Metamorphoses book XIV,* Cambridge Greek and Latin Classics (Cambridge 2009) 11.

[5] Ovid's revision of the *Aeneid*, especially in the last books, has been much discussed; see especially Stephen Hinds, *Allusion and intertext: dynamics of appropriation in Roman poetry* (Cambridge 1998) 104-22; Joseph B. Solodow, *The world of Ovid's* Metamorphoses (Chapel Hill 1988) 110-56; and Garth Tissol, *The face of nature: wit, narrative, and cosmic origins in Ovid's* Metamorphoses (Princeton 1997) 177-91.

[6] On the topos of importing the muses see Hinds, *Allusion and intertext* (n.5, above) 52-63.

own poetic genealogies. If the Tudor myth of English history looks back to Virgil, the poets' accounts of English literary history come from Ovid.[7]

Ovid had of course already come to England through Chaucer and other earlier writers who had drawn on Ovidian figures and *topoi*. But these Ovidian elements began to be reimagined in the late 1530s through Petrarch's reworking of Ovid. Wyatt and Surrey made Petrarchism the dominant poetic love convention for the next 60 years, one which would later reinforce Elizabeth as an unattainable object of desire. At the same time, and in many ways complementing this, Ovidian figures and imagery began to be grafted onto the form of the medieval complaint. Elements of Pythagoras' speech in *Metamorphoses* XV are obsessively replayed throughout Spenser's complaints, as well as many of his minor works, while Jane Shore's speech in the *Mirror for Magistrates* (1563), by Thomas Churchyard – who would later (1587) translate the first three books of the *Tristia* (as *De tristibus*) – shows the growing influence of the *Heroides*.[8] Ovid provided the perfect stories and themes for a generation of writers who were obsessed with change, and who were thinking about their own transformation of classical works as well as the metamorphic powers of desire and poetry itself.[9] This ongoing process of grafting Ovid onto the English literary landscape is the subject of Lodge's *Scillaes metamorphosis*, which brings Ovid's half-fish sea-god, Glaucus, to Britain.

In Ovid, Glaucus is not only divided physically, but also split between *Metamorphoses* XIII and XIV, where he is part of the convoluted sequence of stories which interrupt the journey of Aeneas. The tale of Glaucus and Scylla is triggered when the Trojans arrive at Sicily and prepare to face the monstrous Scylla. Ovid launches into an *aition* to explain the origins of the terrifying threat that might have blocked the Trojans' journey to their new home. Expanding on Virgil's comment that '*prima hominis facies et pulchro pectore virgo* | *pube tenus*' ('Above she is of human form, down to the waist a fair-bosomed maiden', *Aeneid* III. 426-27),[10] Ovid makes Scylla's upper half a kind of remnant of her past, saying that '*et, si non omnia vates* | *ficta reliquerunt, aliquo quoque tempore virgo*' ('and if everything the poets have left us are not fictions, she was once a girl',

---

[7] Other critics have noted how the end of the *Metamorphoses* offers a model for literary succession through the theme of metempsychosis; see esp. Stuart Gillespie, 'Literary afterlives: metempsychosis from Ennius to Jorge Luis Borges', in *Classical literary careers and their reception*, ed. Philip Hardie and Helen Moore (Cambridge 2010) 209-25. Such a use by later writers to claim that they were the incarnation of earlier generations is appropriate, for, as Philip Hardie has shown, Ovid used the speech of Pythagoras to construct his own poetic genealogy; see 'The speech of Pythagoras in *Metamorphoses* 15: Empedoclean epos', *Classical Quarterly* 45.1 (1995) 204-14. While the image of inheritance as metempsychosis is relevant here, my interest is on representations of movement from one place to another.

[8] On Ovid and the English complaint, see esp. Raphael Lyne, 'Writing back to Ovid in the 1560s and 1570s', *Translation and Literature* 13.2 (2004) 143-64, as well as Clark Hulse, *Metamorphic verse: the Elizabethan minor epic* (Princeton 1981) 16-34.

[9] See further my discussion, *Milton and the metamorphosis of Ovid* (Oxford 2012) 13-19.

[10] Citations are from Virgil, *Aeneid,* trans. H. Rushton Fairclough, rev. G. P. Goold, Loeb Classical Library (Cambridge 1999).

Metamorphoses XIII. 733-34).[11] As Philip Hardie has shown, Ovid's aside foregrounds how Scylla 'had become a touchstone for poetic fictiveness',[12] an association that made her appealing for later imitators of Ovid, such as Spenser and Milton. By drawing attention to this commonplace, Ovid also hints that the Trojan journey is impeded by fictions. This is certainly true in one sense: the Trojans are put on hold while Ovid spins a series of tales that lead us far away from Virgil's plot.[13] Ovid claims Scylla was once a beautiful nymph who was courted by the besotted Glaucus, whom she coldly spurned because of his fishy form. She is therefore, rather fittingly, turned by Circe into a monster who is herself divided: a girl on top, a pack of dogs below. This digression explaining the Trojans' enemy contains a further digression, the unsuccessful courtship of Galatea by Polyphemus, which echoes that of Scylla by Glaucus. The intertwining of these parallel stories, all taken from earlier works, turns Aeneas' journey into part of the 'journey through earlier literature' which runs through these books.[14] Moreover, if this tour of literary history interrupts Aeneas' journey it also mirrors it: Glaucus' swim from Aetna along the coast of Italy stands in for the Trojans' journey, while his transformation into a merman (XIII. 951-53) anticipates Aeneas' deification (XIV. 603-04).[15] Glaucus is thus a kind of Ovidian substitute for Aeneas, one of many in the final books, which offer alternative versions of metamorphoses and rebirth.[16]

---

[11] Citations are from Ovid, *Metamorphoses*, trans. Frank Justus Miller, rev. G. P. Goold, Loeb Classical Library (Cambridge 1984).

[12] Philip Hardie, 'The self-divisions of Scylla', *Trends in Classics* 1.1 (2009) 118-47 (122).

[13] See Myers, *Metamorphoses XIV* (n.4, above) 11-18; Joseph Farrell, 'Dialogue of genres in Ovid's "Lovesong of Polyphemus" (*Metamorphoses* 13.719-897)', *American Journal of Philology* 113.2 (1992) 235-68.

[14] Neil Hopkinson, *Ovid Metamorphoses book XIII*, Cambridge Greek and Latin Classics (Cambridge 2000) 8. On the interweaving of stories and their relation to earlier works, see also Farrell, 'Dialogue of Genres' (n.13, above); Myers, *Metamorphoses XIV* (n.4, above), and also her *Ovid's causes: cosmogony and aetiology in the* Metamorphoses (Ann Arbor 1994) 98-104; and Betty Rose Nagle, 'A trio of love-triangles in Ovid's *Metamorphoses*', *Arethusa* 21 (1988) 75-98.

[15] See Tissol, *Face of nature* (n.5, above) 210; Myers, *Ovid's causes* (n.14, above) 101-02; and also Hopkinson, *Metamorphoses XIII* (n.14, above) 35, 235. Solodow's claim that the interrupting episodes 'lack … thematic relevance' (*World*, (n.5, above) 139) is clearly wrong.

[16] See Myers, *Metamorphoses XIV* (n.4, above) 6. For images of rebirth, see: the death and resurrection of Anius' daughters (*Met.* XIII. 644-74); the birth of the heron out of the ashes of Ardea after the death of Turnus (XIV. 573-80); the metamorphoses of the phoenix (XV. 393-407); deification of Aeneas (XIV. 581-608), Romulus (XV. 805-28), and Caesar (XV. 746ff.) and finally, the climax of all these images, the poet's own projected apotheosis (XV. 875-79).

Ovid's creation of a parallel between Glaucus and Aeneas may offer us another way of understanding Dante's famous allusion to Glaucus to describe his 'transhumanization' as he ascends to heaven (*Paradiso* I. 67-72). As Virgil is left behind at the top of Purgatory, Dante starts to return to Ovidian myths previously associated especially with infernal metamorphoses, and reimagine them in light of his own journey (see esp. the allusions to Pyramus in *Purgatorio* XXVII. 37-8; XXXIII.69; Leander in *Purgatorio* XXVIII. 73-74; Phaethon in *Purgatorio* XXIX. 118-20; Prosperina in *Purgatorio* XXVIII. 49-51; Marsyas in *Paradiso* I. 19-20). At the start of his journey, Dante had protested that he was not Aeneas – '*Io non Enëa [...] sono*' (*Inferno* II. 32: I am not Aeneas) – here

In Lodge's poem, the journey of Glaucus to Britain also inevitably recalls that of Aeneas to Rome, and of his British equivalent, Brute, to Britain. Like Ovid too, Lodge makes the episode about the literary tradition: the poem traces the transformation of English verse into the new form of the epyllion itself.[17] The opening is broadly reminiscent of Chaucer's *Book of the Duchess*, and George Gascoigne's more recent experiment in Chaucerian Ovidianism, *The Complaint of Philomene* (1576), in which the narrator strolls out at night to hear the nightingale, and then dreams of the story of Philomela.[18] In Chaucer and Gascoigne, the classical world is imported through dream; Lodge brings the Ovidian story to England in reality and transforms it. Lodge's narrator claims that one day, as he walked weeping by the river Isis, he ran into the equally despondent Glaucus who explains how he came to be both so unhappy and in England. Lodge's Glaucus is not a merman, but a handsome and carefree water god, adored by the water nymphs but defiantly uninterested in girls. However, he unfortunately happened one day to spot and be smitten with the lovely but hard-hearted Scylla who coldly rebuffed his ardent advances, telling him, in effect, go west young man: 'Packe hence thou fondling to the westerne Seas, | Within some calmy riuer shrowd thy head' (373-74).[19] While Ovid's rebuffed Glaucus goes to Italy, Lodge's follows Scylla's directions, swimming till he comes to 'A fruitful Ile begirt with Ocean streames' (395) – England. He settles down to a life of miserable moping near Oxford, which Lodge, who had studied there, clearly assumes to be the right place to pine away.[20]

In Lodge, moreover, Glaucus' geographical journey sets in motion a generic one. When the Ovidian Glaucus first arrives in England, it is in the form of the conventional Petrarchan

the role models for his transformation are drawn from Ovid. As his journey stops being Virgilian it becomes Ovidian. See further Gildenhard above, and my discussion of 'Dante's Ovidian doubling', in *Dantean dialogues: engaging with the legacy of Amilcare Iannucci*, ed. Maggie Kilgour and Elena Lombardi (Toronto 2013) 174-214.

[17] See also Georgia Brown, *Redefining Elizabethan literature* (Cambridge 2004) 107. Such scenes of generic origination are of course common in Ovid: so, for example, the episode of Apollo and Daphne in *Metamorphoses* I. 438-567 and the opening scenes in *Amores* I. 1 and II. 1 show the transformation of epic into elegy.

[18] See William Keach, *Elizabethan erotic narratives: irony and pathos in the Ovidian poetry of Shakespeare, Marlowe, and their contemporaries* (New Brunswick 1977) 38. Charles Whitworth also notes the influence of Chaucer on the solitary poet figure of Lodge's *Truth's complaint over England*; see his 'Thomas Lodge', in *Thomas Lodge*, ed. Charles C. Whitney (Farnham 2011) 29.

[19] Citations are taken from Thomas Lodge, *Scillaes Metamorphosis* (online facsimile) (London 1590), Early English Books Online http://gateway.proquest.com/openurl?ctx_ver=Z39.88-2003&res_id=xri:eebo&rft_id=xri:eebo:citation:24225639 (accessed 15 July 2005)

[20] On the poem as a satire on the educational system see Lynn Enterline, 'On the passions of nymphs in Elizabethan minor epics', in *The Oxford history of classical reception in English literature*, ed. Patrick Cheney and Philip Hardie, II (Oxford 2015, forthcoming). Enterline argues that the poem's substitution of a Virgilian model with an Ovidian one is a means of challenging the ideology of male civility and power inculcated in the Renaissance classroom through Virgilian texts.

186   THE AFTERLIFE OF OVID

lover and complainer, who bemoans his situation and the inconstancy of the world in stock images of Ovidian mutability: [21]

> Unto the world such is inconstancie,
> As sapp to tree, as apple to the eye.
> Marke how the morne in roseat colour shines,
> And straight with cloudes the Sunnie tract is clad;
> Then see how pomp through waxe and waine declines,
> From high to lowe, from better to the bad:
> Take moist from Sea, take colour from his kinde,
> Before the world deuoid of change thou finde.
> With secret eye looke on the earth a while,
> Regard the changes Nature forceth there;
> Behold the heauens, whose course all sence beguile;
> Respect thy selfe, and thou shalt find it cleere,
> That infantlike thou art become a youth,
> And youth forespent a wretched age ensu'th.
> In searching then the schoolemens cunning noates,
> Of heauen, of earth, of flowers, of springing trees,
> Of hearbs, of mettall, and of Thetis floates,
> Of lawes and nurture kept among the Bees:
> Conclude and knowe times change by course of fate,
> Then mourne no more, but moane my haples state. (23-42)

However, while the poem begins as a complaint, it breaks free from the genre when Glaucus is suddenly cured of his love with the help of Venus and Cupid. Even more gratifyingly, at the very moment that his desire for Scylla disappears, Scylla herself turns up in England. As punishment for her previous cruelty, Cupid shoots her, so now she pursues Glaucus, who flees in horror from her. It is now Scylla's turn to pine away from desire and, as a consequence, be transformed. Lodge leaves out the role of Circe, and abridges the metamorphoses of Scylla who in Ovid is first turned into the monstrous dog-lady who is an enemy of mariners, and who is then petrified; of course, because she is a fixed rock she is no threat to Aeneas.[22] Moralist had pounced on the half-human Scylla as an image of lust. Lodge is not interested in this aspect of the story, but rather in exploiting its potential as the Petrarchan lover's revenge fantasy against the unattainable female. Spurned by

---

[21] On the relation of Lodge's poem to the complaint, see Hulse *Metamorphic verse* (n.8, above) 42; Enterline, 'On the passions of nymphs' (n.20, above), and Keach, *Erotic narratives* (n.18, above) 38. Keach argues that Lodge surveys and exaggerates to make fun of 'previous types of amatory poetry', in particular to create 'a parody of the conventional love-complaint' (44, 40). Lodge himself was quite capable of writing quite conventional complaints and did so later in the rhyme royal *Truth's complaint over England*, published in *An Alarum against usurers* (1584); his sonnets of 1593 end with the *Complaint of Elstred* (which copied Daniel's *Complaint of Rosamund*, appended to the sonnet sequence *Delia* (1592)).

[22] While Myers comments that 'Scylla's petrification also effectively ends the possibility of any further literary repetition' (*Metamorphoses XIV* (n.4, above) 14), it clearly does not prevent her from taking many new forms in later writers.

Glaucus, Scylla 'with hideous cries like winde borne backe she fled | Unto the Sea, and toward Sicillia sped' (659-60) – a return journey obviously necessitated by geography, as Lodge does not completely forget that the story is supposed to explain the origins of a Mediterranean landmark, so he can't move Scylla to England as he does Glaucus. Back where she came from, she is put in her place, turning into the conventional abandoned woman whose complaint is played back to her by the figure of Echo (695-714). However, while it briefly looks as if the poem will relapse into the complaint form with which it began, it does not: Scylla is given only 5 lines in which to proclaim her woe (709-14), and at the end, the narrator, Glaucus, and his family head off for a jolly feast of 'pure immortal Nectar' and 'sweete Ambrosia dainties' (757-58). Everyone seems pleased when Scylla is petrified by the intervention of a group of allegorical figures who bind her to the rocks which she becomes:

> Furie and Rage, Wan-hope, Dispaire, and Woe
> From Ditis den by Ate sent, drewe nie:
> Furie was red, with rage his eyes did gloe,
> Whole flakes of fire from foorth his mouth did flie,
> His hands and armes ibath'd in blood of those
> Whome fortune, sinne, or fate made Countries foes.
> Rage, wan and pale vpon a Tiger sat,
> Knawing vpon the bones of mangled men;
> Naught can he view, but he repinde thereat:
> His lockes were Snakes bred foorth in Stigian den,
> Next whom, Dispaire that deepe disdained elf
> Delightlesse liude, still stabbing of herself.
> Woe all in blacke, within her hands did beare
> The fatall torches of a Funerall,
> Her Cheekes were wet, dispearsed was hir heare,
> Her voice was shrill (yet loathsome therewith all):
> Wan-hope (poore soule) on broken Ancker sitts,
> Wringing his armes as robbed of his witts.
> These fiue at once the sorrowing Nimph assaile,
> And captiue lead her bound into the rocks,
> Where howling still she striues for to preuaile,
> With no auaile yet striues she: for hir locks
> Are chang'd with wonder into hideous sands,
> And hard as flint become her snow-white hands.
> The waters howle with fatall tunes about her,
> The aire dooth scoule when as she turnes within them,
> The winds and waues with puffes and billowes skout her;
> Waues storme, aire scoules, both wind & waues begin them
> To make the place this mournful Nimph doth weepe in,
> A haples haunt whereas no Nimph may keepe in.
> The Sea-man wandring by that famous Isle,
> Shuns all with feare dispairing Scillaes bowre;
> Nimphes, Sea-gods, Syrens when they list to smile
> Forsake the haunt of Scilla in that stowre:

Ah Nimphes thought I, if euerie coy one felt
The like misshappes, their flintie hearts would melt. (715-50)

The scene is remarkably similar to the end of *Faerie Queene* III. 12, in which Amoret is tortured by the conventions of love from which she cannot break free and 'bounden fast…, | And her small waste girt rownd with yron bands, | Vnto a brasen pillour, by the which she stands' (III. 12. 30. 7-9). In both poems, allegorical figures – here Fury, Rage, Despair, Woe, and Wan-Hope[23] – represent the Petrarchan love experience which makes lovers' lives a living hell.[24] Spenser and Lodge both attended Merchant Taylor's School, though, the older Spenser would have been ahead of Lodge. Lodge drew on Spenser's *Complaints*, especially *Mother Hubbard's tale*, in his own 1591 complaint, *Catharos, Diogenes in his singularitie*; he refers to Spenser as 'reurend Colin' in *A Fig for Momus* (1595), and in his 1596 prose satire, *Wit's misery and the world's madness: discovering the devils incarnat of this age*, he describes Spenser as the contemporary poet 'best read in ancient poetry'.[25] In return, Spenser might have known Lodge's 1579 spirited *Defence of poetry, music and stage-plays*, the first of the many defences of poetry written at this time. The connections do not present a strong case for influence, however; rather, and perhaps, more interestingly, the parallels between the two works reveal the common concern of a generation eager to experiment with new forms of both poetry and desire, and to break free from the entrenched conventions of Petrarchism. Moreover, the similarities illuminate striking differences. Spenser's solution is to have Amoret freed by Britomart, Knight of Chastity, who destroys the tormenting Petrarchan images of love that have bound the girl. As Pugh has argued, Spenser suggests that Petrarchan conventions distorted not only love, but also Ovid; in freeing Amoret, therefore, Britomart is 'rescuing Ovid from the Ovidian tradition', thus enabling Spenser to imagine a new kind of Ovidian poetry in the metamorphic and generative Garden of Adonis.[26] Lodge, whose subtitle is 'Contayning the detestable tyrannie of Disdaine, and Comicall Triumph of Constancie: Verie fit for young Courtiers to peruse, and coy Dames to remember', will have none of this. While Lodge's work celebrates liberation from restricting love (in the case of Glaucus at least), it does not release the lovers into each other's arms.[27] Spenser's goal is married love, Lodge's is pure revenge; he is primarily interested in torturing the stony lady and teaching the lesson:

---

[23] Spenser's list is much longer, beginning with Fansy, Desyre, Doubt, Daunger, Feare, Hope, Dissemblaunce, Suspect, Griefe, Fury, Displeasure, Pleasaunce, Despight, Cruelty, then breaking down into a jumble of emotions and psychological states; see *Faerie Queene* III. 12. 7-25.

[24] The seminal discussion of *Faerie Queene* III as an attack on Petrarchism is that of Thomas P. Roche, Jr., *The kindly flame: a study of the third and fourth books of Spenser's* Faerie Queene (Princeton 1964).

[25] Andrew Hadfield notes the connection between the two authors and speculates that they may have had some correspondence around this time, even though Lodge was in exile; see his *Edmund Spenser: a life* (Oxford 2012) 392. The allusion to Spenser in *Wit's misery* is cited from Charles Whitworth, 'Thomas Lodge: Elizabethan pioneer', *Cahiers Élisabéthains* 3 (1973) 5-15 (13).

[26] Pugh, *Spenser and Ovid* (n.3, above) 145.

[27] One might compare this with the later anti-Petrarchism of the cavalier poets which by avoiding sexual consummation revived 'repressed Petrarchism in a libertine world'; see William Kerrigan and Gordon Braden, 'Milton's coy Eve: *Paradise Lost* and Renaissance love poetry', *English*

That Nimphs must yeeld, when faithfull louers straie not.
Least through contempt, almightie loue compell you
With Scilla in the rockes to make your biding
A cursed plague, for womens proud back-sliding. (783-86)

We cannot say with absolute certainty that Lodge's was the first epyllion of this kind in England, mostly because of the difficulty of dating Marlowe's *Hero and Leander*. But it would be typical of Lodge to be a pioneer – he wrote the first *Defence of poetry* (1579), the first English satire (1595), the first translation of Josephus (1602), and the first translation of all Seneca's moral essays (1614) – although, as even his greatest defender wryly noted, he blazed 'more trails for others to follow than he left enduring markers of his own'.[28] But if *Scillaes metamorphosis* does not mark the point of absolute origins of the epyllion it clearly offers a highly Ovidian aitiological myth for the genre, creating a genealogy that starts with Ovid and descends through the complaint and Petrarchan love poetry. Moreover, it introduces its central properties, and suggests why it became, for a short time, hugely popular. As William Keach noted, Lodge's 'strategy of adapting Ovidian transformations so that they become part of an ironic and satirical treatment of the conventional conceits of love poetry' was taken up by other poets.[29] Following Lodge also, the mythological narrative was often framed as a seduction poem: so John Marston's 1598 *The metamorphoses of Pigmalion's image* uses the story of the softening of the marble statue to try to warm up his own stony lady; while Francis Beaumont's 1602 *Salamacis and Hermaphroditus* moralizes that 'all creatures that beneath bright *Cinthia* be, | Haue appetite vnto society' (887-88).[30] In England, the prototype for the unattainable Petrarchan lady is less Daphne (the guiding myth for Petrarch himself) than Narcissus, which had the great advantage of making it seem that any girl who did not leap into bed with the poet was clearly a narcissistic pervert, or as Scylla's example suggests, a monster at heart.[31] William Barksted's 1607 *Mirrha the mother of Adonis; or, lustes prodegies* – written as a

---

Literary History, 53.1 (1986) 27-51 (37). Lodge does and can imagine conventional happy endings in *The delectable history of Forbonius and Prisceria* (published in *An Alarum against usurers*, 1584) and *Rosalynde: Euphues golden legacie* (1590, which Shakespeare famously used for *As you like it*).

[28] Whitworth, 'Thomas Lodge, Elizabethan Pioneer' (n.25, above) 14.

[29] Keach, *Erotic narratives* (n.18, above) 49.

[30] Citations from Francis Beaumont are from *Salmacis and Hermaphroditus* (online facsimile) (London 1602), Early English Books Online http://gateway.proquest.com/openurl?ctx_ver=Z39.88–2003&res_id=xri:eebo&rft_id=xri:eebo:image:8089 (accessed 17 Aug. 2005).

[31] On the ubiquitous figure of Narcissus in Renaissance love poetry, see my *Milton and the metamorphosis* (n.9, above) 184-96. In Ovid, the stories of Daphne, Narcissus, and Scylla are complexly (and narcissistically) linked; on the relation of Daphne and Narcissus, see Philip Hardie, 'Approximative similes in Ovid. Incest and doubling', *Dictynna: revue de poétique latine* 1 (2004) 83-122. Like Daphne and Narcissus, Scylla rejects love; moreover, her discovery of her own metamorphosed body, reflected back to her in the water, clearly replays the episode of Narcissus.

prequel to Shakespeare's hit *Venus and Adonis* – thus makes Myrrha's incestuous desires a direct result of her earlier unnatural scorning of normal love. It is rather as if the stories from the *Metamorphoses* were retold by the *Magister amoris* from the *Ars,* and of course in Shakespeare's *Venus and Adonis* the mythic figure of Venus from *Metamorphoses* X becomes a version of the *praeceptor*. (Much of the comedy in the poem stems from the fact that, while it is hard to imagine a better authority on the subject of love, she turns out to be surprisingly ineffectual). Moreover, Scylla's metamorphosis triumphantly marks the transformation of the cold and aloof lady of Petrarchan poetry into the firey and enamoured female who rages through the epyllion: Oenone in Heywood's *Oenone and Paris* (1594); Diana in Drayton's *Endimion and Phoebe (1595);* Aurora in Thomas Edwards *Cephalus and Procris* (1595); Salmacis in Beaumont's *Salmacis and Hermaphroditus* (1602); Myrrha in Barksted's *Mirrha* (1607), and the best and biggest of them all, Shakespeare's Venus who in more ways than one is the prototype for the figure. The popularity of this stock figure suggests that by the 1590s many were pretty fed up with female chastity in poetry and perhaps even more in politics, especially as the consequences of Elizabeth's virginity – the lack of an heir – became increasingly anxiety provoking.[32]

Scillaes metamorphosis thus uses Ovidian figures to construct a genealogy for the epyllion as part of the 'Englishing' of classical forms to produce a new native literature. John Weever extends the line in *Faunus and Melliflora, or the original of our English satyres,* which appeared in 1600 as the popular genre was beginning to dwindle from revolutionary innovation into formulaic cliché. Like Lodge, Weever is interested in imagining Ovidian figures coming to England: in this case, Faunus, the son of the Picus whose story is also told in *Metamorphoses* XIV as part of the series of tales which interrupts and substitutes for Aeneas' journey.[33] Ovid's account of Picus is connected to that of Glaucus through the figure of Circe, the archetypal lusty lady, who transforms both Scylla and Picus in revenge for unrequited love. The two episodes furthermore represent stages of Aeneas' journey; as Glaucus' journey to Italy replaces that of Aeneas, the figure of Picus recalls Aeneas' arrival in *Aeneid* VII, where Virgil describes the Italian king Latinus' descent from Picus and his son Faunus, and alludes to Picus' transformation into a woodpecker by Circe (VII. 45-9, 187-91).[34] Virgil's Picus is thus part of the native Italian world with which the Trojans must unite to become Romans. Ovid takes Virgil's ancient Latin and weaves Picus into a tragic love story in which he is married to the nymph Canens, who as her name suggests,

---

[32] Heather Dubrow sees Shakespeare's Venus as a comment on 'the chaste heroines of Elizabethan love poetry', suggesting also that 'Venus' assertions of power may well reflect resentment of Elizabeth herself'; see *Captive victors: Shakespeare's narrative poems and sonnets* (Ithaca 1987) 34.

[33] Ovid also mentions Picus and Faunus in *Fast.* III. 291ff. as indigenous gods who teach Numa rituals of expiation.

[34] In the *Metamorphoses,* moreover, the story of Picus is told by Macareus, one of Ulysses' men who was left behind on Circe's island where he is picked up by the Trojans, and who is the mirror image of the Greek Achaemenides whom Virgil had invented to link Aeneas' journey with that of Ulysses. The three epic journeys – that of Homer's Odysseus, Virgil's Aeneas and Ovid's Aeneas – briefly intersect in a complex intertextual dialogue. As Hinds notes, 'Ovid thematizes his intertextual dialogue with his epic predecessor... by putting an Odyssean stray of his own into conversation with the Odyssean stray through whom Virgil had thematized *his* intertextual dialogue with *his* epic predecessor', *Allusion and intertext* (n.5, above) 112.

MAGGIE KILGOUR: IMPORTING THE OVIDIAN MUSE TO ENGLAND   191

represents the power of song.[35] The faithful Picus therefore spurns the advances of Circe. While Homer's Circe lets Odysseus return to his wife, Ovid's more venomous jilted deity spitefully turns Picus into a woodpecker, and in grief, Canens dissolves into water (XIV. 431-34). While Ovid claims she turns into a place which the Camenae, the Italian Muses, called Canens in her memory, no one has been able to identify any such place; Sara K. Myers thus suggests he, in fact, invented the figure of the tragic singer to create an *aetion* for the Italian Muses.[36] While Virgil's poem tells of the arrival of Aeneas in Italy, Ovid's shifts our attention to the arrival of the Muses.[37]

Weever's poem rewrites Ovid to tell a similar story of the arrival of muses. While married to Canens, Weever's Picus is not the epitome of married bliss but a spokesman for misogyny who denounces women and love. He warns his son against:

> This vpstart loue, bewitcher of the wit,
> The scorne of vertue, vices parasite:
> The slaue to weakenesse, friendships false bewrayer,
> Reasons rebell, Fortitudes betraier:
> The Church-mens scoffe, court, camp, and countrie's guiler,
> Arts infection, chaste thoughts and youth's defiler.
> And what are women? painted weathercocks,
> Natures ouersight, wayward glittring blocks:
> True, true-bred cowards, proude if they by coide,

---

[35] In Virgil, the relation between Circe and Picus is ambiguous. Arriving in Italy, Aeneas sees a statue of Picus: '*quem capta cupidine coniunx | aurea percussum virga versumque venenis | fecit avem Circe sparsitque coloribus alas*' ('whom his bride Circe, smitten with love's longing, struck with her golden rod, and with drugs changed into a bird with plumes of dappled hue', VII. 189-91). Some versions, like the Loeb here, take this to mean that Circe is Picus' wife, though, as Donatus first noted, '*aurea*' is ironic. Others, including Servius, suggest instead that Circe only wanted to be Picus' wife; rejected by him, she took revenge by turning him into a woodpecker. It is hard not to think that the latter readings were not influenced by Ovid's account of the story. Dryden's translation of *Aeneid* VII certainly sounds Ovidian when he fills in the details:

> For Circe long had lov'd the youth in vain,
> Till love, refus'd, converted to disdain:
> Then, mixing pow'rful herbs, with magic art,
> She chang'd his form, who could not change his heart;
> Constrain'd him in a bird, and made him fly,
> With party-color'd plumes, a chatt'ring pie. (VII. 260-65; citation from Virgil, *The Aeneid of Virgil,* trans. John Dryden, ed. Robert Fitzgerald (New York 1965) 221)

As Elizabeth Ten-Hove pointed out to me, the ambiguity has important implications for the genealogy of the Italians: while Latinus himself traces his family back to Saturn, Virgil leaves open another possible, and somewhat shadier, family tree. As Fordyce notes, Virgil seems to remember that Hesiod had suggested that Latinus was descended from Circe (though with Odysseus); C. J. Fordyce, *Aeneidos libri VII-VIII.* (Oxford 1977) 103.

[36] Myers, *Ovid's causes* (n.4, above) 110-11.

[37] Hinds notes the importance of the Camenae in earlier Roman constructions of 'importing the Muse'; *Allusion and intertext* (n.5, above) 58-63.

192   THE AFTERLIFE OF OVID

A seruile sex, of wit and reason voide:
Shall women moue thee, whom so many loathes,
In gaudie plumes trickte, and new-fangled cloathes? (523-34).[38]

As in Lodge, Circe is written out of the story; when Picus is transformed it is Venus who
punishes him for his contempt of love (1007-20). In both epyllia, the omission of Circe
explicitly makes desire the sinisterly metamorphic force,[39] though Weever's narrator, who
leaps also to the defence of women, stresses the positive side of this, saying love's excellence
'is to transforme the verie soule and essence | Of the louer, into the thing beloued' (554-55).
At the centre of the poem is the popular Renaissance debate about the nature of desire, and
especially its transformative qualities that make men either gods or beasts.

    In Weever, however, Picus is simply the background for the next generation, and the
real story is that of his son, Faunus, and his beloved, Melliflora. Geographical movement
from one place to another is thus mirrored by succession in time: the progression from
the misogynist Picus, who clearly deserves to be turned into a woodpecker, to Faunus
and Melliflora, the happy and ultimately married couple. The poem opens by setting
the action at the time when Jove 'deposed his Syre *Saturnus* from the throne, | And
so vsurpt the Diadem alone' (4-5), drawing attention to generational succession and
the overthrow of an old order. Weever announces a new generation of Ovidian poetics
through lovers whose love is reciprocal and, even more importantly, *consummated*.
While Melliflora's name clearly recalls Ovid's Flora, she is completely made up, a new
woman indeed, as Weever claims when he introduces her as: 'faire *Melliflora*, amorous,
and yong, | Whose name, nor story, neuer Poet sung' (131-32). Her natural amorousness,
and her immediate reciprocation of Faunus' affections, show her difference from the
hard-hearted Scylla.

    However, while Weever insists that he is telling a new story, it is one that by 1600 already
looks familiar. *Faunus and Melliflora* reads like a tour of the greatest hits of English poetry
of the 1590s, although this might seem a polite way of describing what other scholars have
called 'slavish…imitation' or at best 'accomplished parody'.[40] In denouncing love, Picus
recalls Shakespeare's Adonis. Faunus himself begins looking like figures such as Adonis,
Hermaphroditus, and Narcissus: his story starts when he reaches adolescence and wanders
away from his home. Like Ovid's Hermaphroditus and Narcissus, he finds himself at a
body of water. However, where Hermaphroditus and Narcissus reach pools whose stillness

---

[38] Citations taken from *Faunus and Melliflora* (online facsimile) (London 1600), Early English
Books Online http://gateway.proquest.com/openurl?ctx_ver=Z39.882003&res_id=xri:eebo&rft _id
=xri:eebo:citation:99846921 (accessed 2 August 2005).

[39] Keach notes the effect of the omission of Circe in relation to Lodge; see *Erotic narratives*
(n.18, above) 46-47.

[40] Hallet Smith, *Elizabethan poetry: a study in conventions, meaning and expression* (Cambridge
1952), 99; Helmut Castrop, *Shakespeares Verserzählungen: eine Untersuchung der ovidischen Epik
im elisabethanischen England* (Munich 1964), 169; both are quoted (and Castrop translated) by
Keach, *Erotic narratives* (n.18, above) 169. See also Keach's fine reading of the poem, 162-89.
Keach argues that Weever's work marks a new stage in which imitation becomes more selfconscious
and even 'mannerist' in its borrowing.

and untouched surfaces mirror their own virginity,[41] Faunus find a river, whose movement urges him to love:

> Whose wanton streames the bank so oft do kisse,
> That in her lap (at length) he falling is:
> Her bubbling water with slow gliding pace,
> Shews her great griefe to leaue that pleasant place:
> And with a murmure when she goes away.
> Greatly laments she can no longer stay,
> Cause th' vpper streams by violence would come,
> To take possession of that ioyfull roome,
> With swift pursute, and as they gin to chace it,
> The bankes like armes doe louingly imbrace it. (89-98)

As often happens in erotic poetry, nature teaches a human being that desire is natural.[42] The lesson is not lost on Faunus who sees Melliflora at this spot, and is immediately smitten.

The rest of the poem details their courtship, drawing heavily on Spenser, Sidney, Shakespeare, and Marlowe, as well as Ovid himself.[43] Like other Ovidian works of the time, it crams the single episode with many other stories from Ovid: Faunus decides to write to Melliflora in a scene which copies Byblis' writing to her brother (183-98); there are many allusions to the figure of Salmacis (367-78; 821-28); and Faunus looks at a picture of Diana and Actaeon (275-82). Weever also explicitly 'corrects' Ovid, explaining that when the sun scorched the earth it was not because of Phaethon but because Phoebus' infatuation with Melliflora caused him to lose control of his horses (147-52).[44] There are numerous references, especially to the story of Venus and Adonis, which provide a particular contrast for the new love story Weever is imagining. In this case, however, he is correcting not Ovid but Shakespeare whose plot momentarily threatens to derail Weever's happy story, as the courtship of Faunus and Melliflora is interrupted by the sudden appearance of a savage boar (441-68). However, the beast poses no real threat as Faunus is able to kill it 'with a little knife' he happens to have on hand (465). In fact, Weever explains, Adonis was not killed by the boar, but died of love for Melliflora, and Venus was really in love with Faunus (with whom

---

[41] See *Met.* III. 407-12 and *Met.* IV. 297-301. In all three cases, the water reflects the hero's emotional state.

[42] See for example, Venus' interpretation of the meaning of Adonis' randy horse in *Venus and Adonis*, 385- 408.

[43] A scene in which Faunus sees dancing graces is adapted from *Faerie Queene* VI. 10. 5-28; while Keach, *Erotic narrative* (n.18, above) 171, suggests that the description of Diana and Actaeon recalls Spenser's *Mutabilitie cantos* – another place in which Faunus appears – these were not published till 1609. Keach concentrates especially on the influence of Sidney on the central scenes; see 167-68, 170-72.

[44] In this he is copying and correcting Marlowe, who in *Hero and Leander* I. 45-50 had claimed that the dark skins of some races were not caused by Phaethon's fall but by Hero's influence on nature.

194 THE AFTERLIFE OF OVID

Adonis is easily confused several times). When Venus flees the world it is not for grief over Adonis' death, as in Shakespeare, but because Faunus rejects her.[45]

[45] Here is part of Weever's version of what happens:

> Losing himselfe, within a groue he [Faunus] found
> Loue-sicke *Adonis* lying on the ground.
> For hating Loue, and saying *Uenus* nay,
> Yet meeting *Melliflora* in his way:
> Loue made (Loue weepe to see thy tyrannie,)
> *Adonis* frustrate his vow'd chastitie:
> Whilst narrowly vpon her lookes he spide,
> Strooke with loues arrow, he fell downe and dide.
> For by the Bore (as all our Poets faine,)
> He was not kilde, *Faunus* the Bore had slaine.
> But tracing further, who but *Venus* met him,
> Thinking he had beene *Adon*, thus she gret him:
> Welcome *Adonis*, in thy louelie breast
> Now do I see remorse and pitie rest,
> Which to returne my deare *Adonis* moued,
> *Uenus* perswades her selfe she is beloued:
> Hoping to haue some water from the rocke,
> Which shee had pierst, she stript her to the smocke:
> Wrought all in flames of Chrisolite and gold,
> And bout his necke her armes she did enfold:
> So (at the least) shee meaning to haue kist him
> He turn'de aside: then sorie cause shee mist him,
> To *Faunus* said, faire Saint, shun not such kindnesse,
> Can these bright eies be blemisht with such blindnesse?
> If thou wert blind, and *Venus* could not see,
> Yet in the darke best sighted louers be:
> Or giue, or take, or both, relent, be kind,
> Locke not Loue in the paradize of thy mind:
> Is *Venus* louely? then *Adonis* loue her.
> Is she the Queene of loue? then what should moue her
> To sue and not command? Is shee loues mother?
> Shall she be loath'd, which brings loue to all other?
> With that she doft all to the Iuorie skinne,
> Thinking her naked glorie would him winne.
> The shamefac't *Faunus* thereat something smiled,
> *Uenus* lookt on him, knew shee was beguiled:
> Yet would haue lou'd him for *Adonis* sake,
> (Thus women will one for another take.)
> *Faunus* resisted, *Venus* would no more
> Sollicite him, but mounted as before
> In her light Chariot drawne with milke-white Doues,
> *Away she flies.* (471-512, emphasis added)

The ending especially rewrites the last stanza of *Venus and Adonis* in which:

> Thus weary of the world, *away she hies*,
> And yokes her silver doves, by whose swift aid,
> Their mistresse mounted through the empty skies,

While Weever's couple momentarily meet up with Shakespeare's characters, their story follows a different path to a new kind of love. Yet again this love is not really new, as Weever takes the courtship from Marlowe's *Hero and Leander*. Faunus' rhetorical seduction of Melliflora, in which he tells her she must break her vow of virginity (90506), is modelled on Leander's speech to Hero in *Hero and Leander* I. 305-16. Weever copies the shaggy dog story at the end of the first sestiad in *Hero and Leander* (I. 375ff.), when he explains how the love in Faunus' eyes flies to the Destinies to denounce men like Picus who attack it.[46] Like Hero and Leander, Weever's innocent and rather inept lovers court each other and, after some contrived mishaps and a very long authorial digression to deliciously delay the action, are finally united in mutual happiness in a scene that itself compresses the more drawn-out (and funnier) consummation in Marlowe.[47]

> In her light chariot, quickly is conveyed,
> Holding their course to Paphos, where their queen,
> Meanes to immure herself, and not be seen. (1189-93, emphasis added)

Citations taken from William Shakespeare, *The complete sonnets and poems*, ed. Colin Burrow, The Oxford Shakespeare (Oxford 2002).

[46] Other writers who copied Marlowe especially elaborated on his digression; see esp. Beaumont, *Salamacis and Hermaphroditus*, which piles digression on digression.

[47] Again here is Weever:

> *Faunus* alone, with her alone required,
> Alone with him, which she alone desired.
> Yet now she feares to be with him alone,
> Because no further in loues office gone:
> He would haue sealed with the cheefest armes
> Of his desire, the waxe that *Uenus* warmes.
> But as she did the contrarie command,
> He was afraide, durst not her words withstand.
> Did not the boy therein a coward proue?
> Nay rather valiant, to withstand such loue.
> The marriage was by one of *Vestaes* Nuns
> Solemnized. She *Faunus* neuer shuns:
> *He giues, she takes, and nothing is denide,*
> *She his, he her loue's force and valor tride.*
> *And still they striue,* but who obtainde the day,
> Let him be iudge that er'e fought such a fray:
> But faint and breathlesse here the quarrell ends,
> Loues cause being righted, both againe are friends. (989-1006, emphasis added)

Compare with the two stages of consummation in Marlowe, which requires two separate meetings in Hero's tower. In the first, the lovers swiftly embrace:

> At last he came, O who can tell the greeting,
> These greedie louers had, at their first meeting.
> *He askt, she gaue, and nothing was denied,*
> *Both to each other quickly were affied.*
> Looke how their hands, so were their hearts vnited,
> And what he did, she willingly requited.
> (Sweet are the kisses, the imbracements sweet,
> When like desires and affections meet.) (II. 31-38, emphasis added)

196   THE AFTERLIFE OF OVID

The goal of Weever's lovers is, like that of Marlowe and again Spenser, a happy, even respectable, union. However, the Marlovian digression in which Love flies to the Destinies to denounce the ingratitude of men leads to a prophesy which recalls that at the end of *Venus and Adonis*. We learn that, because of Picus' misogyny, love will always be full of misery. The Fates proclaim:

> That market marriages euermore should be
> Content the best, the worst to disagree,
> That shrewdnesse should possesse the womans heart,
> In stubbornnesse the husband act his part:
> Thus drawing opposite in one yoke, aliue
> Long might they liue, but they should neuer thriue:
> And since that time, all marriages enforced,
> Neuer agree vntill they be deuorced. (665-72)[48]

Moreover, the marriage of Faunus and Melliflora is not the conclusion of Weever's story (as of course the consummation of Hero and Leander's love is not the end of theirs), which goes on to show love turning Picus into a woodpecker. Metamorphosis also takes a dark turn as the poem moves forward to the next generation. Faunus begins as a son but ends as a father, and the originator of an ambiguous line of descent. Faunus and Melliflora's son is cursed by the angered Diana, and turned into a monstrous satyr. At the end, Weever returns to the Virgilian source of Faunus' and Picus, to recall that it is this familial line which will eventually immigrate to England with the Trojan Brute:

While it appears that their love has been consummated, it is only on Leander's second visit that Hero gives in completely:

> *She trembling stroue, this strife of hers* (like that
> Which made the world) another world begat,
> Of vnknowne ioy…. (II. 287-89, emphasis added)

Citations taken from Christopher Marlowe and George Chapman, *Hero and Leander* (online facsimile) (London 1598), Early English Books Online http://gateway.proquest.com/openurl?ctx_ver=Z39.88-2003&res_id=xri:eebo&rft_id=xri: eebo:citation:99840679 (accessed 2 August 2005)

[48] Compare with the end of *Venus and Adonis*, when the frustrated Venus proclaims that:

> Since thou art dead, lo, here I prophesy:
> Sorrow on love hereafter shall attend:
> It shall be waited on with jealousy,
> Find sweet beginning, but unsavoury end,
> Ne'er settled equally, but high or low,
> That all love's pleasure shall not match his woe.
>
> It shall be fickle, false and full of fraud,
> Bud and be blasted in a breathing-while.... (1135-42)

The end of *Venus and Adonis* explains why love can never be satisfied or reciprocal; it is an *aition* of unrequited passion, and indeed Petrarchism, which suggests that this is the inevitable nature of all love.

[Faunus] At length begot *Latinus*, he *Lauinia*:
Aeneas her from *Turnus* tooke away,
Succeeding him, hïs sonne *Ascanius*,
And after him *Aeneas Siluius*,
Him *Brutus* kild, and at our English *Douer*
Landed, and brought some Satyres with him ouer,
And nimble Faëries. As most writers graunt,
London by *Brute* was named *Troynovaunt*.
The Faëries ofspring yet a long time went,
Among the woods within the wild of *Kent*,
Vntill transformed both in shape and essence,
By some great power or heauenly influence,
The Faëries proued full stout hardy knights,
In iusts, in tilts in turnaments, and fights,
As *Spencer* shewes. But *Spencer* now is gone,
You Faëry Knights, your greatest losse bemone.... (1049-64)

The *translatio* here is Virgilian, but what is being carried across – not *lars penatesque* but satyrs and fairies – is not. The presence of the former may perhaps not seem too surprising in a poem concerned with generic descent. From the start, the epyllion, evolving out of and against Petrarchism and the complaint, had verged on satire.[49] Lodge's *Scilla* was published in a collection which included a satire called 'The Discontented satyr', and Lodge went on to write the first full blown English satire, *A Fig for Momus*, in 1595.[50] Describing Hero's disappointed lovers, the narrator of *Hero and Leander* wryly observes that 'some (their violent passions to asswage) | Compile sharpe satire' (I. 126-27). Love poetry always leads to satire. In the end, Weever's epyllion shows that the genre ends in satire, as it turns into a satire on satire itself. The narrator protests that 'I was borne to hate your censuring vaine, | Your enuions [sic] biting in your crabbed straine' (1085-86), a claim that is ironized by the fact that the rest of the volume in which the poem appeared consists of satires and that Weever would go on to write more satires.

But Brute also brings fairies with him from Italy - specifically, fairies who, after a bit of time in the healthy English woods, bulk up and turn into Spenserian knights. Chaucer had simply translated pagan gods into English fairies, a tradition that was continued by other writers, including Golding. Golding, however, also keeps the two mythological systems distinct. This allows him to make comparisons; for example, Philomela is 'in beautie farre more rich, even like the Fairies which | Reported are the pleasant woods and water springs

---

[49] As also argued by Keach, *Erotic narratives* (n.18, above) 48-49, who notes how in the late 1590s 'the Elizabethan delight in languid eroticism and extravagant artificiality gave way to an increasingly satirical and parodic approach to Ovidian fable' (119). The burlesquing of Ovid gained further popularity in the 17th century with works such as James Smith's smutty parody of both Ovid and Marlowe, *The loves of Hero and Leander: a mock poem* (1651), Matthew Stevenson's *The Wits paraphrased, or paraphrase upon paraphrase in a burlesque* (1680), and Alexander Radcliffe's *Ovid Travestie: a burlesque upon Ovids epistles* (1681).

[50] Whitworth notes that in his *Defence* Lodge had called for 'some satirical poets nowadays... to decipher the abuses of the world' (cited from Whitworth, 'Thomas Lodge' (n.18, above) 8); he returned to satire and complaint in other works such as *Truth's complaint* and *Wit's misery*.

198   THE AFTERLIFE OF OVID

to haunt' (VI. 579-80).[51] But it also allows him to give fairies priority over the pagan gods when, in Book XIV, he slyly sneaks in the claim that Pan's bower 'heertoofore… was the fayryes bowre' (XIV. 586). The juxtaposition of fairies and pagan myths is complex also in Spenser, as well as in Shakespeare's *A Midsummer night's dream*, where the two worlds meet and yet stay separate. For later writers, Shakespeare's and Spenser's bringing together of fairy and Ovidian elements showed how the classical and the indigenous could be creatively combined. Thomas Edwards' 1595 *Cephalus and Procris* which rewrites Ovid through Shakespeare and Spenser (as well as Marlowe),[52] has a fairy interlude in which Procris is taken in by Lamia, queen of the fairies.[53] A mixing of classical and native

[51] Quoted from *Shakespeare's Ovid: being Arthur Golding's translation of the* Metamorphoses, ed. W. H. D. Rouse (Carbondale 1961).

[52] Aurora is based on Venus, and Cephalus, who wants to hunt the boar (243-44), on Adonis, although, unlike Adonis, he is not chaste but a figure for (Spenserian) married chastity. The scene of Marlowe's lovers' consummation, reworked by Weever, also is echoed here when Cephalus tries to leave Aurora: 'He striuing to be gone, she prest him downe | She striuing to kisse him, he kist the growne, | And euermore on contrarieties' (215-17). Citations taken from Thomas Edwards, *Cephalus & Procris* (online facsimile) (London 1595), Early English Books Online http://gateway.proquest.com/openurl?ctx_ver=Z39.882003&res_id=xri:eebo&rft_id=xri:eebo:citation:99848471 (accessed 12 September 2005).

[53] *Lamie* by chaunce some sacred herbe to vse,
   On deere compassion of some louers plaintes,
   Among the woods and moorie fennes she hauntes,
   Such euill pleasing humours, fairie elues,
   Obserue and keepe autenticke mong'st themselues;
   And now was she of purpose trauailing,
   Intending quietly to be a gathering
   Some vnprophane, or holy thing, or other:
   Good Faierie Lady, hadst thou bene loues mother,
   Not halfe so meny gallants had bene slaine,
   As now in common are with endlesse paine,
   This Lady compassing her secret fauour;
   Procris espi'd wondring at her behauiour,
   Amaz'd she stoode at such a heauenly sight,
   To see so debonary a saint at such a hight,
   Her haire downe trailing, and her robes loose worne,
   Rushing through thickets, and yet neuer torne,
   Her brest so white as euer womans was,
   And yet made subiect to the Sunnes large compasse:
   Each so officious, and became her so,
   As *Thames* doth Swannes, or Swans did euer *Po*,
   Procris in steede of tearmes her to salute,
   With teares and sighes, (shewing her toung was mute)
   She humbly downe vnto her louely feete,
   Bow'd her straight bodie *Lamie* to greete:
   Therewith the Lady of those pretie ones,
   That in the twylight mocke the frozen zone,

is taken for granted in William Percy's 1603 *The Faery pastorall*, in which Oberon is married to Chloris, Queene of the Faeryes.[54]

Ending with the arrival of Spenserian fairies to England with Faunus and the satyrs, Weever's poem brings me back to where I started: Spenser and the foundational myth of Brute. For Weever, Spenserian epic is part of the same family tree as the epyllion, which is not surprising given that Spenser wrote Ovidian complaints, including an early epyllion, '*Muiopotmos*', and, like epyllion writers, rejected Petrarchan forms of desire.[55] The complex genealogy through which classical works become English is suggested also in John Milton's *A Masque performed at Ludlow Castle*, or *Comus*, (performed 1634, published 1637 and 1645), a work which offers a retrospective on the process I have been mapping, as well as a glimpse of its future. Like Lodge and Weever, Milton follows the movement of classical figures to England. However, the mask sets up opposing kinds of journey and lines of descent, centred on the two main characters of the enchanter Comus and the chaste Lady. Like Faunus, Comus is part of the later generation of the ancient gods; he is the son of Circe (once again from Ovid's *Aeneid* in *Metamorphoses* XIIIXIV), who has moved to Britain. The Lady is an Aeneas figure who is leaving England to go to a new home in Wales on a journey that is both a story of personal growth and part of the expansion of empire.[56] Her link to Aeneas is reinforced by the presence of Sabrina, nymph of the River Severn, which the Lady must symbolically cross to reach her destination. Sabrina is herself of Trojan descent; she is identified by her birth as 'virgin, daughter of Locrine | Sprung of old Anchises line' (922-23).

> And hand in hand daunce by some siluer brooke,
> One at another pointing, and vp looke,
>   (Like rurall Faunes) vpon the full fa'st Moone,
> Intreating *Venus* some heroicke boone,
> Gently gan stoupe, and with her sacred haire,
> Her louely eies, and face so ouer faire,
> She neatly couers, and her vngirt gowne,
> Deafely commits vnto the lowly growne,
> She dandleth *Procris* thereon prettily,
> And chaunteth soueraigne songs full merrily,
> And gins to prancke her vp with many a flower,
> And vow'd she should be *Oboron's* parramore. (480-518)

[54]   Chloris, taken from Ovid's *Fasti* V. 183-354, is a stock name for nymphs in the Ovidian poetry of the 17th century especially; see further my 'Eve and Flora (*Paradise Lost* 5.15-6)' *Milton Quarterly* 38 (2004) 1-17, as well as 'The poetics of time: the *Fasti* in the Renaissance', in *A handbook to the reception of Ovid*, ed. John F. Miller and Carole E. Newlands (Oxford: Wiley-Blackwell, 2014) 217-31. The classical and fairy also seem parallel in the works of Drayton, who writes both 'Nymphidia' and *England's Heroicall Epistles*, and Herrick, whose Ovidian *Hesperides* is punctuated with a series of fairy poems.

[55]   For a further discussion of 'Muiopotmos' in relation to Spenser's revision of Virgil and Ovid, see my *Milton and the metamorphosis* (n.9, above) 277-83.

[56]   On the political subtext, and in particular the relation between England and Wales at this time, see Michael Wilding, '*Milton's 'a mask presented at Ludlow Castle, 1634'*: theatre and politics on the border', *Milton Quarterly* 21.4 (1987) 35-51.

THE AFTERLIFE OF OVID

As in *Faerie Queene* III, an Ovidian figure turns a Virgilian journey into a scene of seduction, as Comus tries to prevent the Lady from reaching her new home. The son of Circe, Comus is clearly related also to the Shakepearean and Marlovian Ovidian line of seducer figures, as well as their English heirs, the rakes who appear in the Caroline poetry of Milton's contemporaries.[57] In contrast, the Lady looks back to Spenser as the heir of Virgil. The latter line of descent is again made explicit through Sabrina, who is taken from another instalment of the history of Britain in *Faerie Queene* II. 10. 14-19. Spenser explains how Locrine, son of Brute, is overthrown and killed by his wife for infidelity. His wife then pursues his illegitimate daughter, Sabrina, and drowns her:

> But the sad virgin innocent of all,
> Adowne the rolling riuer she did poure,
> Which of her name now *Seuerne* men do call:
> Such was the end, that to disloyall loue did fall. (II. 10. 19. 6-9)

Though he included an account in his *History of Britain*, Milton was extremely skeptical of the myth of Brute and his family, which he assumed had been invented 'in affectation to make the *Britan* of one Original with the *Roman*' and which had produced false genealogies: 'those old and inborn names of successive Kings, never any to have bin real persons, or don in thir lives at least som of the part of what so long hath bin remember'd'.[58] In his *History*, Milton makes it clear that the story of Sabrina is an *aition* of the name of the river Severn: 'But not so ends the fury of *Guendolen*; for *Estrildis* and her Daughter *Sabra*, she throws into a River: and to leave a Monument of revenge, proclaims, that the stream be thenceforth call'd after the Damsels name; which by length of time is chang'd now to *Sabrina*, or *Severn*'.[59]

In Milton's *History*, as in Spenser and other earlier accounts, Sabrina simply drowns and is memorialized in the river's name. In *Comus*, however, she actually becomes the river through metamorphosis:

> Sabrina is her name, a Virgin pure,
> Whilom she was the daughter of *Locrine*,
> That had the Scepter from his father *Brute*.
> The guiltless damsell flying the mad pursuit
> Of her enraged stepdam *Guendolen*,
> Commended her fair innocence to the flood
> That stay'd her flight with his cross-flowing course,
> The water Nymphs that in the bottom plaid,
> Held up their pearled wrists and took her in,

---

[57] On the relation of Comus to Elizabethan and Caroline forms of Ovidianism, see *Milton and the metamorphosis* (n.9, above) 74-111.

[58] See Milton's *The History of Britain*, in *The Complete prose works of John Milton*, ed. Don M. Wolfe, 8 vols (Yale 1953-82), V (1971) 8-9, and his account of her story, 8-18. While he raises the question of authenticity, he brackets the issue, explaining that 'to examin these things with diligence were but to confute the Fables of *Britan* with the Fables of *Greece* or *Italy*' (11).

[59] Milton, *History* (n.58, above) 18.

Bearing her straight to aged *Nereus* Hall,
Who piteous of her woes, rear'd her lank head,
And gave her to his daughters to imbathe
In nectar'd lavers strew'd with Asphodil,
And through the porch and inlet of each sense
Dropt in Ambrosial Oils till she reviv'd,
And underwent a quick immortal change
Made Goddess of the River. (826-42)[60]

The episode from the Virgilian *translatio* is itself turned into one of Ovidian metamorphosis, as the scene recalls the baptisms of Glaucus and Ovid's Aeneas in *Metamorphoses* XIII-XIV. While Ovid also has several figures who turn into rivers, the closest Ovidian precedent for Sabrina's change comes from another moment in which he rewrites the *Aeneid*, to tell the story of a journey of a female and Carthaginian exile in contrast to that of the male Trojan/Roman. *Fasti* III. 543-656 explains that Dido's sister Anna was forced to flee Carthage after the death of Dido. Landing in Rome, she was treated hospitably by Aeneas but persecuted by the jealous Lavinia. Warned by her sister's ghost (as Hector had warned Aeneas in *Aeneid* II), she fled once more, to be taken by the river and transformed into its nymph, the goddess Anna Perenna. Like Anna, Sabrina is the Ovidian, female, substitute for the male Aeneas.

For Milton too, the Virgilian *translatio* has been reshaped through Ovid as it comes to England. Moreover, his poem ends with the vision of another journey and family tree. The Lady is saved from the evil Comus and returned to her parents. At the opening of the mask, an Attendant Spirit is sent down from heaven to help her; his job done, he imagines his ascent back home through a series of mythological paradises which lead from the Hesperides, through the Garden of Adonis, to an even higher garden:

To the Ocean now I fly,
And those happy climes that ly
Where day never shuts his eye,
Up in the broad fields of the sky:
There I suck the liquid ayr
All amidst the Gardens fair
Of *Hesperus*, and his daughters three
That sing about the golden tree:
Along the crisped shades and bowres
Revels the spruce and jocond Spring,
The Graces, and the rosie-boosom'd Howres,
Thither all their bounties bring,
That there eternal Summer dwels,
And West winds with musky wing
About the cedar'n alleys fling
Nard, and *Cassia's* balmy smels.
Iris there with humid bow,

---

[60] Citations from John Milton, *Complete shorter poems,* ed. Stella P. Revard (Malden 2009).

Waters the odorous banks that blow
Flowers of more mingled hew
Then her purfl'd scarf can shew,
And drenches with Elysian dew
(List mortals, if your ears be true)
Beds of *Hyacinth* and roses
Where young *Adonis* oft reposes,
Waxing well of his deep wound
In slumber soft, and on the ground
Sadly sits th' *Assyrian* Queen;
But farr above in spangled sheen
Celestial *Cupid* her fam'd son advanc't,
Holds his dear *Psyche* sweet intranc't
After her wandring labours long,
Till free consent the gods among
Make her his eternal Bride,
And from her fair unspotted side
Two blissful twins are to be born,
Youth and Joy; so *Jove* hath sworn. (976-1011)

The final vision especially is a glorious mythological compendium that synthesizes Ovid and Elizabethan poetics to rise above them, just as the Spirit and poem go beyond the figures of Venus and Adonis, associated not only with Ovid but also with Shakespeare and Spenser. Milton creates a new genealogical line, one that can include Virgil, Ovid, and his English precursors, all brought together to form a new family unit, and to create a new kind of journey, one which is not just across seas and time but upwards to the skies. If the poem looks backwards as it rises above these myths it also looks forward to the next generation: Venus' son Cupid and his wife Psyche, and their children, as the poem moves up in time as well as space, from the icon of deadly desire to a happily married couple and their offspring. One glimpses the next generation of this line of Ovidian transmission that will produce a new vision of paradise, as the mutual love of Adam and Eve which is at the centre of *Paradise Lost*. The classical muses are now at home in England, where they have become part of a new mythology.

Department of English, McGill University

MILTON AS READER OF OVID'S *METAMORPHOSES*

PHILIP HARDIE

This paper was prompted by reviewing Mandy Green's excellent book on Milton and Ovid, *Milton's Ovidian Eve* (Farnham and Burlington, 2009). Green takes a single Miltonic character and explores the superimposition on to Eve of a series of characters in Ovid's *Metamorphoses* and *Fasti*: Narcissus, Pygmalion's statue, Daphne, Flora, Proserpina, Ceres, Venus, Pomona, and Pyrrha. The 'many [Ovidian] faces of Eve'[1] allow Milton to explore a range of roles and subject positions that Eve's daughters will be called upon to play in human society, with a particular focus on the relationships between the sexes and on sexual politics. An attention to Ovidian intertextuality also interacts with modern concerns in the interpretation of Eve: whether her marriage to Adam is companionate or patriarchal; whether she is Adam's equal or inferior; whether from the moment of her creation she is trapped in the role of temptress-to-be. Green speaks of the (22) 'comprehensive, shifting balance of opposing forces that is fundamental to [Milton's] conception of his Eve'. The range of Ovidian roles played by Eve also traces a development from birth, through pre-sexual innocence, to sexual experience and marriage, and finally to death, with the possibility of rebirth and regeneration. Thus within the short time-span of the primary narrative of *Paradise Lost*, we start with Eve's birth, of the peculiar kind experienced by Pygmalion's statue, awakening into a fully adult capacity for knowledge of self and of others (4.451-52), 'much wond'ring where | And what I was, whence thither brought, and how'. She rapidly comes to self-awareness, through a Lacanian mirror stage, which replicates the experience of Ovid's Narcissus, before swerving from it into relationships with others; firstly with God, whose voice warns against self-love, and leads her to another individual of whom she is nevertheless a likeness.[2] She is brought to Adam as a coy nymph, inclined like Daphne to flee, but quickly turns from being a nymph-like Diana-double to being a complaisant rape-victim, like Ovid's Chloris-Flora (*Fasti* 5.195 ff.), or, somewhat differently, Pomona pursued by Vertumnus in *Metamorphoses* 14, and then becomes a devoted wife, again a Pomona, or a youthful version of Baucis to Adam's Philemon.[3] This

---

[1] Green, *Milton's Ovidian Eve*, 16

[2] J. Milton, *Paradise Lost*, ed. A. Fowler, in *The poems of John Milton* (Harlow, 1968), 4.471-72 'he | Whose image thou art'; 8.450-51 'Thy likeness, thy fit help, thy other self, | Thy wish exactly to thy heart's desire'.

[3] A youthful Philemon and Baucis in their reception of the heavenly messenger Raphael in *PL* 5: with the store of vegetable produce gathered for their guest by Eve at *PL* 5.321-49 *cf.* the garden produce gathered for their divine visitors by Philemon and prepared by Baucis, *Met.* 8.646 *quodque suus coniunx riguo collegerat horto.*

is a happy marriage, which like that of Ceyx and Alcyone in *Met.* 11,[4] is broken off by death, in this case the spiritual death of the Fall, an event which is also the introduction into the world of mankind's literal mortality.[5]

When Eve eats the apple she repeats Proserpina's self-condemnation to a continued existence in Hades through the plucking and eating of the pomegranate (*Met.* 5.535-38). But this is a 'death' that is followed by regeneration, as Adam and Eve's repentance is met by prevenient grace (*PL* 11.1-14), and our general ancestors now take on the roles of Deucalion and Pyrrha, surviving after the shipwreck of the prelapsarian world, and resolved to (re)populate the world after the catastrophe. This is a prefiguration both of the repopulation of the world after the Biblical Flood,[6] and of the final redemption of mankind through Christ into eternal life.

For the most part Green sees Milton as combining what in Ovid are unconnected stories: for example (53) 'By yoking discrete episodes [Narcissus, Apollo and Daphne] from Ovidian myth into fruitful collaboration, Milton stirs the dry bones of Genesis to strangely independent life and meaning, offering complex emotional insights in the differing trajectories of erotic desire in the first man and woman'. Green's analysis of Milton's practice in combining different Ovidian characters within the single person of Eve is anticipated by Richard DuRocher,[7] and he also talks of Milton as (11) '... recombining scattered mythic figures from the *Metamorphoses* [in order to] highlight distinct stages in Eve's development'.[8]

In this paper I suggest that Milton's 'combinatorial imitation' of a variety of Ovidian characters in the construction of Eve's character reveals a Renaissance reader of Ovid, alert to the kind of intratextualities that modern readers of Ovid multiply in the *Metamorphoses*. 'Combinatorial imitation' is a term I used many years ago in discussions of the imitation of Virgil's *Aeneid* by later Roman epic poets, Ovid, and the Flavian epicists: Valerius Flaccus,

---

[4] With the absolute mutual devotion of Ceyx and Alcyone even in death compare Adam's wish not to live without Eve at *PL* 9.906-16; with the repetitions at 9.908-15 'How can I live without thee ..? ... flesh of flesh, | Bone of my bone thou art' *cf.* the repetitions, albeit in a different context, at *Met.* 11.706-07 '*si non | ossibus ossa meis, at nomen nomine tangam*'.

[5] For the fall as death *cf.* *PL* 9.900-01 'How art thou lost, how on a sudden lost, | Defaced, deflow'red, and now to death devote'.

[6] Green, *Milton's Ovidian Eve*, 203 notes that *PL* 11 is framed by allusion to Deucalion and Pyrrha and Noah's flood, the first and second regenerations of men.

[7] R. J. DuRocher, *Milton and Ovid* (Ithaca and London 1985), ch. 2 'From Proserpina to Pyrrha: Ovidian faces of Eve in *Paradise Lost*'.

[8] *Cf.* for example also DuRocher, *Milton and Ovid* (n. 6, above) 109, 'By the method of comparison employed in the Enna simile, Milton associates Eve with, in turn, the innocence of Narcissus, the responsiveness of Echo, the chastity of Pomona, the passion of Medea, and the piety of Pyrrha. By selecting specific moments from Ovid's fables, Milton dissociates Eve from the egregious faults of these characters, especially the self-enclosure of Narcissus and the dependency of Echo, while the suggestions of vulnerability and limitation in all these Ovidian figures remain to develop suspense and pathos in *Paradise Lost*'.

Statius, and Silius Italicus.[9] I used the term to refer to the imitation within a single passage of the alluding author of two, or sometimes more, separate passages in the *Aeneid*; in many cases passages which modern critics of Virgil read as being in significant relationships within the *Aeneid* itself. This is in line with the now prevailing view that the *Aeneid* is not only a vast echo-chamber of a host of earlier Greek and Latin texts, but also, as it were, an internal, self-alluding, echo-chamber. That Ovid's *Metamorphoses* is also this kind of poem is but one of the ways in which the *Metamorphoses* attempts to meet the challenge laid down by Virgil to subsequent Latin authors of long hexameter narrative poems. 'Combinatorial imitation' can be a way of thinking about how other Renaissance authors respond to their models, classical or otherwise: for example, Shakespeare's intricate weaving together in *The Winter's tale* of a number of stories from the *Metamorphoses*, producing what A. D. Nuttall refers to as 'a complex sequence of unrivalled power'.[10] Nuttall implies that it is Shakespeare's own poetic powers which fuse together a disparate range of Ovidian stories into something greater than the sum of its parts; I want to suggest that Shakespeare is responding to complex relationships which are already operative within the *Metamorphoses*, at least for a particular kind of reader of Ovid. That kind of reader I would venture to say is now the standard kind of reader, at least within my own profession of classical Latinist.

My approach in this paper is also an intervention in an ongoing discussion among students of Renaissance as to the ways in which early modern readers read their classical texts, and the implications therefrom for the practice of imitation and allusion. It has been argued that an emphasis on extracting *exempla* from texts, and the practice of compiling commonplace books, fostered a 'reading in parts rather than as a whole'. The consequent atomization and fragmentation of texts will then be reflected in localized and particularist practices of imitation. This is an attempt to delimit imitative practice by reference to what Colin Burrow, in a forthcoming book on literary imitation labels 'historical intertextuality', *i.e.* a focus on an author's position within contemporary practices and discussions relating to imitation.[11] Such historical contextualization is always salutary, but it should not be used to close down possibilities for ways of reading and imitating, even on the part of readers and authors of average education and abilities, let alone authors as impossible to confine within narrow expectations as a Shakespeare or a Milton. Raphael Lyne offers some persuasive correctives to the 'reading in parts rather than as a whole' approach to Renaissance imitative practice.[12] In her book on Milton and Ovid, Maggie Kilgour gives examples of the combination of 'similar Ovidian characters' within a range of Renaissance texts, going back to the work that Kilgour identifies as the first in 'the deluge of Ovidian

---

[9] P. Hardie, 'Ovid's Theban history: the first anti-Aeneid?', *Classical Quarterly* 40 (1990) 224-35; P. Hardie, 'Flavian epicists on Virgil's epic technique', in *The Imperial Muse. Ramus essays on Roman literature of the Empire.* II *Flavian Epicist to Claudian*, ed. A. J. Boyle (Bendigo 1990) 320.

[10] A. D. Nuttall, '*The Winter's Tale*: Ovid transformed', in *Shakespeare's Ovid. The Metamorphoses in the plays and poems*, ed. A. B. Taylor (Cambridge 2000) 135-49, 141; see P. Hardie, *Ovid's poetics of illusion* (Cambridge 2002) 194-95.

[11] C. Burrow, *Metaphors of imitation* (Blackwell's Lectures) (forthcoming).

[12] R. Lyne, *Ovid's changing worlds. English Metamorphoses, 1567-1632* (Oxford 2001) 36-53.

writings in the sixteenth century', T. H.'s 1560 *The fable of Ovid treting of Narcissus*, in which a parallel is drawn between the stories of Narcissus and Marsyas.[13] An awareness of the relationships between different stories in the *Metamorphoses* is also central to Paul Barolsky's discussion of the importance of Ovidianism in Renaissance art and literature, what Barolsky calls 'the ancient poet's capacity to metamorphose one myth into another', as, for example, the 'transformation' of the story of Narcissus into that of Pygmalion.[14] Barolsky's claim is that a notion of 'poetic transformation' is determinative for the Renaissance: for example Lorenzo de' Medici's poem the *Ambra* runs together the Ovidian stories of Apollo and Daphne, Arethusa, and Deucalion and Pyrrha. This principle of transformation operates, according to Barolsky, at the levels of both form and subject matter: thus the figure of Apollo in Bernini's statue group of *Apollo and Daphne* is a metamorphosis of the Apollo Belvedere; in turn Poussin's painting of Pan's pursuit of Syrinx is a transformation of Bernini's *Apollo and Daphne* (and the thwarted rapes of Daphne and Syrinx constitute a narrative doublet within Book 1 of the *Metamorphoses*).

In the first section of this article I will examine a range of examples of Milton's 'combinatorial imitation' of Ovidian characters in the person of Eve. After which I will explore the link between the relationship of similarity that links different episodes in the *Metamorphoses*, and which is reflected in Milton's 'combinatorial imitation' of those episodes, and Milton's thematization of likeness, reflection, and doubling. Thirdly, I suggest that Milton's construction of the character of Eve through a stratification of different Ovidian characters finds an analogy and perhaps a source in Virgil's construction of the character of Dido.

1. Ovidian Intratextualities

I start with a small example. Mandy Green sees in Eve's report of Adam's words to Eve, when she first catches sight of him after her creation and turns away, an allusion to the Ovidian Apollo's words to the flying Daphne: *PL* 4.481-83 'Thou following cried'st aloud, Return, fair Eve; | Whom fly'st thou? Whom thou fly'st, of him thou art, | His flesh his bone …'. Compare *Met.* 1.514-15 *nescis, temeraria, nescis | quem fugias, ideoque fugis* 'thoughtless girl, you do not know from whom you flee, you do not know, and that is why you flee'. Green notes the echo in the doubled 'fly'st' of the repetition *fugias … fugis*. Green also thinks that the repetition of *nescis* 'may have suggested to Milton a thematic motif peculiar to Narcissus, Daphne and Eve – their lack of essential knowledge'. However in a footnote she rejects Kenneth Knoespel's claim that Adam's words allude to Narcissus' address to his reflection at *Met.* 3.476-79 *quo refugis…?* 'Whither do you flee?',[15] on the grounds that 'Adam's words more closely resemble Apollo's'. I would prefer to keep both Ovidian intertexts in play, and point to the intratextuality whereby the Ovidian Apollo's relationship with Daphne is already highly narcissistic. Apollo's rebuke to the fleeing Daphne that she does not know whom she flees implies that Apollo himself has fully realized the Delphic

---

[13] M. Kilgour, *Milton and the metamorphosis of Ovid* (Oxford 2012).

[14] P. Barolsky, 'As in Ovid, so in Renaissance art', *Renaissance Quarterly* 51 (1998) 451-74 (45758).

[15] Green, *Milton's Ovidian Eve* 61, with n. 14, referring to K. J. Knoespel, 'The limits of allegory: textual expansion of Narcissus in *Paradise Lost*', *Milton Studies* 22 (1989) 79-100 (89).

precept of 'know thyself'. Apollo follows this up with an attempt at erotic persuasion in the form of a list of his own powers that in effect constitutes a hymn to Apollo, but, as a hymn to himself, a thoroughly narcissistic performance. His response to Daphne's final escape from his erotic attentions through metamorphosis into a tree is to appropriate the foliage of the tree to himself, so that the laurel becomes an attribute and identifying mark of his own person. Apollo takes the apparent nodding of the laurel tree, after he has finished speaking, as a sign of the quondam girl's agreement to this perpetual connection with the god in the future; readers of Callimachus' *Hymn to Apollo*, which begins with the shaking laurel as the sign of the epiphany of the god, may however understand that the laurel's nod signifies the presence only of Apollo, and not the continuing presence as a conscious person of the metamorphosed Daphne.[16]

Adam's question to Eve 'Whom fly'st thou?' follows immediately after Eve's narcissistic experience of her own reflection in the pool. Adam persuades Eve to return by emphasizing that she is a part of himself, *PL* 4.486-87 'an individual solace dear; | Part of my soul I seek thee'.[17] Degrees of resemblance is what it is all about: Adam's relationship to Eve is what one might call a legitimate narcissism, a proper desire of like for like (but not too like).

If it is accepted that Milton alludes to both Apollo's and Narcissus' question to their objects of desire as to why they are running away, and it is furthermore accepted that the two questions point to wider connections between Apollo and Narcissus within the *Metamorphoses*, then is it possible that Ovid's intratextuality is intertextual with a Virgilian intratextuality in the use of the questions using the second-person singular *fugis*. The first occurrence is in Dido's first speech of complaint to Aeneas, when she asks bitterly (*Aen.* 4.314) '*mene fugis?*' 'is it me you flee?'. Those words are echoed ironically, and by a kind of poetic justice, in the underworld when, in a scene that contains multiple inversions of the earlier dealings between Dido and Aeneas, Aeneas asks of the stonily unresponsive shade of Dido (6.466) '*quem fugis?*'.[18] However, the exact form of Aeneas' question (*quem fugis*, rather than *mene fugis*) replicates Aeneas' use of those words in the previous book, 5, to address the fleeting dream-vision of his dead father Anchises (5.742) '*quem fugis? aut quis te nostris complexibus arcet?*' 'Whom do you flee? Or who is it that keeps you from my embrace?'. The fact that Aeneas, whose goal in travelling to the underworld is to be reunited with the shade of his father, uses the very same words to the shade of Dido is perhaps a further indication of the depth of his attachment to Dido. A route to a closer

---

[16] See Hardie, *Ovid's poetics of illusion* (n. 10, above) 47-48. On Narcissus himself as one of 'Daphne's male counterparts', a 'male nymph', see G. Davis, *The death of Procris: 'amor' and the hunt in Ovid's Metamorphoses* (Rome 1983) 84-97. Narcissus' *quo refugis?* is intratextual in its immediate context with – is an echo of – his previous question to the unseen Echo, *Met.* 3.383-84 '*quid ... me fugis?*', immediately echoed, in as many words, but now with erotic content, by Echo.

[17] Cf. *Met.* 3.473 *nunc duo concordes anima moriemur in una*. See Hardie, *Ovid's poetics of illusion* (n. 10, above) index s.vv. 'two souls in one'.

[18] The parallel between *Aen.* 6.466 and *PL* 4.482 is noted and discussed by A. Verbart, 'Milton on Vergil: Dido and Aeneas in *Paradise Lost*', *English Studies* 78.2 (1997) 111-26 (111-12); Verbart notes that Adam's first words to Eve are echoed in Aeneas' last words to Dido. For an inventory of verbal parallels between the *Aeneid* and *Paradise Lost* see A. Verbart, *Fellowship in 'Paradise Lost': Vergil, Milton, Wordsworth* (Amsterdam 1995) 261-302.

connection between Virgil's Dido and Aeneas and Ovid's Daphne and Apollo might be traced through the image of the Diana look-alike: Daphne is described as (*Met.* 1.476) *innuptaeque aemula Phoebes* 'the rival of unwed Diana', and this is the appearance under which Dido first presents herself to the eyes of Aeneas in the simile at *Aen.* 1.498-502 (anticipated by Venus disguised as a votary of Diana earlier in the book). There are detailed parallels between Ovid's Daphne and Apollo, and the story of Philomela and Tereus in *Metamorphoses* 6, where Philomela enters with a simile comparing her to a nymph that is modeled on the Diana simile of Dido in *Aeneid* 1.[19]

Milton practices his own further intratextuality with the motif of flight in an erotic context in the perverted foreshadowing of the generation of Eve from the body of Adam, and the ensuing drama of narcissism corrected, in the account of the self-generation by Satan of Sin, who springs from Satan's own head, followed by the incestuous/narcissistic coupling of Satan and Sin, the issue of which is Death, who immediately commits incestuous rape on his own mother. Sin recounts her rape experience to Satan thus: *PL* 2.787-90 'I fled, and cried out Death; | Hell trembled at the hideous name, and sighed | From all her caves, and back resounded Death. | I fled, but he pursued ...'. There is a chiastic doubling of 'I fled' and 'Death'. Compare the chiastic doubling in Adam's appeal to Eve in Book 4 of (482) 'Whom fly'st thou? Whom thou fly'st'.[20] The doubling of 'Death' is here the doubling of echo, in Ovidian terms, given the coupling of the stories of Echo and Narcissus in *Metamorphoses* 3, occurring appropriately enough in a family history that has already included a repetition of the self-love of Narcissus: a few lines before Sin has reminded Satan how (*PL* 2.764-65) 'Thy self in me thy perfect image viewing | Becamest enamoured'. The reference to echo also functions at a textual level: the foul relationship between Satan, Sin, and Death, will be echoed in a fairer version in the first stages of the history of Adam and Eve, and Milton also echoes the doublings of the verb *fugio* in the Ovidian models, and in Ovid's own Virgilian models. Death's pursuit and rape of Sin is the first rape narrative in *Paradise Lost* (and indeed the first in universal history), as Apollo and Daphne is the first in the series of rape narratives in the *Metamorphoses*, and in Ovid's cosmic history.

I return to Adam and Eve, and look now at the Miltonic combination of Ovid's Narcissus with another Ovidian character. Firstly, more on the Narcissistic aspects of Eve; Eve's reluctance to be united with Adam results from her lingering attachment to an illegitimate and sterile form of narcissism. Eve goes to the lake as she wonders (*PL* 4.45152) 'where | And what I was, whence thither brought, and how'. Tiresias prophesies that Narcissus will have a long life 'if he does not know himself' (*Met.* 3.348). On first awakening Eve experiences the delusion of Ovid's Narcissus when she falls in love with her own reflection in the lake (*PL* 4.453-76), but the voice of God ensures that Eve will undergo a happier drama of self-knowledge. This is one of the longest and most complex of Milton's imitations of an Ovidian episode, and the subject of a whole chapter in Maggie Kilgour's recent book. For an account of what happened before she came to consciousness we

---

[19] P. Hardie, 'Approximative similes in Ovid. Incest and doubling', *Dictynna* (2004) 13-16; on the parallels between Apollo and Daphne and Tereus and Philomela see G. A. Jacobsen, 'Apollo and Tereus: parallel motifs in Ovid's *Metamorphoses*', *Classical Journal* 80 (1984/85) 45-52.

[20] *Cf.* perhaps the double doubling of *Met.* 1.514-15 *nescis, temeraria, nescis | quem fugias, ideoque fugis*.

have to wait for Adam's narrative of the same sequence of events in book 8, where the fashioning of Eve from the bone of Adam's rib echoes (or foreshadows: Milton in effect reverses the direction of intertextuality by narrating originary events of which all later narratives are echoes or shadows) Pygmalion's sculpting of his ivory statue, of a shape and beauty unknown in women brought into the world by natural childbirth, *Met.* 10.248-49 *formamque dedit, qua femina nasci | nulla potest* 'he bestowed on her a shape/ a beauty such as no woman can be born with'. The example of Pygmalion is present in two ways: Eve, like Pygmalion's statue, is created by an unnatural birth, because natural childbirth will only become possible once the first woman has come into existence (although after that, Eve, as the general mother, will become the model for the *forma*, in the sense of 'shape' rather than 'beauty', of all subsequent women who come to birth). Secondly, God works as a sculptor, *PL* 8.469-70 'the rib he formed and fashioned with his hands; | Under his forming hands a creature grew'.

The story of Pygmalion's statue offers itself readily as an analogue to the peculiar circumstances of Eve's coming to being. Reading it back into Eve's repetition of the experience of Narcissus in book 4 also makes for an improvement on the Ovidian story of Narcissus, since, unlike the sixteen-year-old Narcissus, it really is 'with unexperienced thought' (*PL* 4.457) that Eve tries to make sense of what she sees in the mirror of the lake, just as Pygmalion's statue comes to consciousness as an adult woman with no previous experience of waking life. As Patrick Hume notes in his 1695 commentary on *Paradise Lost,* Milton 'has made it much more probable, that a Person who had never seen anything like herself, should be in love with her own faint reflected Resemblance, than that a Man acquainted with the World and himself, should be undone by so dull a Dotage'.[21] There may indeed already be an allusion to the Pygmalion story in Eve's own account of her first moments. She comes to (4.455-59) 'a liquid plain … | Pure as th' expanse of heaven; I thither went | With unexperienced thought, and laid me down | On the green bank, to look into the clear | Smooth lake, that to me seemed another sky'. The first things that Pygmalion's statue sees are her lover and the sky, *Met.* 10.293-94 *timidumque ad lumina lumen | attollens pariter cum caelo uidit amantem* 'timidly raising her eyes to his eyes she caught sight of her lover and the sky at the same time'. When Eve looks into the lake she sees what she takes to be another sky, and, immediately afterwards, her own reflection – her own lover.

In the Ovidian lines on the coming to consciousness of Pygmalion's statue there is also a connection with what Narcissus sees in his pool at *Met.* 3.420 *spectat humi positus geminum, sua lumina, sidus* 'lying on the ground he gazes at the twin stars of his eyes'. Here, through the metaphorical equation of his own eyes with the stars, *caelum* and *amans* collapse into one. This is just one of the many connections between the Narcissus and Pygmalion episodes within the *Metamorphoses*, connections that have frequently been noted by Ovidian critics (Rosati's classic 1983 study, *Narciso e Pigmalione*, is absent from Green's bibliography, although in fairness this is a rare bibliographical oversight in her

---

[21] P. Hume, *The poetical works of Mr. John Milton. Containing Paradise Lost, Paradise Regain'd, Sampson Agonistes, and his Poems on several occasions. Annotations on Milton's Paradise Lost* (London 1695) 150.

book).[22] In each case an erotic attachment is formed to an object of desire too close to the lover: himself in the case of Narcissus, and his own creation, in the case of Pygmalion, a statue formed to express his own conception of ideal female beauty. The latent incestuous narcissism in Pygmalion's love is manifested in the erotic attachments of his descendants: firstly, his great-granddaughter Myrrha's love for her father Cinyras, and, secondly, the attraction of Venus to Pygmalion's great-great-grandson Adonis, the spitting image of Venus' own son Cupid.

A further Ovidian intratextuality helps to point out the Miltonic intratextuality, already noted, between the asexual generation of Eve out of the body of Adam, and of Sin out of the body of Satan, and between the lustful couplings of Satan with Sin, and of the postlapsarian Adam with Eve. Satan's narcissistic and incestuous impregnation of Sin leads to the birth of Death, whose violent birth transforms Sin's nether half into serpentine folds surrounded by the hell hounds in turn fathered on Sin by her son Death, so making of her a more terrifying version of the Ovidian Scylla. Green argues for a further connection between Scylla, allegorized in the Renaissance commentary tradition as the effects of lust on virginal beauty, and Eve's fall into a creature of excessive appetite.[23] This connection is reinforced by the inverted reflection of Narcissus in Ovid's Scylla, who tries to flee from her other half, her monstrous lower parts in the water, but cannot escape from herself (*Met.* 14.62-63 *refugitque abigitque timetque | ora proterua canum, sed quos fugit attrahit una* 'she shrinks from, she drives away, she fears the shameless mouths of the dogs, but those she flees she drags along with her'), where Narcissus complains that what he gazes down upon in the water flees from him (3.477 *'quo refugis?'*).[24] And, looking further ahead, Eve's fall is itself a further reflection of her originary episode of narcissism, since the serpent's temptation begins with Petrarchan flattery of Eve,[25] appealing to her sense of pride as 'sole wonder' (9.533) of the world.

For another example of Milton's yoking of Ovidian narratives already in a significant relationship within the *Metamorphoses* take the first episode in Eve's relationship with Adam, which threatens to turn into the first in the sequence of Ovid's narratives of rape, the pursuit of Daphne by Apollo. Some even see a hint of a forceful conquest of Eve in *PL* 4.488-89 'with that thy gentle hand | Seized mine, I yielded ...'. But the yielding Eve quickly falls into the role of a Pomona happily clinging like a vine to her husband elm, and joined by their shared love of gardening.[26] This gains point if one reflects on the coherence within the *Metamorphoses* of the series of rape narratives, as analyzed in

---

[22] G. Rosati, *Narciso e Pigmalione. Illusione e spettacolo nelle Metamorfosi di Ovidio* (Florence 1983).

[23] Green, *Milton's Ovidian Eve* 170-4; on Sin and Scylla see also 89-94.

[24] P. Hardie, 'The self-divisions of Scylla', in A. Rengakos and J. Grethlein (eds) *Trends in Classics* 1 (2009) 118-47.

[25] See D. S. Berkeley, 'Précieuse gallantry and the seduction of Eve', *Notes & Queries* 196 (1951) 337-39.

[26] Green, *Milton's Ovidian Eve*, ch. 5.

particular by Gregson Davis.[27] The story of Apollo and Daphne is the first of a sequence of rapes which culminates in the story of Pomona and Vertumnus in *Metamorphoses* 14. That story provides closure by inverting and negating the elements of the narrative pattern. Pomona is no huntress-nymph of the wilds, but a cultivator of gardens. When Vertumnus, the god of transformations, finds none of his disguises succeed in his aim of penetrating Pomona's body as well as her garden, he is on the point of using force to get his way. But when he appears in his true shape, force proves unnecessary, since she experiences a mutual wound of love and freely yields to her lover. In Paradise, that is to say, the threat of rape, the Apollo and Daphne model, is instantly averted by the kickingin of the Vertumnus and Pomona model. Furthermore, an awareness of the Ovidian series of violent rapes, or attempted rapes, brought to a conclusion in erotic pursuit overtaken by mutual love, makes more shocking the inversion, or corruption, of that pattern in *Paradise Lost*, when the Fall is engineered by Satan in the guise of a malevolent Vertumnus who enters the garden in changed form, to seduce Eve verbally and figuratively, and so to deflower her (*PL* 9.901) at the point when she herself plucks the fruit.[28] The carefully cultivated Garden of Eden thus turns out to be as dangerous a place as the typical Ovidian *locus amoenus* in the uncultivated countryside, where violence and rape are inevitable. In *Paradise Lost*, then, the Ovidian tales of Narcissus and Apollo and Daphne are replayed in comic mode, while the happy-ever-after story of Pomona and Vertumnus is replayed in tragic mode. Once Satan-Vertumnus has successfully penetrated Eve's defences, Adam and Eve again feel mutual desire, but now of the fallen variety, and the erotic *mutua uulnera* 'mutual wounds' of Vertumnus and Pomona (*Met.* 14.771) turn into 'mutual guilt' (*PL* 9.1042-43 'There they their fill of love and love's disport | Took largely, of their mutual guilt the seal'.

Within the *Metamorphoses* there is a particularly close mirroring between the stories of Narcissus and Echo, and Hermaphroditus and Salmacis, in the consecutive books 3 and 4. In her pool the lustful Salmacis achieves that gratification of a total union with the object of her desire, the hapless Hermaphroditus, which Narcissus is incapable of (for the simple reason, of course, that he is already inseparable from his object of desire, himself). The connection between Narcissus and Hermaphroditus is one frequently made in Renaissance texts.[29] As we have seen, Milton constructs the mutual love of Adam and Eve as a kind of corrected narcissism. Raphael blushes an innocent blush when he answers Adam's questions about angelic sex, *PL* 8.626-29 'Easier than air with air, if Spirits embrace, | Total they mix, union of pure with pure | Desiring; nor restrained conveyance need | As flesh to mix with flesh, or soul with soul'. This is a version of the union of Salmacis and Hermaphroditus: compare *Met.* 4.373-75 *nam mixta duorum | corpora iunguntur faciesque inducitur illis | una* 'for the bodies of the two individuals are mingled and joined, and they

---

[27] G. Davis, *The death of Procris* (n. 15, above) 66-71 'Transcendence of the norm: the conversion of Pomona', the 'norm' being 'the nymph-huntress who remains impervious to *amor*'.

[28] Green, *Milton's Ovidian Eve*, ch. 6; see esp. 153, 160.

[29] Kilgour, *Milton and the Renaissance Ovid* (n. 12, above) 184-88.

take on a single appearance'.[30] It is also a spiritual realization of the origin in one flesh of Adam and Eve. Union by total commingling, a return to their original unity, is something that the unfallen human pair Adam and Eve may hope for in the future, as Raphael told Adam earlier on, *PL* 5.496-97 'And from these corporal nutriments perhaps | Your bodies may at last turn all to spirit'. Had the Fall never taken place, man's ascent up the ladder of being might also have been a progression from a purified form of narcissism to a purified hermaphroditism, in fulfilment of the injunction of Genesis 2:24 that man and woman become 'one flesh' through the institution of marriage.[31]

The interconnectedness of stories in the *Metamorphoses* can also be viewed as an aspect of its quality as a cumulative anthropology, by which I mean a cumulative picture of all ages and conditions of man and woman, built up through the poem. This is the approach of E. A. Schmidt in his 1991 *Ovids poetische Menschenwelt*:[32] 70-78 on '*Universalanthropomorphismus und Weltgedicht*'; (75) 'The *Metamorphoses* is the narrative aetiology of the world in its human significance and as a metaphor for humanity; and as such an encyclopaedia of epic similes, whose genesis is the subject of the epic narrative'. For Schmidt the subject of the *Metamorphoses* is (77) 'not the single epic hero, but mankind of all ages; not individual epic similes, but the world understood as a mirror of mankind'. In other words, Ovid's poem offers us not the life-history of a single hero in his interactions with a small number of other leading characters, but a composite picture of human identity and experience built up through a plurality of partly overlapping and partly contrasting characters, and through the multiple reflections of human experience and emotions in the landscape of metamorphosis. *Paradise Lost* by contrast tells the story of just one man and one woman, the hero and heroine (in some sense of those words), which is also the story of everyman and everywoman, all of us as the descendants of our general ancestors.

2. Likenesses and doubles

Milton compares Eve to Pomona by name at the point when the hands that had first been joined when Eve had been persuaded not to flee like Daphne (4.488-89 'with that thy gentle hand | Seized mine') are parted for the last time before the Fall.[33] Pomona is one in a series of five mythological women to whom Eve is compared in a multiple simile, which, as Alastair Fowler notes *ad loc.*, 'is so discriminating that it consists largely of qualifications'. Both the cast-list (with the exception of Pales in line 393) and qualifications are heavily Ovidian, *PL* 9.385-96:

---

[30] *Cf.* Lucr. 4.1110-11 *nequiquam, quoniam nil inde abradere possunt | nec penetrare et abire in corpus corpore toto.* This is the impossibility made possible in the case of Salmacis and Hermaphroditus.

[31] On the use of the Hermaphroditus myth in the Renaissance as a positive allegory of erotic and marital fulfillment see D. Cheney, 'Spenser's Hermaphrodite and the 1590 *Faerie Queene*', *PMLA* 87 (1972) 192-200; A. R. Cirillo, 'The fair Hermaphrodite: love-union in the poetry of Donne and Spenser', *Studies in English Literature* 9 (1969) 81-95.

[32] E. A. Schmidt, *Ovids poetische Menschenwelt. Die Metamorphosen als Metapher und Symphonie* (Heidelberg 1991).

[33] Eve is implicitly compared to Pomona at 5.377-78 'So to the sylvan lodge | They came, that like Pomona's arbour smiled ...'.

Thus saying, from her husband's hand her hand
Soft she withdrew, and like a wood-nymph light
Oread or Dryad,[34] or of Delia's train,
Betook her to the groves, but Delia's self
In gate surpassed and goddess-like deport,
Though not as she with bow and quiver armed,
But with such gardening tools as art yet rude,
Guiltless of fire had formed, or Angels brought.
To Pales, or Pomona, thus adorned,
Likeliest she seemed, Pomona when she fled
Vertumnus, or to Ceres in her prime,
Yet virgin of Proserpina from Jove.

The effect is to linger on the unfallen and, in a sense, still virginal beauty of Eve just before the Fall; the lingering is also that of Adam's gaze, as we realize when we read on to find he is still looking after her departing form, 397-98 'Her long with ardent look his eye pursued | Delighted, but desiring more her stay'. The multiplicity of comparands asks the reader to reflect on degrees of likeness between Eve and her classical avatars; 'like', 'surpassed', 'goddess-like', 'though not as she ...', and 'likeliest', and at the same time to think about similarities between the classical females. This passage is about comparing and contrasting. The difference between the visual lingering of Adam and that of the reader is that Adam has no other woman with which to compare Eve; the accumulation of allusions which build up a composite picture for the reader reminds us of the impossibility of ever recapturing Adam's vision of a truly incomparable Eve (or at least comparable only to himself (*PL* 8.471 'manlike') – the absence of other women with which to compare her makes of that likeness to her male 'original' something unique). These similarities are largely Ovidian approximations.

Milton's multiple simile begins with the comparison of Eve to a nymph, and, more specifically, a nymph 'of Delia's (*i.e.* Diana's) train'. Daphne, the first in the series of nymph rape-victims in the *Metamorphoses*, is introduced as (1.476) *innuptaeque aemula Phoebes*, the first also in a series of Diana look-alikes in the poem.[35] Milton also has in mind the famous simile in *Aeneid* 1 when Dido, as Aeneas first catches sight of her, is compared to Diana (*Aen.* 1.498-502). This simile is modelled on the simile in *Odyssey* 6 (102-08) comparing Nausicaa to Artemis. Unlike Nausicaa, whose chastity remains unassailed, Dido will become the 'victim' of a coupling in the wilds, like the typical Ovidian nymph (and the Virgilian simile in turn is a model for Ovid's comparison of Philomela to a nymph at *Metamorphoses* 6.452-54: see below). The Homeric and Virgilian Artemis-Diana is distinguished from her company of nymphs, in other respects similar to herself, by her

---

[34] 'Oread or Dryad': *cf.* the pairing of *Naides* and *Dryades* in Ovid, *Met.* 3.506-07, 6.453, 11.49, 14.326-28.

[35] The slippage from Diana to nymph is anticipated at *Aen.* 1.329 *an Phoebi soror? an Nympharum sanguinis una*: this is an addition to the Homeric model, *Od.* 6.149-55, where the alternatives for Nausicaa's identity are only god (Artemis) or mortal.

214   THE AFTERLIFE OF OVID

superior height; Eve's distinction is that she is like a nymph who surpasses her goddess, in gait and deport, rather than height (*Od.* 6.107; *Aen.* 1.501).[36] So, Milton's simile is similar to, but swerves from, its Homeric and Virgilian models. Lines 390-92 'Though not as she with bow and quiver armed, | But with such gardening tools as art yet rude, | Guiltless of fire had formed, or angels brought', prepares us for the explicit mention of Pomona in line 393, through allusion to *Met.* 14.625-28 (Pomona) *nec fuit arborei studiosior altera fetus; | unde tenet nomen. non siluas illa nec amnes, | rus amat et ramos felicia poma ferentes. | nec iaculo grauis est, sed adunca dextera falce* ... 'No other [nymph] was keener in the care of orchard trees. Thence came her name. For in her heart she loved not woods nor rivers, but a plot of ground and boughs of smiling apples all around. She had no spear, only a pruning-knife'.[37] Pomona is a Hamadryad (14.624), and so sister to other Ovidian nymphs who suffer the attention of divine rapists, Syrinx, Callisto,[38] but she is also different from others in the series, firstly in that she is a Latin Hamadryad (*Met.* 14.623-24), and secondly in her dedication to horticulture. *Arborei* points to the etymology of *hama-dry-as* ('together with an oak-tree'), before our attention is drawn to the etymology of the name 'Pomona' (*fetus*, the noun with which *arborei* agrees, and then the word *poma* itself), signifying a fruitfulness antithetical to the lifestyle of the huntress-nymph. *Non siluas illa nec amnes ... nec iaculo* correct the reader's initial inclination to line up Pomona with the other nymphs whose lifestyle and fate have become so familiar to us in the preceding books. She is an 'anti-nymph'. There is a telling divergence from the Ovidian model in Milton's reference to Pomona, 'To Pales, or Pomona thus adorned, | Likeliest she seemed, Pomona when she fled | Vertumnus ...'. In Ovid Pomona does not flee from Vertumnus. However our memory of all the other nymphs in the *Metamorphoses*, in the series that culminates with Pomona, might lead us to expect that this too would be a narrative of attempted rape and flight.

   Milton folds the contrast between the activities of Pomona and of other nymphs into another Ovidian intertext, or rather class of intertext. By presenting the contrast between Eve's gardening tools and the bow and quiver of Diana as an appendix to a simile, Milton makes of it an example of what I have labelled an 'approximative simile', a simile, of a kind typically Ovidian, which makes a point of judging the exact degree of approximation of tenor to vehicle.[39] An approximative simile takes the form 'A was like B, were it not for detail x or y'. The closest Ovidian parallels for the present passage are, firstly, the simile used of Philomela when Tereus first catches sight of her (a simile that is modelled on and comments on the Virgilian simile comparing Dido to Diana at *Aen.* 1.498-502), *Met.* 6.451-54: *ecce uenit magno diues Philomela paratu, | diuitior forma, quales audire solemus |*

---

[36]   Ovid reverts to the simple Homeric distinction of height in his description of Diana at *Met.* 3.18182 *tamen altior illis | ipsa dea est colloque tenus supereminet omnes.*

[37]   Milton's allusion is noted by S. A. Brown, *The metamorphosis of Ovid* (London 2002) 111; Green, *Milton's Ovidian Eve*, 142-43.

[38]   *Met.* 1.690-91 *inter Hamadryadas celeberrima Nonacrinas | Naias una fuit* (Syrinx); *Fasti* 2.15556 *inter Hamadryadas iaculatricemque Dianam | Callisto sacri pars fuit una chori.* These are the only two instances of *hamadryas* in the *Met.*, and only one in the *Fasti* (Davis, *Death of Procris* (n.15, above) 68 n. 69).

[39]   Hardie, 'Approximative similes' (n.19, above).

Naidas et Dryadas mediis incedere siluis, | *si modo des illis cultus similesque paratus* 'See, here comes Philomela, rich in her royal attire, but richer still in beauty, just like the Naiads and Dryads who, we are told, walk through the middle of the woods, if you were only to give them similar adornment and dress',[40] and, secondly, the description of Syrinx, *Met.* 1.694-98 (although formally this is not a simile) *Ortygiam studiis ipsaque colebat* | *uirginitate deam; ritu quoque cincta Dianae* | *falleret et posset credi Latonia, si non* | *corneus huic arcus, si non foret aureus illi;* | *sic quoque fallebat* 'In her pursuits and her dedication to virginity she cultivated the goddess of Delos; dressed in the manner of Diana, as well, she might cause confusion and be taken for Latona's daughter, were it not she had a bow of horn, and the goddess a bow of gold'.

I have argued that in Ovid these approximative similes, with their careful calibration of likeness and unlikeness, and their concern to preserve discriminations, are related to an Ovidian obsession with doubles and incest, operative at the levels both of theme, and of the poet's anxiety about his relationship to his own work, and about the relationship between art and nature, representation and reality. Furthermore, the tendency for stories with similar themes to merge into one another, and the consequent pressure on the poet to maintain distinctions between them, are phenomena related to the approximative simile. Ovid draws attention to this affinity in the first two narratives of this kind in the *Metamorphoses*, the stories of Daphne and Syrinx, so close in characters and story-pattern that the narrator concludes the latter in brief summary fashion in order to avoid sending the reader to sleep with boredom, as the internal audience, Argos, is sent to sleep by the internal narrator, Mercury. Not coincidentally Mercury starts off his tale of Syrinx with the first in the series of approximative similes in the poem (or, to be more precise, what is formally an approximation to an approximative simile), in this respect, as in others, Mercury is a highly Ovidian narrator.

My claim is that in *Paradise Lost* this interest in likeness between different stories, and Milton's alertness to the Ovidian patterning of similarity and difference in the *Metamorphoses*, should not be restricted to the narratological level, but are connected to, and reflect, a central theological and anthropological theme, that of the correct relationship between original and model, with consequences for the proper regulation of interpersonal relationships. *Paradise Lost* is an epic about relationships, the relationship between the persons of the divinity, between God and man, and between human beings, man and wife, and parent and child, which includes the relationship between Adam and Eve and 'us', as well as the comparability of ourselves to our general ancestors (4.324 'the fairest of her daughters Eve', like Diana superior to her look-alike nymphs). At the intertextual level *Paradise Lost* is in the business of judging, and asking the reader to judge, its relationship to its own literary models, not the least important of which is Ovid's *Metamorphoses*.

---

[40] For a Spenserian precedent to Milton *cf. FQ* I. vi. 16.6-9 'Sometimes Dame Venus selfe he seemes to see, | But Venus neuer had so sober mood; | Sometimes Diana he her takes to bee, | But misseth bow, and shaftes, and buskins to her knee'.

The relationship between the Father and the Son is the model for an ideal resemblance of likeness to original.[41] The relationships into which Satan enters, both with himself and with his own progeny, Sin and Death, are parodic and perverted images both of the perfect relationships within the Trinity, and of the perfectible relationships of human beings. Viewed as Pygmalion's statue, Eve is in the likeness of both her maker and Adam, in the likeness of God at two removes, in the likeness of Adam at one remove, since she is physically made of the same substance as Adam, his bone: 8.471 'Manlike, but different sex'. At her creation Adam recognizes in her, 8.495-99 'Bone of my bone, flesh of my flesh, my self | Before me; woman is her name, of man | Extracted; for this cause he shall forgo | Father and mother, and to his wife adhere; | And they shall be one flesh, one heart, one soul'.[42] Eve is in the relationship to God of a likeness of a likeness, the likeness of Adam who himself was created 'in the image of God' (7.527), although as together constituting mankind Adam and Eve are both in the likeness of God: 4.291-92 'for in their looks divine [both Adam and Eve] | The image of their glorious maker shone'; 7.519-20 'Let us make now man in our image, man | In our similitude, and let **them** rule …'.[43] In the words of a discussion of the varieties of narcissism in Dante, whose *Commedia* is another very important model for *Paradise Lost*, God is 'the Ultimate and Original Narcissist. God gazes eternally upon His Image, loving Himself, yet His self-love implies perfect self-knowledge'.[44]

It is immediately after her creation that Eve is called upon to exercise proper discrimination in the matter of her relationships with the only two humans in the world, herself and Adam. Deluded, like Narcissus, by the sight of her own reflection, it is through things heard, the voice of God, that she is instructed in the need to turn towards another person to whom she stands in the relationship of an image: 4.467-74 'What thou seest, | What there thou seest fair creature is thyself, | With thee it came and goes: but follow me, | And I will bring thee where no shadow stays | Thy coming, and thy soft embraces,

---

[41] *PL* 3.63-66 'The radiant image of his glory sat, | His only Son; on earth he first beheld | Our first two parents, yet the only two | Of mankind'. 3.138-40 'Beyond compare the Son of God was seen | Most glorious, in him all his Father shone | Substantially expressed' (the Biblical model is Hebrews 1:3 on the Son of God, 'the brightness of his [Father's] glory, and the express image of his person'; *cf. PL*. 3.384-86, 6.680-82, 7.196 'all his Father in him shone', 10.63-67 'So spake the Father, and unfolding bright | Toward the right hand his glory, on the Son | Blazed forth unclouded deity; he full | Resplendent all his Father manifest | Expressed'.

[42] These lines are a lightly adapted version of Gen. 2:23-24; *cf.* Matth. 19:4-6; Mark 10:6-8. *Cf.* also *PL* 8.449-50 'What next I bring shall please thee, be assured, | Thy likeness, thy fit help, thy other self'.

[43] Gen. 1:26 'Let us make man in our image, after our likeness; and let **them** have dominion …' E. Miner (ed.), *Paradise Lost 1668-1968. Three centuries of commentary* (Lewisburg 2004) 284, 'This is the first biblical account of human creation, taken to be liberal for its identification of Adam with Eve, "them", with "Man". From the second, related in Genesis 2.21-23, Eve is deemed inferior for being created from Adam's rib'.

[44] R. McMahon, 'Satan as infernal Narcissus: interpretive translation in the *Commedia*', in *Dante and Ovid: essays in intertextuality*, ed. M. U. Sowell (Binghamton 1991) 65-86 (82), cited in Kilgour, *Milton and the metamorphosis of Ovid* (n. 13, above) 193.

he | Whose image thou art, him thou shall enjoy | Inseparably thine, to him shalt bear | Multitudes like thyself ...'. 'Invisibly led' Eve falters once more as a result of something seen, 477-80 'Till I espied thee, fair indeed and tall, | Under a platan, yet methought less fair, | Less winning soft, less amiably mild, | Than that smooth watery image'. Eve judges degrees of likeness ('fair indeed ... less fair'). Once again it is a voice, that of Adam, who corrects her and instructs her how to relate to a likeness of herself, 482-88 'Whom thou fly'st, of him thou art, | His flesh, his bone; to give thee being I lent | Out of my side to thee, nearest my heart | Substantial life, to have thee by my side | Henceforth an individual solace dear; | Part of my soul I seek thee, and thee claim | My other half.' Eve's vision (now a mental kind of seeing, one able to see the non-physical beauty of wisdom and compare it with visible beauty) now sees things straight, 489-91 'from that time [I] see | How beauty is excelled by manly grace | And wisdom which alone is truly fair', closing with the fifth and final instance of the word 'fair' in her narrative (468 'fair creature', 477-78 'fair indeed ... less fair', 481 'Return fair Eve').

At the level of Milton's Ovidian models, Eve reaches this point of correct relationship to Adam, her 'most resembling unlikeness, and most unlike resemblance' as Milton describes the relation of man to woman in the *Tetrarchordon*,[45] through the narrator's adroit negotiation of a path through the like and unlike Ovidian stories of Pygmalion, Narcissus, and Apollo and Daphne. Eve will fall when she once again strays in her relationship to herself, tempted into the sin of pride, and to God, and Adam will follow her when he in turn is tempted to overvalue the closeness of his relationship to Eve.

Adam reverts to his first acknowledgement of his inseparable likeness and attachment to Eve as he resolves to share in the Fall with her, 9.907-16 'Certain my resolution is to die; | How can I live without thee, how forgo | Thy sweet converse and love so dearly joined ... no no, I feel | The link of nature draw me: flesh of flesh, | Bone of my bone thou art, and from thy state | Mine never shall be parted, bliss or woe'.[46] 952-59 'However I with thee have fixed my lot, | Certain to undergo like doom; if death | Consort with thee, death is to me as life; | So forcible within my heart I feel | The bond of nature draw me to my own, | My own in thee, for what thou art is mine; | Our state cannot be severed, we are one, | One flesh; to lose thee were to lose myself'. To which Eve replies, 961, 'O glorious trial of exceeding love', and describes their union as, 967, 'One heart, one soul in both'.

---

[45] *Complete prose works of John Milton*, vol. 2, *1643-1648* (New Haven and London 1959) 597, cited by H. James, 'Milton's Eve, the romance genre, and Ovid', *Comparative Literature* 45 (1993) 121-45. This is a rather Ovidian chiasmus: cf. *Ars amatoria* 2.24 *semibouemque uirum semiuirumque bouem*.

[46] T. Newton (ed.), *Paradise Lost. A poem in twelve books. The author John Milton. The third edition, with notes of various authors*, 2 vols (London 1754) *ad loc.* thinks that Milton has in mind the speech of Aristophanes in the *Symposium*; J. H. Todd (ed.) *The poetical works of John Milton with notes of various authors*, 4th ed., 4 vols (London 1842) disagrees, citing *Tetrachordon* (*Complete prose works* 2.589), alluding to Gen. 1:27, 'It might be doubted why he saith, In the Image of God created he him, not them, as well as male and female them; especially since that Image might be common to both, but male and female could not, however the Jewes fable, and please themselves with the accidental concurrence of Plato's wit, as if man at first had bin created Hermaphrodite: but then it must have bin male and female created he him'.

218   THE AFTERLIFE OF OVID

The conjugal conceits of Ovid, with parallels in the language of Deucalion and Pyrrha and of Ceyx and Alcyone, have been diverted to the emotional effusions of a romantic love in which the heart rules over the intellect. Alistair Fowler notes on 9.967 'One heart, one soul in both' that Eve's words are in contrast with the formulation of the relationship as it was before the Fall, 8.604 'Union of mind, or in us both one soul': 'Intellect (*mens*) has been replaced by the more passionate *heart*'. It will be through a painful process of self re-discovery after the Fall that Adam and Eve will re-establish their proper dependence, as husband and wife, on the God in whose likeness they had been created, setting to order the hierarchy of relationships that flows from the chain of likenesses through which the world had been constituted after the fall of the rebellious angels.

3. Virgil's Dido as a model for constructing an intertextually layered character

For the construction of a full picture of female identity Ovid's *Metamorphoses* serves Milton's purposes better than the *Aeneid* does. Through the several leading ladies of his epic Virgil offers a partial and largely pathological picture of womanhood, being deficient most notably in images of fulfilled and harmonious marriage. Echoes of Dido, unsurprisingly, occur mostly at ominous or tragic moments.[47] When Adam looks longingly after Eve for the last time before the Fall there is an echo of Aeneas' last view of Dido in the Underworld: with *PL* 9.397-98 'Her long with ardent look his eye pursued | Delighted, but desiring more her stay' (cited above) compare *Aen.* 6.475-76 *nec minus Aeneas casu percussus iniquo* | **prosequitur** *lacrimis* **longe** *et miseratur euntem* 'Aeneas was no less stricken by her unjust fate, and long did he gaze after her (literally 'followed'; English 'pursue' is derived ultimately from Latin *prosequor*), weeping and pitying her as she went'.[48] An awareness of the Miltonic lines retrospectively lends fresh point to *casu ... iniquo.* The most emphatic allusion to the Dido and Aeneas story comes at the eating of the apple, first by Eve, and then by Adam, now united with Eve in original sin, as he knowingly eats of the apple: *PL* 9.781-84 '... she plucked, she ate: | Earth felt the wound, and Nature from her seat | Sighing through all her works gave signs of woe, | That all was lost'; 9.1000-04 'Earth trembled from her entrails, as again | In pangs, and Nature gave a second groan; | Sky loured, and muttering thunder, some sad drops | Wept at completing of the mortal sin | Original.' Both passages allude to the elemental accompaniments to the 'wedding' of Dido and Aeneas in the cave, Dido's 'fall', *Aen.* 4.166-70 *prima et Tellus et pronuba Iuno* | *dant signum; fulsere ignes et conscius aether* | *conubiis summoque ulularunt uertice Nymphae.* | *ille dies primus leti primusque malorum* | *causa fuit* 'Earth and Juno, giving away the bride, first gave a signal: lightning flashed and sky witnessed the wedding, and the Nymphs cried out on the mountain top. That day first brought death, that day first

---

[47]   For a survey of the parallels from the story of Dido and Aeneas in *Paradise Lost* see Verbart, 'Milton on Vergil' (n. 18, above).

[48]   Contrast the happier occasion at *PL* 8.59-63 'With goddess-like demeanor forth she went; | Not unattended, for on her as queen | A pomp of winning Graces waited still, | And from about her shot darts of desire | Into all eyes to wish her still in sight.' (where 'all' might suggest an audience larger than that of just Adam and Raphael – we the readers?).

brought woe'.[49] For images of mutual love and fulfilled marriage, as we have seen, Milton goes to Ovid rather than Virgil. At the same time Virgil's construction of the character of Dido through a kaleidoscopic intertextuality with characters in earlier Greek and Latin literature offers a parallel with, and perhaps a model for, Milton's combinatorial imitation of a range of Ovidian females (of course only a part of the totality of models in Biblical, classical and post-classical literature that go to make up the Miltonic Eve). Virgil uses the same multiply allusive technique in the construction of other characters in the *Aeneid*, not least Aeneas, but Virgil's Dido is unusual in the concentration of so many models within a relatively compressed section of the text (*Aen.* 1 and 4, and the meeting with Aeneas in the Underworld in 6). Furthermore Dido experiences within the *Aeneid* something like Eve's accelerated life-history. She enters as a woman with a past, a majestic queen with a marriage already behind her, but she has in a sense returned to a pre-married virginal state, from which she falls once more into sexual experience, what she, if not Aeneas, calls a *coniugium*, to be followed shortly by death, and a posthumous existence in an afterlife, once more happily married (after a fashion) to Sychaeus. Dido in fact has two afterlives, the second in the shape of the avenging Fury, into which she promises to transform herself in her second accusing speech to Aeneas (4.384-86); as love turns to hate the fair Dido turns into a foul monster, an analogy and possibly source for Milton's doubling of Eve and Sin. For Eve, too, there is life after the death of the Fall, and a second chance of building a happy marriage. At the same time the Fall is the occasion for the entry of Sin and Death into the world.

The Virgilian figure of Dido is refracted through a multiplicity of Ovidian women, beginning with Daphne, the archetypal follower and imitator of Diana, the goddess in whose likeness Dido first appears in *Aeneid* 1.[50] Ovid produces a multiplicity out of the single person of Dido; in his Eve Milton reassembles a unity out of a plurality of Ovidian women.

Trinity College, Cambridge

---

[49] On the allusion, first noted by Addison, see W. Porter, *Reading the Classics and Paradise Lost* (Lincoln, Nebraska, 1993) 112; Verbart, 'Milton on Vergil' (n. 17, above) 113-14. The line *ille dies primus leti primusque malorum* | *causa fuit* may also echo in the third line of *Paradise Lost*, 1.3 'Brought death into the world, and all our woe'. For the day that first brings death *cf. PL* 8.329-30 'The day thou eat'st thereof, my sole command | Transgressed, inevitably thou shalt die'; 9.762-63 (Eve) 'In the day we eat | Of this fair fruit, our doom is, we shall die'. 'Day' and 'die' resonate against each other in both these passages; the Latin for 'day' spells 'dies' in English; *malum* (with a difference in quantity in the first syllable) is the Latin for both 'apple and 'woe, misfortune'.

[50] See Hardie, *Ovid's poetics of illusion* (n. 10, above) index *s.v.* 'Dido'.

THE TRANSFORMATION OF OVID IN COWLEY'S HERB GARDEN: BOOKS 1 AND 2 OF THE *PLANTARUM LIBRI SEX* (1668)

VICTORIA MOUL

Abraham Cowley, educated at Westminster and Cambridge, was a major poet of his day and had come to prominence very early – aged only fifteen – for a precocious collection of English verse, *Poetical Blossomes* (1633). If his works are read at all today, it is likely to be either his Pindaric odes, which are important in the history of English imitation of Greek, or perhaps his fine prose essays. He wrote in both Latin and English, both poetry and prose, throughout his career. He had greater contemporary prominence and a wider literary reach than most of the 'Cavalier' poets, he was, like them, a Royalist and indebted in particular to Ben Jonson for his understanding of English literature; but also, he was closely involved with the newly founded Royal Society and the emergence of modern science. Despite this interesting combination, his work today is extremely unfashionable.

This short article goes some way to explaining why the *Plantarum Libri Sex*, or *Six Books of Plants*, published in its final form in 1668, a year after Cowley's death, has no modern translation, and has attracted almost no scholarship.[1] It appears in a volume entitled *Poemata Latina*, the great bulk of the book is taken up by work on plants, which runs to 362 pages in that edition, and comprises enormous variety both in theme and form. The outline below offers an overview of the work:

---

[1] An edition of the *Plantarum Libri Sex*, edited by Daniel Kinney with introduction, notes and facing translation, is in progress (*The Complete Works of Abraham Cowley*, forthcoming from the University of Delaware Press). An interesting selection of material relating to the *Plantarum*, including a rich store of images, is to be found at Kinney's text and image archive: http://etext.lib.virginia.edu/kinney.

The complete Latin text (though with occasional errors of transcription, and without Cowley's notes) can be found on Dana Sutton's website, www.philological.bham.ac.uk/plants/.

Currently, the main discussions of the work as a whole remain Leicester Bradner's useful chapter on Cowley in *Musae Anglicanae: a history of Anglo-Latin poetry, 1500-1925* (New York, 1940); chapter VIII of Robert B. Hinman's *Abraham Cowley's World of Order* (Cambridge, MA 1960); Ruth Monreal, *Flora Neolatina. Die Hortorum libri IV von René Rapin S. J. und die Plantarum libri VI von Abraham Cowley. Zwei lateinische Dichtungen des 17. Jahrhunderts* (Berlin, 2009) and Victoria Moul, 'Abraham Cowley, *Abrahami Couleij Angli, Poemata Latina. In quibus Continentur, Sex Libri Plantarum, viz. Duo Herbarum, Florum, Sylvarum, Et Unus Miscellaneorum* [...] (London: T. Roycroft and Jo Martyn, 1668; Wing C6680)', *EEBO Introductions*, http://eebo.chadwyck.com/intros/htxview?template=basic.htx&content=index.htm.

Book 1: Herbs: Miscellany of pieces in elegiac couplets – twenty-seven poems on twenty different herbs (several have more than one poem).[2]

Book 2: Herbs: Eleven elegiac poems, each spoken by a different herb, set in the herb garden at Oxford.[3]

Book 3: Flowers: Ten flowers, each with her own ode, linked by narrative in elegiac couplets; gathering presided over by Flora. Set on the banks of the Thames in 1660.

Book 4: Flowers: Long introduction of epigrams, followed by eight further flower odes.

Book 5: Fruit and nut trees: Hexameter verse describing around forty types of fruit and nut tree – latter ten all trees of the new world. Rivalry between the (classical) gods of Europe and those of Mexico. The book concludes with a prophecy by Apollo of the fall of Europe and the rise of America.

Book 6: Woodland trees: Hexameter verse describing around thirty further woodland trees, with a long speech by the oak concluding the work and telling of the regicide, civil war and Restoration.

There are many facets of this work which deserve much greater comment than they have previously received, including its political and nationalistic force, the engagement with the New World and the rise of America, and its scientific seriousness, as well as the gathering of multiple genres (ode, elegy, epigram, and epic) within a didactic frame, and its deployment of a commentary composed by the poet. This paper focuses upon the first two of the six books, devoted to herbs, and the complexities of their engagement with Ovid in particular.[4]

Nahum Tate's description of the *PLS*, taken from his preface to the English translation published in 1689, identifies Ovid's significance as a model for these first two books:

[2] Vettonica (Bettony), Capillus Veneris (Maidenhair Fern), Salvia, Melissa (Lemon Balm), Cochlearia (Scurvy Grass), Cassytha (Dodder), Absinthium (Wormwood), Nymphea (Water-Lily), Asplenum (Spleenwort), Lactuca (Lettuce), Euphrasia (Eyebright) x 2, Vesicaria (Winter Cherry), Rorella (Sundew) x 2, Cyclaminus (Cyclamen) x 5, Lens Palustris (Ducksmeat), Rosmarinus (Rosemary), Mentha (Mint), Viscus Quernus (Mistletoe), Chelidonia (Celandine) x 2, Euruca (Rocket) x 2.

[3] Artemisia, Pulegium (Pennyroyal), Dictamnus (Dittany), Plantago (Ribwort Plantain), Rosa (Rose), Laurus (Laurel), Aristolochia (Birthwort), Lentiscus (Mastick tree), Sabina (Savin), Artemisia, Myrrha (Myrrh).

[4] Note that books 1 and 2 – with which I am concerned here – were initially published separately in 1662 as *Plantarum Libri Duo*, with the later books added for the 1668 posthumous edition. I have discussed elsewhere Cowley's deployment of models drawn from Horatian lyric (Victoria Moul, 'Horatian Odes in Abraham Cowley's *Plantarum Libri Sex* (1668)', in *Neo-Latin Poetry in the British Isles*, ed. L. B. T. Houghton and Gesine Manuwald (London 2012) 87-104 and from Latin elegy (Victoria Moul, 'Latin and English elegies in the seventeenth century', *Cambridge Companion to Latin Love Elegy*, ed. Thea S. Thorsen (Cambridge, 2013) 306-19).

The two first Books treat of Herbs, in a Style resembling the Elegies of *Ovid* and *Tibullus*, in the sweetness and freedom of the Verse; but excelling them in the strength of the Fancy, and vigour of the Sence.[5]

Tate makes similar observations about the rest of the work, commenting on the Horatianism of Books 3 and 4, and the imitation of Virgil in particular in the hexameter Books 5 and 6. The ascent from relatively low-status genres (elegy and epigram), via lyric, to didactic and ultimately epic hexameters tracks the literal increase in scale in the plants in question: herbs are small and grow close to the ground, flowering plants are a little larger, fruit and nut trees taller still, and the lofty trees of the woodland the mightiest of all. Certain subdivisions lend individual books additional coherence: book 2 is set in the physic garden at Oxford and dramatizes an assembly of herbs used specifically for female ailments – each herb (and they are all female themselves) speaks *in propria persona* of her own myth and utility. Similarly books 3 and 4 are arranged as a kind of 'beauty competition' on the banks of the Thames, supervised by Flora, as the flowers compete for ruler-ship of the floral kingdom at the time of the restoration. Book 5, set in Mexico, stages a competition for dominance between the trees of the old world and those of the new; and book 6 offers an epic-style assembly of trees, led by the dryad of the oak: his speech telling of the civil war and the restoration takes up the final half of that final book.

What this description omits is the didactic seriousness of Cowley's project: the plants are selected not simply for their beautiful appearance or literary or mythological associations, but for their utility – and in particular for their use in medicine. All the herbs of book 2, for instance, are of use in relation to menstruation, conception, childbirth and related matters, and footnotes written by Cowley himself run right through the work, offering details on etymology, common English names and appearance, how to distinguish between different related species and the preparation of these plants as remedies as well as more conventional poetic matters such as myth and literary allusion.[6] This is a work intended to be memorable for scientific as well as literary reasons, and it is also a thorough demonstration of the seventeenth-century conviction of the unity of knowledge: poetic and scientific authority complement one another, and belong together.

Given the limitations on space, a single example of the style and content of this commentary is offered here. In this case, a translation of the opening lines of '*Aristolochia*' ('Birthwort') in book 2, followed by the commentary. I have added a few glosses in square brackets.

---

[5] Abraham Cowley, *The third part of the works of Mr. Abraham Cowley* (London 1689); Wing C6665, a2ʳ.

[6] These notes were not included in the 1689 translation of the *PLS*, resulting in a rather different overall effect. They are also not included in Sutton's online database. They are however reproduced (without translation) on Daniel Kinney's web archive, where they are usefully keyed to Sutton's text: http://etext.lib.virginia.edu/kinney/works/notes.htm.

224 THE AFTERLIFE OF OVID

Et Florem, & Baccas virides, & Semina fundo,
     Patronámque Uteri non sterilem esse decet.
Sed magìs est altè mea summa recondita virtus,
     Et Fructus Radix maximus ipsa mihi est.
Hanc Natura Uteri signavit cauta figurâ,
     Nec passa est vires dissimulare suas.
Indè vocor *Terrae Malum*; tam nobile Malum
     Non ipse *Hesperidum* lucidus Hortus habet.
Dignius hoc tolli (tu Nupta fatebere) cursum
     Quàm quod tardavit, pulchra *Atalanta*, tuum. [7]

I pour forth my flowers, my green berries, and my seeds –
     It is not fitting for the Womb to have a sterile Patroness.
But on the contrary my greatest virtue is deeply buried,
     And my root is my greatest source of power, my finest fruit.
Cautious Nature has marked this root with the sign of the Womb,
     And she has refused to disguise its particular properties.
This is why I am called *Apple of the Earth* [*Terrae Malum*]; not even the brilliant
     Garden of the Hesperides holds so noble a fruit.
This fruit, beautiful Atalanta, would more properly have delayed you
     As you stopped to pick it up (now you are married you will admit it!).

V. 1. In English, Birthwort (*Aristolochia*) is useful in several ways. It induces both menstrual periods and the delivery of the afterbirth, and when mixed with myrrh and pepper, either as a drink or applied directly, it expels unborn children who have died in the womb; it also prevents prolapse of the womb, as a warm poultice, or by using the fumes, or by direct application, especially the slender variety, *Plin. Book* 26.15. Our authorities call it 'Earth Apple' and record four sub-types – all of them are the colour of boxwood, with slender stems, and a purple flower; they bear small berries like that of the caper. Only the root is powerful – the scent of each type is medicinal, but more effective in the type with the oblong and more slender root – the chief glory of the oblong variety is this: if it is applied to the womb mixed with raw beef immediately after conception, it ensures male offspring, so it is said; *Plin. Book* 25.8. The last point is more appropriate to this poem than a work of philosophy; this is certainly the more fitting context for it. Fernelius [Jean François Fernel, 1497-1558, French physician] sees fit to add that both types of *Aristolochia* help to expel

---

[7] For Latin text: Cowley, *Poemata Latina*, 86-87. Translations throughout are my own unless otherwise noted. Quotations throughout this article are taken from the 1678 edition of the *Poemata Latina* (Abraham Cowley, *Abrahami Coulelii Angli, Poemata Latina: in quibus continentur Sex Libri Plantarum, Viz. Duo Herbarum. Florum. Sylvarum. Et Unus Miscellaneorum.* (London 1678)), hereafter *Poemata Latina*. I have used this edition, rather than the earlier editions of 1662 (first two books) or 1668 (all six books), for three reasons: the 1678 edition provides page and line numbers; it corrects several minor typographical errors of the 1668 edition; and it is the edition available on the *Early English Books Online* digital database, and now cheaply in a facsimile print form in the *EEBO* 'Early English wit, poetry & satire' print-on-request series.

menstrual blood, the afterbirth, and the foetus when prepared with myrrh and pepper; the same plant is best when applied from below, and it purges filth from the womb.

V. 5. Crollius (Oswald Croll, *c.* 1563-1609, German alchemist, chemist and professor of medicine) who is much experienced in the distinctive features of plants, has observed this resemblance between the shape of the Uterus and that of the root of the round *Aristolochia* – and I think he was the first to do so. What power these marks have in fact I do not know; but they are certainly poetic.

V. 9. A well-known story: see *Metam.* 10.

Literary authority and patterns of reference: Ovidian citation and allusion in the Plantarum libri duo

As this example indicates, the most obvious way in which Ovid is important to these books is that he is one of the Latin poetic authorities cited directly in the footnotes Cowley has added to his work. More than that, we can say he is in some sense the most important of these authorities, as he has the largest number of citations. Ovid's works are referenced (with or, as in the example above, without a quotation) six times in the notes to book 1 and seventeen times in book 2; references to the *Metamorphoses* predominate, but we find also references to the *Fasti, Amores* and *Ars Amatoria.* (The quantities of footnoted references to Virgil in these books are reversed: he is mentioned eleven times in book 1 and only five times in book 2).[8] Counting explicit citations of this sort is a rather crude measure of influence – and as we shall see it by no means conveys the full extent of Cowley's engagement with Ovid – nevertheless, it offers an indication of Ovid's prominence in these books, and the extent to which the reader is invited to connect Cowley's Latin with Ovidian models.[9]

Some of the footnotes to Ovid seem to be simply a matter of citing an authoritative precedent for an unusual term. The first of five epigrams on Cyclamen in book 1, for instance, uses a link to a fairly familiar piece of Ovid (the very beginning of the *Fasti*) to gloss two unusual terms ('*Patulcius*', 'the opener' and '*Clusius*', the closer), both applied to the god Janus in *Fasti* 1.129-30. In the epigram these names are applied to the cyclamen, and remind us of the medicinal application of the plant – in this case, it is useful both for stopping a nose-bleed and for draining blood that has gathered behind the nose. That is, it both 'opens' and 'closes'.[10]

A more self-conscious device sees the plants themselves cite Ovid, even by name, to bolster their personal authority and veracity. We find this motif three times in the first two books. In her poem, for instance, the Mint plant ('*Mentha*') has told how she used to be a girl, who was raped by Pluto, and caught in the act by Proserpine. Apparently worried she might not be believed, she cites Ovid as evidence of the truth of her story:

---

[8] Other authors cited as authorities include Persius, Horace, Homer, Lucretius, Statius, Catullus, Martial, Juvenal, Claudian, Valerius Flaccus, Lucan, Cicero and Tibullus, as well as scientific authorities both ancient and modern – chiefly Pliny and Fernelius, but also Aristotle, Columella, Crollius.

[9] By contrast, Ovid is cited in this way only four times in book 3, nine in book 4, five in book 5 and just three in the epic book 6.

[10] The first epigram on Cyclamen (Cowley, *Poemata Latina*, 38).

226   THE AFTERLIFE OF OVID

Nè quis mentiri me fortè existimet, ore
Veridico meminit Naso poeta mei.

Lest anyone should think that I am lying,
      The poet Ovid, who does not lie, has told my story.

V. 58.   Foemineos artus in olentes vertere menthas,
      Persephone, licuit? Ovid. Met. 10. Fab. ult.[11]

Ovid, then, is appropriated both by Cowley (as the scholarly author of the footnotes) and by the plants themselves, the characters of the poem. Linked to this rather pointed – even overdetermined – use of Ovid, is Cowley's choice of epigraph for the work as a whole. The phrase '*Habeo quod Carmine sanet & Herbis*' appears on the title page of all the editions, followed by 'Ovid. Met. 10.'. The quotation – 'I have means of healing both by song [or spells] and by herbs' – functions as a neat summary of the parallel and equal importance of the literary and scientific content and ambitions of the work. The source of the citation is also worth noting; it is taken from the speech of Myrrha's nurse, when she discovers Myrrha about to commit suicide, driven to despair by her passion for her father. Myrrha's story of despair and destruction might seem an unedifying one: but the Myrrh plant takes up the final section of Cowley's second book with a long poem of marked scientific optimism which also mentions (in passing) her own history. In the 1662 publication of the first two books, Myrrh's story effectively begins (with the epigraph) and ends (with her poem) the work. As we shall see, Cowley's deployment of Ovid is alive to the potential to re-contextualize these mythological tales in a scientific context, but also to the literary suggestiveness of the myths themselves.

The epigraph is both explicitly Ovidian and an example of a kind of tacit Ovidianism – of unmarked but significant themes, allusions, and favourite stories – with which Cowley structures his first two books. We find tacit Ovidianism of unmarked allusions being used to create atmosphere and to bring into play the wide range of tones and voices of which Ovid is capable, and perhaps especially the combination of narrative, entertainment and didactic we find in the *Fasti* and the *Ars Amatoria*.

Cowley exploits just that association early on in book 1, in the poem delivered by the Maiden Hair fern (Capillus Veneris):

Funditur augurio noster meliore capillus,
   Et non de nihilo nomen amoris habet.
Ipsa mihi multum scit se debere venustas,
   Ipse meis telis reia nectit amor.
A me formosi lasciva volumia crinis,
   Plaudentisque humeros umbra decora comae.
Me cole quisquis amas; laetam nutrire memento
   Caesariem, & toto vertice tende plagas.[12]

---

[11]   Cowley, *Poemata Latina*, 49, ll. 57-58 and associated footnote. The quoted lines from Ovid are *Metamorphoses* 10.729-30.

[12]   Cowley, *Poemata Latina*, 9, ll. 11-18.

My hair was born of far better origins [*than other ferns*], it is not for nothing that it has the name of love. Beauty herself knows that she owes me much, and love ties his nets from my threads. Wanton curls of beautiful hair come from me, and shoulders finely shaded by sweeping locks. Whoever you are, worship me if you are in love; remember to nourish your fine hair and spread your nets around your whole head.

The plant's aetiological explanation here alludes to her own most common Latin name (*'Capillus Veneris'*, 'Venus' Hair'), and offers an explanation and *aide-memoire*: the plant is called *'Capillus Veneris'* because it resembles a beautiful woman's long hair; but also – so we are told at greater length in a note to line 14 – because it is an effective conditioner, which promises to make your hair more curly and luxuriant. The poem links these two points: a fine head of hair is an asset in courtship, so the plant 'belongs' to Venus – to the erotic realm – in this sense as well. Typically, Cowley strengthens the literary effect of this blend of botanic, cosmetic, and erotic instruction by allusion to Ovid. The third book of the *Ars Amatoria* (addressed to women rather than men) includes some discussion of hair care, and describes a range of hairstyles that suit different women, including long hair worn down.[13] This generally Ovidian register is combined in these lines with a specific allusion, which, in accordance with Cowley's usual practice, goes unmarked in the notes.[14] This is from a well-known passage in the first book of the *Ars*: '*Prima tuae menti fiducia, cunctas / posse capi; capies, tu modo tende plagas*' (*Ars Amatoria* 1.269-70); 'first be assured, all women can be caught; only spread your nets, and you will catch them'.

The joke is that whereas Ovid, in *Ars Amatoria* 3, describes *women's* hairstyles, here in Cowley a female herb redeploys Ovid's own words (from *AA.* 1) to instruct *men* on the optimal look for courtship. The self-consciousness about gender here is as we shall see a peculiar feature of Cowley's reading and recasting of Ovid throughout *PLS* I and II.

Science, medicine and the female body: Ovidian transformations reimagined

Several of the examples described above combine a strikingly authoritative female speaking voice – itself a feature of Ovid's *Heroides* – with a self-conscious deployment, by the female plants themselves, of Ovidian myth, drawn particularly from the *Metamorphoses* (as in Birthwort's mention of Atalanta, and Mint's allusion to her own Ovidian story). The combination of these two features, however, is a marked redeployment of Ovidian tropes; especially as so many of Cowley's female plants represent themselves as speaking, as it were, post-Ovid and in the aftermath of their own metamorphosis. (By contrast, Ovidian transformations are marked by the, often heartrending, *loss* of bodily autonomy and, very

---

[13] *AA.* 3. 132: '*munditiis capimur: non sint sine lege capilli: / admotae formam dantque negantque manus*'. '*alterius crines umero iactentur utroque: / talis es adsumpta, Phoebe canora, lyra*'. (14142). *Cf.* also *Amores* 1.14 on the damage done by elaborate hair-care regimes.

[14] In general, mythological references and occasional unusual items of vocabulary are marked with notes, whereas sophisticated intertextuality of this kind is not. Perhaps because part of the pleasure (and didactic effect) of the lines resides in the satisfaction of appreciating the wit for ourselves.

often, of coherent speech).[15] When Mint alludes to her story of rape and transformation, but goes on, cheerfully, to recount her scientific efficacy in her new form, we understand that both the comedy and the didactic force of these very memorable re-workings relies upon Ovid, and our Ovidian expectations of a text of this sort, but also presents a concerted challenge to that Ovidian perspective.[16]

The challenge presented to Ovid by a female plant who tells of her own rape and transformation as only the beginning of an ultimately triumphant story of medicinal utility is obvious. Rather more complex examples are offered by the regular Ovidian 'asides' which, especially in book 2, incorporate Ovidian material in a less direct form. A particularly rich example of this sort of interaction is developed over several poems in book 2, beginning with the poem ascribed to Rose. At this point in the book, the assembled herbs – all of particular use for women – are debating the nature and purpose of menstruation. Rose claims that a mother's milk and the blood that is lost at menstruation are composed of the same material, and are both designed to nourish an infant: one after birth, and one before. But she is also responding to – and mocking – the argument made by Dittany earlier in the book that menstrual blood is in fact highly poisonous.[17] In doing so, she alludes to the story of Nessus, Deianira, and Hercules, while a footnote points us to that story in *Metamorphoses* 9:

> Ille veneficii reus actus, lethifer ille,   45
>   Cui tu Nessaeum virus inesse putas,
> (Et mirum est sanè nisi Vestem tinxerit illo
>   Quâ miserum occîdit Deïanira virum)
> Componit teneri sanguis primordia foetûs,
>   Et dat per menses blanda alimenta decem.

---

[15] Most of the women transformed into plants or animals in Ovid are rendered mute or reduced only to inarticulate cries by their transformation. Some significant exceptions (which were no doubt important models for Cowley) include the speech of the crow in *Metamorphoses* 2.549-95 and of Arethusa in 5.577-641. On the female voice and experience in Ovid more generally, see: L. Enterline, *The rhetoric of the body from Ovid to Shakespeare* (Cambridge 2000), K. L. McKinley, *Reading the Ovidian heroine: 'Metamorphoses' commentaries 1100-1618* (Leiden, 2001), and P. Salzman-Mitchell, *A web of fantasies: gaze, image, and gender in Ovid's* Metamorphoses (Columbus, OH 2005) 150-206.

[16] A more sustained example of this trope is found in the poem spoken by '*Nymphea*', the Water Lily, who tells of her seduction and abandonment by Hercules, and her subsequent transformation into an aquatic plant which is (it turns out) an effective remedy against excessive lust. Botanical knowledge of this plant, in other words, could avoid a repetition of her fate. The poem includes several specific allusions to Ovid, and is discussed further in Moul, 'Latin and English elegies', 2013 (n. 4 above).

[17] This ancient idea, derived in particular from Pliny's *Natural History*, is roundly mocked by the other herbs. Laurel for instance comments on the argument at the opening of her poem: 'Did you hear what Dittany said? In no month need any woman / Draw down the moon, witch that she is, with poisons: / Nor need she mix herbs, or deadly spells; / She is quite capable of playing Medea simply by her own blood' (Cowley, *Poemata Latina*, 81).

That substance [the blood] is charged with poisoning [or witchcraft], and accused of
   being deadly,
And you suggest that the poison of Nessus is found within it,
(And indeed I'd be surprised if Deianira had not used that liquid to soak the tunic,
   With which she killed her wretched husband);
But that same blood constitutes the first beginnings of the tender embryo,
And provides pleasant food [for the embryo] through the course of ten months.

V. 48. Herculem: Vide fab. *Ovid. Met.* 9.[18]

The mythological reference here requires some comment. Nessus was a centaur who
carried Deianira, the wife of Hercules, across a river and then tried to steal her. On seeing
this, Hercules shot him with an arrow tipped in poison from the Hydra. Believing it would
keep Hercules faithful, Deianira soaked a shirt or tunic in the blood and gave it to her
husband, who died in agony as a result. The remarkable (albeit ironic) suggestion seems to
be that the dread poison in question was a woman's menstrual blood.

The rather striking appropriation of Ovidian myths for a debate about female
reproductive physiology continues in the following lines. Rose goes on to describe how the
menstrual blood that sustains the foetus in the womb is miraculously re-routed to become
the milk that feeds the baby after birth:

Nec satis hoc illi, chara inter brachia matris,
   Hospitis occurit rursus ad ora sui.
Mutato occurrit mutatus tramite & ipse,
   Secretam emensus qualem Arethusa viam;
Mammarúmque duplex gemino de fonte resurgit,
   Flumine vel ripis candidiore suis.

Nor is this [feeding the embryo in the womb] enough for it [the blood], for between
   the mother's dear arms,
It rushes again to offer help to its own guest's mouth [*i.e.* the baby's].
Itself transformed, and with its route also changed, it hurries,
   Having measured out a secret path of the sort traced by Arethusa;
And from the twin fountain of the breasts it rises in a double flow,
   A fountain purer than the river or its own banks.

The nymph Arethusa, who relates her story at some length towards the end of
Metamorphoses 5 (ll. 577-641), escaped twice from the river god Alpheus – first by
transformation into a stream herself, and then (when Alpheus returned to his river form) by
following a secret subterranean path to emerge as a fountain in Sicily. Here the combined
transformation (of blood into milk) and its redirection by mysterious means (*'per venas
hypogastricas'*, Cowley specifies in the footnote) are related to Arethusa's transformation
and subterranean escape.[19]

---

[18]   Cowley, *Poemata Latina*, 79, ll. 45-50 and associated footnote.

[19]   This suggestive comparison draws a fascinating parallel between the typical female experience
in the *Metamorphoses* (of the threat of sexual violence, pursuit and transformation) and what is
going on *inside* women once they have conceived. Cowley's interest in the mechanics of human

THE AFTERLIFE OF OVID

By this point in the debate, Dittany has claimed that a menstruating woman is poisonous and Rose that a woman's menstrual period discharges a source of food for the growing embryo. Laurel in response says this doesn't make sense – since only human females menstruate, and plenty of other mammals are much more prodigiously fertile. She claims, in another strange (and strangely Ovidian) passage that menstrual blood is neither poisonous, nor designed to feed a growing embryo, but that its loss each month is related instead to the fact that human females excel the male 'in form and softness', in contrast to other animals, in which the sexes are more evenly matched:

> Non equa vincit equum, non taurum vacca; sed ista
> Si digna est Io, dignus & ille Jove est.
> Si leo tu torvus visu, tua torva Leaena est;   85
> Terribilésque minùs non quatit illa jubas.
> Nec magìs ursa rudi concinnè lambitur urso,
> Nec nitido magìs est apta figura polo.
> Foemina nec tigris maculâ est ornatior unâ,
> Et sus fulmineo conjuge foeda magis.[20]   90

> For the Mare does not outdo the Stallion, nor the Cow the Bull; but
> If the Cow is worthy of Io, the Bull is of Jove.
> If you, Lion, are ferocious in appearance, so too is your Lioness;
> She shakes her dread mane no less than you.
> Nor is the She-Bear groomed more neatly than the shaggy male,
> And she is no more fit to adorn the shining heaven.
> The Tigress is not by a single spot more decorated than the male,
> Nor the female Boar more foul than her husband with his thunderbolts.

> V. 84. Iö in Vaccam; vide Fab. *Metam*. 1. Jupiter in Taurum, *Met*. 2.

> V. 88. *Callisto à Junone in ursam commutata, à Jove in caelum translata, efficit Ursam Majorem quae Arctos dicitur*, Fab. *Met*.

> V. 90. Apro.
> *Fulmen habent acres in aduncis dentibus Apri.* Ovid, and passim alii.[21]

Something odd is happening here; the learned adumbrations of the footnotes do not at first appear to add very much, and if anything the insistent reference, *via* the notes, to erotic pursuit and metamorphosis seems if anything to blur the argument. But in fact Laurel's account of female physiology, like that of Rose, is riddled with myths of metamorphosis – not least by our awareness of the story of Daphne (Laurel) herself, once a nymph pursued by Apollo and transformed into the tree from which the wreaths of victory are made (Ovid,

---

reproduction is obviously not Ovidian, but some stimulating recent work has attended more closely than before to the motif of birth itself as metamorphosis in the poem (see for instance Mairéad McAuley, 'Matermorphoses: Motherhood and the Ovidian Epic Subject', *Eugesta* 2 (2012) 123-68).

[20] Cowley, *Poemata Latina*, 84, ll. 83-90 and associated footnotes.

[21] The quoted line here is Ovid *Met*. 10.550, part of the story of Venus and Adonis.

Metamorphoses. 1.452-566). Laurel does not recount the story herself, though she alludes to it in passing:

> Sed, cui chara feror, nisi me deludat *Apollo*,
> Simque sacrum frustrà cingere sueta caput . . . [22]

> But, if Apollo, to whom I am dear, does not delude me,
> And as long as I do not bind his sacred head in vain . . .

There is no note here. We are expected to remember the story ourselves. The relevance of metamorphosis to Laurel's argument eventually emerges when she offers her own interpretation of menstruation, explaining that what makes women so beautiful, soft and hairless (compared to men) is the loss of excess blood each month (ll. 111-16). Typically, she goes further with a rather startling corollary to this claim, complete with Ovidian flavour:

> Quòd si impura suis decurrere flumina rivis
> Fors vetet, & magnus digerat ille calor,
> Paulatim formam mulier solidata virile
> Induit, & stupor est qui fuit, Iphi, tuus.
> Sic Phaethusa pilis sibi totum horrescere corpus
> Mirata est, densas & fruticare genas.[23]

> But if chance happens to suppress the running of those impure waters
> In their proper channels, and excessive heat dissipates them,
> Then little by little the woman grows hard, and takes on
> A manly appearance, and experiences the same dumb astonishment as you, Iphis.
> In the same way Phaethusa was astonished, as her whole body
> Began to bristle with hair, and her cheeks sprout dense shoots.

Iphis, whose story (one of the more positive transformations in Ovid) is told at the end of *Metamorphoses* 9 (ll. 666-797), had been raised as a boy in order to avoid disappointing her father, and was eventually betrothed to Ianthe, whom she loved. In despair, her mother prays to Isis the day before the wedding, and Iphis is transformed into a young man just in time. In a typical example of Cowley's blend of sources, the case of Phaethusa – whose periods stopped, as she grew a beard and body hair, and her voice was lowered – is reported in Hippocrates. The rather startling argument is that a woman's monthly bleed is all that *prevents* her from being transformed into a man (though Laurel does not account for why this does not happen during pregnancy). This is a rather dramatic extension of the 'capacity for mutation and multiplication' which Mairéad McAuley sees reflected in Ovid.[24]

In the course of book 2, as the debate about the purpose of menstruation unfolds, a woman's essential power of transformation is progressively re-defined: from the

---

[22] Cowley, *Poemata Latina*, 81, ll. 15-16.

[23] Cowley, *Poemata Latina*, 85, ll. 111-22.

[24] McAuley, 'Matermorphoses', 127.

232   THE AFTERLIFE OF OVID

destructive and magical power of menstrual blood, to 'change' (that is, erode or destroy) almost anything with which it comes into contact, according to Dittany (and Pliny);[25] to a mocking Ovidian reprise of this idea in Rose's poem, followed by a stress upon the miraculous transformation of blood into milk; and finally a claim that menstruation is all that prevents a woman actually becoming a man.

Female transformation and the advantages of metamorphosis

These female speaking plants are both very Ovidian (female subjects of metamorphosis and the victims of sexual violence) and also very un-Ovidian in their eloquence, their scientific knowledge (remember, these ideas about menstruation are presented as a learned debate in an entirely female company) and their medicinal utility. Whereas the herbs of book 1 have a range of uses, often associated with love and its problems, the majority of herbs in book 2 are described as useful for labouring women – and, in fact, their assembly is interrupted at the end of the book when Robert, the gardener, arrives to collect some herbs to help his wife who is in labour. This usefulness in labour extends to a variety of related problems, such as treating a retained placenta, uterine haemorrhage or prolapse of the womb, which can result from a difficult birth or multiple pregnancies.[26] Birthwort ('*Aristolochia*') even claims to be the goddess Lucina herself.[27] Moreover, as the herb Savin (Sabina) makes clear in her poem, this distinctive female power (of reproduction) extends to destruction as well. Her poem alludes to this power 'to destroy', and the notes clarify what she means: the herb can be used to 'bring on' a period (an ancient euphemism for an early termination) or induce the birth of a miscarried baby, potentially saving the mother: '*partus emortuos apposita extrahit*', 'once applied it draws out dead offspring'.[28] But it is also a frank abortifacient: '*foetum etiam viventem enecat & mortuum ejicit*', 'it both kills a living foetus and ejects a dead one'.[29]

Many of these plants say the same thing, more or less directly. They can get girls who have been raped or foolish 'out of trouble': avoiding more practically exactly the fate that their mythological personae were transformed to escape. Book 10 of the *Metamorphoses* – with its complex series of childbirths, and the book to which Cowley most often alludes – wouldn't have got very far if the nymphs and girls had been able to terminate their pregnancies. The president of the assembly, Mugwort, even points out how many great men might not have existed if knowledge of herbal remedies had been more available.[30]

Nor is that the last of these ways in which Cowley's apparently Ovidian plants challenge their classical model. Ultimately, the challenge is extended not only to Ovid's characters, but to the poet himself, when Savin describes how she, along with a host of herbs of book

---

[25] The objects and persons subject to disease, decay or destruction if tainted by menstrual blood include: men, dogs, pregnant women, crops, vines, fruit, young girls, wine, swords and metal (Cowley, *Poemata Latina*, 73-74).

[26] See the extract from the commentary added to '*Aristolochia*' given at the beginning of this article.

[27] Cowley, *Poemata Latina*, 87, ll. 27-28. She compares herself to Bacchus, who is identified with the vine, and Ceres, with corn.

[28] Cowley, *Poemata Latina*, 94, note 1.

[29] Cowley, *Poemata Latina*, 94, note 1.

[30] Cowley, *Poemata Latina*, 101, ll. 21-34. She mentions Caesar and Alexander in particular.

VICTORIA MOUL: OVID IN COWLEY'S HERB GARDEN

2, is threatened with exile. (For this longer extract, I have quoted from the 1689 translation, though with some additional glosses where the translation does not make the meaning of the Latin clear).

At centum praestant operam bona germina eandem;
  Exiliúmque ideo si meruisse putor,
Exilii comites video non defore nostri;
  Ibimus in *Cretam* quàm bene magna cohors?
Ibis, *Myrrha*, simul mecum, Virgo impia quondam,
  Nunc *pia*, supplicio nunc pretiosa tuo.
Sed labefactâsti neque tunc, licèt impia, foetum:
  Quem Foetum? & crimen quem peperisse fuit.
Et *Panaces* magno Mortem quod nomine terret,
  Cúmque *Ammoniaco Galbana* flava suo;
Divitibúsque *Laser* planta inficianda Cyrenis,
  Ni simul & Lucri dulcis adesset Odor.
Ibis, *Thus Terrae* (nec *Thura Sabaea* moramur)
  Ibis tu *Luto* quem, *Croce*, tinxit Amor.
Ibis *Ereuthodanum, & Colocynthis* fellea, mecum,
  Pictáque quae varii terga *Draconis* habes:
Eminus & tacitis *Cyclaminus* noxia telis,
  Nec temero gravidis transilienda pede:
Antidotúsque aliis, sed Foetibus ipsa Venenum,
  In coetu nulli *Ruta* secunda pio.
Quid memorem reliquas? Agmen sumus; ipsa quoque ibis
  Quae meritum à Lochiis Optima nomen habes.
Sed neque tu tandem, *Praeses* veneranda, manebis:
  Surge, age, & Exilium concomitare meum.[31]

But many other Plants the same can do,
Wherefore if banishment you think my due,
Companions in it I shall have, I know,
And into *Creet* a troop of us shall go.
Thou, Myrrh! for one shalt go, who heretofore [*i.e.* as Myrrha the girl]
For lewdness [*i.e.* incest] punish'd now deserv'st the more.
But thou, though lewd didst not prevent the birth,
Though 'twas a Crime to bring the Infant forth.
And *All-heal* too, who Death affrights, must pack,
With *Galbanum* and *Gum-Ammoniack*,
And *Benzoin* to *Cyrenians* never sold,
Unless they brought the sweeter smell of Gold.
Ground-pine and *Saffron* too will Exiles prove,
Saffron, once *Crocus*, yellow dy'd by Love.
Madder, and *Colloquintida* with me,
And *Dragon* too the *Cretan* shore must see.

---

[31] Cowley, *Poemata Latina*, 98-100.

234 THE AFTERLIFE OF OVID

> And *Sowbread* too, whose secret darts are found
> Child-bearing Women distantly to wound.
> And *Rue*, as noble a Plant as any's here,
> Physick to other things, is Poison there [to a pregnancy].
> What shou'd I name the rest? We make a throng.
> Thou *Birthwort* too with must troop along.
> Nor must you, President, [Mugwort] behind us stay,
> Rise then and into Exile come away.[32]

The 'crime' here is their abortifacient action, though from a didactic perspective this compressed list is a useful memorandum, and the English translation of 1689 (which does not include the footnotes) has even added 'Plants that procure Abortion' in the margin.[33] The imagined location of their exile – Crete – is not chosen at random. The ancient model is that of Daedalus, exiled to Crete after he threw his nephew Talus off the Acropolis. The story is mentioned in *Metamorphoses* 8, but more significant than this is Ovid's insistent identification, in his own exile poetry, of himself at Pontus with the craftsman Daedalus on Crete.[34] So these Ovidian female characters, who strikingly outdo their models by their knowledge, eloquence, and good cheer after metamorphosis, end their book by taking aim at Ovid himself. Like him, they are threatened with exile; but unlike him, they appear to avoid this fate, in order to be cheerfully useful in the botanical gardens at Oxford.

Conclusion

Books 1 and 2 of Cowley's *Plantarum Libri Sex* are rooted in Ovid generically, by their elegiac form; thematically, in the use of female mythological figures and their transformations; and tonally, with their distinctive blend of humour, myth and didacticism. The importance of Ovid to Cowley's poetic scheme is highlighted by the choice of epigraph and the repeated explicit references to Ovid both in footnotes and in the body of the text. Myrrh, the final plant to speak in book 2, says she need not retell her story in detail because it is told in the *Metamorphoses*. But at the same time these books are a radical challenge to Ovidian poetics: the female plants not only survive their transformations with their voice intact, but they wield and express the power to prevent exactly the sorts of calamities from which they have suffered: seduction or rape, various difficulties of gestation and birth, and even pregnancy itself. Ovid's heroines could have made use of Cowley's *Six Books of Plants*.

King's College London

---

[32] Cowley, *The third part of the works*, 52-53.

[33] In the original Latin publication, the footnotes are particularly dense in this passage, with a wealth of information about different species and names, and references to Pliny, Fernelius, Ovid, Catullus, Tibullus and Virgil.

[34] Usefully collected in A. R. Sharrock, *Seduction and Repetition in Ovid's Ars Amatoria 2* (Oxford 1994) 168-73.

INDEX

abduction 168-70 (*see also* rape)
Achilles 5, 49, 102, 105, 165-67, 88-90, 92
Adam 10-12, 202, 203, 207-18
    Master Adam 31-33
Adonis 63, 78, 182, 188-90, 192-98, 201-02, 210
Aeneas 5, 26, 77, 109, 119, 181-86, 190-91, 197-99, 201-07, 207-08, 213, 218-19
Alberti, Leon Battista 23-24, 41, 75, 152
Alcina 35-39
Apelles 28
Apollonius Rhodius 5
Ara Grimani 142-43
Arethusa 206, 228-29
Ariosto, Lodovico 25, 30-31, 36-38, 40-41, 148
Armida 39-41
art 18-21, 23, 25-31, 34-41, 110, 144-46, 157, 215
Asinius Pollio 6
Atalanta 107-08, 224
Augustus 6, 46, 103, 108-13
autobiography 2, 106

Barolsky, Paul 206
Baucis 6, 14-15, 203-04
Beatrice 1, 12, 17, 20, 34-35
Beaumont, Francis 189-90, 195
Bernard of Clairvaux 1, 13, 20, 104
Bible 1, 4, 6, 9, 10-11, 14-18, 85, 97, 99, 105, 116, 118, 159
    Old Testament 17
    New Testament 10-11, 14, 17
Bonsignori, Giovanni dei 118, 125, 129-30
Boyd, Mark Alexander (Bodius) 61, 96, 107-14
Britomart 182, 188
Brute 181-82, 185, 196-200

Caesar, C. Julius 92-3, 111 *cf* 112
Calderini, Domizio 56-58
calendars 82-3, 85, 90
Candida 73-74
Carbone, Girolamo 75
Carmen de Ovidio 46, 59

carmen perpetuum, idea of 115
Chaucer, Geoffrey 32-33, 183, 197
Chiaravacci, Girolamo 82, 89-93
Chiron 166-67
Chrysippus 76
Cicero, M. Tullius 2, 23-24, 46, 49-52, 76, 78, 110
Colard (Bruges) 118-19, 121, 129
commentary 31, 43-57, 124, 129-30, 134, 150-51, 153-54, 164, 209-10, 222-23
Conradus de Mure (mythographer) 46, 54
conversion 11, 38, 63-64
Correggio, Antonio Allegri da 137-58
Cowley, Abraham 221-34
Creation 7-9, 12, 14, 62, 68, 88, 90, 125, 203, 206, 216,

Daedalus 234
Dante 1-21, 25, 30-41, 184, 216
Daphne 19, 63, 71, 81, 185, 189, 203-13, 215, 217, 219, 230
Deianeira 103, 172, 228-90
deification 13, 19-20, 71, 184
Deucalion (and Pyrrha) 6, 9, 161-62, 204, 206, 217
Dido 104, 109, 201, 206-8, 213, 215, 218-19

Emmanuel 97-98, 101-04, 109, 114
Ennius 5, 49
epic, anthropological 1-21; Renaissance 29-41; Ovidian 203-19
Epicureanism 71
epistles, Neo-Latin 95-114
Eve 202, 203-19

Fabianski, Marcin 155
Faunus 182, 190-99
ficta 78-79
flood, accounts of 7, 9, 85, 91, 162, 200, 204
Fracco, Ambrogio 85-93
Freedman, Luba 153-54

Glaucus 12, 14, 20, 183-88, 190, 201 (*see also* Scylla)

236   THE AFTERLIFE OF OVID

Hercules 103, 127, 172, 228-29
Hermaphroditus 192, 195, 211-12 (*see also* Salmacis)
Hesiod 7, 9, 46, 64
Hessus, Helius Eobanus 96-109, 114
Homer 1, 5, 7, 46, 49-50, 57, 150-51
humanitas 72, 78
humanity 4-14, 71, 84, 91, 212
Hume, Patrick 209

illusion 24-9, 37-41
Illustrations, of *Metamorphoses* 115-35
Image 85, 141, 151-52, 175, 186, 208, 210, 216
    archaeology of 145-46, 150-52,
    original and 7-8, 10, 13, 23-24, 25-27, 29,
    32, 38, 208, 210, 216-17,
    text and 115, 117, 119, 121, 127, 130,
    134-35, 145-46 150-51, 153, 158
imagery 54-55, 145, 172, 179, 183
imitation, combinatorial 204-06,
incredulity, anticipation of 14-15
intertext, interextual, intertextuality 3, 9, 20, 71,
    88, 203, 207, 209, 214-16, 219
Io 2, 112, 137-58, 230
Iphis 231

Janus 81-93, 225
Jesus 3, 11-12, 14, 91
Julia 108-14
Jupiter 20, 48, 71, 91-92, 102-03, 139-42,
    156-57, 230

Lapini, Bernardo 153
Lazzarelli, Lodovico 82-85, 88, 92-93
Leto, Pomponio 45, 81
Leucippids 167-68
lietezza 146, 148, 156, 158
Livy 48-49, 52, 100
Lodge, Thomas 185-92, 197, 199,
Lucretius 7, 71

Mantuanus, Baptista (Mantuan) 82, 84-85, 88,
    92
manuscripts (of Moretti) 44-45, (of the *Ovide moralisé*) 116-17, 121
Marlowe, Christopher 193, 195-98
Marston, John 189
Marsyas 18, 151, 205-06
Mary, Virgin 2, 97-98, 101-05, 109, 114
Melliflora 182, 190, 192-96 (*see also* Faunus)

menstruation 223-24, 228-32
metamorphosis 4, 10-13, 66-69, 70-74, 78, 81,
    139, 170, 182-83, 189-90, 196, 200-01,
    206-07, 227, 230-32, 234
    scepticism about, 14-15
Milton, John 184, 199-202, 203-19
Moretti, Bernardo 43-57
Moses 18, 89-93
Muses 16, 27, 89, 182, 191
Mussato, Albertino 19, 46, 50
myth 2, 5, 7, 9, 14, 17, 25, 37, 41, 46-47, 50,
    53-54, 56, 61-63, 67-68, 71-72, 78, 83, 97,
    115, 137, 142, 152-53, 155, 158, 181-83,
    189, 199-200, 204, 206, 212, 223

Nagel, Alexander 145
Naples, Neapolitan 61, 68-69, 75, 78,
Narcissus 2, 23-41, 74, 125-27, 189, 192-93,
    203-11, 216-17
Nausicaa 213
Neoplatonism 153-54
Nessus 228-29
Noah 9, 84-85, 88, 91-92

Ovid *passim*
    Amores 46, 66, 165, 225
    Ars amatoria 45-46, 98, 165, 167-68,
    225-27
    Epistulae ex Ponto 46, 79, 109-10
    Fasti 46, 65, 71, 81-93, 165, 170, 174, 176,
    178-79, 201, 203, 225-26
    Heroides 46, 95-114, 117-18, 165, 183, 227
    Ibis 43-59, 155
    Medea 46,
    Metamorphoses 1-21, 23-41, 46, 50-51,
    54, 61-79, 81, 90, 115-35, 137-58, 159-79,
    182-86, 190, 198-99, 201, 203-19, 225-34
    Remedia Amoris 46
    Tristia 45-46, 79, 98, 103, 109-10, 183
    Ovide moralisé 116-18, 121

Panofsky, Erwin 150-51
Parma. Cathedral of 156-57
Paul (St.) 11, 16, 18,
Peter (St), as Janus 83-84, 88
Petrarch 19, 61, 63, 71, 189
Phaeton 63-67, 75-78,
Philemon see Baucis
Philomela 107, 162-63, 185, 197, 208, 213-15
    (*see also* Procne, Tereus)

INDEX

Philostratus, *Imagines* 28-29, 175-76
Piacenza, Giovanna 148
Pico della Mirandola 10-11
Pirithous 14-15
Plantin Press 159-61, 164
Pliny the Elder 23, 27, 232
poesia 152
Pomona 203-4, 210-14
Pontano, Giovanni 61-79
pride 29-30, 34-35, 210, 217
Procne 162-63 (*see also* Philomela, Tereus)
Pygmalion 25, 206, 209-10, 217
Pyrrha, *see* Deucalion
Pythagoras 171-72, 183

Rangone, Ginevra 146-48
rape 167, 170, 203, 208, 210-11, 213-14, 228, 234
Raphael 141, 144, 156, 211-12
reality 15, 101, 185, 215, *see also* illusion
reason, recall to 31-41,
reflection 23-35, 40-41, 75, 206-10, 216
relationship 4, 90, 98-99, 103-04, 109-10, 116-17, 206-08, 210, 215-18
Rinaldo 31, 37-41
Romano, Giulio 141-42
Rubens, Peter Paul 159-79
Ruggiero 31, 35-41

Sabrina 199-201
Salmacis 65, 190, 193, 211
Satan 102, 208, 210-11, 216

Scylla 183-87, 190, 192, 210 (*see also* Glaucus)
Septuagint 4, 6, 8
Shakespeare, William 193-95, 198, 202, 205
    Venus and Adonis 182, 190, 194, 196,
sin 34-35, 38, 208-10, 216-19
Siren 343-5, 38-41, 68-69
Socrates 27
Spenser, Edmund 82, 181-85, 188, 193, 196, 198-200, 202

Tasso, Torquato 25, 30-31, 38-41
Tate, Nahum 222-23
Tereus 6, 160, 162-64, 170, 208, 214-15 (*see also* Philomela, Procne)
Tiberius Caesar 46, 92, 112-13
Titian 137, 145, 152, 175-77, 179
Tomi 45, 57
transgression, Ovidian 3, 13, 18, 33, 65, 76
Trinity 85-88, 216,

Varro 52
Venus 65, 77, 105, 107, 174-79, 186, 190, 193-94, 202
Verheyen, Egon 141, 153-54
Vertumnus 203, 211-14 (*see also* Pomona)
Villa della Farnesina 144
Vinci, Leonardo da 155
Virgil 1-7, 15, 17, 48, 50, 150, 164, 183, 190-91, 200-02, 205, 218-19, 225, 199, 202, 208, 210, 227,

Weever, John 190-99